Mumbai & Goa

timeout.com/mumbai

Published by Time Out Guides Ltd, a wholly owned subsidiary of Time Out Group Ltd.
Time Out and the Time Out logo are trademarks of Time Out Group Ltd.

© **Time Out Group Ltd 2006**

10 9 8 7 6 5 4 3 2 1

This edition first published in Great Britain in 2006 by Ebury Publishing
Ebury Publishing is a division of The Random House Group Ltd,
20 Vauxhall Bridge Road, London SW1V 2SA

Random House Australia Pty Limited 20 Alfred Street, Milsons Point, Sydney, New South Wales 2061, Australia
Random House New Zealand Limited 18 Poland Road, Glenfield, Auckland 10, New Zealand
Random House South Africa (Pty) Limited Isle of Houghton, Corner Boundary
Road & Carse O'Gowrie, Houghton 2198, South Africa

Random House UK Limited Reg. No. 954009

Distributed in USA by Publishers Group West
1700 Fourth Street, Berkeley, California 94710

Distributed in Canada by Penguin Canada Ltd
10 Alcorn Avenue, Toronto, Ontario, Canada M4V 3B2

For further distribution details, see www.timeout.com

To 31 December 2006: ISBN 1-904978-71-1
From 1 January 2007: 9781904978718

A CIP catalogue record for this book is available from the British Library

Colour reprographics by Wyndeham Icon, 3 & 4 Maverton Road, London E3 2JE

Printed and bound in Germany by Appl.

Papers used by Ebury Publishing are natural, recyclable products made from wood grown in sustainable forests

"Are the plane tickets available?

Is it a good price?

What about the hotel?

Didn't your cousin stay there once?

Aren't holidays supposed To be stress free?"

Say hello to yatra, discover a world of convenience.

The cheapest air fares and hotel reservations are now only a mouse click or phone call away.

We're talking about real time availability and instant confirmation here.

Precise information and shared experiences of fellow travelers on the site ensure you never end up at a place you would rather not.

All this, comes with the added convenience of payment options of your choice: cheque, credit card or cash.

You see, when we claim the future of travel is here, we're really not exaggerating.

Buy Online at www. yatra.in or call +91-93100-31313

Contents

Edited & designed by
Time Out Mumbai
Paprika Media Pvt Ltd
Essar House
11 KK Marg
Mahalaxmi
Mumbai 400 034
Tel +91 22 6660 1111
www.timeoutmumbai.net

For
Time Out Guides Limited
Universal House
251 Tottenham Court Road
London W1T 7AB
Tel +44 (0)20 7813 3000
Fax +44 (0)20 7813 6001
Email guides@timeout.com
www.timeout.com

Editorial

Editor Iain Ball
Editorial Assistance Ismay Atkins
Proofreaders James Mathew, Meher Marfatia
Researchers Suhani Singh, Nikhil Subramaniam
Indexer Shirley Khaitan

Editorial/Managing Director Peter Fiennes
Series Editor Ruth Jarvis
Deputy Series Editor Lesley McCave
Business Manager Gareth Garner
Guides Co-ordinator Holly Pick
Accountant Kemi Olufuwa

Design

Art Editor Arindam Dutt Gupta
Senior Designer Shirley Khaitan
Picture Editor Chirodeep Chaudhuri
Digital Imaging Pravin Pereira

Advertising

Sales Manager Anil Shah

Production

Group Production Director Mark Lamond
Production Manager Brendan McKeown
Production Co-ordinator Caroline Bradford

Time Out Group

Managing Director Mike Hardwick
Financial Director Richard Waterlow
Director/Group General Manager Nichola Coulthard
Director/Managing Director of TO Magazine Ltd and TO Communications Ltd David Pepper

Director/Managing Director TO Guides Ltd Peter Fiennes
Group Art Director John Oakey
Group IT Director Simon Chappell

Contributors

Introduction Iain Ball. **History** Jerry Pinto (*'This ship was built by a d—d black fellow'* Chetna Mahadik; *Bombay's first boom* Chetna Mahadik; *Empire Falls* Chetna Mahadik; *Mumbai or Bombay?* Iain Ball). **Mumbai Today** Iain Ball. **Communities** Jerry Pinto. **Bollywood** Nandini Ramnath, Rachel Dwyer (*Taste Bollywood's masala* Iain Ball). **Where to Stay** Iain Ball. **South Mumbai** Chetna Mahadik (*Mr Twain checks into Watson's* Chetna Mahadik; *The Japanese attack that wasn't* Chetna Mahadik; *A Beatle in Bombay* Iain Ball). **Suburbs** Jerry Pinto, Iain Ball. **Day Trips** Naresh Fernandes, Jerry Pinto. **Restaurants & Cafés** Iain Ball, Divia Thani-Daswani, Vikram Doctor and contributors to *Time Out Mumbai* (*Café Society* Che Kurrien; *Eat this* Vikram Doctor; *Street eats* Iain Ball; *Pan handling* Iain Ball; *Off Carter Road* Che Kurrien). **Pubs & Bars** Che Kurrien and contributors to *Time Out Mumbai.* **Shops & Services** Divia Thani-Daswani. **Festivals & Events** Nikhil Subramaniam. **Galleries** Srimoyee Mitra, Jerry Pinto. **Gay & Lesbian** Vikram Doctor. **Mind, Body & Soul** Tanvi Chheda, Divia Thani-Daswani. **Music** Amit Gurbaxani. **Nightlife** Che Kurrien. **Sport & Fitness** Jamie Alter, Che Kurrien. **Theatre & Dance** Pronoti Datta (theatre), Amit Gurbaxani, Suhani Singh (dance). **Goa** Vivek Menezes, Iain Ball (nightlife). **Getting Around** Suhani Singh, Nikhil Subramaniam. **Resources A-Z** Naresh Fernandes (media), Suhani Singh, Nikhil Subramanian (*Malaria* Iain Ball; *What's on the menu?* Vikram Doctor). **Further Reference** Naresh Fernandes, Nandini Ramnath.

Maps mapsofindia.com

Photography pages 5 (top), 24 (left), 26, 61 (bottom), 75, 77 (top right & bottom), 79, 91, 100, 105, 106, 126, 134 (both), 136, 137, 150, 155, 159, 170 Poulomi Basu; pages 3, 5 (bottom), 19, 22 (right), 23, 27, 34, 59, 61 (top), 63, 68, 72, 78 (bottom), 82 (top), 92, 94 (both), 95 (top), 97, 99, 119, 127, 128, 131, 133, 135, 139, 140, 141, 142 (both), 143, 145, 147, 149, 152, 153 (bottom), 158, 161, 227 Chirodeep Chaudhuri; pages 7, 9, 43 (both), 46, 48 (left), 55, 58, 62, 67, 71, 73, 74, 77 (top left), 78 (top), 80, 82 (bottom), 85, 89, 95 (bottom), 103, 107, 108, 111 (both), 114, 115 (both), 116, 121, 122-23 (box), 124, 130, 153 (top), 156, 157, 160, 162, 163, 164, 165, 169 Apoorva Guptay; all Goa images Vivek Menezes.
Others pages 24 (right), 81 Ambika Bhatt; pages 104, 202 (top) Iris Dreams; pages 12, 14 Philips Antiques; pages 15 (A city's legacy – Indian Navy's Heritage in Mumbai), 16 (Bombay – The Cities Within), 21 (Bombay The Cities Within), 22 (left) (Bombay The Cities Within) Eminence designs; pages 11, 17 Naresh Fernandes Collection; page 186 Dominic D'Souza; page 187 Bjorn Skolen & Pam Donaldson; page 83 Dinodia Picture Agency.

The Editor would like to thank: Sharada Dwivedi, Naresh Fernandes, Farooq Issa, Neelam Kapoor, Smiti Ruia and all at *Time Out Mumbai.*

Introduction

A chaotic, 13-million-strong melting pot of ethnic groups from all over India, Mumbai – still called Bombay by many who live there – is India's economic engine and home to Bollywood, the world's largest film industry. Hooked on money, glamour and corruption, the city is now beginning to reinvent itself as the financial capital of a superpower-in-waiting. Economic reforms have given rise to a growing and thriving middle class. New bars, restaurants and shopping malls are multiplying; new construction is frenzied; and TV, radio and print media are booming. Mumbai now even has its own *Time Out* magazine. In many ways, it is returning to the status of a global city it once held, as a crucial trade hub under British rule.

But with half its population living in slums, Mumbai remains a city of brutal inequality and shocking poverty. Its infrastructure is crumbling, space is at a premium and urban planning is shunted aside in favour of corrupt deals between politicians and the city's powerful builders' lobby. A protracted battle over how to redevelop Mumbai's sprawling, defunct cotton mills – as desperately-needed public housing and open spaces, or as shopping malls, luxury apartments and offices – reflects a larger struggle for the soul of a city rushing into an uncertain future.

Over the last decade, Mumbai has weathered political extremism, riots, terrorist bombings and catastrophic flooding; but despite the gargantuan scale of their city's problems, Mumbaikars are rarely downcast, bouncing back from disaster with seemingly irrepressible

energy and optimism. On July 26, 2005, when Mumbai nearly drowned in its worst-ever floods, the city's stock market didn't even flinch; instead it rose 53 points.

370 miles away, the beaches of ultra-laid-back Goa feel like another country. A Portuguese colony until 1961, Goa has a unique identity in India, with low population density and relatively advanced development, a culture of tolerance and a long history of openness to the outside world. The world continues to visit in droves. Recent growth has been dramatic, with international arrivals rising by over a third every year. Goa is the preferred holiday destination of the Indian middle class, with domestic traffic increasing exponentially as the economy surges. Goa's famed drugs-and-trance rave culture has come under increasing attack from authorities as the state attempts to go upmarket, restoring its capital, Panjim, turning heritage sites into boutique hotels and hosting an annual international film festival aspiring one day to rival Cannes.

Together, Mumbai and Goa are perfect partners – one a concentrated dose of cutting-edge urban India, the other an unashamedly relaxed beach party getaway. Enjoy them both.

ABOUT TIME OUT CITY GUIDES

Time Out Mumbai is one of an expanding series of Time Out City Guides, produced by the people behind the successful listings magazines in London, New York and Chicago. Our guides are all written and updated by resident experts who have striven to provide you with all the most up-to-date information you'll need to explore the city or read up on its background, whether you're a local or a first-time visitor. The guide contains detailed practical information, plus features that focus on unique aspects of the city.

THE LIE OF THE LAND

We've divided this book into two parts – a Mumbai city guide and a guide to Goa beginning on page 171. In Mumbai, we focus on the historic southern part of the city, the most interesting area for visitors, but we've also cast an eye over the up-and-coming suburbs to the north. Finding your way through it all is notoriously difficult; street names are infrequently used and locals usually navigate by reference to landmarks. Many street names have changed but locals continue to use the old names. To make life easier, we've put landmarks in our listings under 'Taxi' wherever possible and used old street names. We've also indicated whether the entry is on the east or west side of the local train station, for example, 'Bandra (W)'. Sights also have a grid reference and page number that points to street maps at the back of the book (starting on page 247).

ESSENTIAL INFORMATION

For all the practical information you might need for visiting the area – including emergency phone numbers and details of car hire and local transport, turn to the **Directory** chapter at the back of the guide. It starts on page 227.

THE LOWDOWN ON THE LISTINGS

We have tried to make this book as easy to use as possible. Addresses, phone numbers, local train stations, opening times, admission prices and credit card details are included in the listings. However, owners and managers can change their arrangements at any time – and they often do. Some restaurants and bars close to the public for private parties. Arts and cultural events are often finalised late and liable to change. We would advise you wherever possible to phone ahead and check opening times, ticket prices and other details. While every effort has been made to ensure accuracy, the publishers cannot accept responsibility for any errors it may contain.

PRICES & PAYMENT

We have listed prices in rupees (Rs) throughout and noted where venues such as shops, hotels, restaurants and bars accept the following credit cards: American Express (AmEx), Diners Club (DC), MasterCard (MC) and Visa (V). Few places except major hotels accept travellers' cheques.

The prices in this guide should be treated as guidelines, not gospel. It's not uncommon for taxi drivers and street vendors to double or quadruple prices for foreign visitors. Elsewhere, if they vary wildly from those we've quoted, ask if there's a good reason. If not, go elsewhere. We aim to give the best and most up-to-date advice, so we want to know when you've been badly treated or overcharged. Wherever possible, we have factored in the sales tax (VAT), which many restaurants and hotels leave out of the advertised rates.

TELEPHONE NUMBERS

The country code for India is 91. The area code for Mumbai is 022; numbers usually have eight digits. The area code for Goa is 0832, usually followed by a seven-digit number. If you're dialling from abroad, use the country code 91 for India, followed by 22 or 832 as appropriate (thereby dropping the zero from the area code) and the number.

MAPS

The map section at the back of the guide includes an overview map of Mumbai and its suburban train network. There are also some more detailed street maps of south Mumbai and part of the suburb of Bandra. There's also a comprehensive street index. The Goa section also contains an orientation map of the state and more detailed maps. The Mumbai map section begins on page 247, and pinpoints specific locations of hotels (❶), restaurants (❶) and pubs and bars (❶).

LET US KNOW WHAT YOU THINK

We hope you enjoy the *Time Out Mumbai & Goa guide*, and we'd like to know what you think of it. We welcome tips for places that you consider we should include in future editions and will take note of your criticism of our choices. You can email us at guides@timeout.com.

Advertisers

There is an online version of this book, along with guides to over 45 other international cities, at www.timeout.com.

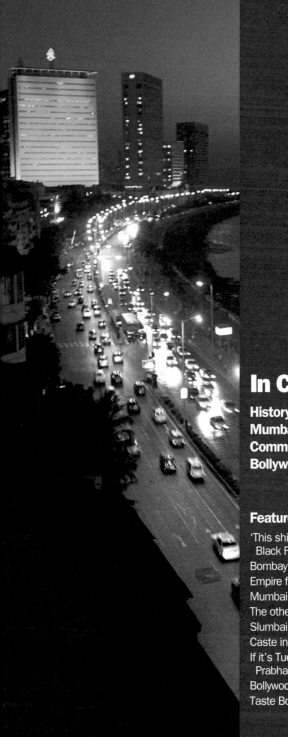

In Context

Western Railway Headquarters – built in 1899.

History

How seven islands became one.

For centuries, the islands that eventually became Mumbai must have seemed like an afterthought. If the Japanese lived here, they might have described the cluster of unremarkable islands off India's western coast as seven ink drops from the pens of the gods. History has forgotten whatever name its aboriginal inhabitants, the Koli fisherfolk, gave their home. For centuries the islands remained mosquito-infested spits of land separated by creeks and swamps, but blessed with plentiful mangroves that provided coastal protection and attracted large volumes of fish. Despite their ordinariness, Ptolemy marked the islands in his maps and the ancient Greeks knew them as Heptanesia (literally, 'Seven Islands').

The only remaining records of Mumbai's early history indicate occasional scraps of activity in between centuries filled with what we can only suppose was the incessant hiss of the Arabian Sea, the swear words of mosquito-bitten Kolis and the thump of falling coconuts. The channels between the islands were so deep they must have been often impossible to cross, with monsoon storms leaving each island isolated from the others. Even when the

legendary warrior king (and later Buddhist) Ashoka – ruler of the Mauryan Empire – turned his attention to the region in the third century BC, he ignored the islands, instead colonising areas located beyond the northern limits of modern Mumbai. In those days, Nalla Sopara (now a 30-second commuter stop for trains on their way north to Virar) was a bustling town, located at the crossroads of ancient trade routes. It became a patronage centre for magnificent Buddhist monasteries – you can still see the remnants of some of them in the Kanheri caves at Borivali.

What is known is that around the fifth century AD, a prince of the Chalukya Dynasty – a political dynasty that ruled large parts of the western and southern regions of the country – constructed the breathtaking cave-temples at Gharapuri, now called Elephanta Island, with an iconography that represents an early dialectic between Buddhism and Shaivism (the worship of Shiva). Some 400 years later, in the ninth century, the Silhara kings of the Konkan region in the south moved north to take control of all seven islands. It was the first of what was to be many battles for control of the region, with the seven islands being batted between competing powers like a tennis ball over the next 1,000 years. Even with the Silharas in control, the islands and their Koli inhabitants remained undisturbed; the Silharas instead established their regional capital in Thane, on the northern limits of present-day Mumbai.

In 1127 the Walkeshwar Temple, in what is now Malabar Hill, was constructed by Lakshman Prabhu, a minister in the court of the Silharas. It was an extraordinary achievement and a measure of the Silharas' devotion to Lord Ram, the Hindu god and hero of the epic Ramayana, who is supposed to have created its sacred Banganga tank by shooting an arrow into the ground and bringing forth the waters of the Ganges. The terrain was difficult and extensive infrastructure was required to transport masonry from one island to another. The Silharas managed to retain control of the islands until 1343, when the Sultan of neighbouring Gujarat took over and ruled it for the next two centuries.

Over the following five centuries, the islands of Mumbai underwent an extraordinary metamorphosis into the contiguous finger of land that now stretches westwards from the mainland. The story of that transformation begins with the Portuguese.

WHITE MAN AHOY

Portuguese explorers had already arrived in Goa in the 16th century, on a mission to wrest control of the near-priceless spice trade from the Arabs and win souls for Christendom. One of the first recorded visits of the Portuguese to Mumbai was in 1508, when a ship halted briefly at Mahim Island while travelling to an outpost at Diu in Gujarat. For the next two decades the Portuguese made many short visits to the islands and in 1532 they finally seized Bassein (now Vasai in northern Mumbai) from Sultan Bahadur Shah of Gujarat. From there the Portuguese took the entire region, including the seven islands. At that time, the Arabian coast was a bustling region of trading ships and seaside outposts. The Portuguese already possessed Goa, Daman and Diu, and Vasai became an important part of their maritime trade network.

To protect their shipping routes, the Portuguese fortified the islanded region, establishing cannon-equipped outposts at Mahim, Sion, Bandra and of course in Bassein. It was around this time that the region got a new name – 'Bom Baia', meaning 'Good Bay' in Portuguese. When the Portuguese first came to the place they called 'Bandora', now Bandra, they found an ideal spot: a strategically important point overlooking the sea, amply

supplied with drinking water from nearby freshwater springs. In 1640, they stationed a permanent garrison of troops here and built a small fort, which they called the Castella de Aguada ('Sea Castle'). Armed with a pair of cannons, the garrison kept watch over sea lanes crucial to Portuguese trading interests. Anxious about the spiritual well-being of their troops, they also built the Chapel of Nossa Senora de Monte ('Our Lady of the Mount') nearby and cut a road linking it to the fort.

Over the next 100 years the region's social history was shaped by Portuguese religious, economic and political impulses and resembled other Portuguese outposts – including Goa and Daman and Malacca in South East Asia. Many village communities from Mahim to Vasai converted to Christianity and the landscape became punctuated with churches and chapels. The Portuguese destroyed the Walkeshwar Temple, which was eventually rebuilt in 1715 by a wealthy Hindu trader. Over 350 years later, the Nossa Senora de Monte church – now known as Mount Mary – is still a place of worship. At the fort, only ruins remain. Thane, to the north east of the islands, became an attractive township of villages, temples and churches nestled between lakes and coconut groves.

> **'Charles II was not exactly sure where his wedding present was located; he initially thought Bombay was somewhere in Brazil.'**

For all the development, the Portuguese still didn't see much trade potential in the area and it remained a backwater. Instead it was their rivals, the British East India Company, who cast a covetous eye over the area from the company's headquarters in Gujarat. They considered it a perfect natural harbour for the Company's first Indian port. The main attraction, of course, was the deep bay on the eastern waterfront over-looking the mainland. The Surat outpost began pressing its London headquarters to purchase the islands from the Portuguese. They finally got their hands on the islands in 1661, when they were given to King Charles II as part of his dowry for his marriage to Portuguese princess Catherine de Braganza. Apparently, Charles was not exactly sure where his wedding present was located; he initially thought that the islands were somewhere in Brazil. In 1668, he leased the islands to the British East India Company for the sum of ten pounds a year and the company quickly

established a colony in and around an existing Portuguese fort, which grew rapidly from 10,000 people in 1661 to 60,000 by 1675. In 1687 the East India Company transferred its headquarters from Surat to what the British now called Bombay.

BIRTH OF A TRADE HUB

Bombay's early population mostly comprised Koli fisherfolk, East India Company officials and migrants from Gujarat who set up shop to service the outpost. Among the migrants were an émigré community of Iranian Zoroastrians known as Parsis (*see p28*), who were to become a decisive commercial and political force in Bombay's development. That was foreshadowed early in the colony's history by the actions of a Parsi trader, Rustomji Dorabji. Just two years after the Company moved to Bombay, the outpost was beset by a plague outbreak; at the same time, a nearby Africa-descended tribe called the Siddis launched an attack on the colony from their base down the coast in Janjira (near present-day Alibaug). Despite the chaos caused by the plague, Dorabji managed to raise an impromptu army from the local Kolis and repelled the Siddis in a counterattack – saving the colony and killing the Siddi chief in the process.

That the size and influence of the Parsi presence was strong very early in Bombay's history is proved by the fact that a Tower of Silence – a traditional Parsi funeral place, where bodies are left to be consumed by vultures – was built on Malabar Hill in 1672. In 1708 the first Parsi *agiary* (fire temple) was built, the Banaji Limji Agiary, with a second established in 1733. Two years later, the Parsis established a shipbuilding industry which later became one of the largest suppliers of ships to the British Royal Navy. A young Parsi shipbuilder from Gujarat, Lowji Nusserwanji Wadia, was invited to Bombay by the British East India Company to build them ships, in an enterprise that led to the Wadia dynasty of shipbuilders (*see p15* **This ship was built by a d—d black fellow**).

The Parsis remained at the forefront of the city's development and in 1777 Rustomji Kashaspathi published its first newspaper, the *Bombay Courier*. The city's main role was as an import-export hub: diamonds, tea, paper, porcelain, raw silk, calicoes, pepper, herbs and drugs sailed out to Britain and lead, quicksilver, woollen garments, hardware and bullion sailed in. Bombay's status was further boosted by an increase in cotton trade with China after 1770, an exchange that continued over the next century.

During this period the city saw a continuous migration of traders from Surat that further energised the economy. Some historians suggest that the rise of Bombay as a successful trading hub precipitated the decline of Surat, which soon lost its cherished status as a major seaport. In subsequent years, the islands began to attract many Gujarati traders (both Hindu and Muslim), including Parsi shipbuilders from the mainland. Most people lived in and around a fort at the heart of the colony, originally built by the Portuguese and further developed by the British. Known as Bombay Castle, it was essentially a walled township in the area of the city today known as Fort. A fragment of the fort wall still exists next to St George's Hospital. By 1813, almost half of the 10,000 people who lived in the Fort area were Parsis. As it became more and more crowded and often prone to disease, its richer inhabitants began to move out to new townships beyond the walled city, building bungalows and mansions in the city's first suburbs: Byculla, Mazagaon and Malabar Hill.

SHAPING THE CITY

By the beginning of the 19th century, business in Bombay was booming – so much so that in 1801 the British Government sent a reporter to document the extent of the city's trade. His reports convinced them in 1813 to end the East India Company's monopoly on trade, encouraging even greater commercial expansion. A few years later, a massive civil engineering project to reclaim land from the sea was commissioned, its aim to fuse the disparate islands of Bombay into a single land mass. Over the next few decades, as the city took shape, a large middle-class population emerged that drove a huge demand for newspapers, schools and colleges.

> **'The British commissioned a massive project to reclaim land from the sea and fuse the islands into a single land mass.'**

In 1822 India's first Indian-language newspaper, the Gujarati daily *Mumbai Samachar*, was published in Bombay. Still running today, it's the country's oldest newspaper. The first copy of the *Bombay Times* (the forerunner of the *Times of India*) rolled off the presses in 1838. Grant Medical College was founded in 1845 and within another 15 years, Wilson College and Bombay University were established. Other colleges like Elphinstone College and St Xavier's came up within a decade. Both the new media and colleges were largely patronised by children of Gujarati merchants and traders, the indigenous Christian populations and Maharashtrians. Middle-class suburbs sprung up in the new neighbourhoods of Kalbadevi, Girgaum,

Bombay University's **Rajabai Clock Tower**.

'This ship was built by a d—d black fellow'

A trademark barley-twisted railing in front of the cabins on the gun decks gave away their makers: the Wadia shipbuilders of Bombay. The name was a byword for high quality for 18th- and 19th-century mariners – an assurance that the ship they were sailing was of prodigious speed, agility and durability. Legend has it that one Wadia ship sailed for years with a proud, defiant message carved on her stern by the chief shipwright, Jamshetji Wadia: 'This ship was built by a d—d black fellow AD 1800'.

The Wadia shipbuilding dynasty was born in 1735 when the British East India Company called Lowji Nusserwanji, a Surat-based Parsi shipbuilder, to Mumbai. Initially, he was only expected to open a trade in teak with the local forest tribes. But his skills impressed the Company so much that he was appointed the master shipbuilder of the fledgling Bombay Docks. He supervised the docks' modernisation and established superb standards of craftsmanship. By the time of his death in 1775, 20 warships and 14 merchant ships had set sail from the docks. In honour of his services, the British gave him the title 'Wadia', Gujarati for shipbuilder, which he adopted as his family name.

HMS Asia, built in Bombay.

Blame it on the genes, but for the next 150 years, a Wadia remained at the helm of the Bombay Docks. Their teak ships were so strong that many of them lasted for 50 to 60 years, compared to the average 12 years of British-built oak ships. With teak being so much cheaper than oak, Wadia ships went on to dominate the British Navy, seeing action in the Napoleonic Wars.

Between 1735 and 1863, the family built 170 warships and other vessels for the East India Company, 34 warships for the Royal Navy and 87 merchant ships for private firms. Over the years, Wadia-built ships witnessed and participated in plenty of world history. Sitting aboard *HMS Minden*, Francis Scott Key composed *The Star Spangled Banner*, the American national anthem, as the ship stood off Baltimore Harbour in 1814. In 1842 the Treaty of Nanking, ceding Hong Kong to the British, was signed on board the Wadia-built *HMS Cornwallis*.

The last Wadia master builder was Khan Bahadur Jamsetji Dhanjibhoy, who retired in 1885 with the family unable to adapt to a new era of shipping. The Industrial Revolution replaced sails with steam and teak with iron, and Bombay's shipbuilding boom came to an end.

Gowalia Tank, Mohammad Ali Road, Thakurdwar and Walkeshwar.

By the middle of the 19th century, the knitting together of Bombay's islands through land reclamation was nearly complete. Causeways linked Bombay, Sion, Salsette and Colaba. Mahalaxmi and Worli were joined. In 1845, Mahim and Bandra were connected by the Mahim causeway thanks to a rich Parsi, Lady Avabai Jamsetjee Jeejeebhoy, who paid Rs 157,000 for it. Legend has it that she prayed at several religious sites for the survival of a sick child. When the child recovered after she prayed at Mount Mary Church, Lady Avabai

built the causeway to allow more devotees access to the Virgin Mother without having to bother with a ferry.

As the physical landmass came together, Bombay's political and commercial links with the Empire were tightened with the beginning of a regular steamship service between the city and London in 1843. Fifteen years later, direct British Government control of the Indian colony was established following the First War of Indian Independence (the 'Indian Mutiny') in 1857. All of the East India Company's formal political powers were handed to the Crown.

Bombay's first boom

Renowned Bombay businessman Premchand Roychand and his friend George Birdwood, the editor of the *Times of India*, were at a meeting in March 1865 when Roychand received a telegram announcing the end of the American Civil War. 'This, Birdwood, means beginning my life all over again,' Roychand told his friend. He wasn't the only one forced to start over. The surrender of Lee's Army at Appomattox was a terrible shock to nearly all of Bombay's leading business families; within a year dozens of companies would be wiped out by bankruptcy.

But it had been fun while it lasted. The outbreak of war between the states in 1861 had seriously disrupted America's bumper cotton exports, forcing the textile industry in Britain and Europe to look for an alternative source. Bombay, as a seaport well connected to cotton fields, was the obvious choice and quickly supplanted America as the world's foremost supplier. Bombay gorged itself on cotton money, earning around 75 million pounds over the next four years. By 1865, Bombay had 31 banks, eight reclamation companies, 16 cotton pressing companies, ten shipping companies, 62 joint stock companies and 20 insurance companies. Property prices skyrocketed.

Roychand was the leader of the pack of speculators who grew rich off the boom, thanks in part to some dubious practices. He would send out small boats to meet mail ships and learn the latest cotton prices in London before the ships docked. He then bought or sold before anyone else and made a killing when the prices were announced. And as the director of the Bank of Bombay and six other financial institutions, he could draw on huge amounts of money to feed the boom.

Most other speculators simply followed Roychand, buying when he bought and selling when he sold. In his notes, Arthur Crawford, one of Bombay's municipal commissioners, describes the euphoria of the times: 'It was a common thing, in strolling from your office to the dear old Navy Club, to stop a moment in the seething Share Market and ask your broker, "Well, Mr B or Bomanji! What's doing?" "Oh Sir! So-and-So Financials are rising – they say Premchand is buying." "Ah well, just buy me fifty or a hundred shares" (as your inclination prompted you). You went to your "tiffin" or luncheon, at the memorable long table; you ordered a pint of Champagne – no one ever drank anything but Champagne in those days… Four o'clock saw you on your way back to the office, and you stopped to ask your broker how your financials stood. "Rising slowly, sir!" would be the answer; with a calm acceptance you said, "Then please sell mine," and the morrow brought you a cheque of fifty or a hundred or two hundred rupees as the case might be.'

When the bubble burst, Bombay became a bankruptcy graveyard. Roychand's Bank of Bombay crashed. The shockwaves were felt

Horniman Circle – paid for by cotton.

as far as London, where Overend Gurney Bank failed and many smaller companies collapsed. Although the crash seemed devastating, Bombay quickly recovered. The vast injection of money paid for new roads and institutions like the High Court and Elphinstone Circle (now Horniman Circle), the Public Works Office and Central Telegraph Office. Roychand took much of the blame for the extent of the crash, but quickly got back on his feet, later bankrolling the Bombay University at Fort (the university library clocktower is named after his mother, Rajabai). Many business houses made a strategic shift from cotton trading into cotton spinning, which fuelled Bombay's economy through the first half of the 20th century.

URBS PRIMA IN INDIS

By 1845, the basis of a modern city had been created with land measuring 170 square miles – a complex landscape of fields, coconut groves and outsize colonial structures, of cosmopolitan enclaves and sleepy villages. Bombay was the starting point of India's first passenger railway line in 1853, connecting the city to Thane.

In the 1860s the British began a construction programme, erecting architecture that was designed to signal to the natives that they were here to stay – a direct response to the Indian uprising of 1857. Victoria Terminus, the Prince of Wales Museum, Rajabai Tower, Bombay University, the General Post Office, the Old Customs House, Elphinstone College, the Public Works Department Building – all were begun in the 1860s. With typical imperial hyperbole, they began to refer to Bombay as 'urbs prima in Indis' – the first city of India.

'Bombay's first cotton mill was vociferously opposed by Lancashire mill owners anxious to avoid the outsourcing of cotton spinning.'

In 1864, the Bombay, Baroda and Central India Railway (later merged with other railways to form what is now the Western Railway) was extended to Bombay, boosting the flow of cotton from the hinterlands. Cotton now dominated trade in Bombay. Raw cotton from Gujarat was shipped to Lancashire in Britain, processed into cloth and then shipped back via Bombay to be resold in the Indian market. Although cotton trading was the city's main activity, city businessmen began to recognise that bigger profits could be made by spinning the cotton themselves. In 1854 the first cotton mill, the Bombay Spinning Mill, was opened by a Parsi, Cowasji Nanabhai Davar. It was met by vociferous opposition from Lancashire mill owners anxious to avoid the 'outsourcing' of the cotton spinning business, and was only pushed through thanks to the influence of the British manufacturers of the cotton looms. In 1870, around 13 mills were in operation in the city. The shipping of raw cotton was still the main engine of the city's economy, however, and was given a massive filip when the American Civil War broke out in 1861 (*see p16* **Bombay's first boom**). The war forced global markets to look for an alternative source of cotton for the booming textile industries of Britain and other countries in Europe. Bombay became the world's

Bombay Municipal Hall – built in 1893.

foremost cotton supplier. Money poured into the city until the war ended.

Yet, within a year of the war's end in 1865, most of the companies were liquidated and many speculators went bankrupt. In spite of this, the city continued to grow, using the wealth generated during the boom to make itself over by shifting more and more into cotton spinning. The city's strategic location as a trade hub was given a further boost with the opening of the Suez Canal in 1869. By 1895 there were 70 mills in the city, rising to 83 in 1915 before stagnating in the global recession of the 1920s. Despite continued British political control, most of Bombay's cotton mills were owned by Indian families. In 1925, only 15 mills were British-owned, and even then the management was mostly Indian.

With the growth of the mills, Bombay's population rapidly increased as thousands of Maharashtrians migrated to the city to work the looms. The workers, usually male, initially lived in hostels and dormitories but eventually the 'chawl' (a tenement still in use today in which each family has one room, with all sharing a common verandah and toilets) emerged as basic housing for workers and their families. The workers settled close to the mills, with new neighbourhoods springing up in Byculla, Lalbaug, Parel and Worli. These neighbourhoods were often referred to by one name – Girangaon – the 'Village of Mills'. It was a dynamic cultural space and spawned generations of writers, poets and dramatists in Marathi and Gujarati. As the city grew, more land was reclaimed and more roads, causeways and wharves were built. The population had already increased from 13,726 in 1780 to 644,405 in 1872. By 1906 it had become 977,822.

The British continued to develop the city's infrastructure, with innovations like a drainage system, which continues to serve the city today. It was in 1860 that piped water began to flow to the city from Tulsi and Vihar lakes. Several city railway lines were unified into the Western Railway, with imposing headquarters built at Churchgate in 1899. The Bombay Port Trust was officially formed in 1870. The Princess Dock was built in 1855, followed by Victoria and Mereweather Dry Docks in 1891 and Alexandra Dock in 1914.

'The British maintained their control by both a reputation for evenhandedness and a shameless policy of divide and rule.'

LIVING TOGETHER, LIVING APART

From its early beginnings, Bombay had been a vibrantly diverse city of Europeans and Indians from across the subcontinent, and by the 19th century, the lines between communities had been drawn – but an uneasy tolerance prevailed. Europeans socialised among themselves in sports clubs, with cricket as the main recreation. The Bombay Gymkhana was set up in 1875, exclusively for Europeans, spurring other communities, including Muslim, Hindu and Parsis, to set up their own gymkhanas, all in a line by the sea along Marine Drive. A friendly rivalry developed between them, with a regular 'Pentangular' cricket tournament, as it was called, never failing to make headlines in city newspapers.

The British maintained their control in the city through a paradoxical combination of a reputation for evenhandedness and a shameless policy of divide and rule. In the 1880s, the commander of the Bombay police was a British superintendent named Charles Forjett, who was greatly admired by Indian residents for his harsh treatment of corrupt policemen and for conducting regular operations against the Parsi mafia who controlled the illegal liquor business in the Falkland Road region. The British were concerned about the power of religious festivals to encourage a desire for political independence, and tried to manage them, albeit tentatively.

The nationalist freedom fighter Lokmanya Tilak saw the same potential and transformed the Ganpati festival, once celebrated on a small, domestic scale across Maharashtra, into a large-scale, outdoor event. He brought his supporters to Mumbai's beaches, ostensibly to immerse idols of the elephant-headed Ganesha in the sea as per tradition, and then gave fiery speeches about their political responsibilities and the dream of *swaraj* (self-government). The British were checked from interfering too much in religious issues by the lessons of 1857, in which a rumour about rifle cartridges being made with pig and cow fat (thereby offending both Muslims and Hindus) had sparked an army rebellion which nearly lost them the colony. The British left Tilak largely alone and mass immersions during the Ganpati festival continue to this day, with its freedom-movement origins largely forgotten.

Instead of direct action, the British responded to such challenges to their authority with the same divide-and-rule policy they had used all over the country – by playing Hindus and Muslims off against each other. It was hardly difficult for the British in Bombay, a city where communities were already naturally divided into different enclaves. With so little official thought put into planning residential neighbourhoods for the poorer or even middle-class populations, the only support network for those looking for homes or the means to build them came from within their own ethnic groups. As the city became more and more politicised, communal riots began to plague Bombay for the first time.

TURNING THE CENTURY

Bombay was still a city among other Indian cities. But in 1875, the basis for its current status as India's economic capital was established with the Bombay Stock Exchange – then referred to as the Native Share and Stockbrokers Association. As the cream of India's professional talent flooded into the city, political movements began to flourish (*see p19* **Empire falls**). Political ferment saw the establishment of the Indian National Congress – the first Indian political party – in 1885 at the Gokuldas Tejpal College in South Mumbai.

By this time a lack of adequate urban planning was causing large parts of the city to choke from over-congestion, a problem that became disastrous just a few years before the end of the 19th century, when bubonic plague broke out, possibly carried by rats on grain ships from Hong Kong. Thousands fled the city and Indian and foreign ports quarantined all goods arriving from Bombay, with ruinous consequences for the city's economy. The tragedy was compounded by the failure of the monsoon in 1899, leading to one of India's worst-ever famines. The British authorities responded to the catastrophe by setting up

Empire falls

The political force that would shape India's destiny was born in Bombay on a mild December day in 1885. A delegation of 70 Indian lawyers, professors and journalists congregated at the Gokuldas Tejpal College to establish the Indian National Congress (INC), India's first national political party. There was no formal political forum in which it could speak or debate legislation – Indian independence was still 62 years away. But the Congress led over 70 million Indians in the struggle against British rule and, after freedom finally came in 1947, dominated independent India's politics for the rest of the century. In Delhi, the Congress is still in power today.

Had he lived to see it, the Congress's founder would have been shocked. His name was Allan Octavian Hume, a retired civil servant from Kent. An ardent but puritanical social reformer, Hume served as the INC's General Secretary until 1908, during which time its official stance was not outright opposition to British rule, but just a demand for greater say for Indians in government. It was only after repeated British refusals that their politics became radicalised.

Bombay remained at the centre of events throughout the Indian freedom struggle, despite being much younger and smaller than Calcutta or Delhi. Lacking the rigid social structures that prevailed in other cities, social reform was already underway in Bombay. The city admired ability and rewarded merit, attracting India's best and brightest. It had a cosmopolitan and enlightened middle class and an array of colleges and cultural institutions. This combination allowed Bombay to take the lead in making Indian political history, like producing the first Indian to be elected to the British Parliament in 1893, a Parsi named Dadabhai Naoroji.

Mohandas Gandhi, commonly known as the Mahatma ('Great Soul'), chose Bombay as his base upon his return from South Africa, living in the now-famous Mani Bhavan in Gamdevi. It was from here that Gandhi planned and co-ordinated non-cooperation and civil disobedience movements, and first introduced his revolutionary concepts of non-violence, *satyagraha* ('truth force') and *swadeshi* (loosely, 'buying Indian'). Be it money or manpower, Gandhi found enthusiastic support from the people of Bombay.

When the fatal blow to British rule finally came, it was struck from Bombay. Gandhi launched the Quit India movement on August 8, 1942 at Gowalia Tank, with Congress support. Gandhi urged Indians to act as citizens of an independent nation and use non-violent civil disobedience to frustrate British control. Hundreds of thousands across India responded. Soon after, Gandhi and other members of the Congress Working Committee were arrested. It was too late – Gandhi's call spread like jungle fire across the city and a large crowd gathered at Gowalia Tank the next day. Just five years later, the British Empire fell in India.

Gandhi on the march – clay depictions of the freedom struggle at Mani Bhavan.

a City Improvement Trust to encourage the development of the suburbs and relieve pressure on the southern part of the city.

By the beginning of the 20th century, the first outlines of the character of modern Bombay had begun to emerge. By 1906, the city's population had topped one million. It quickly became a hotbed for the new politics that would lead to Indian

'The Indian film industry was born, kicking, screaming and running around trees.'

Independence, fired up by Mahatma Gandhi's return from South Africa in 1915. Gandhi took a house called Mani Bhavan in Gamdevi, from where he began to rally citizens to the cause. Prominent Bombay businessmen, traders, workers and professionals became his votaries. Technological innovations that had slowly emerged in the West were implanted in Bombay in rapid order, with the first transmission lines of the Tata Power Company criss-crossing the city's skyline in 1915. In 1926 the first motorised bus service started between Afghan Church and Crawford Market. The first electric train started in 1927, an intercity service from Bombay to Pune and Igatpuri. A few years later the first electric commuter trains (still known in Mumbai as 'EMUs' – Electric Multiple Units) rolled out. In 1932, the Parsi industrialist JRD Tata flew the first scheduled airmail flight from Karachi to Bombay via Ahmedabad, landing his single-engined De Haviland Puss Moth on a grass strip at Juhu Aerodrome.

In 1896, the Lumière Brothers Cinematographe showed four silent short films at the Watson's Hotel in Bombay, charging an entry fee of one rupee. It was a phenomenon that the *Times of India* described at the time as 'the marvel of the century', and quickly fired the imaginations of a generation of Indians. The Indian film industry was born, kicking, screaming and running around trees, in Bombay a few years later. A man named HS Bhatavdekar filmed the city's first documentary in 1899, of a wrestling match, which he showed across the city to general acclaim. The first full-length feature film, *Raja Harishchandra*, was made in 1913 by Dadasaheb Phalke and shown at Bombay's Coronation Cinematograph. By 1920, the Indian film industry was fully formed, with Bombay at its heart. By 1931 about 207 films were being made every year. But it wasn't until the 1990s that the term 'Bollywood' was coined.

POST-INDEPENDENCE UPHEAVAL

After 'freedom at midnight' gave birth to independent India on August 15, 1947, Mumbai continued to expand beyond the suburbs of Mahim and Bandra – erstwhile Portuguese areas – swallowing up everything as far north as Mankhurd, Mulund and Dahisar. The city became the capital of Bombay State, a political creation that included the whole of what are now the two separate states of Gujarat and Maharashtra. Over the following years Bombay became a battlefield for political movements based on language, mainly for Gujarati- and Marathi-speaking populations. The Samyukta Maharashtra Andolan was a major political force of socialists, trade unions and artists that fought fiercely for the formation of an independent state for Marathi-speaking people, with Bombay as its capital. They finally achieved their wish and Bombay State was split in two in 1960, but only after 105 of the movement's supporters had been shot dead by

Mumbai or Bombay?

In 1995 the Shiv Sena, a far-Right Maharashtrian political party, changed the city's official name from Bombay to Mumbai, the Marathi name for the city. It was the centrepiece of a drive to eradicate British Raj-era place names across the city, which included renaming the Victoria Terminus as Chhatrapati Shivaji Terminus. 'Mumbai' is derived from *Mumba*, a name for the Hindu goddess Mumbadevi and *aai*, meaning 'mother' in Marathi.

Visitors often assume that it's politically incorrect to use the old name and are surprised to discover that almost every English-speaker in Mumbai – of whom there are millions – still calls the city Bombay. The fondness for the old name is mostly just a case of old habits dying hard, but for some it's also a rejection of the Shiv Sena and their violent, anti-outsider politics. But it's even more complicated, as each name also carries distinct class connotations – 'Bombay' implies the English-speaking elite, 'Mumbai' the middle and working classes. Either way, as an outsider you're unlikely to upset anyone whichever name you use.

Bombay's western bay in the 1880s...

...and in the 1990s.

police during tumultuous political protests around Flora Fountain earlier the same year. A memorial at what is now called Hutatma Chowk commemorates the dead with an eternal flame.

Bombay's politics in the 1960s and 1970s remained dynamic and dominated by the Left, with the working-class mill areas of central Bombay as a Communist heartland. But a splinter of the Samyukta Maharashtra Andolan morphed into a nativist movement – the Shiv Sena ('Army of Shivaji'), which won continued influence with its Right-wing anti-outsider politics in the face of growing slum encroachment by immigrants from outside the city. During the 1970s the city overtook Calcutta as the most populous city in the country. A lack of political will, cushioned by a healthy economy benefiting from cheap labour, allowed slums to proliferate on a scale that had never been seen before (*see p26* **Slumbai**). In the process, the Shiv Sena fired the imagination of the working class, displacing the old dominance of the Left. Its founder, a former cartoonist named Bal Thackeray, came to dominate the city's political landscape using a combination of

brutal mafia-like force and a string of local election victories. The decline of the textile industry contributed to this political shift and, after a catastrophic 1982-83 mill workers' strike, the century-old cotton-spinning industry effectively died in Mumbai. With its passing, the mill workers lost their key position in the city's economy and politics.

The 1970s and early '80s were an exciting decade in the city's cinematic history, with the emergence of filmmakers determined to differentiate themselves from the mainstream Hindi film industry. They began to make realist and neo-expressionist films with strong elements of social commentary. Shyam Benegal's *Ankur* (*The Seedling*), released in 1974, introduced the stunning actress-turned-MP Shabana Azmi and was the first film to articulate the new conflict between India's educated, urbane city dwellers and the feudal traditions of the countryside. Rabindra Dharmaraj's *Chakra* in 1981, was a searing look at the slums of Bombay, seen through the smouldering eyes of actress Smita Patil.

City authorities made few infrastructure improvements in the 1970s and '80s, despite the alarmingly rapid growth in the city's population. The largest was a plan to create New Bombay (now known as Navi Mumbai) – a parallel city across the harbour on the mainland – to decongest the island city. It began slowly, faltered, and even today has yet to live up to the original aims.

'The riots and bombings were a shattering blow to Mumbai's self-image as a cosmopolitan, secular city.'

The Shiv Sena continued to rise throughout the 1980s, thanks to the decline of the Left and increasingly visible corruption in the Congress. It was a political combination that proved to be lethal, culminating in the horrendous Bombay Riots of 1992-93 – incidents that were in fact state-sanctioned and party-sponsored pogroms against Muslims. The violence erupted after the Babri Mosque was razed by Hindu militants in the city of Ayodhya, in the North Indian state of Uttar Pradesh. Hundreds of Muslims were killed by Hindu fundamentalists during the riots. On March 12 the same year came 'Black Friday', when ten bombs exploded in one day at locations across the city, including the Bombay Stock Exchange and the Air India Building. 257 people were killed in what were revenge attacks by a Muslim group for the slaughter two months previously. The riots and bombings were a shattering blow to Mumbai's self-image as a cosmopolitan, secular city that for years had avoided the communal violence that afflicts other Indian cities. It paved the way for the Shiv Sena's rise to power at both city and state levels and, in 1995, they changed the official name of the city to Mumbai (*see p20* **Bombay or Mumbai?**). Since then, Mumbai has been the victim of sporadic terrorist attacks, most recently in August 2003, when bombs at the Gateway of India and at Zaveri Bazaar killed 52 people.

Since 1991, a series of economic reforms have liberalised India's economy, unleashing Mumbai's entrepreneurial energy. It has become a new global city with a modern spirit close to that of its former identity as a trade hub. But while Mumbai may be the financial capital of a superpower-in-waiting, its citizens are still waiting for a transformation of its infrastructure, social housing and polluted air.

Marine Drive in the 1930s.

Indian art deco – Mahatma Gandhi Road.

Mumbai Today

Bombay dreams are still a long way from being realised.

On July 26, 2005 it started to rain and it continued heavily for six days. In the first 24 hours, almost a metre of rain fell on northern Mumbai, nearly twice the highest-ever recorded rainfall on a single day in the city. Flooding is routine every monsoon. The city's storm-water drains are frequently clogged and its sea outfalls have no floodgates, so seawater flows into the sewer system during high tide. But this was different: Mumbai began to drown. Electricity supplies failed. The suburban rail network – the city's lifeline – ground to a halt. Roads became impassable. Houses were flooded and slum dwellings washed away. All the while, the city's meagre emergency services were paralysed and government officials absent. As the rains continued to batter the city, hundreds of thousands of stranded citizens were left to fend for themselves, spending the night and the next day in choked railway stations and on the top decks of stalled buses, relying on the kindness of strangers for food and water. Thousands more attempted walking home through chest-high floodwaters choked with sewage, garbage and the carcasses of thousands of drowned goats and buffaloes.

Over 400 Mumbaikars died in 'Terrible Tuesday' and its aftermath. Over 200 drowned; others were killed by landslides, collapsing walls and electrocution. Some were drowned in their cars, trapped by rising floodwaters. More died later from diseases caused by the influx of sewage into the water system. Overall, the cost of the disaster was estimated to be $3.5 billion. As the rains eased and the floodwaters receded, an angry citizenry, led by Mumbai's lively media, lashed municipal and state leaders for the disaster and their incompetent response. 'It was unprecedented,' complained Maharashtra Chief Minister Vilasrao Deshmukh, leader of the Congress Party-led state government. 'What could any government do?'

Quite a lot, actually. Despite the record rainfall, the devastation of Terrible Tuesday was payback for years of chaotic urban development, with successive city and state governments offering no coherent plan on how the city should modernise. One of the main causes of the catastrophe was ill-conceived land reclamations along the Mithi River, a waterway running through the centre of the city. Once a navigable river fringed with mangroves, the Mithi (ironically, the name means 'sweet') is now a cesspool of sewage, garbage and toxic chemicals dumped by unauthorised industries along its banks. Despite warnings from environmentalists, the government reclaimed one-and-a-half square miles of land from the

Out: A defunct mill in Girangaon.

In: A midtown shopping mall.

Mithi in the 1990s in order to build the glittering Bandra-Kurla Complex business park, now home to some of India's biggest companies. Once a natural storm water outlet, the river's mouth was narrowed by 1,300 feet and the natural flood defences provided by mangroves were destroyed. On July 26, the suburbs along its length were the worst hit in the city, with floodwaters reaching as high as five metres.

> **'Mumbai is a city with a lot of problems. But its biggest problem is not money, it's corrupt governance.'**

MILLS & MALLS

Mumbai is a city with a lot of problems. But its biggest problem is not the lack of money, it's incompetent and corrupt governance. With the city's Sensex stock index riding a seemingly endless boom, urban planning in Mumbai is driven by builders and developers for profits, not by city planners. A corrupt nexus between builders, bureaucrats and politicians allows hard cash to ride roughshod over laws designed to protect the city's fragile open spaces and coastal zones. There is a huge demand in Mumbai for space for new construction. Fierce battles have been fought over the city's 54 sprawling cotton mills – which sit on just under a square mile of prime land in central Mumbai worth a staggering Rs 210 billion ($4.74 billion). Once the engine of the city's economy and employer of a quarter of its organised labour, the mills have been shuttered since the textile industry began to die off in the 1980s. Their position is perfect – strategically placed between the city's southern business district and its rapidly growing suburbs. Developers want to rebuild them as shopping malls, offices and apartment blocks, to be sold for fabulous profits. But the mills also offer a unique chance for urban renewal. Half of them are state-owned,

the rest leased to private owners on favourable terms to stimulate employment. It was the government's call on how the lands should be developed, and a 1991 state law stipulated that two-thirds of any mill land sold should be reserved for urgently-needed social housing and green spaces. Predictably, the builder-politician nexus altered the law in 2001 to allow large-scale private development. By 2005 several mills had been sold and building work begun. Before they had even been built, luxury flats were being sold for Rs 10 million ($225,000) each. Phoenix Mills in Parel is now 'High Street Phoenix' – a bustling plaza of cafés, restaurants, bars and shops.

In the weeks after Terrible Tuesday, city newspapers and urban activists expressed the hope that the disaster might be a wake-up call for a city developing so rapidly it threatens to derail. They called for a reform of government to break the cosy relationship between builders and politicians, and to streamline the numerous, unco-ordinated municipal and state authorities. But Deshmukh rejected calls for a New York-style elected mayor with real power and accountability. Instead, his government tinkered at the edges, setting up new committees and departments. In October 2005 developers suffered a stunning reversal when a city environmental group won a crucial Bombay High Court ruling reinstating the original 1991 law. Building was stopped and confusion ensued about the status of the sold mills, before a supreme court ruling in March 2006 yet again turned the tables, upholding the the 2001 law. This ruling now seems likely to determine the future character of the city.

ECONOMIC REBIRTH

Mumbai has been India's economic engine for over a century, but the 1990s saw a pent-up energy unleashed as the 'Licence Raj' – the old era of stifling government regulation of private enterprise – was stripped away. Since July 1991, when India first began to liberalise its economy, the Mumbai stock market has grown from 1,000 points to over 11,000 points in March 2006. Investment has poured into a new economy of financial services, IT and software houses, healthcare, new media and outsourced 'back office' operations from the West. The publishing industry is on a high, with three new newspapers in 2005 and innumerable new magazines, including *Time Out Mumbai*.

In northern suburbs like Powai, entirely new middle-class neighbourhoods have emerged around these new industries. Shiny new multiplexes, bars, and restaurants now service a young middle class flush with cash from call centre jobs. After decades of punishing tariffs on foreign imports, the city is awash with international consumer brands. Nothing signals the increase in wealth more than the increase in traffic. In the 1980s there were just three car models available – there are now over 35. Over 200 new vehicles hit Mumbai's roads every single day, a number that can only go up as Mumbaikars' average incomes increase – currently Rs 62,495 ($1,389) a year, about three times higher than the rest of the country.

MEAN STREETS

Despite these tantalising signs of modernisation life for many Mumbaikars remains hard and, for the poorest, life is getting harder as subsidies are reduced to pay for a liberalised economy. Surveys of world cities routinely rate Mumbai as offering one of the worst qualities of life in the world. Part of the reason is sheer population pressure. Around 13 million people live in Mumbai, with 27,000 people per square kilometre – four times the population density of Hong Kong. Nearly eight million live in slums (*see p26* **Slumbai**) crammed into just six per cent of the city's land area. Six million – almost half the population – are forced to defecate in the open because they have no access to toilets. The city's old commuter trains make sardine cans look positively roomy, with ten people packed into ten square feet of coach space during peak hours. Commuters routinely travel up to six hours a day to and from far-flung northern suburbs to offices around Churchgate and Nariman Point in the south. The system is remarkably efficient, carrying 6.3 million people

The other page 3

You know you've made it in the city of gold when you appear on page 3. And unlike its British counterpart, you don't even have to show off your breasts to get there. 'Page 3' is an essential word in Mumbai's lexicon, referring to the 'Boomtown Rap' page in the *Bombay Times*, a daily supplement of the *Times of India* dedicated to reporting the 24/7 party lifestyles of Mumbai's rich and famous. Hot new restaurant launches, the biggest weddings and the latest Bollywood premières are all covered, with as many photos of models, actors, artists, restauranteurs, authors and industrialists as they can cram into a half-page splash. Gossip and tittle-tattle is included, but nothing too racy – *BT* is all about stoking middle-class aspirations and selling publicity.

Page 3 is frequently ridiculed for its fluffy stories and accused of irrelevance in a city where half the citizens don't have access to toilets. But you can't argue with success; *BT* is one of the city's best-recognised brands. In fact, page 3 stories now spread over the first four pages of the paper. Other city newspapers have nearly all followed suit with their own versions of celeb-and-society reporting; the *Daily News & Analysis* supplement *After Hours*, for example, is little more than a *BT* clone. The Times Group has even launched a page 3-style TV channel called *Zoom*. A recent Bollywood movie, *Page 3*, which tells the story of a reporter uncovering the seedy underbelly of the Mumbai social scene, only served to add to its mystique. *BT* has now become one of the most sought-after papers for advertisers and aspiring celebs alike. The first step to a successful modelling or acting career is getting on page 3. And if you've got enough cash, you can even pay them to cover your party or product launch. It's absolutely fabulous, *yaar*.

Slumbai

Just under eight million of Mumbai's citizens live in *zopadpattis* – slums of varying levels of sophistication. Some are little more than bamboo-and-tarpaulin shacks; others are brick-built rooms with electricity and water connections. Slum dwellers perform vital roles in Mumbai's economy, working as labourers in the city's construction boom or as domestic servants in wealthier households. A staggering 40 per cent of Mumbai's police officers live in slums. Slums are everywhere in Mumbai, and it has the dubious distinction of being home to Asia's largest slum in the suburb of Dharavi, with around a million people living there. But it wasn't always like this. Slums first started appearing in Mumbai in the 1950s, as immigrants from other parts of Maharashtra state, and from poor rural states across India, particularly Uttar Pradesh and Bihar, began to arrive in search of work in a city seen as a land of opportunity. With no low-cost housing available, they began building shanties on patches of empty land.

It was the beginning of Mumbai's transformation into what locals ruefully call 'Slumbai', greased by gangsters, corrupt officials and conniving politicians. As

immigration accelerated, the Mumbai mafia muscled in as slum lords, charging rents to slum dwellers and threatening the private landowners whose land they had stolen. Police, bureaucrats and politicians were paid to look the other way as public land was grabbed. Politicians quickly realised they could benefit from these vast new additions to their electorates and used their clout to protect slums from demolition and provide them with some basic amenities. The slum dwellers became 'vote banks' – blocks of support for any politician who would protect them from the law. By the '70s, the slums had made a major impact on the character of the city, swallowing up many of its green spaces. The smallest patch of land is a potential slum, with shanties even lining the city's railway lines. Every year, around 1,000 slum dwellers are killed crossing train tracks just getting to and from their homes.

Numerous slum rehabilitation schemes have been launched over the years, with little impact. In 1995, the Shiv Sena government promised all slum dwellers free 225-sq ft flats. Their plan called for a million homes in five years, to be built by private developers in exchange for lucrative development rights. Ten years later, the scheme was widely seen as yet another scam, allowing builders to grab prime public land for a pittance, while building less than 40,000 homes. However, the scheme is still in operation. Ironically, free housing is not something slum dwellers have ever asked for – after all, they all pay rent to slum lords. Housing experts say that slum dwellers instead need access to mortgages.

In 2004, the congress government of Chief Minister Vilasrao Deshmukh decided to dispense with rehabilitation altogether. In order to clear space for the construction of a 'new Shanghai', he ordered a vast slum demolition drive, just months after winning an election on a promise to legalise all slums built before 2000. In the space of four months, state bulldozers destroyed 90,000 slum dwellings, leaving 300,000 people homeless. It caused widespread outrage and political pressure from the congress central government in Delhi brought the drive to a halt. With nowhere else to go, the slum dwellers patiently started to rebuild what they had lost.

every day with few service breakdowns. Across the city, roads remain shockingly poor, as a single day's experience makes bone-rattlingly evident to visitors. It's perhaps the only city on earth to have introduced a 'pothole audit' to count the innumerable gashes in its roads that reappear, thanks to poor construction methods and materials, after every monsoon. Fumes from vehicles and industrial emissions have ranked Mumbai as the world's fifth most polluted city. It is said that just breathing Mumbai's air is equivalent to smoking about two packs of cigarettes a day.

CLASS DIVIDES
No wonder then, that Mumbaikars' position in the social strata – poor, middle class or rich – is best defined by how much they are able to insulate themselves from one of the toughest urban environments in the world. Until the city becomes the 'next Shanghai', as Chief Minister Vilasrao Deshmukh promised it would just a few months before Terrible Tuesday, the next best thing is to be rich enough to buy your own first-world environment. Life for Mumbai's wealthiest resembles a series of Western-style, air-conditioned bubbles complete with servants – from elegant home to modern office to smart restaurant and back again, transported in a chauffeur-driven car. The elite rarely travel by train or even walk on the streets. Still, Mumbai is different from other developing world cities like Mexico City in that social class cannot be easily defined by postcode. Different classes

live cheek-by-jowl. On Cuffe Parade in Colaba, for example, the elegant apartments of the city's wealthiest overlook the corrugated iron roofs of slum dwellings. Domestic servants and labourers often live relatively close to where they work.

Despite the city's problems, Mumbaikars rarely seem down in the dumps. Barefoot street urchins play cricket on broken pavements with just the same energy and laughter of kids anywhere in the world. Commuters shrug off with a grin the daily fights to get space on the train. The city may be a mess but the energy, warmth and humour of its citizens are by far its greatest charms. Despite predictions of imminent urban collapse, Mumbai continues to grow and prosper. And despite the increasing chasm between haves and have-nots, there is relatively little resentment of the wealthy and a remarkably low crime rate compared to the capital, Delhi. No one can be sure if that will change, but the first signs of ghettoisation are beginning to emerge. In new middle-class neighbourhoods in the northern suburbs like Thakur Village in Kandivali, for example, vast new gated communities complete with their own shopping facilities have been established, with intense security measures to keep out the poor – except for domestic servants, of course. At current rates of growth, Mumbai is set to become one of the world's great megacities, with an estimated population of 28 million by 2015. By the time it gets there, will Mumbai still be Mumbai?

The daily fight for space on Mumbai's trains.

Communities

Author **Jerry Pinto** leafs through Mumbai's multicultural salad.

First, the ABC charts in primary school did their dirty work, introducing us to apples and zebras. Then the 'Good Habits' chart told us that we should brush our teeth, not with *neem* twigs but with toothbrushes and toothpaste. Next we were shown a 'People of India' chart and we struggled to find ourselves reflected in it.

As a Roman Catholic, I remember being slightly surprised to find that my father's native dress was supposed to be a suit and my mother was supposed to have bobbed hair and wear a dress.

I went home from school that day and asked my father why he didn't wear a suit.

'In this heat?' he asked.

I showed him the chart.

He laughed. 'Well, they couldn't put us in loincloths, could they?'

A cold thrill ran down my snobbish-little-boy spine. Yes, my father had been a tiller of the soil in his native Goa. Yes, he had walked eight miles to school ('Yes, yes, daddy, we know') and back *after* he had watered the red bananas of which his village, Moira, was proud. I remember thanking my stars that we were once-removed from the loincloth and that the chart of the communities of Mumbai had chosen to put us into double-breasted suits and hats.

Today, of course, many years later, it is very chic to be the son of a farmer who actually carried his wares to the market and clawed his way out of poverty. It is chic for everyone to be a typical whatever-they-are. The stereotyped representations on that chart no longer have the power to astonish/amuse/offend us. With our kitsch-tinted glasses, we can see ourselves as others see us and laugh in our new-found confidence as one of the largest consumer markets in the world, as the economic driver of the subcontinent, as the city where the stock market only has to cough for the national antibiotics to be trotted out. Like this city, built on rotting fish heads and palm leaves, retrieved from a history of mosquitoes and amnesia, it is a shaky self-confidence.

THE MUMBAI MYTH

The urban myth of Mumbai's secular and classless self-image reads roughly like this. It was inherited from the older urban history of Surat, a port city in Gujarat situated on ancient trade routes that attracted settlers from across the Asian and African continents. As Surat declined, Mumbai emerged as a regional player and people migrated here in large numbers. Since they had already rubbed shoulders with the world, they brought with them their tolerance.

The city had dismantled the barriers of caste simply by making it impossible to follow traditional prescriptions about purity and avoiding pollution. On the train and on the bus, in the mill and in the canteen, at the mess and on the cricket field, it was impossible to worry too much about who ate beef and who didn't, who was 'clean' and who was 'unclean'. In some ways this was true. Cram millions of people on to a patch of land and they must either learn to co-exist or kill each other. Mumbaikars did not learn the virtue of

Saraswati Chitra Kala's '**People of India**' educational picture chart.

CHRISTIAN खिती

कोळी KOLI

MADRASI मद्रासी

tolerance on their own; they were forced into it by the congestion of the big city.

We were also in the habit of saying that there was only one God in Mumbai and his name was Mammon. No one was sure who actually had ever worshipped Mammon but we were proud of his classicism and, like the penguin-shaped dustbins that the municipality put on our streets because penguins are the only creatures with no religious associations, he was secular. We had not Kuber, the Hindu god of wealth, or even a Calvinist god of capitalism. He was just that ugly monster to whom we could all pretend allegiance so that we could laugh at the rest of the country when it went mad over symbolic acts of desecration, the slaughter of a cow near a temple, the mosque bedaubed with pig's blood. We were far too busy, far too intent on the good life, far too Western-looking, Western-facing to bother about that kind of thing. As Bombayites, we left that to the excitable natives of the subcontinent. Our little finger of land was, we believed, too busy making money.

In 1992, we found that we weren't quite so different after all. Far away, in Ayodhya, in Uttar Pradesh, the forces of the Hindu Right went on a rampage and destroyed a mosque that they claimed stood on the birthplace of Lord Rama, the ninth avatar of Vishnu, the *Purushottam* or perfect man, the hero of one of India's seminal epics, the *Ramayana*. No one ever believed that the mosque would be demolished. Even when the mosque came down, no one believed that the rage and the despair would come home to us. It did.

Mumbai's cosmopolitan façade went up in flames. Riots took over the city, hundreds were murdered, and we put to rest the idea of the national melting pot, the *bhelpuri* city, the idea that Mumbaikars had voluntarily exiled themselves from their roots to float free in the city. The next state election returned a coalition government between two right-wing Hindu parties. The city was renamed Mumbai, another small symbolic act of reversal.

But Mumbai is endlessly volatile and we want to go back to that prelapsarian age when the question 'What's your caste?' was not about whether you were going to be burnt alive or not. In the old days, that question wasn't even about caste. It was about identity, an attempt to place you, geographically, psychologically, socially, sometimes even politically.

'There was only one God in Mumbai and his name was Mammon.'

Declare that you are a Pinto, which puts you firmly into a supposedly casteless religion like Roman Catholicism, and your fellow Catholics will ask you your village. This will help them discover exactly what kind of Pinto you are: whether you are from upper-caste stock or a convert from the lower orders.

As a Pinto, I might be a Goan, one of a large wave of migrants washed in from Goa who settled around the port areas, especially Dhobi Talao (the long-since drained 'Lake of the Laundrymen'). I would speak Konkani at home and the rice cooked in my home would have salt in it. Or I might be an 'East Indian' Pinto, even though Mumbai is on the West Coast of India. The term applies to the many converts the Portuguese made when they arrived here and who chose that name for themselves over the term 'Bombay Portuguese' by which they had been known. 'East Indians', they thought, would endear them to the East India Company, which until 1857 was the representative of colonial British power. As an East Indian Pinto, I would speak Marathi at home. I might even be a Pinto of Koli origin, fiercely proud of being one of the first inhabitants of the islands, perhaps a

राठा · **MAHARASHTRIAN**

मुसलमान · **MUSLIM**

पारसी · **PARSI**

generation away from fishing, but still offering coconuts to the sea on *Nariyal Poornima*, to appease the waves after the storms of the monsoon.

For in Mumbai, as in India, no community is solid, no religious persuasion unites all its members. Thus the Mumbai Hindu is sub-divided according to caste (which still persists) but is also acutely aware of his or her family origins. Village life may be a distant memory for many Mumbai residents but it still, in many ways, determines identity.

And anyway, even if the large majority of the city is Hindu, that's not much of an identity at all, except for outsiders. You have only to read the matrimonial columns of the local newspapers to see how many different ways the term can be sliced, with caste only one of them.

MUMBAI MASH-UP

The term Hindu itself may be seen as a misnomer, an inclusive term created by the British as a bureaucratic convenience to make their censuses easier. Hinduism itself is difficult to define as a religion because it has no single defining text. There are hundreds of Hindu texts of different importance to different communities. The four Vedas (ancient religious

Caste in stone

Caste is an uncomfortable phenomenon that most Mumbaikars just don't want to acknowledge. The word 'caste' is derived from the Portuguese word *casta*, meaning 'category'. The Portuguese and, subsequently, the British, saw caste as a way of organising communities on a hierarchy based on the *varna* system. The *varna* system is derived from classical Hindu texts that divide societies into four parts: **Brahmins**, the highest group, represented by priests and teachers; **Kshatriyas**, warriors and kings; the **Vaishyas** who are the merchants and traders; and the **Shudras** (also known as Dalits), who are at the bottom of the hierarchy as labourers and peasants. Some texts hold the '**untouchables**', later referred to by Gandhi as the *Harijan* – the 'children of God' – as a fifth caste who did jobs considered polluting: handling corpses and collecting excrement from homes without sewage system.

However, many sociologists believe that explanations of caste that rely on the *varna* system are flawed. They argue that castes are not discrete but themselves divided into numerous sub-categories. Even people of the same caste may be forbidden from marrying because of these divisions. Brahmins may be ritually superior, but in wealth and status they may actually be dependent on other castes below them on the *varna* scale.

According to some social historians, caste has served mainly to perpetuate the domination of elite priests, rulers and merchants. Those now regarded as the lower

castes may have originally been forest tribes that were absorbed into larger kingdoms. The theory of karma, in which people are doomed to their status in life by their deeds in past lives, can be seen as just an ideological tool that helped suppress desires for political change. But caste can also be seen in other ways, for example as a means of organising a division of labour that gave rise to highly productive economies in India's past.

In Mumbai, caste still connects the modern city to the ancient history of the sub-continent. The city still relies on 'scavengers' – known as 'ragpickers' – to deal with its waste. Most of these scavengers belong to castes that have always been scavengers. Look harder and you'll find a city in which the majority of its teachers still come from the upper castes, and most businessmen and traders belong to communities that have dominated business for centuries. Caste even shapes where people live: over 75 per cent of slum dwellers are from the lower castes – a far cry from Mumbai's self-image as a meritocratic city of opportunity. No one talks of the slums of Dharavi as a Dalit colony but, effectively, they are.

In many ways, Mumbai does not encourage casteism. Many Dalits see the city as a place that frees them from the oppression of rural caste politics. Mumbai is a major centre of Dalit art and literature, and plays an important role in Dalit politics. In the 19th and 20th centuries, it was a centre of Indian social reform and helped weaken caste-based politics. But Mumbai continues to struggle with caste, and with those who see advantage in dividing people on the lines of their birth.

WANTED BRIDES

BRAHMIN

WANTED brahmin bride for handsome Kanyakubj brahmin Dr/Ms 29/5'8".Seek proposal from good looking fair good natured prefer Dr. or Msc .Height up to 5'3" Send BHP. Con:07324-273214

texts dating back to around 1,800 BC, but this is a contested date) are often held to be central but the epics, the *Ramayana* and the *Mahabharata*, constitute the core of most Hindus' connection with their religion. Hinduism has been called a way of life but this is also misleading about a deeply complex and seemingly self-contradictory religion. Hinduism offers a dualistic path in which God and Man are separate entities and a non-dualistic one in which Man's only duty is to recognise the godhead within him. It sanctions great excess as a route to the divine but encourages great asceticism as well. It has 330 million gods, with their own distinct identities; and a single deity into which all of them can be collapsed. It is possible, as one observer remarked, to say two completely opposing things about Hinduism and find scriptural support for both.

No one ever answers 'Hindu' to the question of caste. One might say one is a Saraswat and immediately that answer would suggest that the speaker is from Goa, migrated to Mumbai and belongs to the Brahmin orders. Or one might say Pathare Prabhu and evoke a group that came to Mumbai in the 13th century with the king Raja Bhimdev from Patan in Gujarat. Or one might say Tamilian Dalit, and order up another lineage of social revolution, of an underclass that is beginning to be mobilised by affirmative action, of the tanneries in Asia's largest slum, Dharavi. Or one might say, 'TamBram', meaning Tamilian Brahmin, and another set of images – of classical Carnatic music concerts and tight-lipped morality – would be set into play. All these are stereotypes and as soon as you bump into the real human being behind them, they begin to fade. But they are a legacy of that school chart.

Islam, you might think, would be an easier deal. Muslims are supposed to be one people in their submission to Allah, their adherence to the Koran, right? But beyond the obvious Shia and Sunni divide there are regional differences as well. There are Dawoodi Bohras from Gujarat, Memons from Kutch and from Halai, Khoja Ismailis (also called Aga Khanis), Konkani Muslims from the Konkan coast, Irani Shias who trace their lineage from Iran, Mapilahs and Khoyas from Kerala.

Walk down Mohammed Ali Road and you'll see an enormous variety of mosques and Muslim groups running businesses, groups who share very little except their submission to the will of Allah. A Muslim from the Malabar coast will not speak the same language as a Muslim from the northern plains of India. They may eat together (each thinking very little of the other's food) but they will not intermarry.

Soak it all up with a wipe and a stereotype.

THE ARCHIVE OF IDENTITIES

But if you're walking around South Mumbai, the imprint of another migrant tribe, the Parsis, will be paramount. The Parsis are Zoroastrians, followers of the prophet Zoroaster, who were driven out of Iran by Muslim persecution. They arrived in Gujarat in the eighth or ninth century and sought asylum from the local king. He is said to have sent them a glass of milk full to the brim – his way of saying that his kingdom was full. The Parsi elders conferred, added some sugar to the milk and sent it back – to suggest that they would mix thoroughly and sweeten the life of the community. Thus the Parsis, true to their word, still speak Gujarati at home. And though, as good businessmen, they have been involved in a fair share of dirty dealing (the opium trade, for one) they have done their civic duty as well. Many of Mumbai's public institutions were built by the Parsi tradition of community service.

Today the Parsi population has tragically declined, with no more than 50,000 left in the city, and a mere 120,000 worldwide. I would often suggest to a Parsi friend that I was going to start Project Parsi, much like Project Tiger.

'Yes, with radio collars to track us wherever we go,' he would retort, with the trademark good humour that gave us Parsi theatre, one of the grand-daddies of the Bollywood film.

'And report on mating habits,' I would add.

'If mating was a habit amongst us, would you need a project?'

Few communities can take so much slander with so much éclat.

The decline of the Parsis has found a sad parallel in the sudden decline of the white-backed vulture in South Asia and beyond. The vulture plays a crucial role in traditional Parsi

If it's Tuesday, it must be Prabhadevi

Ganesha – the city's best-loved god.

Mumbaikars are a naturally tolerant lot. They'll happily worship Ganesha on a Tuesday, Mother Mary on a Wednesday and Allah on a Friday. If it wasn't for the religious right wing, mutual respect would be the norm. Most places of worship will let you in regardless of faith, but make sure you're dressed in a way that won't offend – both men and women should cover their arms and legs. You should also cover your head before entering a Muslim or Sikh shrine – a knotted handkerchief will do. You can usually buy one outside or borrow one within. Be warned that visiting a temple on its most popular day may take up your entire day.

Babulnath

Babulnath is Shiva, the god of destruction and also of generativity, who is often represented by the *lingam* or phallus. Devotees see Monday as sacred to Shiva, and the temple is extremely crowded on that day.
Babulnath Temple, Babulnath Road. Grant Road station. **Map** p254 A15.

Ganesha

Mumbai's most popular God, the elephant-headed Ganesha or Ganpati is the son of Shiva. He is the 'remover of obstacles' – no enterprise should be undertaken without his blessing. His idol is immersed in the sea every year (*see p135*) at a city-wide event called Ganesh Chaturthi. His most famous temple is the Siddhivinayak Temple at Prabhadevi. Devotees arrive on Monday night, often walking miles barefoot, for *darshan* on Tuesday, Ganesha's sacred day.
Siddhivinayak Temple, Prabhadevi. Dadar station.

Haji Ali

Haji Ali was a Muslim holy man who died on a pilgrimage to Mecca. Legend has it that his body then floated across the Arabian Sea and washed up back in Bombay. He is now interred in a spectacular *dargah* (tomb) on a rock off the mainland that can only be reached via a narrow causeway at low tide. If you press your forehead against his tomb and offer a covering (*chaddar*), your wishes will be granted, it is believed.
Haji Ali, Mahalaxmi. Mahalaxmi station.

Mahalaxmi

The reigning deity of a commercial city is naturally the Goddess of Wealth, Mahalaxmi. She is the consort of Vishnu, the Preserver of the Universe. On the nine nights of Navratri, a harvest festival, the goddess' devotees arrive in their thousands for *darshan*, a viewing that has been described as seeing and being seen by God.
Mahalaxmi Temple, Mahalaxmi. Mahalaxmi station.

Mauli Mary/Our Lady of Perpetual Succour

Mauli Mary is the local name for the Virgin Mary at the Basilica of Mount Mary in Bandra. During her feast in September she is offered a variety of odd-shaped wax objects including houses (from devotees with accommodation problems), airplanes (from those who want to emigrate) and body parts (from the sick). Mary's most popular avatar is the Mother of Perpetual Succour, worshipped at St Michael's Church on Wednesdays.
Virgin Mary at the Basilica of Mount Mary, Mount Mary's Road, Bandra (W). Bandra station. **Map** p249 A6.
St Michael's Church, Mahim (W). Mahim station.

Makdoom Shah Baba

Shah Baba Ali Mahimi (1372-1471) was a secular Sufi saint who embraced all religions. He is now the patron saint of the Mumbai police. His *dargah*, which is said to be about

350 years old, is accompanied by the tombs of his mother, his maid servant and his pet goat. Fridays bring the faithful to this spot.
Makdoom Shah Baba Dargah, Mahim (W). Mahim station.

Mumbadevi

When the city was being plagued by a sadistic demon, Mumbaraka, locals offered prayers to Brahma, who pulled a six-armed goddess out of his body. The goddess defeated Mumbaraka, who then pleaded with her to take his name. She did so and became Mumbadevi, a manifestation of Shakti, the female principle.
Mumbadevi Temple, Zaveri Bazaar. Masjid Bunder/Marine Lines station.
Map p253 G14.

Sitladevi

The goddess of small pox, ritually appeased to protect children from infection. She is supposed to be an Ancient One, a goddess who predates the four Vedas that some call the defining texts of Hinduism. Many scholars believe she was probably a tribal goddess, and incorporated later into the Hindu pantheon.
Sitladevi Temple, Sitladevi Temple Road, Mahim (W). Mahim station.

Zoroaster

There are barely 50,000 Parsis left in the city but their religious shrines, *agiaries* (fire temples), are everywhere. Non-Parsis are forbidden from entering, but you can admire a fine example from the outside at Cusrow Baug, a Parsi housing colony in Colaba.
Cusrow Baug, Colaba Causeway, Colaba. Churchgate/CST stations.

Candles at **Mauli Mary** in Bandra.

funerals, in which the body is left at the top of a 'Tower of Silence' where vultures are allowed to pick it clean. This tradition is endangered because the vultures are dying out.

Mumbai's communities define and redefine themselves and each resident can be seen as an ambulatory archive of identities. That taxi driver may be from the northern state of Uttar Pradesh but to most of his passengers, he is a 'bhaiya', a word that used to mean 'brother' but now means a northerner. That nurse may see herself as an Orthodox Syrian Christian but to most of her patients she is a 'Mallu' (someone who speaks Malayalam, the language of Kerala) or just an 'Anda-Gundu' (a name intended to evoke hilarity at the supposedly muddled sounds of a Dravidian language).

For this is a city that has had many visitors. It has been home to groups like the Siddis (with roots in Africa), many of whom still live in Dongri; the Iranis, who created the glorious institution known as the Irani restaurant; the Chinese, who were a significant presence in Mazgaon before the 1962 Indo-China War; along with Anglo-Indians and Armenians. And there were Jews from the Maharashtra coast – referred to as Bene Israelis – believing they are among the lost tribes who arrived in India before the destruction of Jerusalem's Second Temple. They moved to Mumbai in the early 19th century, but today they number less than 5,000; many have moved to Israel since 1947. In the 19th century, Bombay played host to a wave of Jews from Baghdad. The most famous family among them were the Sassoons, who built some of the city's major landmarks.

But if there is one space where Mumbai's ethnic diversity is represented in its full glory, it's the Hindi film industry. It should be a little puzzling that Mumbai should be home to a cinema whose language it does not speak very well. Most northerners flinch at the sound of a Mumbaikar speaking Hindi, as well they might. We mangle the language, throw in words from every tongue (including English) and don't bother with honorifics or subtleties. But then that's why this city made a cinema genre that was so easily portable. Largely cosmopolitan and secular, Bollywood is truly representative of the city's diversity, even if much of it is behind the camera. When communities have been caricatured and stereotyped, it is usually done with an insider's sanction. It was this that ultimately made the Hindi film such a mobile force that spread a little of the spirit of Mumbai across India.

● *Jerry Pinto is a well-known Mumbai journalist and author, most recently of* Helen: The Life and Times of an H-Bomb, *about racial and community stereotypes in Hindi cinema.*

नंद मिलींद

Bollywood

Navigate your way around the stars.

No one knows for sure who coined the term 'Bollywood', which first gained currency in the early 1990s, though there are several candidates – mainly journalists and movie producers – vying for parentage. But it's a semantic tic that's spread through the subcontinent like wildfire. The Bengali film industry, based in the Calcutta (now Kolkata) district of Tollygunje, is now commonly referred to as 'Tollywood', movies made in Madras (now Chennai) are said to come from 'Mollywood', while 'Lollywood' is used to describe the Pakistani film industry centred in Lahore. The term Bollywood is despised by many in the Indian film industry, not least for defining Indian films in relation to Hollywood, but it remains an unrivalled catch-all phrase for describing the farrago of emotion, action, song, dance and humour that animate almost every Hindi film.

Ever since films by the Lumière brothers were first screened at the Watson Hotel in Kala Ghoda in 1896, Mumbai has remained at the heart of the Hindi film industry. The first talkie in Hindi, *Alam Ara*, emerged in 1931 from the traditions of the city's theatre circuit. It was directed by theatre director Ardeshir Irani, and established two pillars of Hindi cinema: it had over ten songs, all mimed, and its plot was drawn from a play. This was an early indication of how Hindi cinema would evolve its form and language from Indian dramatic traditions, from classical Sanskrit theatre to folk forms.

Today, Bollywood continues to beat Hollywood at the Indian box office, with a loyal and passionate fan following for its biggest stars. The melodramatic style that defines the Hindi film industry hasn't changed fundamentally over the past half-century: *sturm und drang* interspersed with song and dance. The 1970s and 1980s saw action movies, multi-starrers and family weepies. With the 1990s came the rise of the so-called 'multiplex film', which refers to a movie that is produced with a relatively small budget, has an urban theme and actors who speak an urbanised Hindi that often weaves in English and slang. But the big-budget Hindi movie continues to thrive – Bollywood has borrowed extensively from Hollywood in attempting to make movies that are slick and punchily written. The song-and-dance routine now resembles MTV – some song sequences in new Hindi movies look like hip hop videos.

Spiced-up versions of Hollywood movies have always been a Bollywood staple, but there's now a marked tendency to borrow extensively from other movies right down to the last reel. The movie *Kaante* (2002) was a remake of Quentin Tarantino's *Reservoir Dogs* and was set in Los Angeles. *Zinda* (2005), by the same director, was a remake of Chan-wook Park's *Oldboy*. A great deal of importance is now given to production design – sometimes at the cost of the plot, another tendency borrowed from Hollywood. Most movies are now shot on sets and in foreign locations. There's a veneer of modernity and urbanity in new Hindi movies. Actors now actually kiss, unlike in the past when the camera would cut away as their faces moved closer. But the basic values remain the same: the family is the core unit of stability and identity; marriage is the goal of romance; women look best when they're standing by their men; and wealth is sexy.

This new love for slickness means that the city of Mumbai is increasingly losing its once-central role in Hindi films. For decades, Mumbai was an evergreen star of Bollywood movies in the same way that Los Angeles is a staple of Hollywood films. The Marine Drive promenade in South Mumbai plays a role as the frontier of journey, hope, liberation, and solace, as have the city's industrial zones, including its mills, factories and docks, the bustling streets and flyovers, the beaches, the brothels, bars and nightclubs. Mumbai's unique character types have influenced and shaped Hindi movies: the smuggler, the industrial worker, the bar dancer/prostitute, the industrialist, the dreamy-eyed migrant, the street-smart small-time criminal, the cop. It's difficult to judge who influenced whom: was the typical swagger associated with Mumbai characters picked off the streets, or do citizens learn their strut from the movies? It's hard to tell any more, but Mumbai's people are a bit like characters from their movies: loud, brash, romantic, anxious, hot-headed, money- and glamour-hungry, foolish at times, but always entertaining to watch.

BOLLYWOOD 101

Hindi films are without equivalent in other cinema traditions. Unlike Hollywood, mainstream Hindi movies have always fused fancy with realism, to the extent that descriptions of them as 'unrealistic' become almost meaningless. Instead, Hindi cinema employs melodramatic conventions that are close to those of opera. Just as in, say, *La Traviata*, a woman with an obviously fine pair of lungs can sing about dying of consumption, the lack of Western-style realism in Bollywood is beside the point; what Hindi films seek to convey is *emotional* realism, taken to its purest form through the use of music. A good Hindi film may lack a logical or original narrative but it will make perfect sense to the emotionally literate. In *Kal Ho Na Ho* (2003), Shah Rukh Khan is dying; his heart is failing, but he teaches others how to have a heart, to love their neighbours and put family and community at the centre of their worlds. He

may run through New York, dance a mean *bhangra* and then linger on his deathbed, all in defiance of medical science, but millions of film-goers have sobbed through these moments because they find them emotionally real; the idea is that emotions lead to moral action.

Hindi films are not just about romantic love but also family love and friendship. Often the dramatic tension arises from conflict between romantic love and family duty. In the enormously successful *Dilwale Dulhania Le Jayenge* (1995), Simran (played by Kajol) is in love with Raj (Shah Rukh Khan) but is already betrothed to the son of her father's friend. Simran loves her family, so eloping is not an option; Raj's goal is to make Simran's father accept him. Often, such conflicts are pushed to melodramatic extremes, so the family will only accept the

Bollywood's best

Andaaz (1949): Mehboob Khan's classic love triangle, starring Nutan, Dilip Kumar and Raj Kapoor, explores the influence of Westernisation on Indian values.

Awaara (1951): Through the story of a dacoit who's actually the son of a renowned judge, Raj Kapoor takes on the nature-versus-nurture debate.

Devdas (1955): A couple should have married but the man is too weak; he subsequently ruins the lives of those around him. Scene stealer: Dilip Kumar, King of Tragedy. The movie was remade on a larger, and gaudier, scale in 2002, and starred Shah Rukh Khan.

Mother India (1957): Mehboob Khan's great rural epic, starring Nargis as a mother who kills her son, was labelled 'flood, mud and blood' by a Western critic.

Pakeezah (1971): A camp classic about an innocent courtesan who's in love with a man she's met only once. Scene stealer: Meena Kumari, the Queen of Melodrama.

Deewaar (1975): The family is wronged by society. The older brother seeks to restore the family's fortunes through crime; the younger brother becomes a policeman. Amitabh Bachchan plays the brooding anti-hero, later dubbed the 'Angry Young Man'.

Dilwale Dulhaniya Le Jayenge (1995): Children teach their parents about Indian values in this romance. Scene stealers: Shah Rukh and Kajol, two of Bollywood's best weepers.

couple when death threatens, such as in *Bobby* (1973), when the couple seem headed for a Romeo and Juliet-style tragedy.

Hindi film stories also often revolve around the breaking and restoration of the moral order. A woman who has sex outside of marriage may do so in an irresistibly erotic moment, but she will have to pay for her sin; the man who has loved another man's wife must die for his transgression. One of the many reasons for the enduring popularity of actor Amitabh Bachchan is his talent for conveying moral outrage; his characters are determined to restore the moral order, even if that means breaking the law or dying in the process.

Unlike Hollywood, Hindi cinema isn't ruled by genre, although many films have elements of different genres rolled into one – the *masala* (mix of spices) summed up by the word 'Bollywood'. The leading man in a Hindi movie must be more versatile than his Hollywood counterparts – he needs to know how to cry buckets as well as land a punch.

Hindi films are often dismissed as escapist entertainment, but there's nothing trivial about that. The Turkish writer Orhan Pamuk wrote in the *New Yorker* that the rest of the world will only understand the changes in India when 'we have seen their private lives reflected in novels'; more likely it is in Bollywood that the obsessions, fantasies and fears of modern India will find their clearest expression.

Amitabh who?

A guide to the Bollywood A-list.

Amitabh Bachchan

Known as 'the Big B', Amitabh Bachchan became a superstar after the gangster flick *Deewar* in 1975. Now in his 60s, Bachchan remains one of the most successful actors ever to emerge in Hindi cinema. His appeal lies in his brooding good looks, versatile acting skills, and a deep voice that's as recognisable to Indians as the national anthem. Bachchan's films are now counted among the contemporary classics: *Sholay*, *Amar Akbar Anthony*, *Don* and *Namak Halal*. His popularity dipped in the 1980s, but he bounced back in the '90s by hosting an Indian version of the TV show *Who Wants to be a Millionaire*.

Shah Rukh Khan

The yuppie update on Amitabh Bachchan is the only modern actor to command a guaranteed box-office opening and worldwide fan following. Born in 1965 in Delhi, Khan studied theatre and acted in television serials before making the leap into

Taste Bollywood's masala

Few Bollywood movies are shot on location any more, so the chances of walking down the street and bumping into Shah Rukh Khan doing a *bhangra* are mighty rare. These days, shoots are done at major studios like Mehboob Studio in Bandra, Yashraj Studios in Andheri and Film City in Goregaon. Sadly, entry to studios is restricted and none of them run guided tours. If you want to see a Bollywood film being shot, you'll either have to know someone in the business (pretty difficult) or get cast as an extra (surprisingly easy). Casting agents frequently scour Colaba Causeway for foreign extras, particularly at Leopold's Café (*see p113* **Pubs & Bars**). They'll usually pay a few hundred rupees for a day's work. Expect to spend a lot of time just standing around between shots. Exercise some caution – ask for a business card and call to check the

agent's credentials, and opt for safety in numbers. Away from the camera, it's often possible to spot stars and starlets shaking their hips at select expensive nightspots, among them Zenzi and Olive in Bandra, and Vie Lounge & Deck, J-49 and Enigma at the JW Marriott Mumbai, all in Juhu.

A shoot at the Asiatic Library.

Bollywood. Khan has experimented with several image changes through the past decade – anti-hero, common man, wealthy businessman – but will forever be remembered as the lover-boy extraordinaire, thanks to blockbusters like *Dilwale Dulhaniya Le Jayenge*.

Aamir Khan

Aamir Khan hit gold with his second starring role in the teenage romance *Qayamat Se Qayamat Tak*. After a series of flops in the 1990s, Khan bolstered his charming looks with scene-stealing performances in films like *Raja Hindustani*, *Rangeela* and *Lagaan*. Adored by fans for his attention to performance over preening, Khan has often been described as a director's nightmare for the extraordinary interest he takes in the making of his movies.

Rani Mukerji

The Rani Mukerji story started in 1997 with *Raja Ki Aayegi Baraat* – a forgettable movie that couldn't sink her talent or quell her ambition. After a memorable turn in Karan Johar's *Kuch Kuch Hota Hai* the following year, Mukerji steadily worked on her acting and appearance. Mukerji's image is that of the girl next door who made it. Her warm good looks, passionate acting and hard work has pushed her into Bollywood's stratosphere.

Salman Khan

The son of Salim Khan, the ace scriptwriter who co-wrote some of Bollywood's most iconic films in the 1970s and '80s, Salman Khan established his credentials as a romantic hero with *Maine Pyar Kiya* in 1989. His career has roller-coasted since then. On screen, Khan is often portrayed as a toughie who's a fool for love.

Aishwarya Rai

A former Miss World, Aishwarya Rai has had an indifferent box-office track record but her near-perfect looks ensure lifelong membership of the A-list. Rai entered films after a successful modelling career, and acted in the Tamil movies *Iruvar* and *Kandukondain Kandukondain* before moving into Hindi films.

Rai has since packaged herself as an Indian crossover actress, in the mould of *Memoirs of a Geisha* star Zhang Ziyi, and has Indo-Brit projects like *Mistress of Spice* and *Betrayed* under her sash.

Kareena Kapoor

The younger sister of actor Karisma Kapoor and a member of one of the oldest Bollywood families, twentysomething Kareena Kapoor is the most camera-friendly actor of her generation. Blessed with strong movie genes, a strong and confident face and tons of ambition, Kapoor's noteworthy roles include *Chameli*, *Kabhie Khushi Kabhie Gham*, *Asoka* and *Fida*.

Preity Zinta

One of the few models to have made it big in the movies, Preity Zinta is the perfect modern miss, who looks out of place in a sari and at home in a singlet and shorts. Zinta's dimpled charm shone through in her debut cameo, in Mani Ratnam's *Dil Se* in 1998, and she excels in light, vivacious roles. *Kal Ho Na Ho*, *Koi…Mil Gaya* and *Veer Zaara* are among her biggest hits.

Kajol

In the fans' eyes, Kajol and Shah Rukh Khan are the perfect modern couple – their coupling in the 1995 hit *Dilwale Dulhaniya Le Jayenge* made them superstars. After several subsequent successes, including *Kuch Kuch Hota Hai* and *Kabhie Khushi Kabhie Gham*, Kajol, who is married to fellow actor Ajay Devgan, took a long sabbatical at the end of the 1990s.

Abhishek Bachchan

Amitabh Bachchan's son has a huge legacy, but he has finally come into his own, and has spun his snarling good looks into saleable box office goods with the movies *Dhoom* and *Bluffmaster!* Bachchan Jr has cultivated an audience from urbanites, especially young women, and while his following may never match his father's, he enjoys shrieks of excitement wherever he goes.

Where to Stay

Features

Mrs. Desai's weakness
for chocolate truffles.
Known only to her
'inner-circle'...
and to
Hotel Marine Plaza.

It's always the small things that make the big difference.

Come, get the taste of a delightfully small, boutique hotel experience.
At Hotel Marine Plaza, Mumbai.

With just 68 rooms and suites to attend to, we can understand
and address your personal needs much better.
And you will experience this everywhere. In your room, at **Geoffrey's** - the pub,
The Oriental Blossom - the speciality Chinese restaurant, **The Bayview** - the 24-hour restaurant,
The Allamanda Terrace - rooftop banqueting overlooking the ocean and **Sin** - the pastry shop...
You will find our service always special, always the same.

Hotel Marine Plaza
MUMBAI

A SAROVAR HOTEL
www.sarovarhotels.com Toll Free Reservations: 1 800 111 222

29, Marine Drive, Mumbai - 400 020. Tel: (022) 2285 1212. Fax: (022) 2282 8585. Email: hmp@sarovarhotels.com
Website: www.hotelmarineplaza.com For reservations contact the hotel or call Sarovar Hotels Sales Offices:
Ahmedabad: (079) 2642 5299/2640 8042. Bangalore: (080) 5115 3344/5588/5599. Chennai: (044) 2826 5566/6644/4488.
Hyderabad: (040) 5546 8187/5578 8888. Kolkata: (033) 2228 0301/7301. Mumbai: (022) 5635 0800. New Delhi: (011) 2691 0544/5/6.
Pune: (020) 2683 0855. Surat: (0261) 241 8300/241 4291-6/98798 57558.

Where to Stay

Snoozing in the city of dreams.

Mumbai's hotel industry has never had it so good. With Mumbai an increasingly hot destination for domestic and international business travellers, hotel occupancy rates are staying sky-high all year round. The growth of new industries in the northern suburbs, away from the traditional South Mumbai business centre, has caused a sharp increase in demand for new five-star accommodation in the north. To meet the influx, a clutch of new high-end hotels – all within a few miles of both the domestic and international airports – have sprung up in Andheri, with over 1,200 new rooms since 2001.

But for tourists, the results of the hospitality boom have been mixed. South Mumbai, particularly around Colaba, Marine Drive and Churchgate, is the first choice of most foreign travellers, but you won't find yourselves spoiled for choice nor will you find rooms as cheap as you might expect. The boutique hotel is almost unknown in Mumbai, with the refreshing exception of the **Gordon House Hotel** (*see p43*), which single-handedly fills the gaping hole between high-end and moderate in Mumbai's hotel offerings.

The landscape is dominated by luxury five-stars, charging a minimum of around Rs 8,000 to Rs 12,000 for a double room, with the top choice being the century-old **Taj Mahal Palace & Tower** (*see p43*), a tourist attraction in its own right perched next to the Gateway of India and the harbour. The five-stars aren't just for tourists or foreign businessmen; these hotels have always played an important role in the city's social life, providing restaurants, bars, nightclubs, shopping and private party venues for Mumbai's wealthiest. Travellers looking for something cheaper can find themselves hitting characterless and unappetising mid-range business hotels built in the 1970s that are often not worth the rates they charge. A better option is to seek out cheaper hotels built in the 1930s and '40s like **Bentley's** (*see p47*), which have the virtue of period character and manage to convey some of the sleepy charm of an older Bombay. That's usually not by design but by default – the managements simply haven't got around to changing anything in the last 60 years. Room rates at such places vary from budget (around Rs 1,500) to moderate (Rs 3,500). We haven't listed anything that isn't scrupulously clean and decently maintained, but be prepared for hotels that are often a little rough around the edges.

INFORMATION AND BOOKING

We've included some Bandra and Khar hotels for those who want to step outside of the mainstream into the Bandra suburb, which has rapidly morphed into the city's hottest shopping-and-partying destination. If it's your first trip to the city, you may want to opt for the more tourist-friendly offerings of Churchgate, Marine Drive, Colaba and Fort in South Mumbai and check out Bandra by train or taxi. We've also listed some hotels close to the airport in Juhu and Andheri for those on brief stopovers. With high demand for rooms across the city, it's imperative to book ahead, especially if you're visiting in the peak winter season. The simplest way is to book via the web – even the cheapest hotels have their own websites. Many hotels in Colaba, Churchgate, Marine Drive and Juhu are close to the Arabian Sea, but not all provide sea views. You need to specify if you want a sea view when you book and you may be charged at a higher rate.

The best Hotels

For shameless luxury
Taj Mahal Palace & Tower (*see p43*) and the **Oberoi** (*see p49*).

For a taste of old Bombay on a budget
Bentley's (*see p47*); **Sea Green Hotel** (*see p50*); **Sea Green South Hotel** (*see p50*).

For boutique style
Gordon House Hotel (*see p43*).

For staying in the suburbs
Taj Land's End (*see p50*) and **JW Marriott Mumbai** (*see p52*).

> ❶ Green numbers given in this chapter correspond to the location of each hotel as marked on the street maps. See pp249-255.

PRICES AND CLASSIFICATION

We don't list official star ratings, which tend to reflect facilities rather than quality; instead we've classified hotels within each area according to the price of a double room per night, beginning with the most expensive. All of the rates we've included are for rooms with air-conditioning and attached bathrooms. Some of the cheaper hotels also offer rooms without these facilities for cheaper rates. A simple breakfast is often included at the cheaper hotels, and many hotels in Juhu and Andheri offer a complimentary airport pick-up and drop-off.

Some hotels sneakily quote prices exclusive of the ten per cent sales tax. Always check. We've included the tax in the rates listed here, but room prices change frequently, so please make sure you verify before you book.

FACILITIES AND ACCESSIBILITY

In this chapter, we've listed the main services offered by the hotel. Concierges can often arrange far more than listed here, including restaurant reservations, dry-cleaning and minor clothes repairs. We've also listed which hotels offer rooms adapted for disabled customers, but these vary and it's always best to ring ahead to confirm the precise facilities.

Colaba

Deluxe

Taj Mahal Palace & Tower

Apollo Bunder (6665-3366/www.tajhotels.com). Churchgate/CST stations. **Rates** Rs 11,550-Rs 25,300 single; Rs 12,650-Rs 26,675 double; Rs 49,500-Rs 137,500 suite. **Credit** AmEx, DC, MC, V. **Map** p251 G5 ❶
Mumbai's most famous, oldest and most beautiful hotel, as much of a tourist attraction as the nearby Gateway of India (*see p44* **Crown prince**). **Photo** *p45*.
Bars (2). Business centre. Concierge. Disabled-adapted rooms. Gym. Internet (wireless). No smoking rooms. Parking. Pool (outdoor). Restaurants (5). Room service. Spa. TV.

West End Hotel. *See p48.*

Sea Green Hotel. *See p50.*

Expensive

Fariyas Hotel

25 Off Arthur Bunder Road, Colaba (2204-2911/www.fariyas.com). Churchgate/CST stations. **Rates** Rs 6,050-8,250 single; Rs 6,600-Rs 9,350 double; Rs 12,000 suite. **Credit** AmEx, DC, MC, V. **Map** p250 G4 ❷
There's not much to distinguish this standard 1970s-built ten-floor five-star aimed at business travellers, although it does fill a useful mid-range gap in Colaba between the Taj Mahal and the cheap hotels that feed on its scraps. Rooms are neat, standard and serviceable, although on the small side – as are the pool and tiny gym. Despite space constraints, they've managed to pack in a perfectly decent sauna and steam room, accessed via a maze-like staircase. The position on a street off Apollo Bunder means only corner rooms get a slice of sea view, with north-side rooms getting a view of the Colaba skyline.
Bar. Business centre. Gym. Internet (wireless). Parking. Pool. Restaurant. Room service. TV.

Gordon House Hotel

5 Battery Street, Apollo Bunder, Colaba (2287-1122/www.ghhotel.com). Churchgate/CST stations. **Rates** Rs 6,050 single; Rs 6,600 double; Rs 11,000 suite. **Credit** AmEx, MC, V. **Map** p251 G5 ❸
Mumbai needs more hotels like the Gordon House. It's the city's only real boutique hotel, single-handedly offering a modern, stylish alternative to the standard five-stars, at a very competitive price. Smart, cool and beautifully designed, the courtyard atrium at its heart is a sanctuary of calming pine wood, wheatgrain-coloured tiles and soothing blues and whites under a high glass roof. Rooms on each of the three floors are themed: vibrant colours and smooth tiles on the 'Mediterranean' floor, cool blues and light woods on the 'Scandinavian' floor and a homely, warm feel on the 'Country' floor. There's no gym, but a Bullworker provided in each room, and internet access is free. This is a very popular hotel and there are just 29 rooms, so book in advance.
Business centre. Concierge. Free parking. Internet (dial-up/wireless). Restaurants (2). Room service. TV.

Crown prince

Taj is Hindi for 'crown', which makes the **Taj Mahal Palace & Tower** – locally known as just 'the Taj' – the crown prince of Mumbai's hotels, situated right in front of the Gateway of India and the harbour. More than a hotel, it's a tourist attraction in its own right, admired for its broad, imposing presence, its grand dome, and an architecture that blends Florentine Renaissance and Moorish styles. The Taj has served innumerable illustrious guests over the years, including Queen Elizabeth II, President Gamal Abdel Nasser of Egypt and John Lennon.

The legend of the Taj is that its creator, the renowned Parsi industrialist Jamsetji Nusserwanji Tata, ordered its construction after being refused entry to the European-only Pyrke's Apollo Hotel, with the aim of running a grand hotel without racist entry restrictions. When it was completed in 1903, it was by far the finest hotel in the city, with the latest imported conveniences such as electric lights, electric passenger lifts and its own soda water factory. An urban myth persists that its architect, WA Stevens, was so appalled when he saw the completed hotel that he leapt to his death from its dome; it's said that builders had misread his plans and built the hotel the wrong way round, with the rear facing the sea. In boring old reality, the hotel is built the way it was originally designed and Stevens died of natural causes.

A second wing (the Tower wing) was added in 1972 but, without doubt, the Palace wing offers the original Taj experience – hence the difference in price, with base-category Palace wing rooms commanding prices Rs 3,850 above the highest-category Tower wing rooms. The Palace wing entrance opens onto a vast stone staircase winding its way around the walls of the dome, which is supported with ornate stone arches reminiscent of a cathedral. At the dome's distant apex, stained glass admits a kaleidoscope of coloured light. The Palace rooms are steeped in period feel, with double doors leading from a marbled entranceway into elegant high-ceilinged rooms with antique furnishings and white marble bathrooms, with widescreen plasma TVs as a concession to the 21st century. Rooms in the modern Tower wing offer elegant, contemporary design in soft cream and pastel shades, with fabulous views of the Gateway.

For the **Taj Mahal Palace & Tower** listing, *see p43.*

Moderate

Ascot Hotel

38 Garden Road, Colaba (6638-5566/www.ascot hotel.com). Churchgate/CST stations. **Rates** Rs 3,300-3,850 double. **Credit** MC, V. **Map** p250 G4 ❹
The Ascot is a little gem: not quite a boutique hotel, but easily superior to most hotels in the same price range, including all of the neighbouring hotels on Garden Road. It resides in a charming 1930s building remodelled inside from top to bottom to create a smart, contemporary hotel, with ample use of light wood floors, mirrors and glass, and a soft, cream colour palette. Rooms are spacious and airy, with checkerboards of orange-and-yellow fabric above the beds, plants and glass tables. Most of the rooms have flat-screen TVs and some have DVD players. Add friendly and efficient staff and the Ascot is easily a top mid-range choice.
Bar. Internet (wireless). Restaurant. Room service. TV.

Garden Hotel

42 Garden Road, off Colaba Causeway (2284-1476/ 2283-1330/gardenhotel@mail.com). Churchgate/ CST stations. **Rates** Rs 2,200 single; Rs 2,750-3,025 double. **Credit** AmEx, MC, V. **Map** p250 G4 ❺

The Garden Hotel looks almost identical to its next-door neighbour, the Godwin (*see p46*); both are glass-and-concrete towers built in the 1970s on a street full of old Colaba buildings from the 1930s and. '40s. What a shame. Inside is not much better, with a breathtakingly ugly three-metre waterfall in the lobby made of plastic climbing plants and artificial tree stumps. Still, the rooms are clean, the staff friendly and the Garden offers a cheap and serviceable option for bedding down for the night. *Internet (shared). Room service. TV.*

Sea Palace Hotel

26 PJ Ramchandani Marg, Apollo Bunder, Colaba (2284-1828/2285-4404/www.seapalacehotel.com). Churchgate/CST stations. **Rates** Rs 1,700-Rs 2,300 single; Rs 3,000-Rs 3,750 double. **Credit** AmEx, MC, V. **Map** p250 G4 ❻
The best feature of the Sea Palace is its location: right on the peaceful waterfront road about ten minutes' walk from the Taj Mahal hotel, with perfect views of the harbour. It's well worth shelling out for the most expensive rooms, which have sea views; open the window and you can lean out and gaze at the Gateway of India. Rooms are plain and simple, and you have to go for a deluxe double (Rs 3,750) for decent furnishings – smart beds,

Taj Mahal Palace & Tower. *See p43.*

lime-green walls and large, airy bathrooms. The garden at the front of the hotel is little more than a narrow strip with tables and umbrellas, but breakfast here is a very pleasant way to start the day: clean sea breezes, bobbing yachts in the harbour and the clipping of the occasional horse-drawn trap carrying tourists to the Gateway.
Parking. Room service. TV.

Cheap

Hotel Godwin

41 Garden Road, Colaba (2284-1226/2287-2050). Churchgate/CST stations. **Rates** Rs 2,900 double; Rs 3,800 suite. **Credit** MC, V. **Map** p250 G4 **7**

A 1970s-built concrete tower similar in external appearance to the Garden Hotel (*see p44*), but a superior option, with smarter decor and a spacious ninth-floor terrace offering sweeping 270-degree views of Colaba, complete with plant pots and plaster pillars wrapped with rope lights. A front-facing room is the best choice, with large windows displaying views of the dome of the nearby Taj Mahal hotel (*see p43*). The suites can sleep five people, six if you request an extra mattress for the floor. The rooms are nothing to get excited about but are spacious, neat and clean, and only slightly marred by the tatty red sofas and dusty plastic chandeliers.
Room service. TV.

Regency Inn

18 Lansdowne House, MB Marg, Apollo Bunder, Colaba (2202-0292/2282-3948). Churchgate/ CST stations. **Rates** Rs 2,150 single; Rs 2,500 double. **Credit** AmEx, MC, V. **Map** p250 G5 **8**

The Regency is a small, 21-room hotel on the first floor of a 19th-century colonial building of high ceilings and ancient wooden staircases. The reception and lounge areas manage to mix some of that Old World charm with modern touches, so we have a 180-year-old Belgian chandelier alongside wood-and-chrome Hunter fans, and modern chairs and tables alongside antique chests and an ornate old mirror. It works well and this could rank as a budget boutique hotel if they paid similar attention to the rooms, which are spacious but lacking in character, with old brown blankets on the beds and rexine-backed chairs. It's clean and neat, though, and one of the better budget options. **Photo** *p48. Room service. TV.*

Regent Hotel

8 Best Road, Colaba (2287-1854/2204-1518/ www.regenthotelcolaba.com). Churchgate/CST stations. **Rates** Rs 2,640 double; Rs 2,860 triple. **Credit** AmEx, MC, V. **Map** p251 G5 **9**

The floors are marble, the walls are marble, the reception desk is marble. They like marble at the Regent – there's acres of the stuff. Add wingtip leather armchairs and prints of horses and Mughal emperors, and the decor practically hits you over the head with a (marble) hammer and screams, 'Classy, isn't it!?' And it is, sort of. The paint is peeling in a few places but the rooms are spacious and the design has a genuine kitsch charm that elevates it above most city hotels in the same price range, with pastel tones, high ceilings, more of those wingtip armchairs and a faux-Edwardian feel. The location is central – just behind the Taj Mahal hotel – and the staff professional and friendly.
Internet (wireless/shared). No smoking rooms. Room service. TV.

Strand Hotel

PJ Ramchandani Marg, Apollo Bunder, Colaba (2288-1624/2288-0059/ www.hotelstrand.com). Churchgate/CST stations. **Rates** Rs 1,500-1,700 single; Rs 1,700-2,500 double. **Credit** MC, V. **Map** p250 G4 **10**

Right next door to the Sea Palace Hotel (*see p44*) is this peach harbour-front hotel, which has managed to hang on to some of its Art Deco charm in the face of 'improvements' like the gratuitous marquee stuck onto its frontage. It doesn't offer much in the way of amenities but the location and value for money make this one of the most popular cheap hotels in Colaba. Rooms are airy and clean, with high ceilings, a cream-and-brown colour scheme and simple furnishings. A few period touches have survived, like ornate designs on some of the windows and Art Deco balconies. Book ahead for one of the six 'super-deluxe' doubles (Rs 2,500) for a wonderful view of the harbour and the Gateway of India.
Bar/restaurant. Room service. TV.

YWCA International Guest House

18 Madame Cama Road, Fort (2202-5053/2202-9161/www.ywcabombay.com). Churchgate/CST stations. **Taxi** next to Golden Gate restaurant at Regal. **Rates** Rs 2,090 double; Rs 3,080 triple. **No credit cards.** **Map** p251 G6 **11**

Pay a Rs 50 temporary membership fee – it doesn't

Bentley's Hotel. *See p47.*

Taj Land's End, Bandra's plushest hotel. *See p50.*

matter if you're male – and you can gain access to the YWCA's international guest house. Simply but comfortably furnished, with attached bathrooms and balconies, the YWCA rooms make a great budget option which includes buffet breakfast, lunch and dinner in the attached dining hall. The prices above are for air-conditioned rooms, but they offer cheaper rates for non-AC rooms, including a single room for Rs 900.
Restaurant.

Budget

Bentley's Hotel

17 Oliver Road, Colaba (2288-2890/www.bentleys hotel.com). Churchgate/CST stations.
Rates Rs 1,340-1,795 double. **Credit** MC, V.
Map p250 G4 ⑫
Nothing quite captures the faded elegance of Colaba like Bentley's, on a quiet, tree-lined street just off Colaba Causeway. Spread over three neighbouring buildings built in the 1930s, Bentley's is a strictly no-frills affair with plenty of period Bombay atmosphere, with antique furniture, wooden staircases and chequered black-and-white floors. A stay at Bentley's is a trip back to an older, less frenetic Bombay, with servants cleaning mosaic-tiled floors with floorcloths under their bare feet, sleepy watchmen on the gate and the only noise the clatter of the cage lift door. Oliver Road looks like a suburban London street, lined with 1930s properties all in need of care and attention, but just five minutes' walk from the bustle of Colaba Causeway. The superior doubles offer views of a nearby park.
Photo *p46.*
Room service. TV.

Hotel Moti

10 BEST Marg, opposite Electric House, Colaba (2202-5714/2202-1654). Churchgate/CST stations. **Rates** Rs 1,500 double; Rs 2,000 triple.
No credit cards. Map p251 G5 ⑬.
Run by the friendly and hospitable Raj, Hotel Moti sits on the ground floor of an elderly building very close to the Taj Mahal hotel and a one-minute stroll from Colaba Causeway. An excellent-value budget option for the price, it's very basic but clean and secure, with 11 spacious rooms all equipped with fridges and attached bathrooms, and a few surviving period touches, including ornate stuccowork on the ceilings.
TV.

Churchgate

Expensive

Ambassador Hotel

Veer Nariman Road, Churchgate (2204-1131/www. ambassadorindia.com). Churchgate station. **Rates** Rs 4,800-Rs 10,000 single; Rs 5,500-11,000 double. **Credit** AmEx, MC, V. **Map** p251 & p252 E8 ⑭
This survivor of the 1970s doesn't do much for the eyeballs – it's essentially a 14-storey tower of dull concrete, but it's famed in Mumbai for being home to the city's only revolving restaurant, the Pearl of the Orient (*see p101*), on the 12th floor, which offers some breathtaking views of the arc of Marine Drive and the Arabian Sea. Inside, a '70s Indian vision of opulence is maintained, with acres of marble and wood panelling, an ornate gold-painted ceiling and golden elevator doors. The Society bar and restaurant on the lobby level sets the local standard for

luxury kitsch against some tough competition. Rooms are standard five-star fare, functional and comfortable, although none offer inspiring views of the sea or the city.

Bar (1). Business centre. Concierge. Gym. Internet (shared). Restaurants (2). Room service.

Moderate

Ritz Hotel

5 Jamshedji Tata Road, Churchgate (2285-0500/ 2282-0141). Churchgate station. **Rates** Rs 3,800-Rs 4,300 single; Rs 4,300-Rs 4,800 double; Rs 6,000-Rs 7,500 suites. **Credit** MC, V. **Map** p251 & p252 F7 ⑮

Mumbai's Ritz isn't at all ritzy, but this 50-year-old hotel offers spacious, clean rooms with decent-sized beds and large white-tiled bathrooms. The furnishings may be staid and the minibar in each room consists of just a single bottle of Kingfisher beer, but it's neat and functional, the bathrooms are roomy, and the location is good – just a few minutes' walk from Churchgate station. Room 408A is a good choice: a standard room but with impressive views of Churchgate station, and its own balcony. Be warned: some of the rooms do not have wall-to-wall carpets, balconies or bathtubs – you have to specify whether you want these when you book. *Room service. TV.*

West End Hotel

45 New Marine Lines (2203-9121/ www.westendhotelmumbai.com). Churchgate/ Marine Lines stations. **Taxi** opposite Bombay Hospital. **Rates** Rs 2,880 single; Rs 3,360 double; Rs 3,840-Rs 4,320 suite. **Credit** AmEx, DC, MC, V. **Map** p251 & p252 F10 ⑯

Built in 1948, the popular West End has retained its mid-20th century charm, with plenty of dark wood and original features. Scrupulously well-maintained, the spacious rooms are very simply but comfortably furnished, with bright whitewashed walls, high ceilings and black marble bathrooms with generously sized bathtubs. Rooms at the front of the hotel have small balconies overlooking the crowded New Marine Lines, always buzzing with traffic to Bombay Hospital, and a nearby temple. **Photo** *p43.* *Bar. Free parking. Internet (wireless). Restaurant. Room service. TV.*

Cheap

Astoria Hotel

4 Jamshedji Tata Road, Churchgate (6654-1234). Churchgate station. **Rates** Rs 2,750 double. **Credit** AmEx, MC, V. **Map** p251 & p252 F7 ⑰

A few minutes' walk from Churchgate station, the elderly Astoria announces its presence with a long-hand-style sign of blue neon. Recently renovated, the Astoria's lobby has been given a contemporary makeover, with soft, diffused lighting, wooden floors and an elegant glass fountain. Sadly, the rooms are not nearly so smart, with the obligatory wobbly fans and plain modern furniture, but they're clean, neat and airy, with high ceilings. Bathrooms are walk-in, Indian style, with showers and toilets sharing the same space. Still, at these prices, the Astoria is one of the better-value deals in South Mumbai. *Internet (shared). Restaurant. Room service. TV.*

Regency Inn. *See p46.*

Oberoi. *See p49.*

Chateau Windsor

86 Veer Nariman Road, Churchgate (2204-4455/
www.chateauwindsor.com). Rates Rs 1,440-Rs 1,890
single; Rs 2,190 double; Rs 2,490 triple; Rs 2,790
quadruple. **Credit** AmEx, MC, V. **Map** p251/2 F8 ⑱
The family that has been running Chateau Windsor
for the last 60 years are not given to understatement,
as the Raj-era grandeur of the name will tell you. In
the brochure they inform us that Chateau Windsor
is a 'luxurious' and 'elegant' corporate hotel, which
it plainly is not. It is, however, a cheap and cheerful
place with a fantastic location – on a main street just
a stroll away from both Marine Drive and
Churchgate station. It's popular with foreign
tourists, budget business travellers and families.
The rooms, spread across three floors of narrow,
sprawling corridors, are basic but clean, with
garish bedcovers and curtains, and cheap 1970s
furniture. Staff are professional and friendly, the
hotel is safe, with a closed-circuit TV system. Your
morning tea or coffee is complimentary, as is a
free shoe shine.
Internet (shared). Parking. Room service. TV.

Marine Drive

Deluxe

Hilton Towers Hotel

Nariman Point (6632-4343/www.hilton.com).
Churchgate/CST stations. Rates Rs 12,220-Rs 14,670
double; Rs 26,900-Rs 47,680 suite. **Credit** AmEx, DC,
MC, V. **Map** p251 D6 ⑲
The Hilton Towers is the sister of the landmark
Oberoi Hotel next door, and it's possible to walk
through from one lobby to the other along various
brass-handled staircases and designer store-
fringed corridors. The Hilton may be the poor sister – rates here start about Rs 4,500 a night cheaper
than at the Oberoi – but it's impressive, with a vast
lobby, some excellent restaurants and a
bougainvillea-fringed swimming pool with sea
views. The superior rooms are comfortable, if a little staid, with city-facing views and the kind of
inoffensive design, fixtures and furnishings that
would make granny feel at home. Deluxe ocean-
view rooms (Rs 13,200) offer a much more civilised
experience, with outstanding views of the Arabian
Sea. **Photo** *p52*.
Bar. Business centre. Concierge. Disabled-adapted
rooms. Gym. Internet (wireless). Non-smoking
floors. Parking. Pool (outdoor). Restaurants (3).
Room service. TV.

Intercontinental Marine Drive

135 Marine Drive (6639-9999/
www.mumbai.intercontinental.com). Churchgate/
CST stations. Rates Rs 15,000-Rs 18,500 double;
Rs 29,300-Rs 34,200 suite. **Credit** AmEx, MC, V.
Map p251 & p252 E8 ⑳
With a prime location right on the 'Queen's
Necklace', it would be a shame not to fork out the

extra cash for one of the Intercontinental's
sea-facing rooms: the views of the Arabian Sea are
second to none. The view and the plush rooms put
the Intercon firmly in the top rank of South
Mumbai's five-stars. Rooms are spacious and smart,
with wood floors, plasma TVs, Bose music systems
and DVD players. You can even have the music or
the TV piped through into the bathroom, which has
Bvlgari toiletries and is walled off with a glass
partition so you can keep watching the TV while
you shower, should you desire. Or you could just go
for a suite, where the bathrooms all have TVs anyway. The Intercontinental is also home to South
Mumbai's coolest rooftop bar, the Dome (*see p113*)
and a couple of the city's most delectable hotel
restaurants.
Bars (2). Business centre. Concierge. Disabled
adapted rooms. Gym. Internet (wireless).
No smoking floor. Parking. Restaurants (2).
Room service. TV.

Oberoi

Nariman Point (6632-5757/www.oberoi
mumbai.com). Churchgate/CST stations.
Rates Rs 17,100-Rs 20,000 double; Rs 41,500-
Rs 117,350 suite. **Credit** AmEx, DC, MC, V.
Map p251 D6 ㉑
The Oberoi vies with the Taj to take the top slot in
the rankings of South Mumbai's luxury hotels. One
of the city's first modern five-stars, it has hosted
Bill Clinton, Bill Gates, Michael Jackson and numerous visiting heads of state in its fabulously ornate
Kohinoor Suite (Rs 117,350), a palatial 2,100-sq ft
apartment with dramatic sea views. The deluxe
ocean view rooms (Rs 20,000) offer a little taste of
that luxury, with broad picture windows and spacious, airy spaces decked out in warm wood tones,
and half-bottles of Moët & Chandon are provided
in the minibar. Each room comes equipped with
a butler, who can be summoned at any time with
the press of a large red button. The Oberoi also
offers a selection of top restaurants, including the
superb Kandahar (*see p91*) and Vetro (*see p100*).
Photo *p48*.
Bar. Business centre. Concierge. Disabled-adapted
rooms. Internet (wireless). Gym. Non-smoking
floors. Parking (free). Pool (indoor). Restaurants (3).
Room service. Spa.

Expensive

Hotel Marine Plaza

29 Marine Drive (2285-1212/www.sarovar
parkplaza.com). Churchgate/CST stations.
Rates Rs 8,250 single; Rs 8,800 double; Rs 13,200
suite. **Credit** AmEx, MC, V. **Map** p251 & p252 E7 ㉒
The five-storey atrium of this seafront hotel just
screams Indian nouveau riche: gold-topped glass
elevators glide up and down walls of black-and-
white marble edged with more gold. On the ground
level sits a glass table supported by the tails of
giant glass fish, with paintings of laughing and
crying clowns on the walls. If that's a bit too much,

just avert your gaze to the atrium ceiling and admire fellow guests' backstrokes in the glass-bottomed rooftop swimming pool. The rooms are not nearly as gaudy: they're modern and smart, with outstanding sea views from front-facing rooms. If the city starts to get to you, just march downstairs to the Marine Plaza's ersatz 'English' pub, Geoffrey's.

Bar. Business centre. Gym. Internet (wireless). Pool (outdoor). Restaurants (2). Room service.

Cheap

Sea Green Hotel

145 Marine Drive (6633-6525/2282-2294/ www.seagreenhotel.com). Churchgate/CST stations. **Rates** Rs 2,000 single; Rs 2,450 double; Rs 2,475-2,900 suite. **Credit** Amex, MC, V. **Map** p251 E7 ㉓

This green-and-white Art Deco hotel located on Marine Drive was originally built in 1940 as quarters for British soldiers, before being converted into a hotel in the '50s. The threadbare red carpets look as if they haven't changed since then but the Sea Green is spotlessly clean and does manage to conjure up period charm, with high ceilings, some original features and the sleepy atmosphere of an older Bombay. Each room has a balcony and is reasonably spacious, although the mattresses are a little hard. Shell out a few hundred more rupees for a corner suite with an attached sitting room arrayed with 1970s furniture, where the views of the Arabian Sea are just as good as the lower floors of the plush Intercontinental a few minutes up the road. If the Sea Green is full, go next door to its sister, the Sea Green South Hotel (*see below*). **Photo** *p43.*
Room service. TV.

Sea Green South Hotel

145 A Marine Drive (6633-6525/2282-1613/ www.seagreensouth.com). Churchgate/CST stations. **Rates** Rs 2,000 single; Rs 2,450 double; Rs 2475-2,900 suite. **Credit** Amex, MC, V. **Map** p251 E7 ㉔

The neighbour of the Sea Green Hotel (*see above*) shares the same building and is identical in almost every respect, right down to the room rates, but run under different management. The 1940s feel is even more pronounced thanks to the gorgeous wood-panelled cage lift.
Room service. TV.

Bandra & Khar

Deluxe

Taj Land's End

Bandstand, Bandra (W) (6668-1234/ www.tajhotels.com). Bandra station. **Rates** Rs 11,500-Rs 16,000 single; Rs 12,500-Rs 17,250 double; Rs 23,000-Rs 75,000 suite. **Credit** AmEx, DC, MC, V.

Without doubt Bandra's most luxurious hotel, the 18-storey Taj Land's End stands close to a 16th-century fort where Portuguese cannons once kept watch over maritime trade routes. It's not uncommon to spot Bollywood stars strolling in for dinner (Shah Rukh Khan lives just down the road) and the restaurants are equipped with private dining rooms for just that purpose. The hotel is so large and self-contained that it's virtually a miniature village, with enough designer shops and restaurants to serve Bandra's elite and keep guests – mostly business travellers – distracted. The vast, plant-festooned central atrium leads through to a large outdoor swimming pool and sprawling landscaped lawns, with fine views of the sea and the nearby fort. Rooms are spacious and, thanks to some cunning design, all offer views of the sea through broad windows. **Photo** *p47.*

Bar. Business centre. Concierge. Gym. Internet (wireless). Parking. Pool (outdoor). Room service. Restaurants (3). Spa.

Expensive

SeaRock Hotel

Bandstand, Bandra (2642-5454). Bandra station. **Taxi** opposite Taj Land's End Hotel. **Rates** Rs 5,500-Rs 6,380 single; Rs 6,050-Rs 6,930 double. **Credit** AmEx, DC, MC, V.

The lobby is suitably imposing, with mock-classical pillars and fields of white marble, but the SeaRock feels sleepy compared to its illustrious neighbour opposite, the Taj Land's End. It does, however, have some of the city's most impressive sea views and they've got the basics right: the rooms are simple but cosy, with a calming white-and-green colour palette, and large, soft beds, although it's a shame that the air-conditioning stops once you step out of your room. The outside area by the pool – fringed with rope-light-wrapped palm trees – is one of SeaRock's most charming features, despite fairly basic poolside facilities. From here a romantic promenade extends along the rear of the hotel, with a steady breeze blowing in from the Arabian Sea, just beyond a stone balustrade.
Bar. Concierge. Gym. Internet (dial-up). Parking. Pool (outdoor). Restaurant. Room service.

Moderate

Hotel Metro Palace

355 Ramdas Nayak Road, Bandra (W) (2642-7311/ www.uniquehotelsindia.com). Bandra station. **Taxi** opposite Globlus shopping centre. **Rates** 2,200-Rs 2,800 single; Rs 2,600-Rs 3,200 double. **Credit** AmEx, MC, V. **Map** p249 D5 ㉕

Considering the price, the Metro Palace offers a decent no-frills deal for a stay in the heart of lively Bandra. Rooms are clean and of reasonable size, but very plainly furnished. A typical decorative touch might be a large colour poster of some kittens in a basket. Some of the rooms are wood-panelled and most have balconies, with views of bustling Waterfield Road nearby.
Room service. TV.

JW Marriott.
See p52.

Ramee Guestline Hotel

757 SV Road, Khar (W) (2648-5421/5422/
www.ramee-group.com). Khar station. **Rates**
Rs 3,850-4,400 single; Rs 4,180-Rs 4,500 double.
Credit MC, V. **Map** p249 D2 ㉖

The Ramee manages to pack quite a lot into a small
space – as well as a hotel, there's an 'Irish' pub, a
Chinese restaurant, hall-for-hire and a discotheque.
There clearly wasn't a lot of room left over for the
hotel lobby, or indeed the rooms, which are highly
compact. Still, this is one of Bandra-Khar's better
options for the price and, despite space constraints,
the Ramee has managed to squeeze in broad,
comfortable beds and some smart, modern design,
including attractive headboards of polished wood.
The hotel has a good central location for access to
Bandra and central Mumbai.
Bar. Internet (shared). Parking. Restaurant. Room
service. TV.

Vile Parle

Deluxe

Orchid Hotel

Near the Domestic Airport, Nehru Road, Vile Parle
(E) (2616-4040/www.orchidhotel.com). Vile Parle
station. **Rates** Rs 11,500-Rs 13,500 double;
Rs 14,500-Rs 18,000 suite. **Credit** AmEx, MC, V.

This pleasant 245-room hotel is Mumbai's only ISO-
certified eco-friendly hotel. It won't knock you out
with sharp design, but the environmentally smart
design is arguably more impressive, with furniture
made with wood from sustainable forests, all-
recycled paper products, smart water-saving bathrooms, and energy-saving air-conditioning, among
other innovations. The seven-storey atrium has an
attractive 70-ft 'waterfall' that is actually a circle of
70ft-high plastic wires carrying individual water

droplets. An open-air rooftop restaurant and bar
offer relaxed dining, and there's a medium-size,
non-chlorinated rooftop swimming pool. The
environmental concern isn't just a gimmick –
Mumbai is under intense environmental pressure
and five-star hotels are notorious producers of waste
and consumers of energy. Fortunately, the Orchid's
example is something that neighbouring hotels have
started to take notice of.
Bar. Business centre. Concierge. Disabled-adapted
rooms. Gym. Internet (wireless). Non-smoking floors.
Parking. Pool (outdoor). Restaurants (3). Room
service. TV.

Andheri

Deluxe

Hyatt Regency

Sahar Airport Road, Anderi (E) (6696-1234/
www.mumbai.regency.hyatt.com). Andheri station.
Rates Rs 9,000 single; Rs 9,500 double; Rs 15,500
suite. **Credit** Amex, DC, MC, V.

Cocooned behind a sweeping wall of glass are the
plush confines of the Hyatt Regency: acres of dark
grey marble, dark wood and frosted glass. Even
standard rooms are of high standards here –
spacious and airy, with step-down showers and
glass basins, and with a design laid out according
to the principles of *vastu shashtra* – the Indian feng
shui. That's why there's a tiny bamboo plant
greeting you as soon as you step into your room, and
why the 8ft by 6ft mirror in the bedroom is
positioned off to one side and not directly in front of
the bed – that would be bad *vastu*. The outdoor
gardens include a large swimming pool and – a
rarity – tennis courts, where you can play opposite
one of the hotel trainers.
Bar. Concierge. Gym. Internet (wireless). Parking. Pool
(outdoor). Restaurants (2). Room service. Spa. TV.

Hilton Towers Hotel. *See p49.*

ITC Grand Maratha Sheraton Hotel & Towers

International Airport Road, Andheri (E) (2830-3030/ www.itcwelcomgroup.in). Andheri station. **Rates** Rs 12,000-Rs 18,000 single; Rs 13,000-Rs 19,000 double; Rs 16,000-Rs 85,000 suite. **Credit** AmEx, DC, MC, V.
From the white jali-style lattice screens that cover the walls of the hotel's tall atrium of Agra red stone, to the ayurvedic shampoos in the bathrooms, the Grand Maratha Sheraton stands out from other new five-stars with a design that works to remind you that you are actually in India. Airy rooms are adorned with modern and traditional Indian art, including fine examples of local Warli tribal painting made with rice paste and straw. The restaurants cover Indian cuisines from north to south, with a nod to the British era in a club-like bar stuffed with wingtip leather armchairs. The happy marriage of five-star luxury and Indian style is tastefully restrained until you get to the outside pool, where they've let rip with six stone lion fountains and a giant iron-and-stone gazebo.
Bar. Business centre. Concierge. Gym. Internet (wireless). Non-smoking rooms. Parking. Pool (outdoor). Restaurants (5). Spa. Room service. TV.

Leela Kempinski

International Airport Road, Andheri (E) (6691-1234/www.theleela.com). Andheri station. **Rates** Rs 8,800 single; Rs 9,900 double; Rs 18,700 suite. **Credit** AmEx, V, MC, DC.
The Leela feels a little past its prime compared to its newer five-star neighbours on the airport road. Its multi-level lobby is a sprawling field of cream marble and brass fittings, with an elderly shopping arcade and a small gallery of works by contemporary Indian artists. The centrepiece is a sunken lobby with a waterfall rushing down to a gold-domed gazebo. Rooms are smart, spacious and tastefully decorated, each with a plasma TV. **Photo** *p53.*
Bars (2). Concierge. Gym. Internet (broadband). Restaurants (4). Room service. Spa. TV.

Royal Meridien

Sahar Airport Road, Andheri (E) (2838-0000/ www.leroyalmeridien-mumbai.com). Andheri station. **Rates** Rs 14,625-16,425 double; Rs 27,000-31,500 suite. **Credit** AmEx, MC, V.
Some nice design touches raise Le Royal Meridien above the five-star herd, most strikingly the Crystal Lounge: a long oval room in silver, white and beige with a series of glass doors opening off to other parts of the hotel under a gigantic chandelier. It's like walking into a Fabergé egg. In the Chinese restaurant next door, tables are arrayed with specially-commissioned dinner plates scrawled with the verse of Indian poet Harivanshrai Bachchan – translated into Chinese. Rooms are smart and contemporary, with wooden floors and spacious bathrooms provided (with rubber ducks provided). The only disappointment is that the view through the broad windows is of neighbouring slums and wasteland.
Bars (2). Business centre. Concierge. Disabled-adapted rooms. Free parking. Internet (wireless). Gym. Non-smoking floors. Pool (outdoor). Restaurants (3). Room service. Spa. TV.

Juhu

Deluxe

JW Marriott Mumbai

Juhu Tara Road, Juhu (6693-3000/ www.marriott.com). Santa Cruz station. **Rates** Rs 10,000-Rs 14,000 single, double; Rs 15,900-Rs 22,000 suite. **Credit** AmEx, DC, MC, V.
The JW Marriott is nothing less than a mini city of five-star luxury, set back from the mad scramble that is Juhu Tara Road behind high walls and the city's toughest hotel security, with no less than five restaurants, two bars and one of the city's best spas. Ninety per cent of the rooms have sea views and

are tastefully and sumptuously decorated, with attractive jute headboards, marble bathrooms prettily stencilled with flower designs and elegant shutters opening from the entranceway into the executive rooms. The Ocean Suite (Rs 19,800), although not the largest nor the most expensive, is arguably the most attractive of the suites, with floor-to-ceiling windows offering fabulous views of the palm tree-fringed beach that are not available in the more expensive Lotus Suite (Rs 21,100). You can even admire the view from the bath and shower, which is arrayed with Bvlgari toiletries. Beach access is closed because of security concerns but the outside area offers no less than three swimming pools, including a children's pool with water slide, a large main pool with stone chairs for aquatic lounging and a saline pool. **Photo** *p51.*
Bars (2). Business centre. Concierge. Disabled-adapted rooms. Gym. Internet (wireless). Non smoking rooms. Parking. Pools (outdoor). Restaurants (5). Room service. Spa. TV.

Sun 'n' Sand

39 Juhu Beach, Juhu (6693-8888/2620-1811/ www.sunnsandhotel.com). Santa Cruz station. **Rates** Rs 9,730-Rs 10,700 single; Rs 10,200-Rs 13,380 double; Rs 14,600-Rs 21,900 suite. **Credit** AmEx, MC, V.
Muscle-bound Bollywood superhunk Hrithik Roshan wanders through the lobby after a photo-shoot on Juhu Beach and no one raises an eyebrow – it's just another day at the Sun 'n' Sand, Mumbai's first five-star-rated hotel and a favoured destination for ad shoots thanks to its easy access to the beach and high service standards. Now over 40 years old, the Sun 'n' Sand retains an aura of 1960s Bombay with pastel shades, an easy-listening lobby sound-track, and furniture and decor that must have been cutting-edge modern when it was built in 1964 – like the hunting lodge-style restaurant. Despite no discernible evidence of a design makeover in the last 40 years, the rooms are spick-and-span with sparkling marble bathrooms and broad windows with excellent sea views. Room rates include airport pick-up and drop-off and complimentary cocktails.
Bar. Business centre. Free parking. Gym. Internet (wireless). Non-smoking rooms. Pool (outdoor). Restaurants (2). Room service. Spa. TV.

Expensive

Hotel Sea Princess

Juhu Beach (2661-1111/www.seaprincess.com). Santa Cruz station. **Rates** Rs 7,700 single; Rs 8,800 double; Rs 11,000 suite. **Credit** AmEx, DC, MC, V.
This 20-year-old hotel is an old Juhu standby, undergoing a major renovation during our stay to remodel its lobby and halls-for-hire. The design and decor don't seem to have changed much since the mid '80s, except for the addition of wall-mounted flatscreen TVs, with loud-patterned bedspreads and carpets, staid furniture and Pre-Raphaelite prints on the walls. The rooms feel a little cluttered, but the

Leela Kempinski. *See p52.*

excellent sea views – Juhu Beach is just behind the hotel – help take the edge off. The outside pool area is calm, spacious and pleasant, with beach access. There's also a separate children's pool.
Bar. Concierge. Disabled-adapted rooms. Gym. Internet (wireless). Non-smoking floor. Pool (outdoor). Restaurant. Room service. TV.

Moderate

Hotel Four Seasons

5 Juhu Tara Road, Juhu (2663-1441). Santa Cruz station. **Taxi** opposite Juhu Church. **Rates** Rs 3,250 single; Rs 3,750 double. **Credit** MC, V.
OK, it isn't fancy. The fans are wobbly, the rooms are plain, cramped and have no views, and the plastic climbing plants in the lobby look like they need watering. But it is clean, the cheapest decent hotel in Juhu, and former patrons include the Nobel Peace Prize-winner Shirin Ebadi, who stayed here during the 2004 World Social Forum. If it's good enough for her, it might be good enough for you. Convenient for both airports.
Restaurant. Room service. TV.

King's International

5 Juhu Tara Road, Juhu Beach (6692-2222/ 2618-4381/www.kingsinternational.com). Santa Cruz station. **Taxi** near Prithvi Theatre. **Rates** Rs 3,300 single; Rs 3,850 double. **Credit** MC, V.
The lift door sticks occasionally and needs a gentle kick to get it to shut, but don't worry, the shambling old commissionaire in a peaked cap will do that for you. This small, 30-year-old hotel won't win any awards but it is perfectly clean and decent, with surprisingly good-sized, comfortable rooms provided with fridges and TVs, and friendly service. Room service includes dishes from the excellent Temple Flower restaurant nearby. The rates include a complimentary airport drop-off.
Free parking. Room service. TV.

SULA

V I N E Y A R D S

INDIA'S FINEST
NEW WORLD STYLE WINES

ESTATE BOTTLED
NASHIK
OF INDIA

750 ml.

Sightseeing

Features

Introduction

Looking for nuggets in the city of gold.

It's hard to just be an observer in Mumbai. This city has a habit of grabbing you by the lapels – usually with a big grin – and demanding that you get involved. Mumbai is a noisy, exhilarating, bewildering, enchanting, exasperating, chaotic, smelly and, sometimes, desperately upsetting city, and it will insist on getting in your face even when – especially when – you don't want it to. Welcome to Mumbai. Let it wash over you at first, then dive in and swim.

Mumbai doesn't have many conventional tourist sights – its museums are generally poor and many of its heritage buildings dilapidated, although even the worst still manage a kind of dissipated charm. More often it's the people, the hectic activity of its train stations, its neighbourhoods and streets and their bizarre cheek-by-jowl contrasts that are the city's real spectacles – like the Koli fisherfolk building boats in the same way they have done for centuries just a few minutes from Nariman Point's corporate towers. And it may not be as pretty, but riding a suburban local train (*see p78* **Train strain**) is just as fascinating as gazing at the Gateway of India (*see p60*).

LIE OF THE LAND

We've divided the city into South and North Mumbai – with the latter known better to locals as just 'the suburbs'. **South Mumbai** (*see p59*) is still where Mumbai's wealthy work and play, and die-hard South Mumbai snobs wouldn't dream of going anywhere near the 'burbs, even though **Bandra** is now the city's hottest nightlife hub. **Nariman Point** continues to be a major corporate centre packed with airline offices, banks and foreign consulates, although these days business is shifting northwards to cheaper, more convenient locations like Parel and Powai in the north. Most of the city's sites of architectural and historical interest are located in the south, especially **Fort** (*see p65* **A walking tour of Fort**), named for the large fortress established by the British in the 17th century that became the nucleus of the city. The British influence is everywhere – not surprising for a city that was built by colonialism – and its oldest and most impressive buildings are all British relics. **University of Mumbai** (*see p61*) looks like an Oxford college with palm trees. Although there has been an effort to clean up some of the city's heritage buildings, many

remain in desperately neglected or wrecked by ill-conceived modifications or obscured by vast advertising hoardings. The **Suburbs** (*see pp74-79*), once villages, have swelled with new businesses, shops, restaurants and entertainment venues, but possess few places of interest for sightseers, although we've picked out a few gems that are worth the trouble. Many sights close on public holidays (*see p238*); ring ahead to make sure.

GETTING AROUND

The intense traffic, crowds, noise, heat, shocking poverty and poor infrastructure can make Mumbai an exhausting and overwhelming city. Be gentle on yourself and don't try to do too much at once. Drink plenty of water. Some areas are best appreciated on foot (*see p65* **A walking tour of Fort**), but

---

The best Sights

For the jewels in Mumbai's crown
Gateway of India (*see p60*); Chhatrapati Shivaji Maharaj Vastu Sanghralaya (*see p63*); Horniman Circle and the Asiatic Society (*see p64*); Chhatrapati Shivaji Terminus (*see p68*).

For serenity amid the chaos
Marine Drive (*see p73*); Mumbai Port Trust Garden (*see p59*); Banganga Tank (*see p73*); Veermata Jijabai Bhonsle Udyan (*see p71*).

For spiritual succour
Haji Ali Dargah (*see p73*); Kenneseth Eliyahoo Synagogue (*see p63*); Mumbadevi Temple (*see p72*); St Thomas' Cathedral (*see p67*).

For going independent
Mani Bhavan (*see p74*); Azad Maidan (*see p68*); August Kranti Maidan (*see p74*).

Worth the jaunt
Elephanta Island (*see p81*); Land's End, Bandra (*see p76*); Sanjay Gandhi National Park (*see p80*).

Take a tour in a 'Victoria'.

most of the time you'll find taxis much easier and a relatively cheap way to get around (*see p229*). Getting out to the suburbs is almost always faster by train but if you can't face those packed carriages, you'll find it isn't that expensive to go by taxi. Many street and place names have been officially changed in the last 20 years but most locals still use the old names. New names are often not recognised, even by taxi drivers, so in our listings and maps we've given both where appropriate and a prominent nearby landmark to aid navigation.

TOUTS AND SCAMS

Mumbaikars are warm and welcoming to foreign visitors, but around tourist-heavy sites like Colaba Causeway and the Gateway of India you're likely to be zeroed in on by persistent hawkers, beggars and the odd hashish dealer, especially in the peak winter season. Some visitors find being repeatedly offered drums and oversized balloons for a 'very good price' distressing and tiresome, but be philosophical and just accept it as the price of admission. Scammers and con artists do operate but tourist muggings are very rare. You might be ripped off by a cute 12-year-old asking you to buy her some powdered milk at a hugely inflated price, or an aspiring shoe-shine boy who just needs a hundred rupees to buy some polish and brushes – but you're unlikely to be robbed at knifepoint. Colaba is by far the worst spot for foreigner-focused hawkers and hustlers. If it's all getting too much, just get out of Colaba for some instant relief. If you go to Bandra, however, do watch out for the fake nuns 'collecting for the orphans'.

City tours

By bus

Bombay Safari, Gateway of India, near Taj Mahal Hotel, Colaba (2281-0139). Churchgate/CST stations. **Tours** 10am-8pm. **Fees** Rs 130. **No credit cards.**
Bombay Safari runs a tour of every conceivable sight across the city, as far as Juhu Beach, although you're welcome to hop off wherever you like. At weekends, Neelambari, an open-roofed double-decker bus, sets off from the Gateway at 7pm for a one-hour evening ride through the historic streets of Fort, for Rs 40-90. The guide's commentary is poorly delivered but this is still a great way to see this part of the city, lit by floodlights.

By foot

Heritage Walks (2683-5856/heritagewalks@ hotmail.com). **Tours** Call for schedule. **Fees** Rs 2,500 for minimum 5 people, Rs 250 each additional person. **No credit cards.**
Bombay Heritage Walks conducts a variety of guided walking tours of various parts of the city from the Gothic treats of Fort to Marine Drive art deco to the Portuguese-style villages of Bandra, with an emphasis on architectural details.

By bike

Odati Adventures, Room No.7, Union Co-operative Insurance Building, above Mocambo Café, Sir Pheroze Mehta Road, Fort (98200-79802). Churchgate/CST stations. **Tours** Call for schedule. **Fees** Rs 650 per person. **No credit cards.**
Odati takes you on a pedal-powered tour of Fort, Ballard Estate, Town Hall, CST, Marine Drive, Nariman Point and Colaba, pausing to learn about the city's history and development. Tours usually happen at weekends and take about half a day.

By boat

Gateway of India, opposite Taj Mahal Hotel, Colaba (2202-3585/6364). Churchgate/CST stations. **Tours** 8am-8pm Mon-Sun. **Fees** Rs 40 deluxe, Rs 30 economy. **No credit cards.**
Harbour cruises from Apollo Bunder in Colaba give great views of the city, from a different perspective. The Taj Mahal Palace and Towers Hotel (*see p44*) also has a luxury yacht available for hire for up to 10 people at Rs 15,000 an hour. Book two days in advance. Call them on 6665-3255.

By carriage

Around the Gateway of India, Apollo Bunder and Marine Drive. **Fees** Rs 250-300/45 mins. **No credit cards.**
A fun way to see some of South Mumbai's heritage sites is from the back of a 'Victoria' – an ornate, silver horse-drawn carriage with enough room for four or more. Hail one like a taxi – they look for fares along the Apollo Bunder seafront by the Taj Mahal hotel, near the Gateway, and on Marine Drive. You'll have to negotiate the route and the fare with the driver, so bargain hard.

South Mumbai

The heart of the city.

Colaba

Map p250

In 1743, Richard Broughton leased a quiet, windswept island called Colaba, just south of Bombay Island, from the East India Company for Rs 200 a year. Those were the days. Today, a three-bedroom flat there will cost you around Rs 20 million. Along with Malabar Hill, Colaba is one of the city's most exclusive districts and home to many of Mumbai's innumerable old-money families. Named after the Koli fisherfolk who inhabited the seven islands that became the Bombay peninsula, Colaba was a recreation area for the British throughout the 18th century and was populated solely by large numbers of deer released by the East India Company. In 1838, the construction of a causeway connecting it to the island of Bombay to the north allowed the island to be developed, initially as a military cantonment. As land values skyrocketed, it became a new centre for the city's cotton trade. In 1847, work began on the Church of St John the Evangelist, known locally today as **Afghan Church**, built to commemorate the hundreds of British and Indian soldiers from Bombay who died in the disastrous First Afghan War of 1838-43. Horse-drawn trams followed a few decades later, lending the island a romantic charm.

Today Colaba remains one of the city's greenest stretches, thanks in part to the sprawling campus of the Tata Institute of Fundamental Research – renowned for its research in maths and physics – and the army and navy installations that dominate the southernmost tip of the peninsula. **Cuffe Parade** was once one the city's most desirable addresses, with mansions and bungalows, many owned by Parsi families, overlooking a genteel seafront promenade. Some of the mansions remain but the promenade has gone, as has the sea, pushed back over a mile by land reclamation in the 1970s. It was quickly built over with apartment blocks, a shopping arcade, the twin towers of Mumbai's own World Trade Centre – and a large slum. A few minutes' walk north is **Gita Nagar** at Back Bay, where the brightly painted wooden boats of Koli fisherfolk, the descendants of the city's original inhabitants, line the beach just as they did for centuries before the Portuguese came.

Colaba also possesses one of the city's finest public parks, the **Mumbai Port Trust Garden** (6-10am, 4-9pm daily), where Colaba's well-heeled go jogging and take in a stunning sea view. A little further north and you hit **Colaba Causeway** – once a bridge connecting two islands, now the city's equivalent of London's Oxford Street. It's crammed with clothes shops, restaurants, bars, cafés, trinket stalls, wandering salesmen and, of course, tourists. The sidestreets here abound with mid-range hotels, handicrafts and jewellery shops, and some of South Mumbai's classiest bars, like perennial favourite **Indigo** (*see p113*), on Mandlik Road. At the southern end of the Causeway there's **Sassoon Dock** – a hectic

Sassoon Dock.

If you only have 48 hours

Day One

Take a stroll down **Colaba Causeway**, then sidetrack down to the harbour to the **Gateway of India** (see *below*) and the nearby **Taj Mahal Palace and Tower Hotel** (see *p44*). From here, stroll back down to **Regal Cinema** (see *p141*) and take in the **National Gallery of Modern Art** (see *p145*), and the impressive domes and balconies of the **Chhatrapati Shivaji Maharaj Vastu Sanghralaya**, formerly the Prince of Wales Museum (see *p63*), across the street. If you're feeling peckish, walk up to **Kala Ghoda** past a stretch of colonial-era heritage buildings and the landmark **Jehangir Art Gallery** (see *p145*) and tuck into some first-class North Indian curries at **Khyber** (see *p102*) or try the outstanding South Indian seafood at nearby **Trishna** (see *p102*). Close by is the faded but beautiful **Kenneseth Eliyahoo Synagogue** (see *p63*) and the cool Indian clothes store **Fab India** (see *p127*). From here, it's a quick stroll down University Road to the **Bombay High Court**, **Mumbai University** and the confusion of cricket at **Oval Maidan** (see *p61*). Still got some energy? Then walk up to **Flora Fountain** (see *p66*) and wander the hawker-packed pavement arcades nearby. Then it's a short walk down Veer Nariman Road to **Horniman Circle** and the **Asiatic Society** (see *p64*).

Day Two

You can't leave Mumbai without a taxi ride down the two-mile **Marine Drive** (see *p73*) for a stroll on the beach at **Girgaum Chowpatty** (see *p74*). From here it's another short taxi ride to Walkeshwar for the ex-colonial enclave of **Malabar Hill** and the holy and serene **Banganga Tank** (see *p73*). On the way back south, drive up Balbunath Marg past the **Babulnath Temple** (see *p75*) to nearby **Soam** (see *p103*) for some fabulous vegetarian Gujarati food. Then it's off to the old **Crawford Market** (see *p69*) for a wander around the city's liveliest and oldest food market. From here, take a cab down to Nagar Chowk and the breathtaking **Chhatrapati Shivaji Terminus** (see *p68*), an Indo-British confection in stone. Pop into the Café Coffee Day across the street for an iced coffee, then amble down Waudby Road to cross the lawns of **Azad Maidan** past the elite **Bombay Gymkhana** (see *p68*) to Mahatma Gandhi Road and the open-air **Fashion Street** clothes market (see *p130*). Before six o'clock, go back to Marine Drive for fabulous cocktails and sunset views of the bay from the **Dome** bar (see *p113*) on the roof of the Intercontinental Marine Drive. Then it's a short hop down the road to the seafront **Salt Water Grill** (see *p103*) for a relaxed dinner on the sand, under softly uplit palm trees.

wholesale fish market where the local Koli fisherfolk bring in the night's catch at around 5am. If you can get up in time, it's an experience (and smell) you won't forget in a hurry. Keep going and the entrance to **Colaba Market** appears, also on the right – an open and lively produce market crowded with fruit and vegetable stalls and a line of jewellery shops. Also on the causeway stands the massive, arched entrance of **Cusrow Bagh**, a housing colony built in 1934 and reserved for members of the city's dwindling Parsi community. A watchman guards the gate, but if you ask nicely he might let you take a peek at its spectacular art deco-style *agiary*, or fire temple (from the outside only; non-Parsis are not admitted). *Baghs* (literally, 'gardens') were built for community living, and with its neat, geometrical buildings and gardens, Cusrow Bagh has since catapulted into a prime Mumbai address.

A right turn at Electric House on the Causeway leads you to the back of the **Taj Mahal Palace & Tower Hotel** (see *p44*), dominating the seafront. The city's most

famous hotel, it was built by Parsi industrialist Jamsetji Nusserwanji Tata in 1903, reputedly out of anger at the Europeans-only policy of the prestigious (and now defunct) Pyrke's Apollo Hotel. Built in a blend of Moorish and Florentine Renaissance styles, it's worth visiting even if you're not planning on staying. The Taj is just yards from the waterfront **Gateway of India**, a towering archway of yellow basalt built by the British to commemorate the visit of King George V and Queen Mary to India in 1911, the only visit of a reigning British monarch to the jewel in the Empire's crown. Designed by architect George Wittet, it provided a ceremonial entranceway to the subcontinent for George and his queen immediately after stepping onto dry land, but the original was made out of papier-mâché – the stone version wasn't completed until 1927. In 1948, the last British troops to leave Indian soil exited through the Gateway. Overlooking the Gateway and its garden is the elegant **Royal Bombay Yacht Club** (Apollo Bunder, 6752-7200, www.royalbombayyachtclub.com), established in 1846 and still one of the city's most exclusive private members' clubs, steeped in colonial-era atmosphere. But you'll need permission from the club secretary to see inside. At the end of Colaba Causeway is **SP Mukherjee Chowk** – a traffic roundabout with an ornate stone fountain. Under British rule it was named Wellington Circle, after the Duke of Wellington, and the base of the fountain is inscribed with an inventory of the Iron Duke's battles. Locally, the roundabout is known simply as **Regal**, after the striking art deco cinema (*see p141*) built in 1934 that sits at the end of the Causeway.

Oval Maidan & Churchgate

Maps p251 & p252

The Arabian Sea once lapped at the edge of **Oval Maidan** (*maidan* means 'ground') until a land reclamation project in the 1920s extended the peninsula nearly half a mile westward to Marine Drive. As a result, there's a striking contrast between the High Gothic buildings on the *maidan*'s eastern side and the art deco apartments to the west. This half-mile-long recreation ground between Maharishi Karve Road (Queen's Road) and Karmaveer Bhaurao Marg (Mayo Road) was once a venue for dog-and-horse shows for the entertainment of British colonists in the 19th and early 20th centuries, before falling into disrepair. Now lovingly restored by residents of Queen's Road, it's the city's premier venue for impromptu cricket matches. On weekends there are dozens of games taking place simultaneously, overlapping to the point where it's almost impossible to tell where one ends and another begins. Visitors are very welcome to join the melée. On the Oval's eastern side is a row of some of the city's most impressive Victorian buildings. Next to the **Old Secretariat** and the **Sessions Court** at the southern end of Mayo Road are the curlicued stones and spiral staircases of the **University of Mumbai**, built in 1874 and reminiscent of an Oxford college with palm trees. Attached to the University Library and looming over the Oval is the **Rajabai Clock Tower** (*see p62*), constructed in 1878. To the left is the **Bombay High Court**, outside, which down-on-their-luck itinerant lawyers in threadbare black suits tout for work. Visitors are allowed inside, which is highly recommended for courtroom scenes straight out of Dickens' *Bleak House*. Inside, look out for the satirical animal sculptures decorating the cornices and tops of pillars, like the monkey judge holding a hopelessly unbalanced scale, and foxes and wolves in lawyer's outfits. Across the street from the

Khada Parsi – the 'Standing Parsi'. *See p71.*

Chhatrapati Shivaji Terminus. *See p68.*

Sightseeing

Churchgate Terminus.

court is the **Bhika Behram Well**, built in 1725. It's a sacred well for the Parsi community, surrounded by green benches where elderly Parsis read their holy book. The canopy above the well features vivid stained-glasswork depicting the winged *Aashofarohar*, a Zoroastrian divine messenger. Only Parsis are allowed in. Westwards along Veer Nariman Road sits the **Western Railway Headquarters**, built in 1899, with white domes rising above dark stone minarets. The staid concrete structure opposite is the **Churchgate Terminus** where the suburban Western Railway line ends. Every weekday morning, around three million commuters arrive here. Opposite Churchgate is the **Eros Cinema** (*see p140*), another art deco gem built in 1938, now run-down but as busy as ever.

Rajabai Clock Tower

University of Mumbai, Karmaveer Bhaurao Marg, next to High Court, Oval Grounds, Churchgate (www.mu.ac.in). Churchgate/CST stations. **Open** 10.30am-6.30pm Mon-Sat. **Admission** free. **Map** p251 G7.

The chimes of the Rajabai clock tower, which rises 280 feet above the University of Mumbai Library, have been sounding across Oval Maidan every half-hour, with a few interruptions, since 1880. Modelled on London's Big Ben, the tower was built with a Rs 400,000 donation from Mumbai's first share fraudster, Premchand Roychand (*see p16* **Bombay's First Boom**). In return, the clock tower was named after his mother, Rajabai. It was designed by Sir Gilbert Scott in Gothic Revivalist style and features stone heads of Shakespeare and Homer peering out from the crossed arches under the main spiral staircase. Look out for the pretty stained-glasswork around the staircase, and the flower-like teak wood library ceiling.

Kala Ghoda

Maps p251 & p252

South Mumbai's art district, **Kala Ghoda** (which means 'Black Horse') sits off the intersection of K Dubash Marg (Rampart Row) and Mahatma Gandhi Road. It's one of the city's most attractive areas, with some well-restored heritage buildings. Kala Ghoda owes it name to a 13-foot bronze equestrian statue of King Edward VII, which was installed here in 1879 in what is now a car park, to commemorate the king's visit three years earlier. Edward sat there for the next 86 years, surviving long after the last British troops departed in 1948. The statue was finally removed in 1965 in a drive to eradicate British-era statues from public places. Edward, unlabelled and stuck on a patch of grass, now greets visitors to the Byculla Zoo (*see p71*).

Today, the only horse at Kala Ghoda is a 25-foot-long painting on the façade of the Khyber Building, overlooking the car park, by contemporary Indian artist Baiju Parthan (prints of it are available from Brinda Miller for Rs 5,000 – call 98200-80555 for details). Since Independence, the area has evolved into Mumbai's premier art district, with eight galleries nearby. The largest is the **National Gallery of Modern Art** (*see p145*) which stands off the Regal Circle, and the **Jehangir Art Gallery** (*see p143*). Artists also display their work on the pavement outside the Jehangir, which stands on one corner of the sprawling compound of the **Chhatrapati Shivaji Maharaj Vastu Sanghralaya** (*see p63*), formerly known as the Prince of Wales Museum, on Mahatma Gandhi Road.

Overlooking Kala Ghoda on the western side of Mahatma Gandhi Road is the **David Sassoon Mechanical Institute and Library**, built in 1870 and named after its founder, a renowned Jewish businessman and philanthropist from Baghdad whose family built many of the city's civic and cultural institutions. Sassoon's face peers out of the building's façade above its arched entrance and there's a life-sized statue of him in traditional Jewish robes inside. Upstairs, a peaceful balcony overlooking Kala Ghoda is a popular spot for readers to while away the afternoons. On its left stands **Elphinstone College**, Mumbai's oldest college, instituted in 1835 and taking up residence in this beautiful building in 1888. The college building had for decades been a dark grey mess until renovation restored the exquisite golden stonework a few years ago. Similar magic was worked on the **Army & Navy Building** to its right, renamed for the Army & Navy Departmental Store it once housed. The Army & Navy recently became a department store once again, named Westside, which has a small but decent café. Next door is the decrepit **Esplanade Mansion** (*see p66* **Mr Twain checks into Watson's**), once the city's most luxurious hotel, Watson's.

Rampart Row, officially named K Dubash Marg, runs along the site of one wall of the 17th-century British fort that became the city's nucleus and was finally demolished in the 1860s. On the other side of the popular **Rhythm House** music store (*see p129*) the narrow Dr VB Gandhi Road (Forbes Street) leads to the sky-blue **Kenneseth Eliyahoo Synagogue**. Another Sassoon family-funded institution, it was built in 1884 for what was once the city's thriving Jewish community. It's faded but still beautiful, especially in the afternoons when its tall, stained-glass windows cast a rainbow of light across the prayer hall. Before Independence, the prayer hall benches were packed elbow-to-elbow for Saturday services; these days only a handful come. Most of Mumbai's Jewish community migrated to Israel and elsewhere after 1948.

From the synagogue, the narrow Saibaba Lane leads back to Rampart Row, which is now lined with a stretch of smart restaurants and shops. Keep an eye out for two mahogany trees in front of **Ador House** – legend has it that they were planted by the famous British explorer and missionary Dr David Livingstone on a visit to Mumbai in 1865. At the end of Rampart Row rises the tall spire of **St Andrew's and St Columba's Church**, built in 1819 and modelled on St Martin-in-the-Fields in London's Trafalgar Square. Mumbai's first Scottish Church, St Andrew's massive doors open onto a carefully preserved interior of Burmese teak and shining brass, surmounted by an antique pipe organ. St Andrew's only opens for Sunday services at 6.30pm. Opposite the church, along Rampart Row, stands the **Bombay Natural History Society**, hidden behind thick foliage at Hornbill House. The society was formed by naturalists in 1884 to document the rich flora and fauna around Mumbai. Today, it conducts environmental projects and is at the forefront of efforts to save India's tigers. It's closed to non-members.

Every February, Rampart Row is closed to traffic for the two-week Kala Ghoda Arts Festival (*see p132*), when art installations, photographs, multi-media works and paintings spill out from the neighbouring galleries on to the pavements. Theatre, music and dance shows are performed on a makeshift stage on the road, which is lined with stalls selling street food, ethnic clothes and jewellery.

Chhatrapati Shivaji Maharaj Vastu Sanghralaya (Prince of Wales Museum)

159 MG Road, Kala Ghoda, near Regal Circle (2284-4519/www.bombaymuseum.org).
Open 11am-5.30pm Tue-Sun. **Admission** Rs 300, Rs 2 children 5-12 years. **Map** p251 G6.
The city's largest museum, the Chhatrapati Shivaji Maharaj Vastu Sanghralaya, was built in 1914, and originally called the Prince of Wales Museum, a name that most locals prefer for its brevity. The building is a fusion of British, Hindu and Mughal architecture – a style called Indo-Saracenic pioneered by British architect George Wittet in

Chhatrapati Shivaji Maharaj Vastu Sanghralaya – aka the Prince of Wales Museum.

the early 1900s. The domes are from Mughal architecture, its sculpted windows resemble those of traditional Rajasthani dwellings, and the balconies and façade are typically British. The museum has over 30,000 artefacts including bronze and stone sculptures, miniature paintings, arms and armour, and Far Eastern art. Don't miss the only Assyrian frieze in India, on display in the Pre- and Proto History Gallery. The explanatory labels are poor, but there is a 45-minute audio tour available for Rs 150. **Photo** *p63*.

Ballard Estate

Maps p251 & p252

Under the Mumbai stink of petrol, dust and spices is that all-pervasive smell of fast money, and nowhere is it stronger than in the area around Ballard Estate, the city's old shipping and financial district. The epicentre is the 28-storey **Bombay Stock Exchange**, which stands at the junction of Mumbai Samachar Marg and Dalal Street. The word *dalal* means broker, and Bombay's first exchange was established here in 1875; the new building was built in the 1970s. On March 12 1993, around 50 people were killed by a car bomb in the Exchange's basement during Mumbai's worst-ever terrorist attack, now known as 'Black Friday' (*see p22*). The narrow lanes around the exchange are lined with brokerages, banks, insurance and other financial institutions, and bulls and bears dominate the conversation at local *chai* stalls.

Mumbai Samachar Marg leads to **Horniman Circle**, a London-style fenced circular garden surrounded by elegant heritage buildings, including the imposing neo-classical **Asiatic Society of Mumbai** (*see below*). The circle was the heart of the city's cotton trade during its early boom years (*see p16* **Bombay's first boom**), and there's still an old trough near the western gate that was used to water the cattle carrying cotton bales to the market. After 1863, the cotton market moved to Colaba, but profits from the boom paid for the Horniman Circle Garden and the buildings around it.

Ahead of the Asiatic Society, Shahid Bhagat Singh Road curves into Mint Road, site of the imposing **Reserve Bank of India**, India's main regulating bank. Hidden behind a wall next to the RBI is the **Bombay Mint**, built in 1827 to produce gold and silver coins and still pumping out the steel rupee coins used today. Close by is the **Monetary Museum** (*see below*), on Sir Pherozeshah Mehta Road.

On Modi Street, parallel to Mint Road, stands the **Maneckji Nowroji Sett Agiary**, Mumbai's oldest Parsi fire temple, first built in 1733 and rebuilt in 1891. You'll have to admire it

from outside, though, as only Parsis are allowed in. Inside burns an eternal flame, carried by Parsi refugees from Persia to India when they fled Muslim persecution around 800AD.

Ballard Road leads to the business district of **Ballard Estate**, a neat grid of elegant office buildings designed by George Wittet (the designer of the Gateway of India). The entire area was reclaimed from the sea around 1910, including the access-restricted **Indira Docks** that stand beyond, where the British munitions ship *Fort Stikine* blew up in 1944 (*see p70* **The Japanese attack that wasn't**). The buildings here housed shipping offices and hotels for arrivals at the docks. Most have closed down, replaced by some of India's biggest corporations, like **Reliance House**, the corporate office of Reliance Industries, a Fortune 500 company. Today, the office of the **Mumbai Port Trust**, which regulates all port activities and is the city's biggest landowner, and the **Customs House**, remain the Estate's most important administrative centres. A **War Memorial** to Mumbai Port Trust employees who died in World War I stands at the junction of Ballard Road, Sprot Road and Narottam Morarji Marg. The tiny **Naval Museum** (*see p66*) on Ballard Road is a recent addition to the landscape.

Asiatic Society of Mumbai

Shahid Bhagat Singh Road, near Horniman Circle (2266-0956). **Open** 10am-6pm Mon-Sat. **Admission** free. **Map** p251 H8.

This milk-white neo-classical building with sweeping steps and imposing pillars has starred in numerous Bollywood films, usually masquerading as the Bombay High Court. The Asiatic Society was formed in 1803 with the purpose of 'studying the Orient' – but 'Orientals' themselves were excluded. It remained a Europeans-only club until Sir Cursetji Maneckji was admitted in 1840, after he pointed out the stupidity of banning Indians when they were free to join the Royal Asiatic Society of Great Britain, its sister organisation. Inside, the library's curving stone staircases and cozy alcoves are filled with life-sized statues of British-era governors, officials and philanthropists. The library is a repository of several rare books, including an original manuscript of Dante's *Divine Comedy*, though sadly it is not on display.

Monetary Museum

Amar Building, Sir Pherozeshah Mehta Road (2261-4043/www.rbi.org.in/scripts/ ic_museum.aspx). **Open** 10.30am-5pm Mon-Fri; 10.30am-1pm Sat. **Admission** Rs 10. **Map** p251 H8.

Did you know that the world's smallest coins were *panams* from Kerala, with a diameter of less than one-sixteenth of an inch? No? Then you need to educate yourself at the Reserve Bank of India's compact Monetary Museum, which offers a short,

A walking tour of Fort

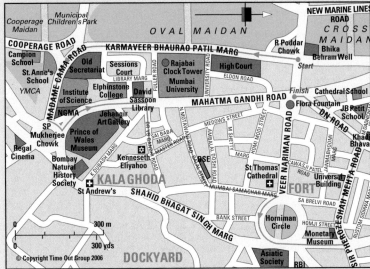

This tour of the area around the south-western part of the site of the old Bombay Fort takes about two hours. Start off at R Poddar Chowk, across from the **Bhika Behram Well** (*p62*), situated between **Oval Maidan** (*p61*) and **Cross Maidan** (so named for the cross put there by the Portuguese). Proceed down Karmaveer Bhaurao Patil Marg, lined with beautiful heritage buildings, including the **Bombay High Court**, **University of Mumbai** (*p61*) and the **Old Secretariat**, once the house of the British governor of Bombay. Turn right onto **Madame Cama Road**, named for Bhikaiji Rustom Cama, a Parsi feminist and freedom fighter, made famous when she unfurled a prototype of the Indian flag at a socialist conference in Germany in 1907. The road curves past the arched façades and gardens of the **Institute of Science**, built in 1920 and affiliated to the university.

At **SP Mukherjee Chowk** (*p61*), better known as the Regal Circle, stands a **fountain**, built in 1865 and dedicated to Arthur Wellesley, the Duke of Wellington, who stayed in Bombay for two months in 1801. On the southern side of the circle stands the art deco **Regal cinema** (*p141*). Turn right onto Mahatma Gandhi Road, which runs along what was once the western wall of the Bombay Fort. On the left are the

horseshoe-shaped galleries of the **National Gallery of Modern Art** (*p145*) and on the right the impressive **Chhatrapati Shivaji Maharaj Vastu Sanghralaya**, or Prince of Wales Museum (*p63*). Continue down past the **Elphinstone College** (*p63*) and the **David Sassoon Library** (*p62*) and take a right into **Kala Ghoda** (*p62*). Keep the **Rhythm House** (*p129*) music store on your right and head down into the narrow Dr VB Gandhi Road, once a covered lane called Ropewalk, filled with rope and cable makers for the city's docks. Just one rope shop remains. On the right is the charming **Kenneseth Eliyahoo Synagogue** (*p63*). Cut left onto the narrow Master Road into the heart of the finance district on **Dalal Street**, near the **Bombay Stock Exchange** (*p64*), still lined with business houses, and one of the best-preserved old streets in Mumbai. Take a left on to Mumbai Samachar Marg past **St Thomas' Cathedral** (*p67*) to the grand **Horniman Circle** and **Asiatic Society** (for both, *p64*). Turn right onto Shahid Bhagat Singh Marg past the **Monetary Museum** (*p64*) and left onto the hectic **Sir Pherozeshah Mehta Road**, lined with lively shops and stalls. From here dive left into the stall-lined pavement arcades of **Dadabhai Naoroji Road** to **Flora Fountain** (*p67*).

Mr Twain checks into Watson's

Esplanade Mansion (144 Mahatma Gandhi Road; *see p63*) at Kala Ghoda is in a state of utter disrepair, but look up at the balconies and you can still see the letter 'W' emblazoned on its railings – 'W' for Watson's, once Bombay's most luxurious hotel, which shut down in 1947. It was famed for its five-storey central atrium, illuminated by a still-intact skylight, which served as a fashionable ballroom. It was in one of Watson's opulent rooms that the Lumière Brothers first took Bombay to the movies in 1896 (*see p20*). And on one of those balconies, 'somewhere high up, on the front', the American novelist Samuel Langhorne Clemens – better known as Mark Twain – fought off recalcitrant crows and recorded his impressions of Bombay for his round-the-world travelogue *Following the Equator*, published in 1897. He found Bombay a bewitching city and threw himself into its whirl, calling on the governor, Lord Sandhurst – at his mansion on Malabar Hill – attending the wedding of a 12-year-old Hindu bride, watching a murder trial, and attending a party thrown by cotton market scamster Premchand Roychand (*see p16* **Bombay's first boom**).

Twain checked into Watson's on 20 January 1896. He recalled: 'The lobbies and halls were full of turbaned, and fez'd and embroidered, cap'd, and barefooted, and cotton-clad dark natives. Some of them rushing about, others at rest squatting, or sitting on the ground; some of them chattering with energy, others still and dreamy; in the dining-room every man's own private native servant standing behind his chair, and dressed for a part in the Arabian Nights.'

'There is a rank of noble great shade trees across the way from the hotel, and under them sit groups of picturesque natives of both sexes; and the juggler in his turban is there with his snakes and his magic; and all day long the cabs and the multitudinous varieties of costumes flock by. It does not seem as if one could ever get tired of watching this moving show, this shining and shifting spectacle...'

Mark Twain at **Watson's Hotel** – an illustration from *Following the Equator*.

stimulating history of Indian money, from barter to credit cards. Some crisp and informative text accompanies the displays, and colourful infographics deconstruct complex concepts for kids. It has an impressive collection of old Indian coins, and a thorough guide to spotting counterfeit notes.

Naval Museum

Naval Museum, Ballard Road, Ballard Estate (2261-4043). **Open** 9am-7pm Mon-Sun. **Admission** Free. **Map** p252 J8.

The tiny Naval Museum was long overdue when it opened in 2005 – the first modern museum dedicated to Mumbai's illustrious maritime history. It's housed in a yellow stone gateway that was once lost behind a high wall after the Indian Navy took over the dockyards. The museum is filled with old black-and-white photographs of maritime Mumbai, compasses, and intricate wooden models of ships and boats built by the Wadia family, once a famous Bombay shipbuilding dynasty (*see p15* **This ship was built by a d----d black fellow**).

Flora Fountain

Maps p251 & p252

The hectic **Flora Fountain** intersection at the junction of Mahatma Gandhi Road, Dadabhai Naoroji Road and Veer Nariman Road is now officially known as Hutatma Chowk, but locals still just call the area 'Fountain', referring to its central ornate fountain mounted with a statue of the Roman goddess Flora, carved from imported Portland stone and erected in 1864. Before that, this was the site of the gates of the original Bombay Fort. There are several other public artworks nearby, including a statue of a 'martyr with a flame' built in memory of the 105 people shot dead here by police in 1960 during a protest for the creation of Maharashtra state (*see p20*). Commerce of all kinds keeps Fountain flowing; the streets are lined with branches of the Hong Kong and Shanghai Banking Corporation, Standard Chartered Bank, the Central Bank of India and Bombay House, the corporate office of the Tatas, one of India's oldest and most respected business houses. Under Fountain's shaded pavement arcades an industry of hawkers peddles everything from second-hand books and T-shirts to bootleg software, Bollywood posters and cheap Chinese vibrators.

The façade of the **Pundole Art Gallery** (*see p146*) is faced with a mural of black horses by the renowned Mumbai artist MF Husain, but even more impressive artwork graces the frontage of the 1930s-built **New India Assurance Company Building**, with a unique art deco-style depiction of rural Indian workers. Along Veer Nariman Road, just before Horniman Circle, stands **St Thomas' Cathedral** (*see below*), the first Anglican Church of Mumbai, built in 1718. On Medows Street, which also runs into the Flora Fountain junction, stands the blue **St Stephen's Armenian Church**, originally built in 1876 for what was once the city's flourishing Armenian community, of whom just four members are left.

Further along Dadabhai Naoroji Road sits the **JN Petit library**, which features rare stained glasswork depicting Parsi philanthropists of the late 1800s. Nearby is **Khadi Bhandar**, a handicraft store dedicated to Gandhi selling handmade ornaments, furniture and traditional Indian clothes made from homespun cotton.

A little off DN Road along Sir Pherozeshah Mehta Road is the **Universal Building**, where the Beatle, George Harrison, spent five days in 1968 recording a soundtrack for the avant-garde film *Wonderwall* with Indian classical musicians (*see p74* **A Beatle in Bombay**)

There's a stark contrast between the crowded, tangled bylanes to the east of Dadabhai Naoroji Road and the smart, broad roads to the west. Its eastern flank is known as **Bazaar Gate**, a market area that dates back to the early 18th century, when the British Fort enclosed the area. Its character hasn't changed much since then, with teeming alleys filled with shops, tailors, fruit stalls and the occasional massage parlour. The area is dominated by Gujarati Jains, and many of the buildings have Gujarati-style wooden balconies and awnings, now hidden under years of dirt. Clearer evidence of the longstanding Jain influence can be found on Maruti Lane at the 200-year-old **Shantinathji Jain Derasar**, a multi-coloured Jain temple with two moustached stone guards manning its entrance.

The area of the city to the west of DN Road was developed after the fort walls were demolished in the 1860s to make room for urban expansion. This area now has some of Mumbai's most exclusive schools and colleges, including **Cathedral and John Connon School**, **JB Petit High School for Girls**, and the **Alexandra Girls' High School**. It's also home to **Siddhartha College**, set up by Dr BR Ambedkar, the writer of India's Constitution and a champion of the country's lower castes, revered by the city's *dalit* community. An impressive mansion of cream-coloured stone stands out on the approach to Nagar Chowk – **Fort House**, famous for being the place where ice-cream was first served in Bombay, at a party hosted by the wealthy entrepreneur Sir Jamshetji Jejeebhoy in the early 1830s. For a walking tour of Fort, *see p65*.

St Thomas' Cathedral

Veer Nariman Road, near Horniman Circle. **Open** 10am-5.30pm daily. **Admission** free. **Services** 7am, 8.45am Sun. **Map** p251 H8.

The Churchgate area is so named because of this church, built in 1718 near one of the gates of Bombay Fort, where Flora Fountain now stands. It was the first Anglican church in Mumbai, and contains memorials to British colonists, many of whom seemed to have died from malaria before they reached 30. The names include Katherine Kirkpatrick, the mother of James Achilles

Flora Fountain. *See p66.*

Dwarkadheesh Temple. *See p72.*

Kirkpatrick, who scandalised colonial-era India by marrying Hyderabadi beauty Khair un-Nissa, and whose story is told in William Dalrymple's *White Mughals*. The church was recently restored, winning the UNESCO Asia-Pacific Heritage Award in 2004.

Nagar Chowk

Map p252
Dominating Nagar Chowk (meaning 'City Square' in Hindi) is the spectacular **Chhatrapati Shivaji Terminus** (*see below*), Mumbai's main train station and still known to many as 'VT' for its old name, **Victoria Terminus**. This area marks the northern boundary of the old British Fort; the last remnant of fort wall still stands behind the terminus near St George's Hospital, unmarked and hidden behind a public toilet around the corner from the **General Post Office**. Across from the terminus on the corner between Mahapalika Marg and Dadabhai Naoroji Road stands the grand headquarters of the **Brihanmumbai Municipal Corporation** – first set up in 1872 to take care of the city's upkeep, now a byword for inefficiency and corruption. In front of the building stands a statue of Sir Pherozeshah Mehta, the Corporation's creator. More justly than unjustly, the Corporation is the favourite punching bag of most local newspapers, one of which is right next door at the **Times of India Building**, built in 1903 and home to the world's largest-selling daily English-language paper. Down Marzban Road,

past the Barista cafe, sits the ever-popular **Sterling Cinema** (*see p141*).

Next to Sterling Cinema stands **Tata Palace**, once the residence of India's foremost business family, now the offices of Deutsche Bank, mounted with circular galleries, stone lion heads and mock classical columns in the form of Greek virgins. Nearby on Waudby Road stands the 130-year-old **Bombay Gymkhana**, once a whites-only colonial enclave, now a private sports and social club for the city's elite, not open to visitors. On the other side of Azad Maidan, opposite the Gymkhana's front entrance on Mahatma Gandhi Road is the vibrant **Fashion Street** (*see p128*), an open-air clothes market selling fake Levis and reject export clothing to college students.

Chhatrapati Shivaji Terminus
Nagar Chowk. **Open** 4.30am-1am. **Map** p252 H10.
If the central suburban railway line is Mumbai's main artery, then **Chhatrapati Shivaji Terminus**, built in 1808 and formerly known as **Victoria Terminus (CST)**, is its beating heart. Along with the western suburban railway line, which terminates as Churchgate (*see p61*), CST is the city's main transport hub and the busiest train station in Asia, with around three million people passing through on 1,350 suburban and intercity services every day. The building was designed by FW Stevens, who also designed the Brihanmumbai Municipal Corporation office facing the station, and was recently declared a UNESCO world heritage site for its unique Indo-Saracenic architecture. The ornate exterior is a jungle in stone, with a life-sized pair of lions guarding the doors to its admin offices, and peacocks, monkeys, owls, chameleons, rams, elephants and other beasts peering down on commuters from the façade. After the Taj Mahal in Agra, CST is the second-most photographed building in India. **Photo** *p61.*

Around Metro

Map p253
Mahapalika Marg is bordered by numerous Raj-era buildings and the sprawling **Azad Maidan**, or 'Freedom Ground', named so for being the site of so many anti-colonial rallies during India's freedom struggle. It remains a popular site for political protests today. Past the Brihanmumbai Municipal Corporation headquarters is the **Presidency Magistrate's Court** (also known as Esplanade Court), which was completed in 1889, and the Gothic façade of the **Cama & Albless Hospital**, built in 1886. Ahead is **St Xavier's College**, established in 1891, now an elite college. Around the corner of Lokmanya Tilak Marg is the **St Xavier's High School**, the courtyard of which displays a piece of a ship's propeller that landed here

after the *Fort Stikine* dock explosion of 1944 (*see p70* **The Japanese attack that wasn't**).

The road ends at a square called **Dhobi Talao**, meaning 'Washerman's Pond' – once home to a community of workers who laundered the city's clothes in a lake that was long ago filled in. The community now works at the Mahalaxmi Dhobi Ghats (*see p73*). On the eastern side of Dhobi Talao is the **Metro Cinema**, a landmark single-screen art deco cinema built in the 1930s, so named because for years it only screened films produced by the Metro-Goldwyn-Mayer Corporation. It's so famous in the city that many locals call the area around it 'Metro' instead of Dhobi Talao. The cinema is now being turned into a multiplex, but you can still enjoy the art deco charms of the restored **Liberty Cinema** (*see p140*), on Vithaldas Thackersey Marg behind Metro.

On the corner between Girgaon Road and Kalbadevi Road is the triangular **Jer Mahal**, an early 19th-century *chawl* – one of the first examples of the tenements that were built to house the thousands of immigrants who came to Mumbai to work in its cotton mills, with one room for each family. Millions of Mumbaikars now live in chawls. Although dilapidated, Jer Mahal is more attractive than most, with ornate wooden balconies and trellises. The lanes north of Dhobi Talao – Girgaon Road, Kalbadevi Road and Lokmanya Tilak Marg – are densely packed with shops, particularly sports goods and music stores. Lokmanya Tilak Road leads to Crawford Market.

Crawford Market

Maps p253 & p255

Sculptures of vegetable vendors adorn the arched entrance to the noisy and colourful **Crawford Market** (*see p129*), the city's first municipal market, built in 1869 to sell what it still sells today – fresh fruits, vegetables, spices, meats, imported foodstuffs and, in the back, live animals. It takes its name from its creator, Arthur Crawford, Mumbai's first municipal commissioner, who later resigned in a scandal over the market's financial mismanagement. It was the first building in Bombay to be lit by electricity in 1892, but little else has changed since then, although recently the range of foods has increased as import tariffs have been slashed – California plums and Malta oranges now sit alongside Maharashtrian mangoes. There's an old sign asking visitors to only hire licenced porters but the wording is ambiguous and some porters like to suggest to foreigners that it's mandatory to hire them – it's not. Like so many of Mumbai's heritage buildings, Crawford Market is fraying at the edges, but

Victorian touches survive intact, the most impressive being two elaborate fountains by J Lockwood Kipling, the father of Rudyard Kipling. Both have since been given a flamboyant multi-coloured paint job. From 1865-75, Lockwood Kipling was the dean of the **Jamsetjee Jeejebhoy School of Arts**, close to the market on Dadabhai Naoroji Road. Established in 1857, it was the city's first art school and remains one of India's premier art colleges. Rudyard was born in a bungalow on the college campus in 1865 and spent his early childhood there.

A short walk through the crowded lanes across the road from Crawford Market is the pristine white **Jama Masjid** on Sheikh Memon Street. It's an unusual mosque, built on a pond of tranquil green water which has been incorporated into the design. Don't miss the intricate mosaic work on the exquisite marble staircase. North on Sheikh Memon Street, take a detour into the narrow passages of the **Moolji Jetha Cloth Market**, the oldest wholesale cotton market in Asia, built in 1881. Behind its high stone walls is a maze of 800 cotton shops, where shopkeepers and buyers lounge on white mattresses and pillows, negotiating the price of rolls of cotton over steaming glasses of *chai*.

Mohammed Ali Road

Maps p253 & p255

A warren of narrow interconnecting lanes spread out either side of **Mohammed Ali Road**, which bustles in the shadow of the JJ flyover for most of its length. The area is a commercial district dominated by the city's Muslim community, with numerous *dargahs* (tombs of saints), mosques and *burqa* shops along its length. A short distance up Mohammed Ali Road is the green-domed **Minara Masjid**, one of the city's oldest mosques, closed to all but Muslim men. During Ramzan, or Ramadan, every September or October, the lane next to the mosque turns into a hectic open-air barbecue in the evenings as thousands gather to break their fast. A narrow lane to the left of the **Jamsetji Jeejebhoy Hospital** and **Grant Medical College** up ahead leads to **Irani Masjid**, a beautiful mosque covered in a mosaic of blue tiles. Again, only Muslims are allowed to enter.

In the days of the Raj, Mohammed Ali Road was known, along with the Hindu-dominated Kalbadevi area nearby, as the 'Native Quarters'. The stark divide between the Hindu and Muslim communities is most evident at **Bhendi Bazaar**, marked by a Hindu temple named **Gol Mandir**: to its west extends the Hindu colony, and to the east the Muslim precinct, extending

The Japanese attack that wasn't

At 2.30pm on 14 April 1944, the *Fort Stikine*, a cargo ship harboured at Victoria Dock, now Indira Docks (*see p64*), sounded a fire alarm. Fires at the docks were not uncommon, but firemen rushed out from the nearby Alexandra Dock fire station in a frenzy: the *Fort Stikine* was loaded with 1,395 tons of munitions on their way to bolster the British war effort. The firemen knew they were fighting a losing battle and orders were given to scuttle the ship out at sea. It was too late: the first explosion took place at 4.06pm, followed by another.

The massive blast split the *Fort Stikine* in half, knocking down buildings and starting fires in an 800-yard radius, destroying neighbouring ships in the harbour. Munitions were flung into the air and exploded across the city, along with showers of lethal, white-hot shrapnel that sliced through people, animals, cars and buildings, starting fires wherever it landed. The explosion was heard as far as the suburb of Santa Cruz, 12 miles away. Panic reigned as rumours spread that the Japanese had attacked the city. People rushed to railway stations to flee, but the debris and munitions had destroyed the tracks and many trains. Adding to the chaos was a shower of gold: the *Fort Stikine* was also carrying 31 crates

of Bank of England-stamped gold bricks, worth over a million pounds. One smashed through a roof into the front room of a Parsi gentleman, who promptly returned it to the British authorities. Another decapitated a horse, which was then seen to stagger headless down the street. At late as the 1960s, dredging ships were turning up the occasional gold brick from the bottom of the harbour.

It was 45 days before the fires were finally doused, and many months before Bombay returned to normal. 476 military personnel and 71 firemen had been killed, and hundreds more injured. Figures of the civilian lives lost were suppressed by the British government but estimates range from 300 to over 1,500. Thousands more were injured, and 27 ships in the harbour had been sunk or burned out. Now largely forgotten, it was the largest explosion in the World War II's eastern theatre, barring the atomic explosions in Hiroshima and Nagasaki.

There are few reminders of what happened there today, except for a piece of a ship's propeller on display in the courtyard of St Xavier's High School at Dhobi Talao, which landed red-hot in its compound. In memory of the firemen who died, the Mumbai Fire Brigade celebrates Fire Service Week from 14-20 April.

The explosion at Victoria Dock.

Workers flee as chaos reigns.

to Mohammed Ali Road. Near the temple is the famous **Chor Bazaar**, which means 'Thieves' Market' (*see p128*), once a place for fencing stolen goods. Now it's a perfectly respectable place selling everything from recycled car parts to old gramophones. Wander down Mutton Street and you'll come across old coins and postcards, dog-eared film posters and magazines, antique porcelain and furniture, and much more. Be ready for some serious shoulder wrestling in the crowds and intense haggling.

Byculla

Byculla, at the end of Mohammed Ali Road, was uninhabitable until 1793, after the Great Breach at Mahalaxmi was sealed and a new road constructed. It became the city's first real suburb, settled by the British after venturing out from the overcrowded walled city of Fort. They built new streets, lined with spacious bungalows, and the first European social club, the Byculla Club, in 1833. The rural character of the suburb changed dramatically with the opening of the city's cotton mills in the late 19th century. Byculla became part of Girangaon, the so-called 'village of mills' (see p17), and home to a large migrant population of mill workers. As the area became increasingly congested, the British moved out to Malabar Hill (see p72). Nowadays, more than a few residents complain that it has returned to its old uninhabitable state: the mills are closed but Byculla is horrifically crowded and choked with traffic. Reminders of quieter times linger on in the form of the imposing **Gloria Church**, near Byculla Station, and **Magen David Synagogue**, near the police colony. Now in a state of disrepair, and with a small tree growing out of its clock tower, the synagogue was built in 1861 by the Sassoon family, a philanthropic family of businessmen from Baghdad, for the large Jewish community that once lived here. A little ahead in a large compound, hidden behind a tall stone wall, is the **Christ Church**, built in 1833, the city's second Anglican church after St Thomas' Cathedral at Churchgate.

Past Shepherd Road, the Sir Jamshedji Jejeebhoy Road splits at a Y-shaped flyover. Stuck below the forking roads is the **Khada Parsi**, or the 'Standing Parsi', a bronze statue of the Parsi businessman and philanthropist, Sir Cursetji Maneckji (1863-1943), on a 15-foot plinth. The right-hand road leads to the **Bhau Daji Lad Museum** (see below), which stands in the grounds of the **Veermata Jijabai Bhonsle Udyan** (see below), a park and zoo.

Bhau Daji Lad Museum

Jijamata Udyan, Dr BR Ambedkar Road, Byculla. Call 2284-3644 for admission prices & opening times.

The Bhau Daji Lad Museum was built in 1872 and originally named the Victoria and Albert Museum. Like its more famous counterpart for London, the museum was built to showcase Mumbai's industrial skills and craftsmanship. The building was recently restored to its original Renaissance Revival splendour with intricate iron pillars, ornate chandeliers, exquisite gold railings and a dramatic painted ceiling. It won a UNESCO heritage award in 2005 and was due to open as we went to press. Displays will include models and maps of the city as it was in the late 19th and early 20th centuries, and 1,200 original glass negatives that include rare images of the gates of the old Fort. Call heritage conservation group INTACH on 2284-3644 for details.

Veermata Jijabai Bhonsle Udyan (Byculla Zoo)

Dr BR Ambedkar Road, Byculla. **Open** 9am-6pm Mon, Tue, Thur-Sun. **Admission** Rs 5; Rs 2 children under 12.

The Veermata Jijabai Bhonsle Udyan, or Byculla Zoo, has for years been a prime example of how not

Bhau Daji Lad Museum.

to run a zoo: animals caged in tiny enclosures, with little or no information provided for visitors. It's locally known as Rani Baag, meaning 'Queen's Garden', after its original name, Victoria Gardens. Formerly a 48-acre 'pleasure garden', it became a zoo in 1873. The types of animal on display has not changed much since then: lions, leopards, elephants, deer, crocodiles, tigers and hippos – although llamas and kangaroos are no longer in residence. Some of the animal enclosures have been improved but many are depressing; instead, the zoo's best features are its gardens and winding pathways, which are littered with Raj-era artefacts, like an ancient basalt elephant that the British recovered in pieces from Elephanta Island (see p81) and reassembled here. The first animal you encounter on entering is Edward VII's horse, with the king on its back. The statue was made in 1877 by JE Boehm, Queen Victoria's favourite sculptor, and once stood at Kala Ghoda (see p62).

Bhuleshwar & Kalbadevi

Maps p253 & p255

It's said that the Hindu pantheon has about 330 million gods. At first glance, it seems that each one has a temple somewhere in the crowded lanes of **Bhuleshwar** and **Kalbadevi**. In fact, some locals believe that Bhuleshwar is so named because even the gods lose their way in the area's labyrinthine alleys: *bhula* means 'to forget' in Hindi, and *ishwar* means 'god'. But actually the name just comes from the **Bhuleshwar Temple**, which was built by a wealthy fisherman by the name of Bhula. If you are ready to brave heaving crowds, get lost in

It's a cow's life at **Bombay Panjrapole**.

the weaving lanes, evade wandering cows and leap over puddles of mud, then the area offers a wealth of colourful Hindu temples. The biggest is the **Mumbadevi Temple** (*see below*), named after the same god as Mumbai. There's also the fuchsia-pink **Dwarkadheesh Temple**, nicknamed Monkey Temple by the British for the row of monkey statues across its façade; the **Ram Temple**, a one-stop shop for major gods, shared between Lord Ram, Ganesha, Maruti, Durga, Garuda, Vishnu, Laxmi and Hanuman; and the **Nar Narayan Temple**, where women peel peas on the temple porch under delicate carvings depicting stories from Lord Krishna's boyhood (dancing on a serpent's head, flirting with milkmaids and stealing butter). All three temples stand close together on Kalbadevi Road.

The arched green doorway to the **Bombay Panjrapole** stands at the end of the Bhuleshwar Road behind a tight maze of stalls selling flowers, incense, coconuts, puffed rice, milk and other bric-a-brac used in temple rituals. Inside the Panjrapole are dozens of cows – sacred animals for Hindus – who graciously deign to eat the grass given to them by Hindu devotees. Bombay Panjrapole is run by a 170-year-old trust which operates five similar cow sanctuaries across the city.

Mumbadevi Temple

Mumbadevi Road, near Zaveri Bazaar. **Open** 5am-noon, 4-8pm daily. **Admission** free. **Map** p255 G14. If you should get lost searching for Mumbadevi Temple, look out for long lines of flower-holding devotees snaking their way through the lanes, and join in. Mumbadevi is the patron goddess of the Koli fisherfolk, the city's aboriginal inhabitants. The original temple stood at Azad Maidan near Nagar Chowk, but was demolished by the British along with a Roman Catholic church to make way for the city's development. The new temple was

built in the 1830s and is one of the city's most popular. Generous devotees have provided the temple with doors of pure silver. The temple walls teem with sculptures of vibrantly coloured gods and animals. Many temples have wishing wells, but Mumbadevi has wishing woodwork: devotees believe that the goddess will grant wishes if they embed a silver coin in the temple railings. The priests have recently banned the practice (it was wrecking the woodwork), but old coins still shine out from the beams.

Malabar Hill

When you have the governor of the state of Maharashtra as your neighbour, you know you're on the top rungs of Mumbai's lengthy social ladder. The upper-crust residents of **Malabar Hill** – sitting atop a green hillock at the end of Marine Drive – literally look down on the rest of the city. Until the early 1870s, the area was a dense jungle where British officers went fox hunting. But the coming of textile mills to once-posh Byculla (*see p70*) sent the British community scrambling for a new, unsullied suburb. The stretch between Malabar Hill and Worli is still speckled with British-era bungalows, though most have been demolished and replaced with high-rise apartment blocks.

The precinct of **Walkeshwar** at Malabar Hill is lined with temples and Gujarati-style homes that were rebuilt in the 18th century after being destroyed by the Portuguese in the previous century. The largest temple is **Walkeshwar Temple**, dedicated to Lord Shiva, which was rebuilt in 1715. The *shivalingam* inside is made from sand, hence the name of the temple, which means 'sand god'. The district around the temple still has the feel of an older and slower Bombay, with doors to homes left open and Gujarati and

Maharashtrian women dressed in colourful saris exchanging local gossip in the streets. Nearby is the holy lake, or 'tank' of **Banganga**, built sometime between the ninth and 13th centuries, and the oldest sacred Hindu site in the city. *Ban* means 'arrow' in Hindi and, according to legend, the water comes straight from the holy River Ganges some 1,000 miles away, brought forth by an arrow shot from the bow of Lord Ram. It's a place of rare serenity, with ducks gliding on the still green waters and visitors relaxing on the worn basalt steps that lead down to them. Banganga usually becomes crowded in August, during the festival of Shravan, when Hindus come to pay their respects to deceased relatives by shaving their heads and purifying themselves in the tank.

There is also an unusual **Hindu graveyard** near the tank, notable because Hindus usually cremate their dead. But the Goswami community that lives here follows their own unique, centuries-old tradition of burying their dead in a sitting position. Men's graves are marked with a *shivalingam*, and the graves of women with a footprint.

While most of Malabar Hill's greenery has been supplanted by concrete jungle, it still boasts one of the city's largest parks – **Kamala Nehru Park**, which provides a panoramic view of Marine Drive. Opposite the park are the **Hanging Gardens** (*see p138*), another spectacular viewpoint.

Mahalaxmi

Mahalaxmi, between Malabar Hill and Worli, takes its name from the **Mahalaxmi Temple** that stands there. It's an attractive temple, with bright exterior murals and carved wooden lintels. According to local folklore, Laxmi, the Hindu goddess of wealth, appeared in a dream to an engineer working on an ambitious land reclamation project to join the islands of Bombay and Worli in 1784. Laxmi revealed to him that an idol of hers lay at the bottom of Worli Creek, which he recovered and later installed in a temple built on the reclaimed land. Close by is the spectacular **Haji Ali Dargah** (*see p32*), a beautiful shrine of white, windswept domes and minarets built on a tiny island off Worli Seaface to a Muslim saint named Haji Ali. The causeway that connects the island to the mainland is lined with beggars and vendors selling toys and religious images.

Mahalaxmi is often referred to as the city's lungs, thanks to the greenery provided by the 64-acre **Mahalaxmi Racecourse** (*see p164*), and the elite **Willingdon Sports Club**,

which boasts Mumbai's oldest golf course. Both stand either side of KK Marg, otherwise known as Racecourse Road. Entry to the uppity club, established in 1917, is reserved for members only, but the racecourse opens its 2,600-yard track to the public from November to May and is a popular walking spot. We recommend a quick visit to the **Mahalaxmi Dhobi Ghats**, on the left from the Mahalaxmi railway station exit, where over 200 *dhobis*, or laundrymen, wash clothes collected from local households in a maze of concrete wash pens. The *dhobis* then thrash the clothes on flogging stones, toss them into huge vats of boiling starch and hang them out to dry on long, criss-crossing clothes lines. It's become a popular tourist attraction for foreign visitors, with a few vendors now selling trinkets and postcards on the bridge by the station. But locals are mystified why foreigners should take so much interest in what they consider an open-air Laundromat.

Marine Drive & Chowpatty

Maps p251-p255

Ask the average Mumbaikar where Netaji Subhash Chandra Bose Road is and he'll probably give you directions to Thane. Despite the change of name, Mumbai's

Banganga Tank.

A Beatle in Bombay

At 10am on 9 January 1968, a long-haired Englishman walked into the Universal Building on Pherozeshah Mehta Road in Fort (*see p67*) and bounded up the stairs to the third-floor HMV recording studio, then owned by Electric and Musical Industries Ltd. It was George Harrison, the Beatle, here in Mumbai to record a soundtrack for an avant-garde movie called *Wonderwall*, starring Jacqueline Bisset. The recording sessions lasted five days, with contributions from some of India's most outstanding classical musicians, including *santoor* player Pandit Shiv Kumar Sharma.

Universal Building remains – as does a weathered HMV sign high on the outside wall – but the recording studio was long ago replaced by an insurance office. Derek Taylor, press agent for the Beatles for most of the 1960s, later wrote in his notes for a re-issue of the *Wonderwall* soundtrack what Harrison remembered of the Bombay recordings. 'I decided to do it as a mini-anthology of Indian music because I wanted to help turn the public on to Indian music,' Harrison told him. 'It was fantastic really. The studio is on top of the offices but there's no sound-proofing. So if you listen closely to some of the Indian tracks on the LP you can hear taxis going by.

'Every time the office knocked off at 5.30 we had to stop recording because you could just hear everybody stomping down the steps. They only had a big EMI mono machine. I mixed everything as we did it there, and that was nice enough because you get spoiled working on eight and 16 tracks.'

Wonderwall premiered in London on January 20, 1969, but never got a general distribution deal; it has remained a '60s curio ever since. But some of the music Harrison recorded in Mumbai made it on to the B-side of *Lady Madonna* as the psychedelic anthem *The Inner Light*.

---

most famous boulevard is still known as **Marine Drive** – a two-mile, palm-fringed arc sweeping along the western bay from the business district of Nariman Point to the wealthy enclave of Malabar Hill. For most Indians, Marine Drive is an iconic shorthand for the city of Mumbai, made famous by appearances in numerous Bollywood films. The other unofficial name is the 'Queen's Necklace', coined by the British to describe the illuminated curve of the bayfront road at night. The seafront has a broad promenade that's a favourite walking and jogging spot, and popular with young couples looking for romance, anonymity and beautiful sunsets. Marine Drive is lined with art deco buildings built in the 1920s and '30s, most of which are now in need of renovation. Still, this is Mumbai's most exclusive address, and home to some of the city's wealthiest residents. At the southern end stands the luxury **Oberoi** hotel (*see p49*). Fabulous views of the bay and Marine Drive can be enjoyed over cocktails at the elegant **Dome** bar on the roof of the

Intercontinental Marine Drive hotel (*see p113*). The road extends past the lacklustre **Tareporevala Aquarium** (*see p138*) and a line of gymkhanas that host opulent weddings during the winter season.

At the northern end of the promenade is the popular **Girgaum Chowpatty** (*chowpatty* means 'beach' in Marathi), a broad, curved beach where spectacular idols of the elephant-headed god Ganesha are immersed in the sea during the festival of Ganesh Chaturthi (*see p135*). Sunbathing and bikinis are out of place here, and don't bother going for a swim – the water is horribly polluted. Families and couples come to Girgaum Chowpatty for a stroll on the sand, for a stiff working-over by itinerant head masseurs, and for the spicy snacks sold at the lines of stalls.

From Chowpatty, P Ramabai Marg runs north past Wilson College to **Mani Bhavan** (*see p75*), once the Bombay home of Mahatma Gandhi, now a museum dedicated to his life. Nearby, at the western end of Laburnum Road is **August Kranti Maidan** (also known as

Gowalia Tank) where Gandhi launched the Quit India movement on 8 August 1942, a mass movement that spread across India and brought British rule to an end five years later (*see p19*).

A little further ahead, past Chowpatty, Babulnath Marg leads to **Babulnath Temple** (*see p32*), dedicated to Lord Shiva and one of the city's holiest Hindu sites. The steps leading up to it are lined with traditional Gujarati houses for priests and temple employees. A short distance away on Hughes Road is the attractive **Khareghat Colony**, a Parsi housing complex. Behind the colony, higher up the hill, is the **Tower of Silence** – sprawling gardens that house a Parsi funeral site, where bodies are left to be devoured by vultures as per tradition. Rudyard Kipling, who spent his early childhood in Mumbai, once described finding severed human fingers near his house at the **Jamsetjee Jejeebhoy School of Art** (*see p69*); his mother believed they had been dropped by careless vultures returning from the Tower of Silence. Recently, the numbers of white-backed vultures has dramatically declined, and the traditional practice is under threat. The Tower is off-limits to non-Parsis, although visitors are allowed into the attractive gardens around it.

Mani Bhavan

19 Laburnum Road, off Ramabai Marg, Gamdevi (2380-5864/www.gandhi-manibhavan.org). **Open** 9.30am-6pm daily. **Admission** Rs 10. Free for Indian nationals. **Map** p254 A16.
Mani Bhavan was the home of the Mahatma (meaning 'Great Soul'), Mohandas Karamchand Gandhi, from 1917 to 1934, and the base for his civil disobedience movement that helped topple the British Empire in India. The museum contains many of his photographs, personal belongings and over 50,000 books and documents, including copies of his letters to figures such as Franklin D Roosevelt, Winston Churchill and Adolf Hitler. It also has a series of charming tableaux telling the story of Gandhi's life through clay models.

Opera House

Map p254

At the junction of Rajaram Mohan Roy Road and Girgaum Road, the tranquil enclave of **Khotachiwadi** provides a snapshot of what much of Mumbai looked like before the arrival of concrete. Once inhabited mainly by the East Indian community, it's a network of narrow, meandering lanes lined with pretty Portuguese-style bungalows with wooden porches, staircases, and balconies. The inhabitants have held out against intense pressure from local builders to sell up, instead restoring much of this neighbourhood's original charm. Every year, the Khotachiwadi Residents' Association holds a festival to celebrate the neighbourhood.

The area around the junction of Girgaon Road and Sardar Vallabhbhai Patel Road is known as Opera House, after the once-magnificent **Royal Opera House** that stands on the crossroads. Built in 1925, the impressive frontage features neo-classical columns and elaborate sculpture-work of dancing figures playing musical instruments. The timing was terrible – film was taking off and cinema became the city's great passion. The Opera House closed down to reopen as a cinema hall in the late 1930s, and ran for the next 60 years before shutting down in the late 1990s. Now closed to the public, it has become increasingly dilapidated, with plants growing out of its crumbling stonework.

Haji Ali Dargah. *See p73.*

The Suburbs

Venture north.

Why does South Mumbai get all the attention? Tourists rarely venture out of the southern part of the city, and it's really not hard to see why. Once rolling fields and forests dotted with charming villages, much of the city's northern extent has turned into mile after mile of congested, polluted and ugly concrete sprawl. There are some areas worth visiting, however – notably the rapidly transforming suburb of **Bandra**, home to Bollywood stars like Shah Rukh Khan and Aamir Khan, and young professionals with money to burn. Bandra's current status as the city's most favoured suburb is a result of a gradual shifting northwards of the city's centre over the past three decades, accelerated in the last decade by commercial development in the north. New middle-class neighbourhoods have sprung up in places like Powai and Thakur Village around the new industries of the liberalised Indian economy, challenging the dominance of South Mumbai's business district.

Dadar

Dadar station is a 25-minute train ride north from both Churchgate Terminus and Chhatrapati Shivaji Terminus. *Dadar* means 'bridge' in Marathi, and the station was named after an ancient crossing over a now non-existent creek. It was once an area for rice farming and became one of the first suburbs to be developed under the City Improvement Trust set up by the British after the city's bubonic plague outbreak and subsequent famine of the late 19th century. It's now a crowded and hectic heartland for the city's Maharashtrian community, and site of the headquarters of the Shiv Sena, a right-wing nativist political party. Dadar's greatest charm, a short taxi ride from Dadar Station, is **Shivaji Park**, a seven-acre expanse of lawns that has been the training ground for some of India's greatest cricketers, including Sachin Tendulkar. It was created in 1925 by the British who, unusually for them, named it after the 17th-century Maratha warrior-king Chhatrapati Shivaji, a hero to the Maharastrian people. The park became an important venue for political rallies in the Indian freedom struggle and, after 1947, a focal point for the Samyukta Maharashtra movement, which sought and finally won the creation

of Maharashtra state. The park still plays host to scores of overlapping cricket games as well as giant rallies for the Shiv Sena and other political parties. Hundreds come here in the mornings and evening for walks; Jains come here to feed the stray dogs, and laughter clubs gather to cackle madly (*see p150*). The separate Nana-Nani Park (literally, 'Grandad-Granny Park') park is filled with pensioners complaining about delayed cheques or boasting of children doing well in New Zealand. Cricket coaching camps for kids are run regularly here, along with training in traditional Indian sports like *kabaddi*, *kho kho* and *mallakhamb* (*see p165*). Across from the park off Swatantrya Veer Savarkar Marg is the **Mayor's Bungalow**, an attractive colonial home closed to visitors. The mayor holds a merely decorative post in Mumbai and several mayors have complained about the poor state of the bungalow's interior; so much that one even threatened to move into the zoo at Byculla.

Bandra

Once a sleepy collection of mostly Roman Catholic hamlets, dismissed as parochial by the sophisticates who lived in the city to its south, Bandra has recently morphed into Mumbai's hottest postcode. Flat prices have skyrocketed from around Rs 5,000 per square foot ten years ago to current highs of around Rs 10,000. Rural charm has been displaced by urban cool. A large part of Bandra's success is down to its location: it occupies a sweet spot between the south of the city and the new business districts in the north, with the sprawling business hub of the Bandra-Kurla complex on its doorstep. The appeal for new residents is that there is something here for everyone: a tradition of communal tolerance that draws the Muslim community; the gravitational pull of movie-star glamour for hipsters, models and wannabe actors; and a diversity of restaurants, smart bars and nightclubs for young, well-paid professionals. In a choking city, what was once parochial is now seen as part of the charm. The tree-lined roads and public spaces like Jogger's Park, Land's End and the Carter Road Promenade provide a welcome respite from the chaos.

But Bandra has been so successful that its appeal is beginning to eat itself; the new landscape of glass and aluminium-clad towers

Sightseeing

Kanheri Caves, Borivali. *See p80.*

Basilica of Mount Mary, Bandra. *See p79.*

Bandra Fort, Land's End, built by the Portuguese. *See p78.*

Train strain

Whether it's floods, riots or other disasters, Mumbaikars have a single litmus test for the state of their city: 'Are the trains working?'

Mumbaikars spend large chunks of their lives on trains, and a train-borne culture has evolved. They talk of 'train friends', regular co-commuters with whom they sing songs and exchange life stories and who, most

importantly, will 'catch place' for them – keep them a seat, hopefully in the sweet spots. In the morning the best seats are on the west side of the train, facing south for the breeze; in the evening it's the other side, facing north.

Local trains have two classes: the first class has deodorised padded velour seats; the second class has wooden benches. They are almost equally crowded, but those who can afford it will shell out up to ten times the price of a second-class ticket for the fractional comforts of first class. The ladies-only compartment is filled with women cleaning vegetables for dinner and rehashing old arguments about the rival merits of tailors. The 'general compartment' is for the men, where *bhajans* (religious songs) are sung, *prasad* (food blessed by being offered to the gods) doled out and endless card games played.

The compartments are scoured by vendors hawking everything from peanuts to mobile phone slipcovers to English courses. Urchins run through with brushes, sweeping the dirt onto the tracks before begging for tips. On a half-hour journey, you can eat a snack and get your shoes shined, your hair straightened and your soul saved (charity to beggars is good in the eyes of the gods).

The crush of train compartments during rush hours, between 9 and 11am and again between 5 and 9pm, defies description. Sardines have it easy. Around ten per cent of passengers during these hours aren't even in the train – you'll see them hanging out of the sides, courting death by trackside pole. Some young men even climb on to the roof, partly because it's too crowded inside, partly out of sheer bravado. Inside, passengers have to start pushing their way to the door one stop before their station – any later and they'll never make it out in time. In the off-peak hours, though, there isn't a quicker and more efficient way of getting around Mumbai. Travel during peak hours, and you'll have bragging rights for life.

has little to do with the balconies and verandas of the old Bandra. Traffic and pollution levels are spiralling, with Bandra now claiming some of the worst air quality in the city. But Bandrawallahs take some comfort from their tradition of civic pride – a rarity in Mumbai. Determined citizens have greatly enhanced the

suburb's charms with the restoration of **Land's End**, a small peninsula leading to the **Bandra Fort**. Named Castella de Aguada by the Portuguese, who built it in 1640, the fort was equipped with cannons to protect shipping routes, and supplied fresh water from a nearby spring to trading vessels on their way to Goa or

Vasai. Today, even after the construction of two hotels nearby – the Taj Land's End and SeaRock (*see p50*) – the fort is a beautiful spot to take in the sunset. The area behind it has been landscaped with palm trees and an attractive stone amphitheatre. Not far away, **Carter Road** was similarly restored with a cool promenade along the seafront. At the end of Carter Road is Road No.5, better known as just 'Off Carter Road' – a lively strip of shops and restaurants with tables out on the street (*see p104*).

Bandra has numerous churches, the most important of which is the **Basilica of Mount Mary** (*see p32*), on the hill along Mount Mary's Road. A highly popular church, it brings thousands of devotees from across the city during the Mount Mary Fair in September. The original chapel was built in 1640 and destroyed in a Maratha raid in 1738. The life-sized statue of the Virgin Mary was rescued from the sea by fishermen and housed in St Andrew's Church on Hill Road while a new church was being built; it was returned in 1761. Until around 30 years ago, this was Bandra's highest point, visible from Mahim beach. St Peter's Church, also on Hill Road, has some interesting frescoes and stained-glass.

Many of the crosses that dot Bandra's streets are 'plague crosses', built around the turn of the 20th century as bubonic plague swept across the city, killing hundreds of thousands. Bandra residents built crosses near their homes, both to seek protection from the pestilence and later in gratitude that they'd survived. Victims of the disease were often buried in a graveyard by Bandra creek that's still referred to as the Plague Cemetery. Crosses were also built to ward off evil spirits and simply to mark property boundaries. Among Bandra's oldest streetside crosses is the wooden one that stands at the junction of Bazaar Road, Chapel Road and Waroda Road, which dates back to 1698.

Goregaon

Goregaon was a pretty tree-lined village until as late as the 1970s, before it was turned into yet another noxious concrete mess of a suburb. Respite remains, though, in the sprawling greenery of the **Aarey Milk Colony**, a dairy farming area with jungle-crested hills. It takes around 15 minutes to get here by autorickshaw from Goregaon Station, which is about an hour's ride on the train from Churchgate. The milk colony is also home to **Goregaon Film City**, on the Film City Road – a major studio built in 1978 on what was previously rural scrubland. Officially no visitors are allowed in, but the gate watchmen may be persuaded with a big smile and a little largesse. You could also get inside by being cast as an extra in a Bollywood movie (*see p36*). Much like its Hollywood equivalents, Film City tends to be a little surreal, with leftovers from sets scattered about, like the abandoned staircase that leads nowhere, along with a Hindu temple and a helipad.

Cricket camps train up future Tendulkars at **Shivaji Park**, Dadar. *See p76*.

Sightseeing

Borivali

There's only one reason to come this far north – the **Sanjay Gandhi National Park** (Borivali, 8860-0389, closed Mon, admission Rs 20), one of Asia's busiest national parks, with around two million visitors a year. Mumbaikars come here to escape the city, get lost in the greenery with lovers, play cricket, eat vast picnics and just cool off – the temperature here is about four degrees cooler than the city's average. And at 40 square miles, it won't be crowded. The nearest station is Borivali, 75 minutes on the train from Churchgate. From there, it's around Rs 15 in an autorickshaw to the main entrance. To the west lie the townships of Goregaon, Malad, Kandivali, Borivali and Dahisar, and to the east the townships of Bhandup and Mulund. In recent years, the park has been encroached by numerous slum dwellings, which is not only bad for the park but also for the slum dwellers – leopards have now started to acquire a taste for them (*see right* **Cat attack**).

The park's two lakes – Vihar and Tulsi – supply Mumbai with water. The park's forest is a mix of deciduous and semi-evergreen and contains a startling diversity of wildlife, including tigers, leopards, lions, pythons, cobras, spotted deer, black-naped hares, barking deer, porcupines and around 5,000 different kinds of insects. There are also crocodiles in Tulsi Lake. Swimming is not encouraged. The park is also home to 150 species of butterfly and the world's largest moth, the Atlas, which was discovered here. There is a **Tiger & Lion Safari bus tour** (*see below*) which departs regularly from the orientation centre around half a mile from the main entrance.

Also in the park are the **Kanheri Caves** – a total of 109 caves in which remarkable halls have been carved out of the rock and ornate statues and images of Buddha and the Boddhisattvas sculpted from the walls. The caves are located about 450 yards above sea level and command a panoramic view of the forest surroundings and the Arabian Sea in the distance. They date back to the Mauryan and Kushan Empires of the first century BCE, although the carving continued well into the ninth century AD. Outside Cave No.3 are two 60-foot statues of Buddha that date back to the sixth century CE. The history of the caves is incomplete, but as there were also two ports nearby at Kalyan and Sopara, the area around must have been an important Buddhist settlement. Inscriptions found in the caves refer to the area as Krishnagiri, Krishnasila, Kanhasila or Kanhagiri. Their current name

Cat attack

On 24 April 2006, a ranger at the Sanjay Gandhi National Park found the half-eaten body of a man near the centre of the forest. It was the fifth leopard attack of the year, which was a big improvement on 2004, when 19 people were killed by leopards in and around the park, many of them children. Numerous other non-fatal leopard attacks have been reported as far away as Powai and Malad; one Powai student just managed to escape by pedalling away furiously on his bicycle. But the problem is not leopards but humans, around 200,000 of whom have steadily encroached on the limits of the park with slum dwellings that are illegal, but protected by local politicians who want the votes. The dogs and cattle around the dwellings first lured the leopards, and the longer they spent near to the settlements, the more appetising humans started to look. After 33 deaths in two years, the park authorities started to take action in 2005, setting traps and educating slum dwellers about the dangers of wandering into the forest at night to go to the loo.

appears to have derived from the Sanskrit word *krishnagiri*, which means 'black mountain'. Archaeologists believe that the caves began to be permanent residences for Buddhist monks in the first century CE.

Tiger & Lion Safari

Orientation centre. **Fees** Rs 30 for a 10min tour. **Schedule** Every 20mins during park hours.
A rickety green forest department bus takes visitors into two fenced compounds of tigers and lions. The lions tend to look a little bored, but they do occasionally leap into action, with mornings being the best time to see some activity. Some years ago, before grated windows were put on the buses, one visitor opened a window and cheekily waved the edge of her sari at them; one of the lions duly jumped on to the roof and ripped off her scalp.

Day Trips

Get out of town.

Elephanta Island

Around the fifth century AD, a prince of the Chalukya dynasty – a political dynasty that ruled large parts of the western and southern regions of India – is said to have constructed the breathtaking cave-temples at Gharapuri, a small island about seven miles north-west of the Gateway of India, now called Elephanta (admission Rs 250 foreigners; Rs 10 Indians, closed Mon). A trip there and back takes at least four hours, but it's more than worth it.

Indian temples had always been built by erecting base pillars and then laying plinths on top to support the roof, but in Maharashtra the brittle volcanic stone plinths kept breaking. At Gharapuri, the ancients decided that the only way to get round the problem was to find a large chunk of stone and chisel away anything that didn't look like a temple. The island was rediscovered and renamed in the 16th century by the Portuguese. As they approached the island, they saw an elephant waiting for them. It turned out to be made of basalt, the first clue that the island was home to something remarkable. Intrigued, they decided to take it home with them, but ended up dropping it into the sea. Many years later the British recovered it, took it apart and carried it back to the mainland, where it now sits at the Byculla Zoo, or Veermata Jijabai Bhonsle Udyans.

The triple-bayed entrance to the cave doesn't look impressive but inside everyone from Andre Malraux to Auguste Rodin has been struck dumb by the sheer spectacle of Sadashiva ('Eternal Shiva'), a full-relief bust about 20 feet high, showing three faces of Lord Shiva. The central image is one of serene contemplation; the left half-face is the face of Aghora Bhairava, the vengeful, angry Shiva; the right one is Uma, or Vamadeva, the feminine side of this complex god. Some have suggested that a fourth face remains buried in the rock that must be imagined.

The temple sprawls across about 60,000 square feet, with ornate pillars and exquisitely carved sculptures, many of which have been badly damaged. Demonstrating the kind of barbarism that they repeated in Goa, the Portuguese used the caves as a firing range. They must have been not only blind to beauty but hard of hearing as well; the echoes would have been deafening. Afterwards, it is possible to wander up to the top of the natural rock mass

Cave temples on **Elephanta Island**.

to see an old Portuguese cannon. There are
a couple of villages on the island but nothing
of much interest to visitors. A word of warning:
don't be tempted to eat anywhere near the
monkeys who populate the island; they're
a rapacious bunch and have been known
to pounce aggressively on visitors with
food. Some locals will ask you to take their
photographs; if you do, they will expect a tip.

Getting there

Except for during the monsoon rains from
June to October, boats to Elephanta depart
every 30 minutes from the Gateway of India
from 9am until 2.30pm and cost Rs 80-Rs 120.
The journey takes about 50 minutes. The last
ferry leaves Elephanta for the Gateway at
around 3pm. There's nowhere to stay overnight
on the island, so don't miss it.

Matheran

Matheran is a hill station 68 miles from Mumbai
– a small township established in the Sahyadri
Hills by British colonists to escape Bombay's
humid summers. It's still a favourite day and
weekend getaway for Mumbaikars for precisely
the same reason. Once a quiet, wooded place
filled with British bungalows – Surrey in the
heart of western India – these days it's a haven
for commercial tourism, filled with restaurants,
snack shops and ice-cream parlours. But much
of its charm has been preserved thanks to a wise

Sula Wine Tasting Centre. *See p83.*

decision to ban motor vehicles from its broad
streets, and horses are a common way of getting
around – you'll see them tied up wild west-style
outside restaurants. The British also built a
narrow-gauge train from Neral – the so-called
toy train – that curved its way up and down
the hill until it was wiped out by terrible
flooding in July 2006. The railway is currently
being rebuilt and now the only way up to the
hill station is along a long switchback road that
makes a very pleasant walk. In fact, this is the
main thing to do in Matheran: go walking into
the woods along its red laterite paths and take
in the spectacular views of forested hills and
valleys from its viewpoints like Panorama
Point, Echo Point and Monkey Point – all
of which live up to their names. Matheran
is also famous for its leather shoes, made by
a traditional community of cobblers. There
is a Rs 25 fee to enter the hill station.

Getting there

The nearest station is Neral, 55 miles from
Chhatrapati Shivaji Terminus and 13 miles from
Matheran. Return tickets cost Rs 26 for second
class and Rs 300 for first class. The old narrow-
gauge train is unlikely to be running again
before 2008. Other than hiking it, you have no
other option but to take a taxi. Negotiate the
price – around Rs 50 per head is reasonable.

Vasai Fort

At its peak in the 17th century, Vasai was
known as Bassein, a jewel in the Portuguese
crown that boasted impressive public
buildings, private mansions, soaring churches
and an imposing seafacing fort. In 1557 it
was the birthplace of India's only Catholic
saint, Gonsalo Garcia, who sailed to Japan as
a missionary. He was later accused of plotting
to overthrow the Emperor Taiko-sama and
crucified on a hill in Nagasaki. The Vatican
declared him a saint in 1862. Today, the walls

The remains of **Vasai Fort**.

of Bassein Fort still stand, sprawled across 110 acres, although none of the buildings are completely intact. It's a calm, romantic spot of collapsing arches and decrepit belfries, half-overrun with forest. Still standing is the seaward entrance, the Porto da Mar, an iron-clad gateway that resolutely thwarted attackers over the years. Today it's scrawled with boasts of other conquests, like 'Sunil love Sunita'. Nearby, there's a shop with snacks and drinks.

Getting there

Trains to Vasai leave from Churchgate with Virar as their final destination. The first train leaves at 4.15am and takes 90 minutes to reach Vasai Road, the fifth stop after Borivali. The return fare is Rs 26 for second class, or Rs 238 in first class. The fort is 30 minutes from the station by rickshaw and costs around Rs 20-Rs 25. The last train from Vasai Road leaves for Churchgate at 12.10am. By road, it's 47 miles from South Mumbai along the Mumbai-Ahmedabad highway via Borivali, taking two to three hours depending on traffic.

Wine tasting in Nashik

Sula Wine Tasting Centre
Gate No 35/2, Govardhan, Gangapur-Savargaon Road, Nashik (0253-223-1663/www.sulawines.com). **Open** 12.30-8.30pm Mon-Thur; 12.30-10.30pm Fri-Sun.

About 110 miles from Mumbai, Nashik has become Maharashtra's own Napa Valley: it's home to the vineyards of Sula Wines, one of India's leading brands. The vineyard was set up in 1997 on 30 acres and released its first wines three years later – Sauvignon and Chenin Blancs. Some six years later it has grown to 400 acres, growing Shiraz, Zinfandel and Merlot varieties. Sula has now opened a wine tasting centre and offers tours of the vineyard, taking visitors through the wine-making process. You can taste the wines (it's Rs 100 for five tasting samples, which seems a bit stingy) and drink much more of them in their impressive tasting room – an elegant 2,000-sq ft wine bar, with a beautiful balcony overlooking the vineyards. It's a long way back to Mumbai, about four hours by train, but after a few glasses it'll go in a flash. **Photo** *p82.*

Getting there

The first train for Nashik leaves at 6am from Chhatrapati Shivaji Terminus – you'll have to catch this one to make it there and back in one day. Return fares for seats in the relatively comfortable AC chair car cost Rs 575. Get off at Nashik Road station and take a cab to Gangapur Road for around Rs 200-Rs 225. The last train back to CST leaves Nashik Road at 6pm. By road, Nashik is 110 miles and takes about three hours. Check the Sula website (*see above*) for detailed directions and a road map.

Getting away from it all in **Matheran**. *See p82.*

Sightseeing

Eat, Drink, Shop

Noodle Bar

Just when you thought you'd savoured it all.

some exciting
new twists

Welcome to the excit

Pan-Asian eat

that springs some delici

culinary surpri

In a cas

contempor

chic ambie

Discover the differen

Restaurants & Cafés

Mumbai's culinary horizons just keep getting broader.

Mumbai loves food. From ubiquitous street-side stalls serving unique Mumbai snacks (*see p99* **Street eats**) to rough-and-ready 'lunch homes' to elegant five-star restaurants, every class and ethnic group has its own favourites. For decades, the finest restaurants in Mumbai were confined to the insides of five-star hotels that were out of the reach of all but the city's wealthiest diners. Today, the five-star culture persists – it's routine for diners to drive miles out to the cluster of hotels around the airports to sample some of the city's finest (and most expensive) food. But in recent years the five-star culture has been increasingly challenged by a new breed of high-quality, stand-alone restaurants eager to grab a share of the Mumbaikar's skyrocketing disposable income. Many of these have sprung up in and around Colaba, but the biggest explosion has been in the up-and-coming suburb of Bandra, a 30-minute train ride north. Standards vary, but the best of the five-stars and the new stand-alones offer food that compares well with top-quality restaurants the world over – often at more accessible prices.

Indian cuisine is represented abroad by chicken tikka and *rogan josh*, but there's so much more to Indian food than North Indian fare. Indian cuisine is as diverse as the country itself and includes some entirely separate sub-cuisines, such as Bengali cooking. Lucky for us, nearly all of them are available in Mumbai, thanks to the millions of economic migrants who have come to the city from across the country over the last 200 years. The newly arrived émigrés stuck together, initially sharing familiar food in community kitchens or *khanevals*, which in time opened their doors to outsiders and became the city's first real restaurants. For a description of some of the different dishes available and where to find them, *see p94* **Eat this**.

Chinese food is now virtually an Indian cuisine, and even the simplest restaurant offers Indianised hybrids like chicken Manchurian and chop suey *dosas*. In recent years, the increasingly well-travelled Mumbaikar has begun to demand much more variety and sophistication in foreign cooking, with more and more new restaurants serving Italian or Mediterranean food, often prepared by foreign chefs. There's a lot of experimentation going on too, with pan-Asian restaurants throwing together dishes from across the continent, often with Indian twists. The Taj hotel chain has opened several restaurants that offer cunning European twists on traditional Indian dishes, like paneer in roux sauces, and the hitherto unheard-of practice of cooking with olive oil instead of ghee (*see p92* **Masala Craft**).

It remains to be seen how many of the new restaurants (there was around one high-profile opening a month in 2006) will survive the frenzy, but there's no doubt that there has never been a better time to eat out in Mumbai.

For descriptions of common dishes and menu terms, turn to the **menu glossary** (*see p239*).

❶ Purple numbers given in this chapter correspond to the location of each restaurant and café as marked on the street maps. See pp249-255.

The best Restaurants

For killer kebabs
Bade Miya's (*see p89*); Kebab Korner (*see p102*); **Moti Mahal Delux** (*see p99*).

For fine fish
Konkan Café (*see p91*); Mahesh Lunch Home (*see p102*); Sushegad Gomantak (*see p106*).

For curries
Delhi Darbar (*see p89*); Peshawri (*see p108*); Kebabs and Kurries (*see p105*).

For vegetarian cuisine
Friends Union Joshi Club (*see p105*); Soam (*see p103*); Swati Snacks (*see p105*).

For lazy weekend brunches
Indigo (*see p93*); Olive Bar & Kitchen (*see p107*); Theobroma (*see p99*).

For regional delicacies
Howrah (*see p103*); Rice Boat (*see p108*); Kandahar (*see p91*).

THE FINE ART OF NORTHWEST FRONTIER CUISINE.
PERFECTED DOWN TO THE LAST DETAIL.

Welcome to Copper Chimney. A distinguished landmark in Mumbai, renowned for serving a tradition of fine North West Frontier cuisine, in an elegant, contemporary environme Come savour history, a bite at a time.

Worli 24925353   Kalaghoda 26406333   High Street Phoenix 24962333

DOS AND DON'TS

It's always best to book in advance where possible. Mumbaikars usually like to eat late; around 9pm or 10pm is the busiest time. It's easy to spot a decent restaurant – it will be packed. Food poisoning is relatively rare and hygiene is generally not something to worry about unless you're eating from street stalls (*see p99* **Street eats**). Most restaurants don't bother with non-smoking sections – although more expensive and five-star establishments do have them – and smoking is generally permitted throughout. The pricier eateries are liable for sales taxes that are usually not included in menu prices, so be aware that your final bill may include a value-added tax of 12.5 per cent on food and 20 per cent on drinks. This should be stated clearly on the menu, but you can't rely on that so it's better to ask. Most places do serve alcohol, and we've listed where they do not. Tipping is standard practice, although at relatively low rates – generally between five and ten per cent. Service charges are sometimes included in the bill, so make sure you're not tipping twice. It's better to tip in cash; some establishments can't be relied upon to properly divide tips made by credit card to staff.

We've listed a range of meal prices for each place. However, restaurants often change their menus so these prices are only guidelines. For more on the latest restaurant openings in the city, pick up a copy of *Time Out Mumbai.*

Colaba

Indian

Bade Miya's

Tulloch Street, off Colaba Causeway, Colaba (2284-8038/2285-1649). Churchgate station. **Open** 7pm-3am daily. **Main courses** Rs 30-Rs 70. **No credit cards. No alcohol.** Map p251 G5 ➊
Not a restaurant, but a hugely popular streetside stall just off Colaba Causeway serving up fabulous kebabs and rolls to Colaba's post-party crowd. Bade Miya's started as a single stall a decade ago, but grew with its fame; it now consists of a couple of hard-working, skewer-laden grills and a row of plastic chairs and tables. It's not fancy, but it is delicious. Everything's good here but the top choices have got to be the *baida rotis* (spicy mutton, chicken or beef with egg in a grilled wrap), the spicy chicken livers, the *bhuna* mutton and *bhuna* chicken. The vegetarian seekh kebab is also excellent. On Friday and Saturday nights expect lots of traffic, alcohol-fuelled patrons and a wait for tables.

Baghdadi

11 Tulloch Road, off Colaba Causeway, Colaba (2202-8027). Churchgate station. **Open** 7am-1am daily. **Main courses** Rs 50-Rs 80. **No credit cards. No alcohol.** Map p251 G5 ➋

Bade Miya's.

Not so much a restaurant as a huge room with rows of six-seater benches and tables, Baghdadi is known locally as the 'poor man's Taj', after the Taj Mahal Hotel nearby. The portions are large, the food decent and the kitchen surprisingly clean. Even so, the experience is more enjoyable if you leave your aesthetic sensibilities at home. The seating is a great equaliser, with executives sharing tables with couriers, taxi drivers, African students and labourers. If there's space at your table you may be asked to slide a place down. Baghdadi is famous for its chicken biryani, topped with a special Baghdadi masala and buried under rice and browned onions, and the chicken masala fry, served in a sweetish red gravy. To mop it up, go for a plump, soft naan or one of their enormous rotis. Baghdadi is also one of the very few places in Mumbai where you can get a beef biryani.

Delhi Darbar

Holland House, Colaba Causeway, Colaba (2202-0235/ 5656). Churchgate station. **Open** 11.30am-12.30am daily. **Main courses** Rs 100-Rs 150. **Credit** AmEx, MC, V. **No alcohol.** Map p251 G5 ➌
An old-timer (it first opened in 1973) with a huge fan base, Delhi Darbar is nothing much to look at: it dispenses with atmosphere in favour of cooking fumes. Doesn't matter, though – it's the food that has been bringing diners back all these years. Delhi Darbar specialises in Punjabi and Mughlai cuisine with some truly excellent kebabs, curries and biryanis.

Kailash Parbat Hindu Hotel

Sheela Mahal, 1st Pasta Lane, Colaba (2287-4823). Churchgate station. **Open** 11am-11pm daily. **Main courses** Rs 40-Rs 65. **No credit cards. No alcohol.** Map p250 F4 ➍

Eat, Drink, Shop

If you're looking for mouth-watering Indian snacks like *bhel puri* and *ragda pattice* (a deep-fried potato patty in a spicy chickpea gravy), few places do a better job than Kailash Parbat, a 58-year-old Colaba institution. The split-level restaurant is always packed and almost everything on the menu is worth a try. But be sure not to miss their *falooda* (a thick, creamy dessert), *gulab jamun* (milk powder balls in a sweet syrup) and other specialities from the Sindh province.

Kandahar

The Oberoi, Nariman Point (6632-6205). Churchgate station. **Open** 6.30am-11.30pm daily. **Main courses** Rs 300-Rs 700. **Credit** AmEx, DC, MC, V. **Map** p251 D6 ⑤

Why go all the way to Afghanistan when you can sample outstanding North-West Frontier province cuisine in the outrageously plush surroundings of the Oberoi? High ceilings and broad windows with gorgeous views of Marine Drive complement rich, skilfully prepared food including curries, biryanis,

and juicy kebabs. The *raan* (leg of lamb) – a royal feast all on its own – is perhaps the city's finest. In the evenings, diners are treated to a traditional performance of jal tarang: music played on water-filled porcelain cups with wooden sticks.

Konkan Café

Taj President, 90 Cuffe Parade (6665-0808). Churchgate/CST stations. **Open** 12.30-2.45pm, 7-11.45pm daily. **Main courses** Rs 800-Rs 1,000. **Credit** AmEx, DC, MC, V. **Map** p250 E3 ⑥

Far from a café, this is a beautifully planned and striking restaurant with decor that mirrors that of village homes along India's Konkan coast, a region that begins in Maharashtra and extends through Goa into Karnataka. Chef Ananda Solomon is a proponent of 'slow food' – so he sticks to authentic seasonings and methods of preparation, including handgrinding. Although the focus is definitely on seafood (including Mangalorean-style *gassi*, steamed fish in turmeric paste and Malwani shrimp curry – all fabulous), Konkan also

Café society

In Mumbai's unpretentious Irani cafés, time has stood still. Original 1940s furniture and weighing scales stand in the same positions they did 60 years ago, along with some of the same customers – wizened old Parsi gentlemen sipping on cups of tea and nibbling *mava* cakes, and buttered buns under slow-spinning fans. Mumbai's first Irani cafés were established in the late 19th and early 20th centuries by Zoroastrian Iranian émigrés, catering to industrial workers who didn't have kitchens in their chawls. The food was cheap and wholesome, the mood tranquil. After the Shah returned to power in 1953 and the Iranian economy boomed, many sold up and went home; other cafés have since morphed into bars or fast-food joints, like the McDonald's opposite Chhatrapati Shivaji Terminus. But a few survive.

The area surrounding Metro cinema near Marine Lines station has a few famous Irani restaurants like Sassanian Boulangerie and Kayani & Co (*pictured*), famous for its marble-topped tables, mava cakes, watermelon juice and 1940s charm. Kayani's upper level 'family section' is a favourite with young couples from nearby St Xavier's College. Lovers can switch on the wrought-iron table fans, huddle together and sip endless cups of tea.

Britannia

Sprott Road, opposite New Custom House, Ballard Estate (2261-5264). CST station.
Open 11.30am-4pm Mon-Sat. **No credit cards. No alcohol. Map** p251 & p252 J8 ㉗

Café Excelsior

23 AK Nayak Marg, opposite New Excelsior Cinema, Fort (2207-4543). Churchgate/CST stations. **Open** 8am-11pm daily. **No credit cards. No alcohol. Map** p252 H9 ㉝

Café Military

Ali Chambers, Meadows Street, Fort (2265-4181). Churchgate station.
Open 8am-8.30pm daily. **No credit cards. No alcohol. Map** p251 & p252 G7 ㉖

Kayani & Co

Jer Mahal Estate, near Metro Cinema (2201-1492). Marine Lines station.
Open 6.20am-9pm daily. **No credit cards. No alcohol. Map** p253 F11 ㉞

Eat, Drink, Shop

Golden Dragon.
See p93.

serves some exquisite lamb chops in East Indian masala, mustard seeds and curry leaves.

Koyla
Gulf Hotel, NA Azmi Street, Colaba (6636-4727). Churchgate/CST stations. **Open** 8pm-2am daily. **Main courses** Rs 150-Rs 200. **Credit** AmEx, MC, V. **No alcohol**. Map p250 G4 **❼**

When the state government's 2005 slum demolition drive ran into political flak, Koyla was torn down to defuse accusations that only illegal structures belonging to the city's poorest were being targeted. Like many of the slums, it was back in business shortly after. Koyla's best feature by far is its location – on the roof of a hotel overlooking the harbour and the rooftops of Colaba, with its tables laid out under white *shamianas* (canopies). A big hit with college kids, Koyla serves up some decent North-West Frontier dishes cooked over charcoal. There's no alcohol; flavoured tobacco is the substance of choice here, smoked in ornate hookahs.

Masala Craft
Taj Mahal Palace & Tower Hotel, Apollo Bunder, Colaba (6665-3366). Churchgate/CST stations. **Open** 12.30-2.45pm, 7-11.45pm daily. **Main courses** Rs 450-Rs 1,150. **Credit** AmEx, DC, MC, V. Map p251 G5 **❽**

Contemporary Indian cuisine delivered with a western twist, like cooking in olive oil – unheard of in traditional Indian cooking. It works fabulously: try the tandoori pink salmon dipped in sugar cane vinegar, or the paneer in a white sauce (another western import) with black peppers. The combination is reflected in the decor – imposing dark wooden pillars conjure up a regal Indian vibe, contrasted with light pine furniture.

New Martin Lunch Home
Glamour House, Strand Cinema Road, Colaba, (2202-9606). Churchgate/CST stations. **Taxi** Strand Cinema. **Open** 11.30am-3pm, 6.30-10pm daily. **Main courses** Rs 35-Rs 50. **No credit cards**. Map p250 F4 **❾**

Good simple Goan food, served simply – don't expect more from Martin's than five tables with benches and tube-lighting. But it's clean and the food is fresh and tasty. Most of the dishes are subtly different shades of red, but they each taste quite different. The top order here is the Goan sausage: sour, spicy and swimming in tasty fat which you can mop up with *pao* (bread). There's also great vindaloo, prawn curry, and the classic fried fish curry and rice. There are no vegetables – Goans don't believe in them – unless you count the 'tomato plate'.

International

Basilico
Sentinel House, Arthur Bunder Road, near Radio Club, Colaba (6634-5670). Churchgate/CST stations. **Open** 7.30am-1am daily. **Main courses** Rs 250-Rs 300. **Credit** MC, V. **No alcohol**. Map p250 G4 **❿**

This stylish wood-and-glass eatery just off Colaba Causeway specialises in European cuisine with a Mediterranean slant, with some excellent sandwiches and mains, and some truly delightful coolers. There's also a deli section with fresh bread, pastries, and imported cheeses.

Café Churchill
103B East West Court Building, opposite Cusrow Baug, Colaba Causeway (2284-4689). **Open** 11am-5pm, 6pm-midnight daily. **Main courses** Rs 300. **No credit cards**. Map p250 G4 **⓫**

An old favourite on Colaba Causeway, Churchill is a small, friendly eatery usually heaving with diners at both lunch and dinner, with a queue waiting outside. It specialises in 'continental' cooking with a menu heavy on pasta dishes, decently done, and great burgers. The desserts cabinet is a must-visit, filled with terrific cheesecakes, gateaux and mousses. Tables are packed in tight and elbow room is at a premium, but food and atmosphere are abundant.

Café Royal

166 MG Road, Colaba (2288-3982). Churchgate/CST stations. **Taxi** opposite Regal Cinema. **Open** noon-12.30am daily. **Main courses** Rs 100-Rs 450. **Credit** AmEx, DC, MC, V. **Map** p251 G6 ⑫

A smart mid-range restaurant, big on sizzling meat platters, pasta dishes, burgers and fat sandwiches, popular with office buddies and families. It's not big on atmosphere – it has a giant mural of Hollywood stars – but the food is decent and service professional. It also boasts the city's biggest-ever celebrity endorsement: also on the walls are photos of former US President Bill Clinton, who ate here during his state visit to Mumbai in early 2000.

Golden Dragon

Taj Palace Hotel & Towers, Apollo Bunder, Colaba (6665-3366). Churchgate station. **Open** noon-2.45pm, 7-11.45pm daily. **Main courses** Rs 500-Rs 700. **Credit** AmEx, DC, MC, V. **Map** p251 G5 ⑬

The provenance of Golden Dragon's food roams widely, even ocean-hopping to Singapore, but the majority of the dishes originate in China's Sichuan province. Here the Indianisation effect is the reverse of the usual – Sichuan is too spicy even for Indians, so the chillis have been taken out. Their master chef is Shi Xi Lin, a native of Beijing who was awarded the title of 'best Sichuan chef in China' in 1994. The hot and sour soup, served in several versions, is a treat, as is the pepper-and-sesame jio ma chicken. **Photo** *p92.*

Henry Tham's

Dhanraj Mahal, Apollo Bunder, near Regal Cinema (2284-8214). Churchgate/CST stations. **Main courses** Rs 600-Rs 900. **Credit** AmEx, MC, V. **Map** p251 G5 ⑭

This Colaba restaurant, with a downstairs lounge bar, is contemporary in grand fashion, with minimalist decor, subtle lighting and nine-foot chairs. But the real beauty is in the food presentation, like the lightly fried tofu soy sauce served in an olive green, almond-shaped dish that resembles the pupil of an eye. It's good value too: the signature vegetarian and non-vegetarian set meals (Rs 650 and Rs 850) offer five generous courses. This is contemporary Chinese cooking at its best. The showstopper is the fresh fruit platter, called One Tree Hill: slivers of melon and grapes, plus a twig and dry ice, arranged as a miniature enchanted forest. **Photo** *p108.*

Indigo

Mandlik Road, Colaba (6636-8999/8980). CST/Churchgate stations. **Taxi** behind Taj Mahal Hotel. **Open** 12.30-3pm, 7.30-11.45pm daily. **Main courses** Rs 500. **Credit** AmEx, MC, V. **Map** p251 G5 ⑮

Indigo was revolutionary when it first opened in 1999, breaking new ground with a sophisticated European menu of the kind previously confined to five-star hotels. It's still one of the city's finest standalone restaurants, serving dishes like carpaccio, lobster bisque and goat's cheese on grilled apples, all well-executed. Indigo also does an addictive all-you-can-eat Sunday Champagne brunch (Rs 1,400). The open terrace upstairs is without doubt the nicest spot to dine in here in the evenings, but book in advance, Indigo is always busy.

Indigo Deli

Chhatrapati Shivaji Maharaj Street, Colaba (6655-1010). Churchgate/CST stations. **Open** 7am-11pm daily. **Main courses** Rs 225-Rs 285. **Credit** AmEx, MC, V. **Map** p251 G5 ⑯

Indigo's younger sister is not far away, a few minutes' walk from Regal Cinema and opposite Henry Tham's restaurant. There is a deli counter with a wide range of fresh breads, imported cheeses, meats, olives and more, plus a wall full of Indian and imported wines. The main attraction, though, is the sit-down dining area, smartly decked out in dark woods. Service is painfully slow, but the results are impressive, with some superb European-style main courses, soups, salads and tasty sandwiches. A great spot for breakfast, lunch (the eggs benedict here is the best in the city) or a snack, Indigo Deli also has excellent coffees and smoothies.

Ling's Pavilion

19/21 KC College Hostel Building, Landsdowne Road, off Colaba Causeway, Colaba (2285-0023). Churchgate/CST stations. **Open** noon-3pm, 6-11pm Mon; noon-11pm Tue-Sun. **Main courses** Rs 200-Rs 250. **Credit** AmEx, MC, V. **Map** p251 G5 ⑰

Ling's isn't a restaurant, it's an institution. This old-timer just off Colaba Causeway has been feeding South Mumbaikars their favourite Chinese dishes for the last 15 years and shows no signs of slowing down. A large part of its appeal is the decor – a miniature, marbled Chinese bridge crossing a fake stream, cute painted-on ceiling clouds in the Chinese style, and an upper gallery roofed with Chinese tiles. But it's mostly about the food: delectable honey-glazed spare ribs (Rs150), crab steamed with soy sauce (around Rs 800) and whole steamed pomfret garnished with chicken and mushrooms (Rs 600). Not only is the quality consistently high, but most dishes are available for around Rs 200-250, making it one of the city's best-value restaurants.

Piccadilly

Donald House, opposite Electric House, Colaba Causeway, Colaba (2282-3217/2056-1431). Churchgate/CST stations. **Open** 8.30am-11.30pm daily. **Main courses** Rs 200. **Credit** AmEx, MC, V. **Map** p251 G5 ⑱

About a decade ago, the Colaba warhorse Piccadilly transformed itself from an Irani restaurant into an Iranian restaurant. The metamorphosis wasn't just semantic. After recruiting a Lebanese chef who was on holiday in Mumbai, Firoze Kermanian added such Persian delights as chello kebab (rice cooked

Eat this

A guide to the flavours of Mumbai.

Gujarati

Gujarati cuisine is 100 per cent vegetarian, thanks to the Jain influence (see p28) and generally sweeter than other cuisines. The Gujarati thali is renowned for its richness and excessive quantities and is a must-try.

Try these: *dal dhokli* (a sweet and spicy Indian 'pasta' with lentils); *fadhani khichdi* (a savoury wholewheat porridge); *undhiu* (a baked winter stew of vegetables, fritters and green garlic chutney).

Get it at: Friends Union Joshi Club (see p105); Rajdhani (see p104), Swati Snacks (see p105); Soam (see p103).

Maharashtrian

Gujarati's more austere cousin, and much healthier thanks to a liberal use of whole grains and a restrained use of ghee and oil. It's also fairly mild, avoiding strong spices in favour of the more delicate flavours of sesame, turmeric and coriander.

Try these: *poha* (a light snack of beaten rice flakes, spices and peanuts); *sabudana vadas* (chewy tapioca fritters); *kothimbir vada* (deep-fried squares of coriander and chickpea paste).

Get it at: Pansikars Aahar (see p103); Swati Snacks (see p105).

Coastal

A broad term covering the cuisines of India's west coast, from southern Maharashtra right down to Kerala, all sharing a holy trinity of coconut, rice and fish. Malvani cooking from southern

A Maharashtrian eatery in **Girgaum**.

पुरणपोळी
दुधीहलवा
गुलाबजाम
श्रीखंड
आम्रखंड
तेलपोळी
रवा लाडू
बेसन लाडू
डिंक लाडू
मोतीचूर लाडू
माळपोवा

Maharashtra uses coconut milk and the sour *kokum* fruit in simple, delicious curries. Goans add Portuguese colonial influences of vinegar, pork and *pao* (bread). Further down, Mangaloreans grind a thick base of spices and grated coconut for their seafood and chicken curries. And deep in the south, Kerala cooking makes use of banana flowers and stems.

Try these: Goan pork sausages; Mangalorean prawn *gassi* (a kind of curry); *neer dosa* (steamed rice bread); classic Goan fish curry-rice.

Get it at: Excellensea (see p101); Konkan Café (see p91); New Martin Lunch Home (see p92); Mahesh Lunch Home (see p102);

Raan –
a slow-cooked
leg of lamb.

Dosa delights.

Sindhudurg (*see p106*); Sushegad Gomantak (*see p106*); Rice Boat (*see p108*).

Parsi

If Gujaratis ate meat, they would eat Parsi, on account of its similarly heavy nature. Dishes are very rich (recipes routinely start with 'Take a dozen eggs'), heavy on the meat and slightly sweet, thanks to a Zoroastrian Persian tradition of cooking with dried fruits (*see p28*). It's a wonderful mélange of Middle Eastern cooking styles and Indian ingredients.

Try these: *dhansak* (a thick curry of meat, lentils and vegetables); *patra-ni-machchi* (fish cooked in banana leaves); *akuri* (spicy scrambled eggs).
Get it at: Britannia (*see p91*); Jimmy Boy Café (*see p102*).

Udipi

South Indian vegetarian cuisine, renowned for highly popular snacks made from fermented ground rice like *idlis* (steamed rice cakes), lentil batter dishes like *dosas* (savoury pancakes) and more substantial *thalis*.
Try these: *appams* (thick round pancakes); Udipi *thalis* served on banana leaves.
Get it at: Shiv Sagar (*see p101*).

Muslim

Think kebabs and biryanis. Mughlai is an ultra-rich non-vegetarian Muslim cuisine but there are also simpler versions created in casual Chillia Muslim-run eateries. The best time to experience Mumbai's Muslim food is unquestionably the Ramzaan festival (*see p132* **Festivals & Events**) when Muslim neighbourhoods like

Mohammed Ali Road become vast outdoor dining extravaganzas after sunset.
Try these: *raan* (a rich, tender leg of lamb, split so you get at the marrow); *khiri* (grilled udders); *khichda* (thick stew of meat, wheat and lentils).
Get it at: Shalimar (*see p104*); the streets around Minara Masjid (map p253 & p255 G14).

Bengali

Pungent, with liberal use of mustard in both seed and oil form. Combine that with poppy seeds, freshwater fish and an inventive range of sweets made from cottage cheese and you have a strikingly different cuisine.
Try these: *maccher jhol* (basic Bengali fish curry); *chingdi malai-kari* (prawns cooked in coconut cream); smoked *hilsa* or *ilish* (a Bengali freshwater fish); *mocchar ghanto* (stir-fried banana flower); *bhaja mungher dhal* (roast mung beans); *mishti doi* (a fabulous yoghurt dessert).
Get it at: Howrah (*see p103*); Oh! Calcutta (*see p105*).

Eat, Drink, Shop

Kebabs at a **Ramzan** street stall.

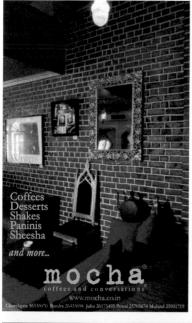

in cream with kebabs). But most of his menu is Lebanese and though the original chef has long completed his stint in Mumbai, he's trained Piccadilly's staff well. The grilled chicken in a lemon and vinegar marinade (Rs 150) remains the signature dish.

Taxi
Jony Castle Building, Khatau Road, off Wodehouse Road, Colaba (2218-4904). Churchgate station. **Open** noon-2.45pm, 7-11.45pm. **Main courses** Rs 400-Rs 700. **Credit** AmEx, MC, V. **Map** p250 E3 ⑲

On a quiet, tree-lined street in deepest Colaba, Taxi is gorgeous to look at – a gothic kaleidoscope of colours and textures amid subdued lighting and lively music. Make a reservation for the private dining room, a cosy space that was once the service quarters of this old bungalow. It's now a mini royal chamber, all red silk drapes, large mirrors and chandeliers, high ceilings, and bunches of roses. The food isn't as stunning as the decor, but it is competently executed European cuisine.

Thai Pavilion
Taj President, Lobby Level, Cuffe Parade (6665-0808). Churchgate/CST stations. **Open** 12.30-2.45pm, 7-11.45pm daily. **Main courses** Rs 1,000-Rs 1,200. **Credit** AmEx, DC, MC, V. **Map** p250 E3 ⑳

The finest Thai restaurant in the city (and quite possibly the whole of India) serves up tender parcels of flavourful chicken steamed in pandan leaves, raw papaya salad and delicate spring rolls tucked with fresh vegetables, all favourites that loyalists swear by. The service is impeccable, and the intricate fruit and vegetable carvings a glorious array of colour.

Wasabi
Taj Mahal Palace and Tower Hotel, Apollo Bunder (6665-3366). Churchgate/CST stations. **Open** 12.30-3pm, 7pm-11.45pm daily. **Main courses** Rs 2,000. **Credit** AmEx, MC, V. **Map** p251 G5 ㉑

For Mumbai's few fans of Japanese cuisine, Wasabi is sacred: its chief chef is Masaharu Morimoto of Nobu fame; his locally recruited chefs maintain his sky-high standards that go with similar prices. Entered only via a narrow spiral staircase from a bar on the Taj's ground floor, Wasabi reeks of exclusivity and elegance. The food is fabulous, but there's only one saké on offer, its appeal extended by using it as a base ingredient in an array of cocktails. Try the Bloody Maro (Rs 325), which substitutes vodka with saké. You'll have to reserve a table several days in advance; request one with a sea view.

Cafés

Barista
Cecil Court, Colaba Causeway, Colaba (6633-6835). Churchgate/CST stations. **Taxi** Regal Cinema. **Open** 8.30am-1.30am daily. **No credit cards. No alcohol. Map** p251 G5 ㉒

A highly successful Indian café chain, modelled on Starbucks, that has now spread across India, Sri Lanka and the Middle East. The snacks and cakes are best avoided, but the hot and cold coffees are top-notch and the decor soothing. This one's usually packed with college kids, shoppers and tourists. **Other locations:** 34 Chowpatty Seaface (2369-0104); Maker Towers, Cuffe Parade (2215-0562); Murzban Road, next to Sterling Cinema, near Chhatrapati Shivaji Terminus; Planet M Store, Times of India Building, DN Road, opposite Chhatrapati Shivaji Terminus (2235-3874); Bandstand Building, Bandstand, Bandra (W) (2643-4287); Pearl Haven, Chapel Road, Bandra (W) (2641-2786); Juhu Princess Hotel, opposite Ramada Palm Grove Hotel, Juhu Tara Road (2614-8022).

Moshe's Café
7 Minoo Manor, Cuffe Parade (2216-1226). Churchgate/CST stations. **Open** 7.30am-11.45pm daily. **Main courses** Rs 250-Rs 550. **Credit** AmEx, MC, V. **Map** p250 E3 ㉓

Hidden behind a hedge on Cuffe Parade is this smart high-ceilinged café with a small garden dining area. Better as a lunchtime stopover than a dinner place, Moshe's offers grilled sandwiches, salads and mains with Mediterranean flavours. There's also a wide range of coffees, desserts and coolers, like a killer limeade made with ginger, fennel and cloves, plus excellent smoothies – the papaya, yoghurt and vanilla are particularly good.

Olympia Café
Rahim Mansion, 1 Colaba Causeway, Colaba (2202-1043). Churchgate/CST stations. **Open** 7am-midnight daily. **No credit cards. No alcohol. Map** p251 G5 ㉔

Olympia, opposite Leopold Café (*see p113*), scores high on the '40s period charm, with old chairs and tables, and lazy fans. It's cheap and popular with

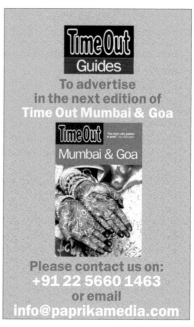

backpackers, office workers and taxi drivers crowded in together. A great spot for a coffee or tea and some respite from the rush of Colaba Causeway.

Theobroma

Cusrow Baug Shop No 24, Colaba Causeway (6629-2929). Churchgate/CST stations. **Taxi** Electric House. **Open** 11am-11pm daily. **Credit** MC, V. **No alcohol. Map** p250 F4

The name means 'food of the gods', and they aren't exaggerating. The decor is strictly terrestrial, but the food is divine; top-quality sourdough loaves, fluffy focaccia, chocolate brownies, danish pastries and freshly made, five-star hotel-quality sandwiches. An excellent lunch and brunch spot.

Nariman Point

Indian

Moti Mahal Delux

102 CR2 Shopping Mall, First Floor, Nariman Point (6654-6434). Churchgate station. **Taxi** INOX Cinema.

Open noon-midnight daily. **Main courses** Rs 150-Rs 300. **Credit** MC, V. **Map** p251 E6 ㉖

Moti Mahal (meaning 'Pearl Palace') is the Mumbai addition to a chain of restaurants that originated in Peshawar in the 1920s. The Mumbai version is neat and contemporary: wooden floors and modern seating, sheer white drapes and a glass-wrapped kitchen. Listen out for the twang of Delhi accents – this is where expat Delhiites come for home-style food. It's pure North Indian cuisine: go for the tender *lasooni* kebabs (Rs 169) and the soft naans (Rs 29). The butter chicken (Rs 169) is worth a trip to the place all by itself. Finish off with a sweet, thick lassi.

International

India Jones

Hilton Towers, Nariman Point (6632-5757). Churchgate station. **Open** 12.30-2.45pm, 7.30-11.45pm daily. **Main courses** Rs 500-Rs 600. **Credit** AmEx, DC, MC, V. **Map** p251 D6 ㉗

China meets Japan via Thailand and Indonesia at India Jones, where the menu includes a mishmash

Street eats

Mumbai's street food is a cuisine in itself, built on Maharashtrian-Gujarati roots, with the added influence of every émigré community. Food stalls are everywhere, serving kids on their way to school, office workers on lunch breaks, commuters grabbing a bite before the train home. The signature street snack is the *vada-pao*, a fried potato fritter in a soft roll with dry chilli-garlic chutney. Another is *bhel puri*, a dry snack of puffed rice, peanuts, chickpea noodles, onions and chutney. Then there's *pao bhaji*, spicy puréed vegetables eaten with buttered bread, and *pani puri* – crispy shells filled with chickpea dumplings, mung sprouts and spiced water. Pop it in, crunch, and it all explodes thrillingly in your mouth. *Buta* is roast corn-on-the-cob dusted with chilli powder and lime. It's all cheap – about Rs 25-30.

You'll find street stalls everywhere, but these aren't always the cleanest places to eat; foreign visitors who aren't used to it will be taking a risk of getting sick. Exercise some common sense: stick to the most popular stalls, like those around Churchgate station and Chhatrapati Shivaji Terminus or at Chowpatty beach. Ensure the cook observes basic hygiene and that the food is piping hot. Alternatively, you can find excellent versions of street cuisine at Swati Snacks (*see p105*), and *vada-paos* are now sold in a branded

fast-food chain modelled on McDonald's called Jumbo King, although purists will tell you that they just aren't the same. Here are some recommended stalls:

Jai Santoshi Ma Bhel Puri Bhandar

20 Bharati Bhavan, 468 Kalbadevi Road, corner of Princess Street & Kalbadevi Road. Marine Lines station. **Map** p253 F12 ㉕

Jumbo King

308 Devji Kanji Street, Princess Street, Marine Lines (98920-23533). Marine Lines station. **Open** 9am-10pm daily. **Map** p253 E12 ㉖

Lokesh & Vedprakash

Opposite Potpourri restaurant, Turner Road, Bandra (W). Bandra station. **Open** 6.30pm-12.30am daily. **Map** p249 C4 ㉗

Vithal Bhelwallah

5 AK Naik Marg, near Sterling Cinema, Fort (6631-7211). CST station. **Open** 11am-11pm daily. **Map** p252 H10 ㉘

Eat, Drink, Shop

of popular dishes from across Southeast Asia, plus some fusion experiments. The *chao tum* (cooked prawn mousse on sugar-cane skewers) is delightful. The appetisers are superb – you could skip the main courses and go straight for the appetiser platter.

Tiffin
The Oberoi, Nariman Point (6632-6205).
Churchgate station. **Open** 6.30am-11.30pm daily.
Main courses Rs 300-Rs 700. **Credit** AmEx,
MC, V. **Map** p251 D6
Another Oberoi restaurant, this one decked out in an understated white-and-grey that exudes off-hand elegance. In other words, the perfect lunch venue for rich and bored South Mumbai housewives – they'll be the ones air-kissing each other's diamond earrings. The menu is short and changes every couple of months, with the emphasis on European cuisine, with some token Indian standards like rogan josh. Tiffin also serves some very decent sushi and sashimi (Rs 300-650). The standard of dishes is uniformly high, although the servings can be a little small.

Vetro
The Oberoi, Lobby level, Nariman Point (6632-5757).
Churchgate station. **Open** noon-3pm, 7pm-1am daily.
Main courses Rs 600-Rs 700. **Credit** AmEx,
MC, V. **Map** p251 D6
Another one of South Mumbai's rapidly mushrooming high-end Italian restaurants, but with beautiful interior design. Row upon row of coloured windows line the walls, reflecting the afternoon sunlight into criss-crossing rainbows. As soon as

you enter you'll be invited for a wine-tasting session before you eat. There's a walk-in antipasti bar, including juicy stuffed olives and very good carpaccio, Parma ham and salads. The starters and salads are outstanding, so good in fact, that they leave the mains a little in the shade.

Churchgate & Marine Lines

Indian

Panchvati Gaurav
Metro Cinema Road, Marine Lines (2208-4877).
Marine Lines station. **Open**
11am-3pm, 7-10.30pm daily. **Thali** Unlimited Rs 145,
Limited Rs 105. **Credit** MC, V. **Map** p252 F10
One of the city's favourite thali places, Panchvati Gaurav specialises in Gujarati thalis. Still a regular joint for the office lunch crowd, it's unbeatable value for money and boasts excellent service. The sweet, milky Gujarati curry is light and tasty, the *farsan* (snacks) delicious with papads and pickles, and dessert is included. And just when you don't think you can stand to eat another bite, they'll finish you off with heaps of rice, dal and a dollop of ghee.

Samrat
Prem Court, Jamshedji Tata Road, Churchgate
(2282-0942). Churchgate station. **Open**
noon-3.30pm, 7-10.30pm daily. **Thali** Rs 160.
Credit AmEx, MC, V. **Map** p251 & p252 F7
Samrat is almost legendary in the city for its Gujarati thalis, attracting big crowds at lunchtimes

Pan handling

There's nothing like a sweet *pan* to finish off a meal. *Pan masalas* are highly popular concoctions made from betel leaves and nuts and numerous other ingredients, sold by tiny panwallah stalls on streets across the city. The key ingredient is shavings of betel nut, or *supari*, a mild stimulant that leaves a characteristic red stain on the teeth. It's chewed slowly and the husk spat out – hence the red stains on streets and walls across Mumbai. Different panwallahs offer different versions, some bitter and some sweet. Common ingredients include lime paste, cloves and cardamom. Others add coconut and sugar, or jellied fruits, dates and honey, all wrapped neatly in a betel leaf and covered in silver leaf. People often favour *pan* as a post-dinner digestive, but others take it for its alleged aphrodisiac properties, with the big daddy of *pan* Viagra being the *palang-tod* ('bed-breaker'). You can find *pan* on any street corner usually for between Rs 5 and 50,

depending on the extravagance of the *pan*. **Pan Palace** in Bandra has a great selection of *pan*, starting at around Rs 25, going all the way up to Rs 1,000 for ones covered in gold leaf.

Pan Palace
4 Jewel Milan, 30 Road, Pali Naka, opposite Toto's Garage Pub, Bandra (W) (93238-74743). **Open** 10am-1am. **Map** p249 C3

from the offices around Churchgate and Nariman Point. The thalis are 'unlimited', with a smartly uniformed waiter on hand to make sure your katoris are constantly filled to the brim with four types of vegetables, two farsan, two sweet dishes, and mountains of puris, papads and rice. It's consistently fabulous – just don't plan on doing anything more strenuous than digesting for a few hours afterwards.

Shiv Sagar

Nagin Mahal, 82 Veer Nariman Road, Churchgate (2282-4862). Churchgate station. **Open** 9am-12.30am daily. **Main courses** Rs 70-Rs 170. **Credit** AmEx, MC, V. **Map** p251 & p252 F8 ❸❷

A neat, clean but hectic Udipi joint serving lunch to the office crowd in the busy Churchgate district. Skip most of the menu and head straight for the South Indian fare – crispy *dosas* and soft *idlis* – and the tasty *pao bhajis*. Shiv Sagar also does a good selection of street-style snacks, hygienically prepared.

International

Oriental Blossom

Marine Plaza Hotel, 29 Marine Drive (2285-1212). Churchgate station. **Open** 12.30-2.45pm, 7.30-11.30pm daily. **Main courses** Rs 500. **Credit** AmEx, MC, V. **Map** p251 & p252 E7 ❸❸

House restaurant of the splendid Marine Plaza Hotel, the Blossom makes a very decent fist of Cantonese cooking. Some of the dishes are a little heavy on the sauces but the freshness of the ingredients wins out. We also appreciate the minimal red and gold Chinoise frippery: instead the place has a clean, modern look. Book in advance.

Pearl of the Orient

The Ambassador Hotel, Veer Nariman Road, Churchgate (2204-1131). Churchgate station. **Open** 12.30-2.45pm, 7.30-11.45pm daily. **Main courses** Rs 350-Rs 1,050. **Credit** AmEx, MC, V. **Map** p251 & p252 E8 ❸❹

Mumbai's only revolving restaurant, on the 12th floor of a 1970s-built concrete tower housing the Ambassador Hotel. It's an East Asian eatery with an emphasis on Hunan, Sichuan and Cantonese dishes, plus some sushi and Thai food – all competently prepared by a chef with a penchant for carving roses out of beetroots. It has spectacular views of the sea, the sweep of Marine Drive and the cityscape through its floor-to-ceiling windows, with the restaurant completing a circuit every 90 minutes. If you're lucky, you'll get an eagle's-eye view of a cricket match at the Brabourne Stadium next door.

Cafés

Mocha

Nagin Mahal, Veer Nariman Road (6633-6070). Churchgate station. **Open** 9am-1.30am daily. **Credit** AmEx, MC, V. **Map** p251 & p252 F8 ❸❺

A trendy hangout for well-heeled college kids, with a Middle Eastern vibe complete with fez-adorned

waiters. The thing to do here is lounge on a bolster passing around a flavoured hookah with your mates, while slurping on a pricey coffee. Mocha also serves wine and Bacardi Breezers (no beer) and a range of workmanlike Euro-dishes.

Other locations: Café Mocha, near Holy Family Hospital, Hill Road, Bandra (W). Bandra station. (2643-3098).

Tea Centre

Resham Bhavan, 78 Veer Nariman Road (2281-9142). Churchgate station. **Open** 8am-10.30pm daily. **Credit** AmEx, MC, V. **Map** p251 & p252 F8 ❸❻

A venture run jointly with the Tea Board of India, the Tea Centre is an eminently civilised showcase of India's finest teas, served by turbaned waiters in stiff uniforms. It's small, decked out in green and white, with walls of sepia-toned photos of former Indian leaders enjoying tea, and information about its benefits (tea improves 'longevity and dental health', apparently). On offer are varieties of Assam, Darjeeling and Nilgiris, both hot and iced, plus a selection of tea 'mocktails' like mint tea with ice cream. Snacks and sandwiches are also served. A pianist plays here on Thursdays, Fridays and Saturdays from 2-4pm.

Fort & Khala Ghoda

Indian

Britannia

Sprott Road, Ballard Estate (2261-5264). CST station. **Taxi** opposite New Custom House. **Open** 11.30am-4pm Mon-Sat. **Main courses** Rs 125-Rs 175. **No credit cards. No alcohol. Map** p251 & p252 ❸❼

Despite the dilapidated wooden interior, complete with wobbly chairs, peeling walls and dusty chandeliers, Britannia, a classic Irani restaurant of a type now slowly dying out (*see p91* **Café society**), manages to exude a homely 1940s charm. Open only for lunch, it's famous for its fabulous berry pulao, a traditional Iranian dish of boneless mutton (Rs 175) or chicken (Rs 150) in a sweet, spicy masala and garnished with tart Iranian berries. If you still have room, follow it with a creamy caramel custard.

Excellensea

Bharat House, Mint Road. (2261-8991/2267-2677). CST station. **Taxi** opposite Fort Market. **Open** 11.30am-4pm, 5.30pm-midnight daily. **Main courses** Rs 300-Rs 400. **Credit** AmEx, MC, V. **Map** p251 & p252 J9 ❸❽

A Mangalorean seafood place with the usual crab butter-pepper-garlic, prawn *gassi*, tandoori pomfret routine, crab legs brought to your table and so on, but well-done and without the airs of Trishna. The kitchen will also make some items not on the menu but available at request, like Konkani *sungta*, a delectable dish of rice cooked with coconut milk and prawns. The noisier, non-air-conditioned section below offers the same food for a little less.

Jimmy Boy Café

*11 Bank Street, Vikas Building, Fort (2270-0880).
CST station.* **Taxi** Horniman Circle. **Open** 11am-
11pm daily. **Main courses** Rs 200-Rs 250. **Credit**
MC, V. **No alcohol**. **Map** p251 & p252 H7 ③⑨

Jimmy Boy is best known for its Parsi specialities,
particularly *lagan nu bhonu*, or Parsi wedding food.
Try the delightful *murghi na farcha* (crumb-fried
spiced chicken), *patra ni machchi* (chutney-stuffed
pomfret wrapped in banana leaves), *jardaloo sali boti*
(boneless mutton cooked with dried apricots and an
onion and tomato gravy) and the signature Parsi
dish, mutton *dhansak* (a lentil and vegetable curry).
A popular joint with Parsis and non-Parsis alike, so
make a reservation.

Khyber

*145 Mahatma Gandhi Road, Kala Ghoda (2267-3227).
Churchgate/CST stations.* **Open** 12.30-3.30pm,
7.30pm-11.30pm daily. **Main course** Rs 250-Rs 350.
Credit AmEx, DC, MC, V. **Map** p251 G7 ④⓪

A sprawling, two-level restaurant grandly furnished
in wood and stone, Khyber is an old favourite of fans
of North Indian cuisine, with consistently high
standards. Top choices here include their tender
raan – a slow-cooked leg of lamb – the biryani and
their paneer korma. After dinner, you can waddle
through a connecting door into the Red Light nightclub (see p158) next door.

Mahesh Lunch Home

*8B Cawasji Patel Street, Fort (2287-0938). CST
station.* **Open** 11.30am-4pm, 6pm-11.30pm daily.
Main courses Rs 150-Rs 250. **Credit** AmEx, DC,
MC, V. **Map** p251 & p252 G8 ④①

Less fancy in its decor than its Mangalorean seafood
sister Trishna, Mahesh nevertheless keeps up with
the competition on their food – excellent Konkan
coastal and Mangalorean cuisine, in particular some
excellent *gassi* and killer curry-rice.

Trishna

*7 Sai Baba Marg, Kala Ghoda (2270-1623). CST
station.* **Taxi** behind Rhythm House. **Open** noon-
3.30pm, 6pm-midnight daily. **Main courses** Rs 150-
Rs 300. **Credit** AmEx, DC, MC, V. **Map** p251 G7 ④②

A popular seafood restaurant famed for its South
Indian Mangalorean dishes. The decor is ornate and
the food good enough to keep the South Mumbai
elite and the odd celebrity coming back. Favourites
include the prawn *gassi*, the butter-pepper-garlic
crab and stuffed pomfret.

International

Joss

*Near Rhythm House, Kala Ghoda (6633-4233).
Churchgate/CST station.* **Open** 12.30-3.30pm,
7.30-11.30pm daily. **Main courses** Rs 320-Rs 975.
Credit AmEx, MC, V. **Map** p251 G6 ④③

A smart, subtly lit pan-Asian restaurant that was
once a Thai restaurant (hence the stunning gold-and-
glass Thai temple-style walls decor, each adorned
with an orchid). Now it's become one of the city's

most impressive pan-Asian restaurants, with a
range of Singaporean, Indonesian, Thai, Chinese,
Japanese and Korean dishes, and fusion experiments
like aki miso-marinated tenderloin thrown in. It's all
good, with an impressive sushi menu as well.

Royal China

*SP Corporation Building, Sterling, Hajarimal
Somani Marg, Fort (6636-5531). CST station.*
Open 12.30-3.15pm, 8.30-11.15pm daily. **Main
courses** Rs 600-Rs 900. **Credit** AmEx, DC, MC, V.
Alcohol served. **Map** p252 G10 ④④

Royal China is arguably the city's finest Cantonese
Chinese restaurant, one of the few places where
Mumbaikars can eat authentic Chinese food. Big
favourites with the local crowd are things in sauces
and with strong flavours, like the crispy aromatic
duck served with paper-thin pancakes and an own-
made plum sauce. Royal China is also the local pioneer of dim sum – nowhere else comes close in terms
of choice or quality – with a dedicated dim sum chef
who prepares up to 50 different kinds daily.

Marine Drive

Indian

Kebab Korner

*Intercontinental Hotel, 135 Marine Drive (6639-9999).
Churchgate station.* **Open** 12.30-3pm, 7.30pm-
midnight daily. **Main courses** Rs 280-Rs 415.
Credit AmEx, MC, V. **Map** p251 & p252 E8 ④⑤

Kebab Korner was an institution that shut down
years ago, before being recreated in 2005 with its
original chefs and traditional cooking style – the
kebabs here are made on a sigri (a kind of coal-fired
grill) instead of a tandoor oven. The results are stunning – tender and subtly flavoured seekh kebabs,
spicy butter chicken (Rs 345) and outrageously tasty
kali dal (Rs 285). The biryani is also to die for, as is
the house special 'Busybee' stuffed chicken kebab
(Rs 345) served with burnt onions and yoghurt chutney. Add a sea view and the sumptuous wood and
marble décor, and you have a Mumbai classic.

International

Corleone

*Intercontinental Marine Drive, 135 Marine Drive
(3987-9999). Churchgate station.* **Open** 6.30am-4am
daily. **Main courses** Rs 200-Rs 750. **Credit** AmEx,
MC, V. **Map** p251 & p252 E8 ④⑥

With grey-washed walls, light wooden floors, venet-
ian blinds and abstract art, Corleone feels a little
corporate, but at least the food – mostly Sicilian
dishes – has plenty of character. Try the 'Corleone'–
an addictive salad of organic rocket, radish, roasted
Sicilian cheese and sun-dried tomato. The restaurant's name has a certain irony: This used to be a
disco called 'RG's' until it closed in the 1990s after a
drunken Mumbai gangster (so says urban legend)
pulled out a gun and ordered a girl to dance naked.

Eat, Drink, Shop

Olive Bar & Kitchen. *See p107.*

Salt Water Grill

*Girgaum Chowpatty, Marine Drive (98925-78494).
Charni Road station.* **Taxi** H20 Water Sports
Complex. **Open** 7pm-1.30am daily. **Main
courses** Rs 245-Rs 400. **Credit** AmEx, MC, V.
Map p254 C14 ❹
The location is unbeatable – right on the Marine
Drive beach. Uplit palm trees sway above white
cotton canopies. *Buena Vista Social Club* croons over
the insistent whisper of the Arabian Sea. Hammocks
loll, lounge chairs beckon, sand shifts underfoot. No
wonder this is the playground of Mumbai's celebrity
Page 3 set. The food is sophisticated Euro cuisine
with an emphasis on seafood. The cocktails are fab,
especially the fresh watermelon-choked caprioskas.

Cafés

Bachelor's Juice House

*Marine Drive, near Chowpatty (2368-8107/2367-8351).
Marines Lines station.* **No credit cards. No alcohol. Map** p254 B15 ❹
Easy to spot from the rows of fruit and parked cars.
This isn't a 'house', but a street stall, although it's a
superior stall on a superior street – the bayfront
Marine Drive. Bachelor's has ice-cream, milkshakes
and fresh juices, all made with fresh fruit.
Everything is superb, but the highlights are the
watermelon, custard apple, mango, roast almond
and green chilli ice-creams (Rs 44 for a large cup).

Chowpatty & Girgaum

Indian

Pansikar Aahar

*Govardhandas Building, JSS Road, Girgaum
(6634-0941, 2386-1211). Grant Road station.*
Taxi Girgaum Church. **Open** 8am-10pm daily.
Main courses Rs 12-Rs 25. **No credit cards.**
Map p254 C15 ❹

Maharashtrian vegetarian food, but Pansikar's speciality is the interesting category of *upvas* dishes,
food meant to be eaten on traditional Hindu fast
days that prohibit the consumption of 'sown' foods,
meaning anything grown in a ploughed field. This
includes fruits, roots and tubers. Pansikar makes
most standard Mumbai snacks in *upvas* form.

Soam

*Sadguru Sadan, Ground floor, Chowpatty (2369-8080).
Grant Road station.* **Taxi** opposite Babulnath
Temple. **Open** noon-midnight daily. **Main courses**
Rs 120-Rs 170. **Credit** MC, V. **No alcohol.**
Map p254 A15 ❺
The true test of a Gujarati snacks joint is its *panki*
chutney (pancakes steamed in banana leaves), and
Soam passes with flying colours. The intense heat
makes it almost difficult to touch, but hold up the
banana leaf and the pancake falls off in one piece –
perfect. Furnished in dark wood, ochre-coloured
walls, bamboo blinds and comfy seating, Soam is
fast becoming a favourite alternative to South
Mumbai's other hugely popular Gujarati snack joint,
Swati Snacks (*see p105*).

Crawford Market

Indian

Howrah

*Sitaram Building, B Block, Dr DN Road, Crawford
Market (2342-4693). CST station.* **Open** noon-4pm,
7-11.30pm daily. **Main courses** Rs 35-Rs 150.
Credit AmEx, DC, MC, V. **No Alcohol.**
Map p253 H12 ❺
Howrah is a restaurant specialising in Bengali
cuisine. Despite being right next to one of the city's
most hectic markets, Howrah's one-flight-up terrace
offers a relaxed dining experience, with old-
fashioned ceiling fans and smiling, unhurried dhoti-
clad waiters. Just think a lazy afternoon in Kolkata,
with an '80s Bengali pop soundtrack to make expat

Kolkattans (who account for most of the customers) feel at home. Howrah is best known for its fish dishes, especially freshwater fish like *ilish*, a regional delicacy flown in specially all the way from Bengal. Styles of preparation vary from a creamy cardamom gravy of *malai* curry to the complex *daab* style where the fish is baked in a coconut shell.

Rajdhani

361 Sheikh Memon Street, near Crawford Market (2342-6919). CST station. **Taxi** opposite Mangaldas Market. **Open** noon-3.30pm, 7-10.30pm daily. **Thali** Rs 125. **Credit** AmEx, DC, MC, V. **No alcohol**. **Map** p253 & p255 G13 ❷

Rajdhani is an oasis of calm in a narrow, frantic side-street a few metres from the bustle of the historic Crawford Market. Getting here requires some Frogger-style negotiation of the local traffic of hand-pulled carts, but if you make it you'll be treated to a superior Gujarati thali with endless refills of *paalak paneer* (spinach and cottage cheese), sweet *kadi* (a gram flour-based curry), *aloo subzi* (masala potato), kidney bean curry and more. Take a glass of *chaas* (buttermilk) and finish off with some *gulab jamun*.

Shalimar

Vazir Building, Bhendi Bazaar, Mohammed Ali Road (2345-6632, 2346-5286). CST station. **Taxi** Bhendi Bazaar Fire Station. **Open** 8am-1.30am daily. **Main courses** Rs 35-Rs 250. **Credit** DC, MC, V. **Map** p253 & p255 G14 ❸

Off Carter Road

The official name is Road No 5 but it's known universally as 'off Carter Road' – a lively strip of modestly priced Bandra restaurants with Parisian street café pretensions, all just a kebab's throw from the Carter Road seafront promenade. Forget the dust and the traffic snarls and concentrate on the food and the people-watching – an endless stream of pretty Bandra college boys and girls, young professionals, wannabe models and actors and the odd Hindi soap opera star. The strip's assorted eateries serve a range of cuisines but few people come for a full meal. Most are here to hang out over a coffee. The outdoor seating resembles a sort of street-long food court. Here are some highlights.

Kareem's.

Café Coffee Day

Gagangiri Commerical Complex (3092-0323). **Open** 9am-1.30am daily. **No credit cards. No alcohol. Map** p249 A2 ❼⓪

Part of a popular café chain with outlets across the city but this one's superior, with fabulous views of the Arabian Sea and the Carter Road promenade and an intimate open-air upper deck. The snacks and sandwiches are decent and the coffee is good. Wander in around 5.30pm and every teenage head will turn to check you out.

Crepe Station Café

8A Gagangiri Commercial Complex (5574-7475). **Open** 8am-12.30am daily. **Main course** Rs 100-Rs 200. **No credit cards. Map** p249 A2 ❼①

Don't bother with the indifferent crepes (the burgers are much better) – it's not really the food that's the draw here anyway. It's owned by Bollywood actor Dino Morea, and a favourite hangout for local TV stars. But the breakfasts are good, including an English breakfast (Rs 70), banana porridge (Rs 40) and muesli with fresh fruits and honey (Rs 50).

Kareem's

A5 Gagangiri Commercial Complex (98198-39391). **Open** 8pm-2.30am daily. **Main course** Rs 50-Rs 100. **No credit cards. Map** p249 A2 ❼②

The best-looking restaurant on the strip, serving excellent Lucknowi-style food. Popular dishes include a paya soup (goat trotter soup) (Rs 50) and a creamy, cotton-soft murgh kali mirch (black pepper chicken) (Rs 90), the city's best.

Zauq

Opposite Café Coffee Day (5579-7969). **Open** noon-1.30am daily. **Main course** Around Rs 200. **Credit** MC, V. **No alcohol. Map** p249 A2 ❼③

Why did nobody ever think of flambéing chicken tikka with Jack Daniels before? Zauq does it and it's fab. Small but sweet, this has to be one of the strip's finest eateries, serving everything from kebabs to curries to soups, salads and pastas. It all works wonderfully. Don't miss the house speciality – melt-in-the-mouth *galauti* kebabs.

Eat, Drink, Shop

Meat, meat, and more meat... this is Mumbai Muslim food at its most carnivorous. Shalimar makes no concessions to health fads, serving up extremely rich and spicy kebabs and other delights. The traditional dishes are great – try the *raan*, a leg of lamb from the restaurant's own livestock, split so you can get at the marrow – but avoid the ill-conceived 'Mexican' and 'Chinese' fusion dishes. It's a little claustrophobic and usually packed, so expect a short wait for a table.

Friends Union Joshi Club.

Mahalaxmi

Indian

Gallops
Mahalaxmi Racecourse, Racecourse Road, Mahalaxmi (2307-1448). Mahalaxmi station. **Open** noon-midnight daily. **Main courses** Rs 275-Rs 375. **Credit** AmEx, MC, V.
The greatest thing about Gallops is the location – next to a tree- and bougainvillea-fringed garden on the edge of the Royal Western India Turf Club, with a view of the racecourse. The restaurant, decked out in acres of stone, wood and brass, offers Indian and 'Continental' – both competently executed, although the Indian is the better option. The ideal spot for lunch before an afternoon at the races.

International

China Garden
Crossroads Mall, Lobby Level, Haji Ali (2353-5588). Mahalaxmi station. **Open** 12.30-3.30pm, 7.30pm-midnight daily. **Main courses** Rs 500-Rs 700. **Credit** AmEx, MC, V.
China Garden tempers Sichuan, Cantonese and Hunan food to the Indian palate, but doing so in an environment that makes it feel not just acceptable, but fashionable. Loyalists swear by the red pepper chicken, bacon-wrapped prawns and steamed vegetarian wontons. Proprietor Nelson Wang claims to have invented Chinese-Indian food's most popular dish, the chicken Manchurian: deep-fried chicken strips that are cooked in soy sauce, ketchup, onions, garlic and green chillies.

Tardeo

Indian

Oh! Calcutta
Rosewood Hotel, Tulsiwadi Lane, Tardeo (2496-3114). Mumbai Central station. **Open** noon-3pm, 7pm-midnight daily. **Main courses** Rs 400-Rs 450. **Credit** AmEx, MC, V.
Oh! Calcutta provides a culinary home away from home for misty-eyed Bengali customers. The must-try dish here is the *ilish maacher apturi* – lightly spiced boneless hilsa fish from the Ganges marinated in mustard paste and green chillies, then baked. And there should be a law forbidding diners from leaving without trying the *mishti doi* – a creamy yoghurt dessert that makes Bengalis go weak at the knees.

Swati Snacks
248 Karai Estate, Tardeo (6660-8405/8406). Grant Road station. **Taxi** opposite Bhatia Hospital. **Open** noon-2.30pm, 7-10pm daily. **Main courses** Rs 50-Rs 80. **Credit** MC, V. **No alcohol. Map** p254 B18 ⑤
Back in the '60s, Swati Snacks was little more than a shack on the street serving Gujarati food. Now, it's a swank, shiny spacecraft of glass and stainless steel. The menu is packed with gorgeous Gujarati staples and some Mumbai street fare like *dahi batata puri* and *idlis*. Everything on the menu is outstanding, in particular the delectable *panki chatni* (rice crêpes steamed in banana leaves) and the *dal dhokli* – a thick lentil curry with a cinnamon flavouring, filled with soft squares of chapati. There's also a good selection of fresh juices. Be warned, lunchtimes here are packed; reservations aren't accepted and 40-minute waits are not uncommon. Try the delicious sugarcane and ginger juice mix while you wait.

Kalbadevi

Indian

Friends Union Joshi Club
381A Kalbadevi Road, Narottamwadi (2205-8089). Marine Lines station. **Open** 11am-3pm, 7-10pm Mon-Sat; 11am-3pm Sun. **Main courses** Rs 60. **No credit cards. No alcohol. Map** p 253 & p255 F13 ⑤
It's been around since before India became independent in 1947, but the FUJC remains tricky to find. Look for a large, bright red neon sign, go through the gateway underneath and take the staircase up to the first floor. It's worth discovering, as the Gujarati shopkeepers who eat there almost daily will tell you. It offers one of the tastiest all-you-can-eat Gujarati thalis in the city.

Lower Parel, Phoenix Mills

Indian

Kebabs & Kurries
ITC Hotel Grand Central Sheraton & Towers, Dr Babasaheb Ambedkar Road, Parel (2410-1010). Lower Parel station. **Open** 12.30-2.45pm, 7.30-11.45pm daily. **Main courses** Rs 450-Rs 1,450. **Credit** AmEx, MC, V.

Sushegad Gomantak.

This sprawling five-star hotel restaurant decked out in light stone and dark wood serves a wide range of Indian cuisines. Choose from Punjabi, Mughlai, Hyderabadi and Keralaite dishes, and more, all of which are usually perfect. Try the rich and tender *murgh aloo qaliya* – chicken and potato in a spicy sauce – and skip the rice for the soft, napkin-sized roomali rotis. There are extensive vegetarian options.

International

Monza
Phoenix Mills, Garden Court Block 16, opposite Quorum, Senapati Bapat Marg, Lower Parel (2495-4852). Lower Parel station. **Open** 12.30-3.30pm, 6.30pm-midnight daily. **Main courses** Rs 250-Rs 400. **Credit** MC, V.
An innovative restaurant, unpretentious but chic, with a stunning decor of black-and-white with copper accents. Try the crêpes stuffed with wasabi-flavoured cottage cheese topped with tomato coulis (Rs 125) – truly excellent. Chicken bruschetta with olives, mushrooms and cheese (Rs 150) arrives on warm, crispy bread and the barbecue chicken wings (Rs 150) are juicy, tasty and basil-topped.

Dadar & Mahim

Indian

Pritam da Dhaba
Hotel Midtown Pritam, Dharamputa, Pritam Estates, Swami Narayan Mandir Road, Dadar (E) (2414-5555). Dadar station. **Open** 11am-midnight daily. **Main courses** Rs 140-Rs 160. **Credit** AmEx, MC, V.
Your *dal makhani* is served in a copper bowl by a waiter clad in a *pathani* suit. You recline on a *charpoy* under open skies as you dine to the thump of *bhangra*. And isn't that a tiger lurking over there, lured by the aroma of your chicken tikka? Don't worry, it's just painted on the walls, along with a perfect pastoral Punjab. Pritam da Dhaba's misty-eyed vision of the motherland may be rose-tinted, but it's fun and the food is gorgeous. Be sure to get a table in the open-air courtyard.

Sindhudurg
Sita, RK Vaidya Road, Dadar (W) (2430-1610). Dadar station. **Open** 11.30am-3.30pm, 7-11.30pm daily. **Main courses** Rs 200-Rs 250. **Credit** MC, V.

This multi-storey, wood-panelled restaurant is an excellent place to experiment with the simple but delicious Malvani-style cuisine, in relative comfort. The basics to order are the prawn, fish and shellfish curries, but the fish biryani, prawn pulao and chicken curry are also good. Ask for seasonal specialities like fried fish roe (*gaboli*) and ask them to make their special flatbreads: *jowari* or *nachni bakhri*. Hearty and healthy bread.

Sushegad Gomantak
Shop No A11, Shiv Sagar Society, opposite Paradise Cinema, Mahim (2444-5555). Mahim station. **Open** 12.30-3.30pm, 7.30pm-midnight daily. **Main courses** around Rs 125. **No credit cards**.
Sushegad serves 'Gomantak' or Hindu Goan cooking as opposed to Catholic Goan cuisine. It's just as preoccupied with fish and rice but with unique masalas. Sushegad breaks out of the pom-fret-rawas-surmai trinity of fishes that most restaurants offer, serving up less famous but no less tasty fish like *mori* (shark), *bhingi* (a kind of bony herring), *tarlya* (sardines), *dhodiyare* (mullet) and *verlya* (similar to whitebait).

International

Tamnak Thai
274 Veer Savarkar Marg, Shivaji Park, Dadar (W) (2447-4646). Dadar station. **Open** noon-3.30pm, 7pm-12.30am daily. **Main courses** Rs 120-Rs 450. **Credit** MC, V.
Tamnak Thai seems to be one of the city's best-kept secrets, despite thousands of motorists passing it every day on their way to and from South Mumbai. That makes Tamnak Thai perfect for a quiet dinner. Authenticity is ensured by a chef from Bangkok and fresh ingredients imported from Thailand and Dubai. Consistently perfect.

Bandra & Khar

Indian

Papa Pancho da Dhaba
Shop No 12, Gaspar Enclave, Dr Ambedkar Road, Bandra (W) (2651-8732). Bandra station. **Taxi** Pali Hill Gold's Gym. **Open** noon-1am daily. **Main courses** Rs 150-Rs 250. **Credit** MC, V. **Map** p249 B4 ⑤⑥
The decor is resolutely rustic: the holes in the plasterwork are fake, the sky is painted on the ceiling and the parrots are plastic. It's a city dweller's idea of rural charm, turned into kitsch. Modelled on a dying breed of Punjabi roadside inns called *dhabas*, Papa Pancho serves up classic, tasty Punjabi nosh like butter chicken, dal makhani and the inevitable chicken tikka. By the way, the restaurant's name is a bit naughty – *pancho* sounds a little like *behenchut*, which is a grievous insult relating to the private parts of a gentleman's sister.

International

Lemon Grass Café
Carlton Court, Turner Road-Pali Road Junction, Bandra (W) (2643-2519/2642-6053). Bandra station. **Taxi** HSBC Bank on Turner Road. **Open** noon-4pm, 7pm-midnight daily. **Main courses** Rs 200-Rs 300. **Credit** MC, V. **Map** p249 B4 ⓗ

Highly popular pan-Asian restaurant in a fashionable part of Bandra, with an emphasis on Thai and Indonesian dishes. It's small but perfectly formed with a lamp-lit entrance and a small fountain. The menu includes an excellent Burmese *khaosuay* and an array of tasty satays. It's consistently good, elevated to greatness by some fabulous mixed fresh fruit drinks like a strawberry and pink guava crush and a kiwi and green mango crush.

Olive Bar & Kitchen
4 Union Park, near Pali Hill Tourist Hotel, Khar (W) (2605-8228). Khar station. **Taxi** Café Coffee Day, Khar Danda Road. **Open** 8pm-1.30am Mon-Sat, 12.30-3.30pm, 8pm-1.30am Sun. **Main courses** Rs 300-Rs 700. **Credit** AmEx, DC, MC, V. **Map** p249 A1 ⓗ

A super restaurant-cum-bar serving top quality Italian cuisine for an endless stream of Bandra models and hipsters. The salads, pastas and risottos are all excellent, as are the funky cocktails. Nights are lively, Sunday brunches are lazy – especially in the coolly-lit outside dining area. Calling ahead for directions and a booking is recommended. **Photo** *p103*.

Pot Pourri
4 Carlton Court, Turner Road-Pali Road Junction, Bandra (W) (2642-9193). Bandra station. **Open** noon-12.15am daily. **Main courses** Rs 190-Rs 250. **Credit** MC, V. **Map** p249 B4 ⓗ

Buy an ancient *New Yorker* from the eclectic newsstand outside and stroll onto Pot Pourri's open-air veranda for a cappuccino and cake, or some well-prepared, well-presented food, from burgers to pastas to their signature chicken stroganoff. The desserts are great. This highly popular lunch and evening eatery was one of the first to capture the mood of modern Bandra – hip, young, with new money to burn. The noisy, auto-rickshaw-choked junction by the veranda is part of the package, unfortunately.

Seijo & the Souldish
206 Krystal, Waterfield Road, Bandra (2640-5555). Bandra station. **Open** 7pm-1am Mon-Sat; noon-4pm, 7pm-1am Sun. **Credit** AmEx, DC, MC, V. **Map** p249 D4 ⓗ

Seijo is 10,000 sq ft of Thailand-meets-Japan via New York's East Village, and one of Bandra's more atmospheric pan-Asian restaurants. Its tall glass walls are offset by winding wrought-iron tubes and dark wooden walkways, all beneath a high, retractable ceiling for open-air dining. It looks stunning, with sprawling idols, candles, even a mini- waterfall. The menu doesn't stray too far from the pan-Asian staples – a bit of sushi, some Thai curries and plenty of noodles, but they're competently done, especially the steamed mussels in Thai coconut sauce.

Zenzi
183 Waterfield Road, Bandra (W) (6643-0670/ www.zenzi-india.com). Bandra station. **Open** 9.30am-1.30am daily. **Main courses** Rs 350-Rs 400. **Credit** MC, V. **Map** p249 D3 ⓗ

Enter through a laid-back reception area of low-slung couches. Bear left for the open-air bar, right for the air-conditioned restaurant, with the two divided by glass partitions. It's smart and it's cool and subtly lit with floor lighters, pin spots and candles. Zenzi offers 'world cuisine' including Italian, Malaysian, Japanese and Spanish. And it works. As midnight nears and the tables are cleared, the music comes to the fore as Zenzi turns into its other avatar – a lounge bar (*see p109*).

Juhu

International

Bohemia
5 Juhu Tara Road, opposite Juhu Church, Juhu (2610-1845). Vile Parle station. **Taxi** Prithvi Theatre. **Open** 11.30am-3.30pm, 7.30-11.30pm daily. **Main courses** Rs 350-Rs 750. **Credit** AmEx, DC, MC, V.

With its 20 ornate chandeliers, you might at first mistake Bohemia for a light fixtures showroom but actually it's a very smart, classy Euro-eatery with a focus on Italian and French cuisine, and a hotspot for Juhu's endless supply of models, actors and celebs. The dishes are uniformly excellent, in particular the delicious port-poached tenderloin with scallion mash and apple.

Don Giovanni
Hotel Bawa Continental, Juhu Tara Road, Juhu (2615-3125/www.dongiovanniristorante.com). Vile Parle station. **Open** 12.30-2.45pm, 7.30pm-11.45pm daily. **Main courses** Rs 500. **Credit** MC, V.

The unofficial 'Italian Embassy in Juhu', run by a former restaurateur from Milan who came to Mumbai to work for a textile company, only to get itchy for the thrill of serving really outstanding food. Chef Giovanni Federico painstakingly trained up a novice Indian crew to create the city's best-value Italian restaurant, aiming for the kind of rustic cooking you'd get in family-run trattorias, except it's all vegetarian. His signature dish, the ravioli di magro, is just brilliant.

Monza.

Temple Flower

Kings International Hotel, 5 Juhu Tara Road, Juhu (6692-2222). Vile Parle Station. **Taxi** Prithvi Theatre. **Open** 11.30am-3.30pm, 7.30pm-12.30am daily. **Main courses** Rs 150-Rs 250. **Credit** AmEx, MC, V.

The menu roams freely across borders but Temple Flower's heart lies in Thailand and Indonesia. The basics are done simply but supremely well – try the richly flavoured Thai yellow curry with prawns. Although modestly sized, it's a good-looking place, with slate floors and lots of dark, chocolatey wood.

Cafés

Prithvi Theatre Café

Prithvi Theatre, Janki Kutir, Juhu Church Road, Juhu (2614-9546). Vile Parle station. **Open** 12.30pm-midnight daily. **Credit** MC, V. **Main courses** Rs 150. MC V.

One of the greatest attractions of Prithvi Theatre, a cozy performance space in the heart of busy Juhu, is its laid-back café. Here pretty orange lamps are as ubiquitous as the small-time film and television stars that like to be seen lounging on the café's bamboo and granite furniture. A perfect place to spend a balmy evening sipping Irish coffee and munching on chocolate brownies, the most popular items on the menu.

Andheri & around the airport

Indian

Peshawri

ITC Grand Maratha Sheraton, near the International Airport (2830-3030). Andheri station. **Open** 7.30pm-11.45pm daily. **Main courses** Rs 400-Rs 500. **Credit** AmEx, DC, MC, V.

The single best import into Mumbai from the North West Frontier Province, Peshawri at the ITC Grand Maratha Sheraton makes the sort of food that connoisseurs across the world fawn over. Food here is prepared authentically (and visibly, in a glass-encased kitchen) in tandoors and gigantic bubbling vats. Kebabs are tender and juicy, rotis soft and crisp and the world-famous dal

Henry Tham's. *See p93.*

Bukhara (now also sold in a ready-to-eat format in branded cans) is cooked just as it should be: overnight, with lots of cream and the subtlest of seasoning. Book in advance.

Rice Boat

Aram Nagar 2, JP Road, Versova, Andheri (W) (2633-6688/2632-6688). Andheri station. **Open** noon-3.30pm, 7pm-midnight daily. **Main courses** Rs 100-Rs 175. **Credit** AmEx, MC, V.

Duck under the shiny temple bell on a chain by the entrance and pretend you're in Kerala. Rice Boat offers a tour of Kerala cuisine, with dishes unique to the state's Syrian Christian community, like *kozhi varuthathu* (tender chunks of chicken roasted on bamboo skewers) as well as more familiar Keralite dishes like *Travancore konju vechathu* – a prawn curry with coconut and garam masala. A must-try is the *aatirachi peralan* – tender mutton and raw banana. If you can, book a table on the terrace or try the upstairs room with a coconut thatch ceiling – Kerala houseboat-style.

International

Celini

Grand Hyatt, Kalina, Andheri (W) (6676-1234). Andheri station. **Open** 12.30-2.45pm, 7.30-11.45pm daily. **Main courses** Rs 400. **Credit** AmEx, DC, MC, V.

This is where to go for the perfect pizza: thin and crisp, with toppings of Italian cheese, fresh vegetables and quality meats. Celini's open kitchen and wood and glass interiors make it contemporary and casual, with a kitchen philosophy focussed on home-style cooking. Don't miss the gorgeous pannacotta.

Pan Asian

ITC Grand Maratha Sheraton Hotels and Towers, International Airport Road, Andheri (E) (2830-3030). Andheri station. **Open** 12.30pm-2.45pm, 7.30pm-11.45pm daily. **Main courses** Rs 150-Rs 250. **Credit** AmEx, MC, V.

A sprawling, gorgeous restaurant and possibly the big daddy of Mumbai's pandemic of pan-Asian restaurants, with no less than five separate kitchens dedicated to different cuisines, including Mongolian, Chinese, Japanese, Thai and Korean. It's also unique in offering tables with built-in grills for authentic Korean barbecues. The Cantonese roasted chicken is a particular treat.

Stax

Hyatt Regency Mumbai, International Airport Road, Andheri (E) (6696-1234). Andheri station. **Open** 7pm-11.30pm daily. **Main courses** Rs 700-Rs 1,000. **Credit** AmEx, MC, V.

Stax deftly combines modern steel-and-glass design with touches straight out of an Italian trattoria, with a live kitchen festooned and a soundtrack of 1960s and '70s Italian hits. The food is top-quality, with a stunning signature dish of seabass and leek fondue in Sicilian sauce and a gorgeous rack of lamb encrusted with pistachios in a bitter chocolate sauce.

Pubs & Bars

There's more to going out in Mumbai than Kingfisher.

The older generation of Mumbai's middle classes may fret about the damage alcohol is doing to the morals, as well as the livers, of 'the youth', but there's no doubt that boozing is in Mumbai's blood. It's packed with bars catering to every level of the social strata: cheap and cheerless 'country liquor' bars (*see p116* **How the other half drinks**) for the very poorest; working-class dives like Café Oval (*see p113*); lively office-worker and college kid hangouts like Gokul (*see p111*); and expensive cocktail bars like Indigo (*see p113*) for the elite. Except in country liquor bars the most popular drink is lager (always sold in 330ml bottles called 'pints', or 650ml bottles). The most famous lager is the ubiquitous Kingfisher, but there's a lot more choice out there, and arguably tastier beers; Castle, Haywards 2000, Amstel and Royal Challenge are alternatives. Cocktails have become hugely popular in recent years, but the default drink for all ages remains the venerable whisky-soda.

A class and sex distinction persists in the city's drinking culture: working-class bars are exclusively male. Women from the upper-middle and elite classes frequent more expensive bars, where it is considered acceptable for women to drink; but in the main, a woman who drinks alcohol is considered immoral. The first years of the new century have seen a growth in the number of new bars opening to soak up Mumbaikars' increasing disposable income, but an uncomfortable tension between boozers and moral guardians persists and the city's pubbing scene remains limited. The Mumbai media, especially the *Times of India*'s page 3 (*see p25* **The other page 3**) loves to bask in the reflected glamour of the city's bar-hoppers and clubbers, but it's something of a fantasy. *Time Out Mumbai* estimates that on an average Saturday night only around 5,000 women will be out in the city's bars and clubs. Mumbai's population is about 13 million.

For the time being, the upper hand belongs to the moral majority. An entire subculture of Mumbai's nightlife known as the 'dance bar' – in which young, sari-clad girls dance to Bollywood numbers, while inebriated patrons frittered currency notes over their heads – was outlawed in 2005. The move forced over 70,000 young women out of a relatively safe and well-paid profession. The ban was reversed by a high court judgement in April 2006, but many of the bars

The best Bars

For stunning city views
Starlit Café (*see p113*); **The Dome** (*see p113*); **11 Echoes** (*see p116*).

For rubbing shoulders with Bollywood beauties
Olive Bar & Kitchen (*see p115*); **Vie Lounge & Deck** (*see p116*).

For the finest cocktails
Bohemia (*see p115*); **Busaba** (*see p111*); **Taxi** (*see p113*).

For the liveliest nights out
Café Mondegar (*see p111*); **Hawaiian Shack** (*see p114*).

For the best live music
Not Just Jazz by the Bay (*see p114*); **Henry Tham's** (*see p111*); **Zenzi** (*see p115*).

had already changed businesses. In February 2006, over 20 of the city's most popular bars were shut in a crackdown over licence irregularities that was driven, in part, by moral concerns.

DOS AND DON'TS
In country liquor bars or working-class haunts, female drinkers – especially foreigners – are likely to be the target of uncomfortable stares or unwelcome attention, so, with a couple of clearly stated exceptions, we've avoided listing them. We've divided bars and clubs on the basis of whether they have a dancefloor or not; for club listings, *see pp157-162*. By law bars are required to close by 1.30am, unless they have special permission to open later or, more frequently, have paid bribes to the local police. Expect to pay the equivalent of western prices at five-star hotel bars and the top cocktail bars, where a 20 per cent sales tax will be added to your bill. Most bars have table service; it's rare

> ❶ Pink numbers given in this chapter correspond to the location of each pub and bar as marked on the street maps. *See pp249-255.*

SERVED IN ALL

LEADING RESTAURANTS

ACROSS INDIA.

AND IN 69 OTHER COUNTRIES.

Made in India from the world's finest grape varietals like Chardonnay, Cabernet Sauvignon, Chenin Blanc, Merlot, Sauvignon Blanc, Shiraz & White Zinfandel, Chantilli goes well with foods of all sorts. Continental, Italian, Oriental, Mediterranean, and of course, Indian. No wonder, Chantilli is a highly sought after wine in 69 countries across the globe.

WINNER OF
THREE BRONZE MEDALS
AT THE INTERNATIONAL
WINE AND SPIRIT
COMPETITION.

CHANTILLI
Loves food as much as you do

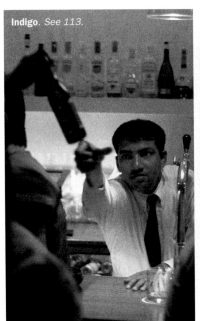

Indigo. *See 113.*

Ghetto.
See p114.

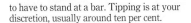

to have to stand at a bar. Tipping is at your discretion, usually around ten per cent.

Colaba

Busaba
4 Mandlik Road, off Colaba Causeway, Colaba (2204-3779/3769). Churchgate/CST stations.
Taxi behind Taj Mahal Hotel. **Open** Noon-3pm, 7pm-1.30am daily. **Credit** AmEx, MC, V. **Map** p251 G5 ❶
Busaba does better cocktails than Indigo next door and they're cheaper. Breeze through the little ante-lounge to the small bar beyond, with sultry red walls, chinoiserie love seats, drapes and the dim glow of table lamps and flickery tea candles. It's a sort of Suzy Wong boudoir look. The adventurous should opt for a www.blowout – a mix of vodka, tequila, tabasco and a whiff of aniseed. But don't come crying to us with your sore head afterwards.

Café Mondegar
Colaba Causeway, Colaba (2202-0591). Churchgate/ CST stations. **Taxi** Regal Cinema. **Open** 8am-midnight daily. **Credit** MC, V. **Map** p251 G5 ❷
It's always ten degrees hotter inside Mondy's than outside. It must be all the bodies they cram in: four to each checker cloth-covered table and as many tables wedged in as possible. The ear-splitting chatter from college students, foreign travellers and office workers competes with a chunky Wurlitzer-type jukebox at the back, where Floyd and the Doors

seem to be on permanent rotation. The cute wall murals by Goan caricaturist Mario Miranda make this a local landmark.

Gokul
Nawaz Building, 10 Tulloch Road, off Colaba Causeway (2284-8503). Churchgate/CST stations.
Open 11am-1am daily. **No credit cards**.
Map p251 G5 ❸
Once a haven for the city's gay community, these days the crowd at Gokul is far less easy to bracket – an easy-going mix of foreign travellers, students, office workers and habitual drunks. It's a dim back-room haunt attached to a budget dining hall, where the air is permanently fugged with cigarette smoke. Spirits come in bottles with names we've never heard of, but the beer's safe and cold.

Henry Tham's
Dhanraj Mahal, Apollo Bunder, Colaba (2202-3186/ 2284-8214). Churchgate/CST stations. **Taxi** Regal Cinema. **Open** 1-3.30pm, 7.30pm-1.30am daily.
Credit AmEx, MC, V. **Map** p251 G5 ❹
Amid the plant pots and warm black, brown and beige decor of this sweet and petite lounge bar sits an automated massage chair. Grab your kiwi Margarita, recline, and get a 15-minute massage. Cosy and laid-back, Henry Tham's is one of the few Colaba venues holding a regular Friday night live music event. The energy levels of the wealthy twenty- and thirtysomething South Mumbai crowd really bump up around midnight.

Eat, Drink, Shop

THE WORLD'S YOUR OYSTER

Indigo

4 Mandlik Road, off Colaba Causeway, Colaba. (6636-8999). Churchgate/CST stations. **Taxi** behind Taj Mahal Hotel. **Open** 12.30-3pm, 6.30pm-1.30am daily. **Credit** AmEx, DC, MC, V. **Map** p251 G5 **5**
South Mumbai's premier watering hole for the well-heeled, Indigo is pretty much an institution. On weekends it's packed wall-to-wall with strutting girls in strapless, backless dresses, and their pumped-up boys in print shirts. Nobody gets too comfortable as seating is limited, and the ambience is chic hotel lobby. After 11pm, the crush can make a rush-hour local train seem positively roomy, so head for the upstairs lounge, or, even better, the beautiful, candlelit terrace.

Leopold's Café

Colaba Causeway, Colaba (2202-0131). Churchgate/ CST stations. **Taxi** near Electric House. **Open** 7am-1am daily. **Credit** AmEx, MC, V. **Map** p251 G5 **6**
The default drinking destination for foreign travellers. Established in 1871, Leo's is undeniably appealing, with arcaded doors that open on to the street, a high ceiling with indolently whirring fans and a general similarity to a grand old railway station waiting room. The fruit juices are fresh and the beers cold (though not as chilled as those served in the dark and arctic 'couples' bar upstairs). Shame about the surly service.

Sports Bar

Regal Cinema Building, Shahid Bhagat Singh Road, Colaba (6639-6684). Churchgate/CST stations. **Taxi** Regal Cinema. **Open** noon-1.30am daily. **Credit** MC, V. **Map** p251 G5 **7**
This Mumbai bar chain has all the required trappings: plasma monitors tuned to the cricket, a couple of basketball hoops, a pool table, a huge poster of Sugar Ray Robinson delivering a KO, diner-style booths and masala peanuts for Rs 65. And the college kids just love the '80s rock soundtrack.

Starlit Café

Hotel Harbour View, Apollo Bunder, Colaba (2282-1089). Churchgate/CST stations. **Taxi** Radio Club. **Open** 24 hrs daily. **Credit** MC, V. **Map** p250 G4 **8**
An open-air rooftop bar with a stunning view of the harbour and the Gateway of India. It never closes, thanks to some creative negotiation with the local cops. The only drinks are beers and Bacardi Breezers, but the mood is so relaxed that it's not uncommon for wasted patrons to stagger from table to table baring their souls.

Taxi

Jony Castle Building, Khatau Road, off Wodehouse Road, Colaba (2218-4904). **Taxi** Colaba Post Office. **Open** 12.30-2.45pm, 7pm-1.30am daily. **Credit** AmEx, MC, V. **Map** p250 E3 **9**
With its 20-foot-high ceilings, stucco walls bathed in dim gold light, towering candle-stands, and copper-topped bar, Taxi feels like a Gothic dungeon, albeit a swanky, sensual one that serves great cocktails. Expect plenty of posing and scoping after 10pm, when it fills up with upstart fashionistas, and bankers with their trophy wives.

Why dry?

On election days and other special occasions known as 'dry days', bars are forbidden to serve alcohol, usually out of respect for the occasion. Even the days when votes are being counted are 'dry', making India's tortuously long general elections a nightmare for those of us who like a tipple. By law, foreigners are exempt from the ban, but many bars just stop serving alcohol altogether. Most five-star hotel bars will continue to serve alcohol to foreigners on production of a passport (a non-Indian complexion will usually do).

26 January Republic Day
30 January anniversary of Gandhi's death
1 May Maharashtra Day
15 August Independence Day
August-September Ananta Chaturdashi and Gauri Visarjan (Ganesh celebrations)
2 October Gandhi Jayanti (Gandhi's birthday)
8-15 October Gandhi Week

Churchgate

Café Oval

Eros Cinema, Churchgate (6634-5721). Churchgate station. **Open** 9am-11pm daily. **No credit cards.** **Map** p251 & p252 F8 **10**
This tiny, Irani-run bar opposite the Oval Maidan is bare and spare but has its own 1940s-style Bombay charm, with the waiters sliding onto the old wooden benches to chat with regulars – mostly working-class gents and Parsi old-timers. Its no-frills philosophy is inscribed on an ancient sign below the television: 'No TV channel choice'. Be aware, this is an exclusively male hangout.

Czar Bar

Intercontinental, 135 Marine Drive (6639-9999/ www.intercontinental.com). Churchgate station. **Open** 6.30pm-1.30am daily. **Credit** AmEx, DC, MC, V. **Map** p251 & p252 E8 **11**
Three sparkling chandeliers and a gold, black purple colour scheme aim for a Russian reg~ at Mumbai's only vodka bar. It's all vodka here; try the test-tube shots caviar on a bed of ice. Shame abou~ soundtrack.

Dome

Intercontinental, 135 Mo~ www.intercontinental.~ **Open** 6pm-12.30am da~ **Map** p251 & p252 E8 **12**

Eat, Drink, Shop

Dome. *See p113.*

Undoubtedly South Mumbai's finest hotel bar, accessible to the public. It's a bar/grill occupying the Intercontinental's eighth-floor rooftop terrace, overlooking the fabulous arc of the seafront promenade. Walls are white, the tiled floor is white and the abundant sofas and armchairs are all wrapped in white cotton. A raised platform holds the aqua-blue swimming pool, while a corner rotunda houses a sleek aluminium-and-glass bar counter with matching stools. It's totally Miami. Be sure to drop in before 6.30pm for the glorious pink-orange sunset.

Not Just Jazz by the Bay
Soona Mahal, 143 Marine Drive (2285-1876). Churchgate station. **Open** 12.15-3.15pm, 6pm-1.30am daily. **Credit** AmEx, DC, MC, V. **Map** p251/2 E8 ⑬
Locally known simply as 'Jazz', this sole survivor of Bombay's '50s jazz era is among the handful of live music options left in the city. Wednesdays, Thursdays, Fridays and Saturdays (entrance fee Rs 200) draw the thirty- and fortysomething crowd for bands usually dishing out jazz, country and rock; Sundays, Mondays and Tuesdays are reserved for the wildly popular karaoke nights (entrance fee Rs 150), for students and young professionals seeking therapy on stage.

Opera House

Karma
534 SVP Road, Opera House (2361-7171). Charni Road station. **Taxi** Sukh Sagar Restaurant. **Open** noon-1.30am daily. **Credit** AmEx, MC, V. **Map** p254 B15 ⑭
With its diffused red lighting, soft leather sofas, beanbags and tea lights on the tables, the vibe at Karma is relaxed enough to get buttoned-up Gujarati families in for dinner at 7.30pm, noisy college kids in ...0pm and even the occasional gaybombay.org ...g (*see p146*). Tasty snacks and decent cocktails ...to the appeal.

Breach Candy

Ghetto
30B Bhulabhai Desai Road, near Mahalaxmi Temple, Breach Candy (2353-8418). Mahalaxmi station. **Taxi** Mahalaxmi Temple. **Open** 7pm-1.15am daily. **Credit** MC, V.
This smoky rocker's cove has been boozing for 12 years, making it the city's oldest existing bar, with a fanatical band of regulars permanently fixed to its barstools. The college pub-like atmosphere has walls with graffiti and Jim Morrison murals and is illuminated by UV tube-lights. Expect an obligatory '80s rock soundtrack. **Photo** *p111.*

Lower Parel

Lush Lounge & Grille
Phoenix Mills Compound, 462 Senapati Bapat Marg, Lower Parel (6663-4601). Lower Parel station. **Open** 6pm-1.30am daily. **Credit** AmEx, MC, V.
Lush is the great middle ground: it brings the upscale Bandra and Colaba crowds onto neutral territory, hence the crowds. It isn't a nightclub but it's not just a bar, with a stark industrial look and a DJ spinning hip hop, house, pop and Bollywood tunes. For a few inches of personal space, push your way either to the discreet upper section or to the back end of the long bar, the one the waiters set on fire for fun.

Bandra

Hawaiian Shack
16th Road, Bandra (W) (2604-1749). Bandra station. **Taxi** opposite Mini Punjab. **Open** 6.30pm-2am daily. **Credit** MC, V. **Map** p249 C3 ⑮
What makes Hawaiian Shack Bandra's most popular pub? Is it the outstanding service? The resemblance to the inside of an old wooden ship? Or could

Eat, Drink, Shop

it be that a large number of Mumbaikars still think the 1980s had the best pop music? In any other country, a bar that played so much Madonna and Boney M would surely be a gay joint, but this is India, where the two men holding hands or dancing together next to your table are probably just good friends.

Olive Bar & Kitchen

4 Union Park, near Pali Hill Tourist Hotel, Khar (W) (2605-8228). Khar station. **Taxi** Café Coffee Day, Khar Danda Road. **Open** 8pm-1.30am daily. **Credit** AmEx, DC, MC, V. **Map** p249 A1 ⑯
Bandra's swishest spot for those who want to see and be seen, packed to the gills with models, actors and Bandra's rich and shameless. The Pulitzer prize-nominated author of *Maximum City*, Suketu Mehta, maintains that on Thursday nights the most beautiful women in Mumbai come to Olive. Pretty faces and Pilates-toned bodies certainly abound, but one regular patron calls Olive a gay bar and 'one of the best places in the city to pick up men'. Then again, his female friends seem to agree. This place can be tricky to find, so call ahead for directions.

Seijo & the Souldish

206 Krystal, Waterfield Road, Bandra (W) (2640-5555). Bandra station. **Open** 7.30pm-1.30am daily. **Credit** AmEx, MC, V. **Map** p249 D4 ⑰
Aimed at the professional 30-and-up crowd, Seijo (pronounced say-joe) looks like a bar in New York's East Village. Red and black hues, a 20-foot aquarium inhabited by shark and catfish, and Japanese pop art splashed up against sunken panels lend a Tokyo-meets-Manhattan edge. Tasty cocktails and some of the city's best live music help elevate Seijo into Bandra's top ranks.

Temptation

Hotel Metro Palace, 355 Ramdas Nayak Marg, Bandra (W) (2642-7311). Bandra station. **Open** noon-midnight daily. **Credit** AmEx, MC ,V. **Map** p249 D5 ⑱
This faux-tavern's tag-line, 'the devil's alternative', doesn't really go with the warm dark blue decor, but the music does – the jukebox is permanently stuck on death metal. But aside from the smattering of long-haired metalheads, the crowd is mostly made up of working twentysomethings. Temptation scores points simply for being different (read: for not playing Bryan Adams).

Toto's Garage

30 Lord's Heaven, Pali Junction, Bandra (W) (2600-5494). Bandra station. **Open** 6pm-1.30am daily. **Credit** AmEx, MC, V. **Map** p249 C3 ⑲
Engine parts, hubcaps and number plates emblazon the walls of Toto's Garage. One of the city's most popular watering holes with office workers and students, with an air as casual as the waiters' denim overalls. The playlist segues from the Doors to Duran Duran to Ramstein without an eyebrow being raised. It's super cheap, too – a beer pitcher costs just Rs 220. Once you're done here, pop across the road to Pan Palace for a pan masala (*see p100* **Pan handling**).

Zenzi

183 Waterfield Road, Bandra (W) (6643-0670/www.zenzi-india.com). Bandra station. **Open** 11.30am-1.30am daily. **Credit** MC, V. **Map** p249 D3 ⑳
This gorgeous bar/restaurant is a perennial upmarket Bandra favourite. It extends deeply off the street into a long bar/dining area split by glass, and decked out in natural woods lit by candlelight. Even better, the city's best bands play here on Thursday nights, with top DJs spinning strictly non-commercial sounds the rest of the week.

Juhu

Bohemia

5 Juhu Tara Road, Juhu (2610-1845). Vile Parle station. **Taxi** Prithvi Theatre. **Open** 7.30am-1.30am daily. **Credit** AmEx, MC, V.

11 Echoes. *See p116.*

Toto's Garage.

Bohemia offers welcome relief from the rickshaw gridlock on Juhu's main strip, with a dark bar section lit by soothing blue and purple spots and a spartan, candlelit lounge. Bohemia's drinks menu is a revelation, featuring a comprehensive list of cocktails and lesser-spotted aperitifs like Pernod. The DJs promise to spin 'no Hindi, only house'.

11 Echoes

Opposite Palm Grove, Juhu Tara Road, Juhu (2618-4040). Santa Cruz station. **Open** 7pm-1.30am daily. **Credit** AmEx, MC, V.

This vintage bungalow opposite the beach has been made over into a lounge bar (what else, in this town?), with great care to retain the charm of the original structure. The results are spectacular. The open-air courtyard is lit to perfection by soothing orange lanterns and lined with tables illuminated by flickering candles. Best of all is the terrace, where patrons sip on stellar cocktails and gaze on to Juhu beach. **Photo** *p115.*

Vie Lounge & Deck

102 Juhu Tara Road, Juhu (2660-3003). Santa Cruz station. **Taxi** opposite Little Italy restaurant. **Open** 8pm-1.30am daily. **Credit** AmEx, DC, MC, V.

One of the city's premier page 3 celeb hangouts and a popular party destination for the Bollywood elite and wannabes alike. Vie's location, right on Juhu Beach, is a killer for a start, but the design really makes the most of it. Sloping glass planes intersect with gnarly palms and the luminescent back-lit panels of the open-air deck glow under starlit skies. Providing you can get in (the place is all too often reserved for private parties), there is absolutely no finer place for a fruit cocktail than leaning against the railings high above the sand, watching the landing lights of incoming aeroplanes slither across the silvery waves. It's set back a little from the road and can be tricky to find, so it's best to call ahead for directions.

How the other half drinks

Desi daru (literally 'country liquor') is the drink of choice for Mumbai's working classes, served at the city's 300 licensed country liquor bars – many of which are clustered around Dhobi Talao – for as little as Rs 20 a quarter-pint. *Desi daru* is a clear spirit made from molasses infused with essences like narangi (orange), mosambi (sweet lime) and santra (a kind of mandarin orange) and referred to by these names. It's usually drunk neat or mixed with water.

The bars are male-dominated, no-frills establishments with a few benches and tables in a stark room, with a television blaring songs in the background. Patrons are mostly menial workers and lower-level office staff, with each clique having its own drinking rituals. A labourer will usually top up his glass with liquor, dip a forefinger into the glass, splash two drops onto the floor, down the booze at one go, then sprinkle some salt on his tongue.

It's true that *desi daru* is not the most sophisticated or tasty drink in the world – its main appeal is that it sells for about half the price of other spirits – but that's not the only reason it's avoided by Mumbaikars higher up the social scale. The common myth is that it is extremely potent and that a couple of glasses will render you incapable; in fact, it's about 75 per cent proof, the same as most spirits.

Desi daru is also often confused with the illicit but cheaper 'hooch' that's manufactured

Country living, Mumbai style.

in forests outside the city and in fishing villages like Khar-Danda. Hooch (sometimes called 'snake juice') can be fatal: in December 2004 a batch containing methanol claimed 91 lives in Vikhroli, just a few days after another batch killed 20 people in Mahalaxmi. But *desi daru* is legal, regulated and safe. It's available at bars and liquor stores for about Rs 25 per 180ml. If you're feeling brave, try Devkar Distilleries' Lucky No 1 Santra Punch or VK Distilleries' Super Lemon Punch.

Shops & Services

Don't forget to haggle.

Retail in Mumbai is a young but booming industry. Most locals still head straight to speciality street markets (*see p127*) for everything from kitchen utensils to silk saris to antique chandeliers. But not a day goes by without news of a new 'high-end lifestyle store' catering to the rapidly internationalised tastes of the urban middle class, which, if these stores reflect it correctly, has an unquenchable desire for Buddha statues, coffee makers and Indo-Western fusionwear.

Colaba is the hotspot for kitsch and trinkets, as well as a good offering of mid-range and expensive shops, but other areas have sprung up that are great to shop around, and also make for an interesting portrait of the city's changing socio-economics and geography. Mumbai's glamour industry lives primarily in **Bandra**, where boutique stores abound with eclectic mixes of imported jeans and T-shirts, as well as home-grown designerwear. **Lower Parel** has become a hub of activity since its dilapidated mill areas were sold to private developers and converted into prime retail and residential spaces. The outsourcing boom has also made once-sleepy **Malad** a hot shopping destination, with the city's best-looking mall, Inorbit. With Mumbai's heat, dust and crowds, you should take the phrase 'shop till you drop' a little more literally than you would at home – give yourself plenty of time and take plenty of water.

THE BASICS

Most stores open at 11am and close at 8pm. Visa and MasterCard are accepted almost everywhere, except at markets and street stalls, where cash is king. Expect some marketwallahs and street vendors to double, triple or quadruple their prices for foreigners.

Haggle in Hindi

Ye kitne ka hai? How much is this?
Aap pagle ho gaye hai kya? Have you gone crazy?
Bahut zyaada hai That's very expensive.
Theek bhao bolo Give me a fair price.
Thoda kam karna Drop the price a little.
Dhanyavaad! Thank you!

The best Shops

For fine Indian fashion
Amara (*see p119*); the **Courtyard** (*see p121*); **Fab India** (*see p123*).

For manic Mumbai markets
Chor Bazaar (*see p128*); **Crawford Market** (*see p129*); **Mangaldas Market** (*see p129*).

For jewellery
Amrapali (*see p124*); **TBZ** (*see p124*).

For glittering Indian sweets
Brijwasi (*see p125*); **Camy Wafer** (*see p125*).

For the latest Indian sounds
BX Furtado & Sons (*see p129*); **Rhythm House** (*see p130*).

Friendly but frenzied haggling is required and a few Hindi phrases may come in handy (*see below* **Haggle in Hindi**). A good rule: bargain everywhere except in air-conditioned shops.

Books

Crossword
Mohammed Bhai Mansion, Hughes Road, Kemp's Corner (2384-2001). Grant Road station. **Open** 11am-9.30pm daily. **Credit** AmEx, DC, MC, V. The flagship store of Mumbai's best-known bookstore chain also sells music and movies, toys and games, and has a great café with pastries, sandwiches and coffee. It also organises author readings, forums and children's events. Crossword has a good selection of Indian writing in English, plus mainstream international fiction.
Other locations: Noor Mahal, ground floor, Turner Road, Bandra (W) (3956-5547). Bandra station. (Taxi: near Tavaa Restaurant); Inorbit Mall, ground floor, Malad (W) (6645-0950). Malad station.

Nalanda
Taj Mahal Palace & Tower, Lobby Level, Apollo Bunder, Colaba (2202-2514). Churchgate/ CST stations. **Open** 8am-midnight daily. **Credit** AmEx, DC, MC, V. This is where to go for glossy coffee table books on Rajasthani palaces, Benarasi textiles and the Kama

Oxford Bookstore.

Sutra. Nalanda is small but has a strong India focus and a smattering of international publications.

New & Second-hand Bookstore
Near Metro Cinema, Kalbadevi (2201-3314).
Marine Lines station. **Open** 10am-7.30pm daily.
No credit cards.
Now in its 100th year, New & Second-hand Bookstore is sadly in danger of shutting shop. It's a treasure trove of collectibles, odds and ends, and out-of-prints. This one's for those who love quaint bookstores almost as much as the books themselves.

Oxford Bookstore
Apeejay House, ground floor, 3 Dinsha Vachha Road, Churchgate (6636-4477). Churchgate station.
Open 10am-10pm daily. **Credit** AmEx, DC, MC, V.
Better known in its hometown of Kolkata, Oxford Bookstore has a good selection, particularly of fiction and travel, plus handmade paper stationery and international publications, including newspapers. At the petite-but-sweet Cha Bar you can sup on delicate teas and chicken tikka wraps while you read.

Strand Book Stall
Dhannur, Sir PM Road, Fort (2263-0154/2261-4613). Churchgate/CST stations. **Open** 10am-8pm daily.
Credit AmEx, DC, MC, V.
The favourite of journalists and novelists, this city institution is tiny, and stuffed with piles and piles of assorted books. While the space is not very conducive to browsing, it does have a range of lesser-known writers and the staff let you linger as long as you like. Most important, you can't beat the prices: it offers an average discount of 20 per cent on every purchase. Stock up.

Department stores

Lifestyle
Inorbit Mall, Goregaon Malad Link Road, off SV Road, Malad (W) (6675-4275/4276). Malad station.
Open 10.30am-9.30pm daily. **Credit** AmEx, DC, MC, V.

Pantaloon
High Street Phoenix shopping mall, 462 Senapati Bapat Marg, Lower Parel (6666-4848). Lower Parel station. **Open** 11am-9pm Mon-Fri; 11am-9.30pm Sat, Sun. **Credit** AmEx, DC, MC, V.

Shoppers' Stop
211 Swami Vivekanand (SV) Road, Andheri (W) (2624-0451/0455). Andheri station. **Open** 10.30am-8.30pm daily. **Credit** AmEx, DC, MC, V.

Westside
Army & Navy Building, Kala Ghoda (6636-0499/0500). Churchgate/CST stations. **Open** 11am-9pm daily. **Credit** AmEx, DC, MC, V.
Other locations: R Mall, LBS Marg, Mulund (W). Mulund station.

Electronics

Vijay Sales
Shiv Ashish, Near Irla Bridge, SV Road, Andheri (W). Andheri station. **Taxi** opposite Bank of Maharashtra, Andheri branch (2624-8447).
Open 10.30am-8.30pm daily. **Credit** DC, MC, V.
Vijay Sales is a one-stop shop for gadgets of almost all kinds, ranging from refrigerators and television sets to iPods and mobile phones.
Other locations: 3 Bhatia Building, Zarina Co-op Society, Swami Vivekanand (SV) Road, Bandra (W) (2642-2119) Bandra station; 108 Lady Jamshedji Road, Mahim (2445-7959). Mahim station; 225 Pandurang Bhuvan, LJ Road, Shivaji Park (2430-9660). Dadar station.

Fashion

Indo-Western designerwear

Amara
Hughes Road, Kemp's Corner (2387-9687/2530). Grant Road station. **Open** 10.30am-7.30pm daily.
Credit AmEx, MC, V.
A large, ambitious project located on prime South Mumbai property selling a range of exclusive designers. Plans are afoot to open a restaurant and a spa here too.

Ananya
Shop 3, Pluto Building, Turner Road, Bandra (W) (2655-3327). Bandra station. **Taxi** near Moti Mahal Restaurant. **Open** 11am-8pm Mon-Sat. **Credit** MC, V.
A fashionista favourite, Ananya was originally started up in London by sisters Ansuya and Nandita Mahtani. Showcasing a range of high-profile Indian designers as well as its in-house label, it has some of the country's most colourful and quirky looks.
Other locations: Burani Mahal, 59 Nepean Sea Road, behind Kotak Mahindra Bank (5571-4888).

Aza
21 Altamount Road, off Pedder Road (2381-1212). Grant Road station. **Open** 10am-8pm daily.
Credit AmEx, MC, V.

Eat, Drink, Shop

Leafy green Altamount Road is better known for its famous residents (think old, old money) than its fashion quotient, but that's all changed with the recent arrival of Aza. This large store stocks a large range of up-and-coming designers from across the country. The staff are courteous, the fitting rooms roomy and alterations are done while you wait.

Barefoot

House No 30, Anand Villa, Palimala Road, Bandra (W) (3296-5067). Bandra station. **Taxi** Carter Road Police Station. **Open** 11.30am-8pm Mon-Sat. **Credit** MC, V.
Undoubtedly one of Bandra's best stores, Barefoot isn't just about shoes (although the leather slippers are fabulous). It's about funky clothing, with plenty of cool accessories and striking jewellery as well.

Be

F6 Quorum, first floor, High Street Phoenix, Block 2, 462 Senapati Bapat Marg, Lower Parel (6661-2509). Lower Parel station. **Open** 10.30am-8.30pm daily. **Credit** AmEx, DC, MC, V.
India's only chain store carrying prêt collections from designers like Priyadarshini Rao and Aki Narula. Be is packed with fusionwear for both men and women.
Other locations: Inorbit mall, Malad (2878-8811). Malad station.

Courtyard

Minoo Desai Marg, Apollo Bunder, Colaba. Churchgate/CST stations. **Open** 11am-8pm daily. **Credit** AmEx, MC, V.
This chic enclave houses a mix of designer and boutique stores that sell everything from bridalwear to gold jewellery, Aigner handbags and bar accessories. Some top designers also have stand-alone stores here, including Suneet Verma and Narendra Kumar Ahmed.

Cypress

Windward Apartments, 21st Road, Khar (W) (6646-1747). Khar station. **Taxi** off Linking Road. **Open** 2-8.30pm Mon-Sat, 11am-8.30pm Sun. **Credit** MC, V.
At 1,400 sq feet, Cypress houses prêt collections from a mix of Mumbai- and Delhi-based designers, including Sabina Singh (*see p128* **The fab three**).

Ensemble

Great Western Building, 130/132 Colaba Causeway, Colaba (2284-3227/5167). Churchgate/CST stations. **Open** 11am-8pm Mon-Sat. **Credit** AmEx, DC, MC, V.
The pioneer in Indian clothes retailing, Ensemble was the first store to stock high-profile Indian designers in a luxurious space – at mostly unattainable prices – and the Lion's Gate location still symbolises exclusivity and quality for many Mumbaikars. Ensemble currently carries big label names such as Monisha Jaisingh and Manish Malhotra and Tarun Tahiliani, who is also an owner.
Other locations: Crossroads Mall, Haji Ali (6660-3072). Mahalaxmi station.

Cotton World Corporation. *See p123.*

Ishnaa

Sagar Fortune, 184 Waterfield Road, Bandra (W) (2640-1002/1008). Bandra station. **Open** 11am-8.30pm Mon-Sat. **Credit** AmEx, MC, V.
Bandra's answer to Kimaya and Ensemble, Ishnaa stocks top Indian designers like Sabyasachi Mukherjee, Manish Malhotra and Priyadarshini Rao.

Kimaya

2 Asha Colony, Juhu Tara Road (2660-6154). Santa Cruz station. **Taxi** near Hotel Sea Princess. **Open** 11am-8pm Mon-Sat. **Credit** AmEx, MC, V.
Juhu's film crowd loves Kimaya – it saves them a trip to South Mumbai to buy all their favourite Indian designers.

Melange

33 Raj Mahal, Altamount Road (2385-4492). Grant Road station. **Open** 10am-7pm Mon-Sat. **Credit** AmEx, DC, MC, V.
This pretty store is tucked away on Altamount Road, but has a dedicated crowd of buyers that prefer more sober and grown-up clothes than those you'll find at most other boutique stores.

Mogra

10 Quorum, first floor, High Street Phoenix, 462 Senapati Bapat Marg, Lower Parel (2496-0808). Lower Parel station. **Open** 10am-8.30pm daily. **Credit** AmEx, MC, V.
Glitter and glam is the rule at Mogra, which stocks dozens of young designers, and packs stuff in tight.

OMO

204 Sagar Fortune, second floor, Waterfield Road, Bandra (W) (6698-1804). Bandra station. **Open** 11am-7.30pm Mon-Sat. **Credit** AmEx, DC, MC, V.
OMO was doing folk way before it became trendy, and it's still doing it better than most. It also has the most die-hard loyalists we've seen of any store in Bandra.

Oak Tree

18 Cusrow Baug, Colaba Causeway, Colaba (2281-9031). Churchgate/CST stations. **Open** 11am-8pm Mon-Sat. **Credit** AmEx, MC, V.
A small Colaba boutique packed with funky shoes, belts, bags, jewellery and Indo-Western clothes.

You

2 Cornelian, Kemp's Corner, 104 August Kranti Marg (2382-6972/73). Grant Road station. **Open** 10.30am-7pm Mon-Sat. **Credit** AmEx, MC, V.
Kitsch is cool at You, which stocks summer dresses, T-shirts and a changing assortment of accessories including sequinned suitcases and greeting cards stitched with miniature dresses.

Other Indian designers

Abu Jani-Sandeep Khosla

Loving Mother, Arvind House, 9 Darabsha Road, off Nepean Sea Road (2367-3401). Grant Road station. **Taxi** near St Stephen's Church. **Open** 10.30am-6.30pm daily. **Credit** AmEx, MC, V.

India's most exclusive designer duo, Abu Jani and Sandeep Khosla have dressed innumerable stars and celebrities, including creating an Oscar ceremony dress for Dame Judi Dench.

Azeem Khan

Shop No 1, Usha Sadan Building, Colaba (2215-1028/0372). Churchgate/CST stations. **Taxi** next to Colaba Post Office. **Open** 10.30am-7pm Mon-Sat. **Credit** AmEx.

Make a statement with glitter.

Manish Arora

The Courtyard, Minoo Desai Marg, Apollo Bunder, Colaba (6638-5464). Churchgate/CST stations. **Open** 11am-7.30pm daily. **Credit** AmEx, MC, V.

Designer Manish Arora recently showed at London Fashion Week with a collection that bears his signature style – gaudy colours that magically work together, over-the-top embellishments and a distinctly Mumbai feel.

Ritu Kumar

Phoenix Block 9, Annexe Phoenix Mills, 462 Senapati Bapat Marg, Lower Parel (6666-9901).

Lower Parel station. **Open** 10am-8pm daily. **Credit** AmEx, DC, MC, V.

The empress of traditional craft and colour, Kumar's creations are the kind you've seen in countless Bollywood wedding sequences.

Rohit Bal

The Courtyard, Minoo Desai Marg, Apollo Bunder, Colaba (6638-5478/5479). Churchgate/CST stations. **Taxi** near Fariyas Hotel. **Open** 11am-7pm daily. **Credit** AmEx, MC, V.

Best known for dressing India's most high-profile grooms, Bal's prêt line includes excellent shirts and Nehru-style tunics.

Satya Paul

C204/205 Crossroads Shopping Mall, 28, Pandit MM Malviya Road, Haji Ali (6660-3880). Mahalaxmi station. **Open** 11am-8pm daily. **Credit** MC, V.

Satya Paul is always doing something new with his trademark printed saris and hip ties. Both make great gifts.

Tarun Tahiliani

Villar Ville, ground floor, 16 Ramchandani Marg, Apollo Bunder, Colaba (2287-0895/2285-4603). Churchgate/CST stations. **Open** 11am-7pm Mon-Sat. **Credit** AmEx, MC, V.

India's reigning king of design, Tarun Tahiliani's been around for years and has mastered the art of sexily draping women in yards of fabric. And getting them to pay the earth for it. Also check out his range of jewelled Maharani T-shirts.

Mumbai to a tee

Kolhapuri kool

Now in heavy metal shades and with a kitten-heel, these classic sandals from Kolhapur just got a modern makeover. They're the Jack Rogers sandals of India.
Metro, 9 Metro House, Colaba Causeway (2284-8198). Churchgate/CST stations. **Open** 10.30am-10.30pm daily. **Credit** AmEx MC, V. Rs 550 and up.

Tantra mantras

With quips like 'Welcome to Bihar. Set your watch back 20 years' and a picture of a leering Rajput prince over the words 'Your palace or mine?', Tantra has tapped into local humour and slapped it across T-shirts for men, women and kids alike.

The Bombay Store (see p126).
Narisons (Khubsons),
49 Colaba Causeway, next to Leopold Café (2202-0614).
Churchgate/CST stations. **Open** 10am-8pm, Mon-Sat. **Credit** AmEx, DC, MC, V.
Rs 220 and up.

Jumbo presents

Wooden, brass, and marble elephants turned into bookends, planters and side-table ornaments. How have you lived without one?
Cottage Industries, Colaba Causeway (2281-8802).
Churchgate/CST stations.
Open 9.30am-8pm Mon-Sat; 9am-6pm Sun.
Credit AmEx, MC, V.
Rs 14,000 and up.

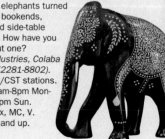

Casual

Chemistry

CR2 shopping mall, Nariman Point (6654-7966).
Churchgate station. **Open** 11am-8pm Mon-Sat.
Credit AmEx, DC, MC, V.

Chemistry's got the formula right, with good basics, such as office shirts, fun tees and occasionally denim.
Other locations: 210 Govindham, Waterfield Road, Bandra (W) (2640-6601). Bandra station.

Cotton World Corporation

201 Ram Nimi Building, Mandlik Road, Colaba
(2285-0060). Churchgate/CST stations. **Taxi** near
Indigo, behind Taj Mahal Hotel. **Open** 10.30am-8pm
Mon-Sat. **Credit** AmEx, DC, MC, V.

Mumbai's answer to the Gap, CWC has a host of basics like T-shirts, pants, capris, shorts and shirts that are perfect for the warm, humid climate. Shame there aren't more stores like this. **Photo** *p121.*
Other locations: Phoenix Mills, Lower Parel (2491-8801) Lower Parel station; Vipul Apartments, Tagore Road, Santa Cruz (W) (2605-1602) Santa Cruz station.

Fab India

137 MG Road, Kala Ghoda (2262-6539).
Churchgate/CST stations. **Open** 10am-8pm daily.
Credit AmEx, DC, MC, V.

A very popular store selling stylish, high-quality Indian casualwear – from kurtas to salwar kameez – with a wide range in cotton and silk. There's also a home furnishing section.

Other locations: Navroze, Pali Hill, Bandra (W) (2646-5286). Bandra station; Inorbit Mall, Malad (W) (6641-9989). Malad station; Nirmal Lifestyles, Mulund (W) (2591-9301). Mulund station.

Peppertree

Shop No 3, Vaidya Mansion, opposite Crossroads,
Tardeo (2494-1905). Mahalaxmi station. **Open**
11am-8pm Mon-Sat. **Credit** AmEx, DC, MC, V.

Think Goa: bright colours, tie-dye, flowing skirts, large pants and affordable prices.
Other locations: R Mall, Mulund (W) (6649-2907). Mulund station.

Men's chain stores

Color Plus

Cusrow Baug, Colaba Causeway, Colaba (2284-1821). Churchgate/CST stations. **Open** 10.30am-9pm daily. **Credit** AmEx, MC, V.

Excellent quality trousers and khakis; this is a chain of stores that says 'export quality' and means it.
Other locations: Phoenix Mills, Lower Parel (2496-4464) Lower Parel station; Shops 1 & 2, Satyam, Linking Road, Khar (W) (2648-2731) Khar station.

Millionaire

132 Damodar Mahal, Breach Candy (2382-5555/
2388-6018). Grant Road station. **Taxi** opposite
Shalimar Hotel. **Open** 11am-9pm Mon-Sat.
Credit MC, V.

Millionaire has an excellent selection of ready-to-wear versions of this classic Indian formalwear.

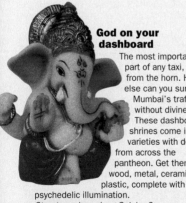

God on your dashboard

The most important part of any taxi, apart from the horn. How else can you survive Mumbai's traffic without divine help? These dashboard shrines come in all varieties with deities from across the pantheon. Get them in wood, metal, ceramic and plastic, complete with psychedelic illumination.
Street vendors along Colaba Causeway.
Rs 30 and up.

Past cards

Take back a piece of Old Bombay. Phillips Antiques has old prints, postcards and maps dating back to 1556.

Phillips Antiques,
opposite Regal Cinema,
Colaba (2202-0564).
Churchgate/CST stations.
Open 10am-7pm Mon-Sat.
Credit AmEx, MC, V. Rs 2,000 and up.

Bollywood in a bottle

Pop culture creations by Bharati Pitre appeal in terms of both aesthetics and humour. It's Andy Warhol meets Bollywood, with caricatures of Bollywood stars on bottles and cushions in all shapes and colours. The range isn't available in the shops, so give her a call.
Bharati Pitre (93255-24791). Rs 1,500 and up.

Salim Asgarally.
See p127.

Salim Asgarally.
See p127.

Raymonds

RNA House, Veer Nariman Road, Fort (2204-5912).
Churchgate station. **Open** 10.30am-8.30pm daily.
Credit AmEx, DC, MC, V.
Raymonds is one of India's best-known 'suiting'
stores, and for good reason: the staff can tailor-make
a suit in just a few days for a fraction of the price
you'd pay in Europe or the US, and the quality is
outstanding.
Other locations: 59A Bhulabhai Desai Road,
Breach Candy (2351-1644). Mahalaxmi station.

Tuscan Verve

1 Lotia Palace, Linking Road, Bandra. (2648-
0385) Bandra station. **Taxi** Khar Danda Junction.
Open 10.30am-9pm daily. **Credit** AmEx, MC, V.
Tuscan Verve shirts are as colourful, loud and as
funky as it gets; stay far away unless you have the
chutzpah to carry them off.

Zodiac

The Taj Mahal Hotel, Apollo Bunder, Colaba
(2202-6211). Churchgate/CST stations. **Open** 10am-
8pm daily. **Credit** AmEx, DC, MC, V.
Zodiac has crisp shirts, great patterns and prints,
cool ties, and prices that will make you want to buy
them all.
Other locations: Linking Road, Bandra
(5581-7121). Bandra station; Grand Hyatt
Mumbai, Santa Cruz (5581-7130). Santa Cruz
station, Inorbit Mall, Malad (W) (5581-7139).
Malad station.

Jewellery

Amrapali

Shops No 39 & 62, Oberoi Shopping Arcade,
Nariman Point (2281-0978/0981). Churchgate/CST
stations. **Taxi** The Oberoi Hotel. **Open** 10.45am-
8pm daily. **Credit** AmEx, DC, MC, V.
This Jaipur institution creates fine gold and silver jewellery, combining Indian tradition and craftsmanship
with contemporary design and aesthetics. Jennifer
Lopez and the Prince of Morocco seem to like it.

Curio Cottage

19 Mahakavi Bhushan Marg, Colaba (2202-2607).
Churchgate/CST stations. **Taxi** near Regal Cinema.
Open 11am-8pm Mon-Sat. **Credit** AmEx, MC, V.
A favourite for both locals and visitors, Curio
Cottage sells semi-precious jewellery that fills the
pages of fashion magazines as well as tiny trinkets
your friends back home would love.

Orra

Zariwala Mansion, August Kranti Marg, Kemp's
Corner (2368-0606). Grant Road station.
Open 11.30am-8pm daily. **Credit** AmEx, MC, V.
This chain of stores is a reliable place to buy gold,
diamond and platinum jewellery, as well as Indian
mythology-inspired pendants.
Other locations: 2 AN Chambers, Turner Road,
Bandra (2643-3423, 3291-6064). Bandra station.

Sia

37 Maskati Corner, 110/112 Altamount Road
(2381-2628). Grant Road station. **Open** 11am-8pm
daily. **Credit** AmEx, MC, V.
Sia sells stunning replicas of the kind of ornate,
heavy Indian jewellery you see at lavish weddings.

TBZ

Zaveri Bazaar, Bhuleshwar (2342-5001/2343-5001).
Charni Road station. **Open** 11am-7.30pm Mon-Sat.
Credit AmEx, DC, MC, V.
One of the city's oldest goldsmiths, TBZ is known
for its solid gold jewellery and for not having copy-
righted its name. Dozens of inferior imitators have
the same name, but this is the real deal.

Food & drink

Bakeries

Paris Bakery

278 Cowasji Hormusji Street, Marine Lines (2208-
6619). Marine Lines station. **Taxi** near Our Lady of
Dolours Church. **Open** 8am-9.30pm Mon-Sat, 8am-
2pm Sun. **No credit cards**.

On a tiny street-side stall on a narrow potholed lane up from the church sits Paris, a well-loved institution with gorgeous cashew macaroons and garlic-butter breadsticks among many other treats.

Kayani & Co
Jer Mahal Estate, Dhobi Talao (2201-1492). **Taxi** near Metro Cinema. **Open** 6.20am-9pm daily. **No credit cards.**
The baked delights on offer here have a sort of period charm to them – custard puffs, sweet buttered buns and other treats of the sort dreamed of by Billy Bunter. Don't miss the chicken patties and the cardamom-flavoured *mava* cakes beloved of Parsis. **Photo** *p127*.

Theobroma
Cusrow Baug Shop 24, Colaba Causeway, Colaba (6629-2929). Churchgate/CST stations. **Taxi** Electric House. **Open** 11am-11pm. **Credit** MC, V.
The name means 'food of the gods', and they mean it. Top-quality sourdough loaves, fluffy focaccia, chocolate brownies and freshly made sandwiches.

Beverages

Philips Tea & Coffee
Shop No 8, Usha Sadan, Colaba Causeway, Colaba (2207-4793). Churchgate/CST stations. **Taxi** near Colaba Post Office. **Open** 9am-8pm daily. **No credit cards.**
Cheap, super quality fresh Indian teas and coffee beans are available at this sleepy store.

Shah Wines
Sitaram Building, ground floor, Fort (2342-7996/ www.shahwines.com). Churchgate/CST stations. **Taxi** near Crawford Market. **Open** 10am-8.30 Mon-Sat. **Credit** MC, V.
One of the city's biggest wine shops, selling a good range of Indian wines, spirits and beers.

Indian sweets

Mishty Bela
Krishnaraj Building, Walkeshwar Road, Malabar Hill (2361-6690). Grant Road station. **Taxi** near White House. **Open** 9am-8pm daily. **No credit cards.**
A wide range of traditional Indian *mithai* (sweets), including sugar-free, all-natural fruit *mithai* made from almonds, raisins, walnuts, figs and more . Don't miss the tiny *rasmalai* – sweet, milky and juicy.

Brijwasi
Narayan Building, near 1st Pasta Lane, Colaba Causeway, Colaba (2282-0963/ www.brijwasi.in). Churchgate/CST stations. **Open** 9am-9.30pm daily **No credit cards.**
A top choice for a glittering array of silver-wrapped *mithai* (Indian sweets) in all their glory – try the *kaju anjeer* (cashew and fig) rolls and ghee-soaked *ladoos* (sweet balls). Brijwasi also has a range of delicious fresh milk sweets and Bengali treats like *sandesh* – dry on the outside, sweet and juicy on the inside.

Other locations: Raj Mahal Building, near Ambassador Hotel, Veer Nariman Road, Churchgate (2282-2368).

Camy Wafer
5-6 Oxford House, near Colaba Market, Colaba Causeway, Colaba (2282-8430/ www.camywafer.com). Churchgate/CST stations. **Open** 9am-9pm. **No credit cards.**
More *mithai* than you can shake a candy cane at, all superb quality. Camy also has an outstanding selection of savoury snacks, including *chivda* – dry snacks of puffed rice, raisins nuts and spices.
Other locations: 2nd Taj Building, August Kranti Marg, Gowalia Tank (2389-2288). Grant Road station; Shop 1 & 2, Crystal Building, Junction of 16th Road, Khar Danda Road (2604-1178). Khar station.

Gifts

Cheemo
Mangal Darshan, Waterfield Road, Bandra (W) (2603-5566). Bandra station. **Open** 11am-8.30pm Mon-Sat. **Credit** AmEx, MC, V.
Handbags galore – from bejewelled, embroidered and studded clutches that will turn heads back home, to 'Prada-inspired' purses.
Other locations: High Street Phoenix shopping mall, Lower Parel (2493-0495). Lower Parel station.

Shawl Art
Shankar Mahal, Sophia College Lane, Bhulabhai Desai Road (2351-6252). Grant Road station. **Open** 10am-7pm Mon-Sat. **No credit cards.**
This speciality store for shawls, scarves and stoles is happy to send a trunk full of wares based on your requirements and tastes, so you can shop from your hotel room. Or pop in for a look. There's a lot of variety in embellishments, weaves and embroideries.

Hidesign
India House, Kemp's Corner (2386-9188). Grant Road station. **Open** 10am-8pm Mon-Sat. **Credit** AmEx, DC, MC, V.
All manner of leather goods, from cool satchels to belts and jackets, made in Pondicherry and exported to fine stores across the world.
Other locations: CR2 shopping mall, Nariman Point (6654-8907/8908). Churchgate station; High Street Phoenix shopping mall, Lower Parel (2496-4309). Lower Parel station.

Ravissant
131 August Kranti Marg, Kemp's Corner (2363-7003, 2368-4934). Grant Road station. **Open** 9.30am-8pm Mon-Sat. **Credit** AmEx, DC, MC, V.
One of India's oldest fine brands, Ravissant is best known for its silver items that are handcrafted in Holland, Germany and Switzerland. If you're looking for a one-of-a-kind three-foot-high Ganesh statue or an actual swing set for your bedroom (both in silver), this is the place.

Jaipur chic

It used to be difficult to find stylish, comfortable and reasonably priced ethnic clothing in Mumbai. But all that's changing with the arrival of the Jaipur trinity: Anokhi, Soma and Cottons. All three chains have long attracted block-print-loving congregations of devotees from across the nation and the globe. Now you can have them all: soft cotton, paisley and floral motifs, straight-cut kurtas with arch collars, crushed skirts, brightly coloured stoles, and restyled jodhpurs, and the comfort of spending the summer in as much elegance as the humidity permits.

The three labels are flag-bearers of the school of modern Jaipur design, which the founders of Anokhi – UK-born Faith Hardy and her husband JP Singh – established in 1970. Each of the three retailers is distinctive: Anokhi is the place for more expensive, refined block prints in earthy colours and rich reds and blues. Cottons is bright and brash, and aims for a funkier and younger look. Soma also does block prints but in softer shades, with a preference for pastels. Soma and Anokhi also sell furnishings like curtains, bed and table linen, as well as largely useless but irresistible knick-knacks: napkin holders, coasters, make-up bags and handbags that carry little more than a mobile phone and credit cards.

Aside from the trinity, don't miss Fab India and Bandhej, both of which use traditional textiles, motifs and design methods – like the always in fashion tie-dye *bandhani* and *leheriya* style – but innovate with style and shape for clothes that merge the old and new.

They're as perfect for a night on the town in Colaba as they are in Knightsbridge.

Anokhi
See p127.

Cottons
Alexandria, St Sebastian Road, near Barista, Mount Carmel Church, Bandra (W) (2651-8408). Bandra station. **Open** 11am-8pm daily. **Credit** DC, MC, V.

Soma
A2 Amar Chand Mansion, above Golden Gate Restaurant, 16 Madam Cama Road, Colaba (2282-6050). Churchgate/CST stations. **Open** 10am-8pm daily. **Credit** AmEx, DC, MC, V.

Fab India
See p123.

Bandhej
F26 Quorum, Phoenix Mills, Senapati Bapat Marg, Lower Parel (2497-4050). Lower Parel station. Also at Grand Hyatt, Kalina (3060-1011). **Open** 10.30am-8pm daily. **Credit** MC, V.

Cottons.

Other locations: Navy India Building, Mahatma Gandhi Road, Colaba (2287-3405/3406) Churchgate/CST stations; Taj Land's End Hotel, Bandstand, Bandra (W) (6668-1364). Bandra station.

The Bombay Store
Western India House, Sir Pherozeshah Mehta Road (2288-5048, 2288-5049). CST station. **Open** 10.30am-7.30pm Mon-Sat, 10.30am-6.30pm Sun. **Credit** AmEx, DC, MC, V.

Perfect if you want to get a taste of everything, with plenty of potential for interesting presents and souvenirs – like the modernistic stone Ganesha statues small enough to sit on the palm of your hand. The Bombay Store brings together artefacts, home accessories, clothes, jewellery, stationery and various trinkets that proudly bear a Made in India stamp.

Hairdressers

b:blunt
Block No 1, ground floor, 29 Hughes Road (98197-25868). Grant Road station. **Open** 11am-6.30pm Tue-Sun. **Credit** MC, V.

Adhuna Bhabani, the woman behind b:blunt, sets the biggest hair trends in Bollywood. This new salon also houses a Kerastase centre.

Hakim's Aalim
Pali Hill, Bandra (W) (2646-0044). Bandra station. **Taxi** opposite Shatranj Restaurant. **Open** 11am-7pm daily. **Credit** MC, V.

This shiny salon looks more like a sports bar spread over 2,500 ft, with plasma screens and a resident DJ. But don't let the fluff distract you – it's high quality.

Nalini & Yasmin
Sagar Fortune, Waterfield Road, Bandra (W)
(6668-2614). Bandra station. **Open** 11am-6.30pm
Mon-Sat. **Credit** MC, V.
Nalini and Yasmin are pioneers in every sense of the
word and were around long before hair styling was
considered a 'cool' thing to do in Mumbai. Best
known for their signature clean style, great service
and excellent hands-on training.

Raih: Hair Reinvented
Arunodaya Building, 20 Nepean Sea Road (2363-5599).
Grant Road station. **Taxi** opposite Contemporary
Arts & Crafts. **Open** 11.15am-6.30pm daily.
Credit MC, V.
This is one of the city's swankiest hair salons. To
proove it Raih: Hair Reinvented boasts a client
rolodex stuffed with Mumbai's rich and beautiful,
including industrialist wives, page 3 celebrity
regulars, sportspeople and fashion editors.

Home

Anokhi
Rasik Niwas, Metro Motors Lane, off Hughes Road
(2368-5308/5761). Grant Road station. **Open** 11am-
8pm Mon-Sat. **Credit** AmEx, MC, V.
Rajasthani prints abound here on bed and table
linens, easy-to-wash curtains and seat covers.
Other locations: Govinda Building, Waterfield
Road, Bandra (W) (2640-8263). Bandra station.

Contemporary Arts & Crafts
Opposite BPL Mobile Showroom, Nepean
Sea Road (2363-1979). Grant Road station.
Taxi St Stephen's Church. **Open** 10am-8pm
Mon-Sat, 10am-7pm Sun. **Credit** AmEx, MC, V.
CAC makes knick-knacks and essentials for the
home, ranging from brocade cushions to Christmas
lights, candle-stands and lampshades. Cool design
with subtle Indian influences.

Dhoop
Radha Sadan, junction of 18th and 1st Roads, Khar
Danda (6691-9352). Khar station. **Taxi** opposite
Khar Danda Police Chowki. **Open** 10.30am-8.00pm
Mon-Sat. **Credit** DC, MC, V.
Dhoop's focus is on handicrafts made of natural
materials, but this isn't your average jute bag shop
– think coconut shells, bamboo, banana, sugar cane
and water hyacinth, and many more intriguing
materials.

Fab India
137 MG Road, Kala Ghoda (2262-6539).
Churchgate/ CST stations. **Open** 10am-8pm daily.
Credit AmEx, DC, MC, V.
Indian textiles and artistry at their best in a range
of cool home furnishings and accessories, all very
affordable.
Other locations: Navroze, Pali Hill, Bandra (W)
(2646-5286). Bandra station; Inorbit Mall, Malad (W)
(6641-9989). Malad station; Nirmal Lifestyles,
Mulund (W) (2591-9301). Mulund station.

Good Earth
Raghuvanshi Mills, Lower Parel (5572-0345,
5572-0342). Lower Parel station. **Open** 10.30am-
7.30pm daily. **Credit** AmEx, DC, MC, V.
This large, pretty store sells everything from dining
tables to chandeliers, spa products to coffee cups.
None of it is overtly ethnic, but all of it is lovely.

India Weaves
Near Cymroza Art Gallery, Bhulabhai Desai Road
(2368-6366). Grant Road station. **Open** 10am-8pm
Mon-Sat. **Credit** MC, V.
For that majestic look and feel that comes from
luxurious Indian silks and rich tissues, head to India
Weaves where staff can help you to create just that.

Salim Asgarally
99 Abde Villa, SV Road, Khar (W) (6629-5265).
Khar station. **Open** 11am-8.30pm daily.
Credit MC, V.
Furnishings that are wildly decadent and jewel-
toned home accessories. Turn your home into an
Indian palace. **Photo** *p125*.

Yamini
380 Shanti Nivas, 14th Road, Khar (W)
(2646-3645/3647). Khar station. **Open** 10.30am-
7.30pm daily. **Credit** AmEx, DC, MC, V.
Yamini is the best place to go for very affordable,
Indian-inspired linens, textiles, bags, home accessories and delightfully fun lamps.
Other locations: Wodehouse Road, Colaba
(2218-4143/4145). Churchgate/CST stations.

Markets

Mumbai's mercantile instinct is nowhere
better evident than in its wide range of
specialised markets that sell everything from
pickles to zebra-striped fabric. Credit cards
are very definitely not accepted, and don't
expect a money-back guarantee. Here's a
selection of the city's most colourful and
quirky trading zones.

Kayani & Co. *See p125.*

Antiques at Chor Bazaar

Mutton Street, opposite Null Bazaar. Marine Lines/CST stations. **Open** 10.30am-7pm Sat-Thu. From ancient 78 rpm records by Gauhar Jaan to elaborately carved cupboards, from ships' wheels to 1950s Bollywood posters and old cameras, Chor Bazaar ('Thieves' Market') has something for everyone. It is thought to have its origins as a market where stolen goods were fenced, but today it's a warren of respectable stores peddling antiques and an interesting assortment of bric-a-brac. *Photo p130.*

Books at Fort

Around Flora Fountain & Mumbai University, Mahatma Gandhi Road. Churchgate/CST stations. **Open** 10am-7pm daily.

Walk around Flora Fountain and behind the university to browse through a random assortment of old English books, magazines and periodicals on the street. You are guaranteed to come across at least half a dozen *Mein Kampfs* amid old *Vogues* and innumerable dog-eared paperbacks of yesteryear.

Clothes at Fashion Street

Mahatma Gandhi Road, near Azad Maidan. CST station. **Open** 10.30am-7pm daily. Wondering why shopping in Mumbai isn't as inexpensive as you expected? Head to Fashion Street, the unofficial name for a stretch of Mahatma Gandhi Road near Azad Maidan, where stalls sell all kinds of clothing for cheap prices. Some export surplus makes its way here. Don't forget to bargain, hard.

The fab three

Local designers we love.

Deepika Gehani

Gehani's clothes are as easy as her attitude: superbly wearable and perfect for occasions when nothing else seems right. Her background in textile design contributes to her understanding and comfort with mixing materials and styles. She blends fluid cuts with subtle ornamentation, blurring the lines between East and West for a look that's at once both modern and traditional.
Available at: **Ensemble** *(see p121)*; **Kimaya** *(see p121).*

Sabina Singh for Horn OK Please

An eye for the quirky – and a good dose of humour – gives Sabina Singh our vote for the designer who gets the most out of Mumbai. Her funky designs celebrate quirky localisms and transform them into hip Mumbai icons. Right from her brand name, Horn OK Please, to the sequinned double-decker bus T-shirts and tutu skirts, Singh's work identifies, adopts and develops unique elements of Mumbai. 'It's usually something visual that I pick off the street that inspires me – a slogan on a truck, for example,' she says. 'They're just catchy, everyday experiences that I try to translate and capture and take to another level. I'm a complete Bombay girl'.
Available at: **You** *(see p122).*

Surily Goel

It's hard to believe that Surily Goel launched her own brand, Surily, only in 2004. Since then she's dressed celebrity Bollywood director Karan Johar for his mega-successful

A Deepika Gehani top.

Koffee with Karan television chat show, outfitted Mumbai's page three regulars, shown a collection at the India Fashion Week and even styled a few Bollywood blockbusters. But Goel's is a refreshing and complex mix of humility and high class, with generous use of embellishments like turquoise, coral, shells, coins and even metal. Her garments are bold and geometric with a focus on a single striking component in the design, usually a belt or a motif. And, like the designer, they're young, trendy and loads of fun.
Available at: **Aza** *(see p121);* **Shlok** Shop No 11, Quorum, High Street Phoenix, Senapati Bapat Marg, Lower Parel (6661-0428). Lower Parel station. **Open** 11am-8.30pm daily.
Credit AmEx, MC, V.

Everything at Crawford Market
Opposite Police Headquarters, Fort. CST station.
Open 11am-7pm Mon-Sat.
Crawford Market, which opened its iron gates to the public in 1865, is a Mumbai institution not to be missed. As well as the four broad lanes packed with stalls selling fruit, vegetables, kitchenware, spices, dry fruits and foreign foodstuffs, you'll find bloody warehouses for poultry and mutton and even pet stores. Watch out for the wigs at the Hair House for the Bald and Beautiful, just one of the oddities.

Fabric at Mangaldas Market
Sheikh Memon Street, near Chhatrapati Shivaji Terminus. CST station. **Open** 10am-7pm Mon-Sat.
A glorious array of colours and textures and a somewhat chaotic atmosphere make this the city's most vibrant and frantic fabric market.

Fireworks at Mohammed Ali Road
Near the junction of Paltan Road and Mohammed Ali Road. CST station. **Open** 10am-8pm Mon-Sat.
Last Diwali saw a Tsunami, a Katrina and a Rita hitting this market simultaneously – natural-disaster-inspired brands of aerial fireworks. During Diwali, temporary stalls stretch down the pavement for kilometres. The rest of the year, weddings and other festivals keep the road's five firework shops in business.

Jewellery at Zaveri Bazaar
Bhuleshwar. **Open** 11am-7pm Mon-Sat.
India is said to consume about one-third of all the gold produced in the world – roughly 800 tons every year – and one visit here is all you need to believe it. Zaveri Bazaar offers customers highly competitive rates for an astonishing variety of gold and silver jewellery. Larger stores sell diamond jewellery as well, making this a one-stop shop for brides-to-be.

Leather at Dharavi
Sant Rolida Marg, Sion-Bandra Link Road, Sion (W). Sion station. **Open** 11am-8pm Tue-Sun.
Die-hard leather fans swear by Dharavi, where world-class leather products are produced in innumerable dingy workshops. Better known as Asia's largest slum, Dharavi houses over 125 shops that retail and export leather goods to Europe and the Middle East. This is where Indian fashion designers source accessories like handbags, jackets and shoes for ramp shows. Those hot pink knee-high leather boots would find little use elsewhere.

Saris at Dadar
NC Kelkar Road, near Dadar Station, Dadar (W). Dadar station. **Open** 9am-9pm daily.
During the winter wedding season, the Dadar sari market – 25 sari shops packed into a half-mile stretch – is packed with women taking saris out onto the street to ensure that it is the exact shade of lemon yellow or parrot-green they desire. Prices start at Rs 150 for synthetics and go up to Rs 40,000 for hand-woven Paithani saris from Aurangabad.

Shoes at Linking Road
Linking Road, Bandra (W). Bandra station.
Open 11am-6pm daily.
Hundreds of slippers, stilettos and sandals for men, women and children. A steady river of people flows along its periphery, selling everything from fruit trays to silk pouches and fluorescent yo-yos.

Snacks & pickles at Lalbaug
Chivda Galli & Achar Galli, off Dr B Ambedkar Road, Lalbaug. Chinchpokli/Lower Parel stations.
Open 10am-7pm daily.
Ten fragrant outlets line Chivda Galli, a lively lane near Lalbaug market The *chivdas* sold here are made out of *dagadi poha* (thick rice flakes), with chillis and raisins deep-fried and tossed together with a spice mix in a round-bottomed *kadhai*. They sell for Rs 56-80 per kilo. Next door is Achar Galli, which sells the traditional Maharashtrian *loncha* (made out of lime) as well as pickles of raw mango, chillies and berries.

Wedding cards at Girgaum
Khandilkar Road, opposite Gaiwadi, Girgaum, Charni Road (E).Charni Road station. **Open** 10am-8pm Mon-Sat.
Before you walk down the aisle take a stroll down Khandilkar Road, for a look at its dizzying array of thousands of ready-to-print wedding invitations. There are around 200 stores, each with hundreds of clever samples on display. Most are adorned with the elephant-headed Ganesha, who symbolises new beginnings and good luck. But stores also feature at least one wall of 'Muslim, Catholic and non-religious wedding cards'. Fun to browse even if you're not planning on tying the knot.

Music

CDs

Planet M
Times of India Building, Dr Dadabhai Naoroji Road, Fort (6635-3872). CST station.
Open 12pm-8pm Mon-Sat; 11am-9pm Sun.
Credit MC, V.
The country's largest music chain store has ten outlets spread across Mumbai. Modelled on successful international chains such as HMV and Virgin Megastore, this 10,000-sq ft flagship store has an impressive range – you'll find music from all genres – but not in-depth. A good place to pick up the latest releases. It also has a café upstairs.

Rhythm House
40 K Dubash Marg, Fort (2284-2835). CST station.
Open 10am-8.30pm Mon-Sat; 11am-8.30pm Sun.
Credit MC, V.
One of Mumbai's oldest music stores, this city institution is the best place to find old Hindi film soundtracks. In addition to current chart hits, it also stocks a wide range of Hindustani classical and

Eat, Drink, Shop

fusion/lounge music. Best of all, most of the red jacket-clad shop assistants actually know their music.

Musical instrument shops

Bhargava's Musik
4/5 Imperial Plaza, 30th Road, Bandra (W) (2641-1842). Bandra station. **Open** 10am-1pm, 2-7.30pm Mon-Sat. **Credit** MC, V.
Bhargava Musik is a one-stop shop for all Hindustani and Carnatic musical instruments, including sitars, tablas, sarods and more. This 52-year-old shop counts renowned santoor player Shivkumar Sharma and flautist Hariprasad Chaurasia among its clientele.

BX Furtado & Sons
Jer Mahal, Dhobi Talao (2201-3105). Marines Lines station. **Taxi** near Metro Cinema. **Open** 10am-7.30pm Mon-Sat. **Credit** MC, V.
Around since 1865, Furtado's focus is on Western music instruments but it also sells Indian classical instruments, a large collection of music books, music software, speakers and amplifiers, plus pedals and processors. Its two stores, BX Furtado and LM Furtado, are around the corner from each other. BX is also the only place in the city that stocks albums by local rock bands.

Shoes

Catwalk
Crossroads shopping mall, Haji Ali. Mahalaxmi station. **Open** 10am-9pm daily. **Credit** AmEx, DC, MC, V.
Diamante-studded stilettos, strappy wedges and other shoes for a night on the town are the stock in trade at Catwalk.
Other locations: Kemp's Corner (2351-5890). Grant Road station; Ramdas Naik Marg, 43 Hill Road, Bandra (W). Bandra Station; Grand Hyatt Plaza, Santa Cruz (6676-1234). Santa Cruz station.

Inc 5
Breach Candy (2361-8616). **Open** 10am-9.30pm Mon-Sat. **Credit** MC, V.
Inc 5 carries a mix of party shoes, labels like Guess and Tommy Hilfiger, and a small but practical range of boots, which, despite the climate, Mumbai can't seem to get enough of. Also at Phoenix Mills, Lower Parel (2495-1352).

Metro Shoes
534 Linking Road, Bandra (2649-2899). Also at Metro House, Colaba Causeway (6656-0444). **Open** 10am-10pm daily. **Credit** AmEx, MC, V.
Swarovski crystals on your toes? Look no further than Metro Shoes.

Rinaldi
67/68 Sea View Terrace, 118-B Wodehouse Road, Colaba (2215-1394/2215-2513). **Open** 11am-7.30pm Mon-Sat. **Credit** AmEx, MC, V.
Accessories designer Rina Shah makes glam shoes that work.

Antiques at the **Chor Bazaar**. *See p128.*

Travellers' needs

Dry cleaning

American Express Dry Cleaners
Hill Road, Bandra (W) (2643-1743). Bandra station. **Open** 8.30am-1pm, 3.30-8pm daily. **No credit cards**.

Beauty Art
Shop No 7, R Mall, LBS Marg, Mulund (W) (2555-0825/0835). Mulund station. **Open** 10.30am-10pm daily. **Credit** AmEx, DC, MC, V.

Opticians

Colaba Opticians
A/8 Fatima Manzil, Near Sasoon Dock, Colaba (2287-4244). Churchgate/CST stations. **Open** 9.30am-9pm Mon-Sat. **Credit** AmEx, MC, V.

Lawrence & Mayo
Dr Dadabhai Naoroji (DN) Road, Fort (2207-6049). Churchgate/CST stations. **Open** 11am-2pm, 4pm-9pm daily. **Credit** AmEx, MC, V.

Lotus Opticians
Oberoi Shopping Arcade, Nariman Point (2282-9565). Churchgate station. **Open** 10.30am-7.30pm daily. **Credit** AmEx, DC, MC, V.

Travel agents

Akbar Travels of India
Terminus View, 169 Dr Dadabhai Naoroji (DN) Road, Fort (2340-3434). CST station. **Taxi** Crawford Market. **Open** 10am-5pm Mon-Sat. **Credit** AmEx, DC, MC, V.

Atlas Tours and Travels
53 Haji Mahal, Mohammed Ali Road (6636-1000). CST station. **Taxi** near Noor Hospital. **Open** 10am-8pm Mon-Sat. **Credit** AmEx, DC, MC, V.

Riya Travels & Tours
Atlanta Arcade, ground floor, Marol Church Road, Andheri (E) (2830-4799). Andheri station. **Taxi** near Leela Kempinsky Hotel. **Open** 9.30am-6.30pm Mon-Sat. **Credit** AmEx, DC, MC, V.

Arts & Entertainment

Features

Festivals & Events

Party time, all the time.

With practically every single religion on earth represented in Mumbai's population – except maybe Rastafarianism – almost every day is a festival day for someone, somewhere in the city. In the recent past, the vast number of national holidays and religious festivals (government offices shut for 17 of them in 2006) have provided fodder for thunderous newspaper editorials blaming them for India's poor economic growth. Indians, it was claimed, were too busy celebrating their festivals to get any work done. The theory doesn't hold much water – most Indians work six-day weeks, so the time lost evens out – and got soundly kicked into irrelevance by 21st-century India's economic boom.

In Mumbai the biggest and most widely celebrated festivals are **Holi**, the festival of colours, the noisy and spectacular **Ganesh Chaturthi** around September and the firework frenzy of **Diwali** in October or November – all Hindu festivals, but marked in some form by nearly every community.

January-March

Banganga Music Festival

Banganga Lake, Walkeshwar. Grant Road station. **Date** Jan.
A two-day live music festival featuring the top names in Hindustani classical music from across India on the banks of the Banganga tank.

Gudi Padwa

Across the city. **Date** Late Mar or early Apr.
Also known as Ugadi, Gudi Padwa marks the beginning of Basant or spring. It's also celebrated as the start of the New Year for Maharashtrians. *Gudis* – poles decorated with silk, marigolds, mango leaves and coconuts, with upturned metal pots sitting on the end – are hung out of windows and displayed in traditional households.

Holi

Across the city. **Date** 3-4 Mar, 2007; 21-22 Mar, 2008.
One of the city's most popular festivals, celebrating the death of the demoness Holika. On the morning of Holi, the festival of colours, Mumbai becomes an interactive Jackson Pollock painting, as Mumbaikars gleefully spray each other with brightly coloured water – called 'playing Holi' – and eat and drink dishes made with a kind of marijuana called *bhaang* which is sold at temples on the day of the festival. Cars, tourists, anyone out on the street on Holi is fair game – so grab your colours and join the meleé.

Kala Ghoda Arts Festival

Kala Ghoda, Fort. www.kalaghodaassociation.com. CST/Churchgate stations. **Date** Jan or Feb.
Started in 1999 to promote the Kala Ghoda district in Fort as an art district, this ten-day arts festival is the city's premier showcase for painting, sculpture, film, music, dance, literary events and, of course, lots and lots of food.

Mahashivratri

Across the city. **Date** 16 Feb, 2007; 6 Mar, 2008.
When the dreaded *halahala* poison threatened to kill them all, both gods and demons prayed to Lord Shiva to save them. On the night now known as Mahashivratri, Shiva drank the poison and held it in his throat, turning his throat blue and earning himself two new names in the process – Vishakantha ('The One Who Held Poison in His Throat') and Neelakantha ('The One With a Blue Throat'). That night is now celebrated every year with offerings of *bhel* leaves to Lord Shiva, and fasting. But the highlight of the festival is a night-long vigil when devotees sing *bhajans* in homes and temples to honour Lord Shiva.

Makar Sankranti

Across the city. **Date** 14 Jan.
Makar Sankranti is a harvest festival celebrating the transition of the sun from Sagittarius to Capricorn, according to Hindu astrology. Across the city, children and adults go kite flying, using strings embedded with crushed glass to try and cut each other's lines in friendly dogfights. Kites are sold at shops across Mumbai, with some of the most intense aerial battles taking place at Chowpatty beach. **Photo** *p134.*

Muharram

Bhendi Bazaar, Mohammed Ali Road, Nagpada. **Date** 20 Jan 2007; 10 Jan, 2008.
An important festival in the Shi'a Muslim calendar, Muharram marks the anniversary of the Battle of Karbala when Husayn bin Ali, a grandson of Muhammad, was martyred. The mourning reaches its climax on the tenth day, known as Ashura, when processions of devotees walk the city's Muslim areas flagellating themselves with razor-tipped chains to experience the pain of Husayn bin Ali.

▶ For music festivals, *see p155* **Music.**

Arts & Entertainment

Ganesh Chaturthi at
Chowpatty Beach. *See p135.*

Janmashtami. *See p135.*

Making kites for **Makar Sankranti**.
See p132.

Mumbai Festival

Across the city. **Date** Jan.
Founded in 2004, the Mumbai Festival aims to bring all things Mumbai under one banner, with auto-rickshaw races, arm-wrestling challenges, fishing-trawler pulling contests, concerts, dance performances, handicrafts and, of course, lots of local food.

Mumbai International Film Festival

Various venues. (www.filmsdivision.org/ www.miffindia.org). **Date** Feb.
The Mumbai International Film Festival is a biennial competitive event showcasing films from across the world. It's also a rare platform for independent Indian films, with a programme that includes documentaries, shorts and animated films. Delegate passes are available for around Rs 100.

Pongal

Across the city. **Date** 14-18 Jan.
The four-day long Pongal festival is a South Indian harvest festival traditionally celebrated in the home. Pongal means 'to boil over' in Tamil, representing abundance. On the second day, Surya Pongal, the sun-god Surya is worshipped for protecting and nurturing crops throughout the previous year.

Ramnavami

Across the city. **Date** 27 Mar, 2007; 14 Apr, 2008.
Celebrating the wedding day of Rama and Sita, as well as Rama's birthday, Ramnavami sees devotees performing mock wedding ceremonies for small idols of the deities. In the evening, the brightly adorned statues are paraded through the streets.

April-June

Good Friday

Holy Name Cathedral, Colaba; St Michael's Church, Mahim; St Andrew's Church, Bandra & across the city. **Date** 6 Apr, 2007; 21 Mar, 2008.
Christian prayer services across the city mark the day of Jesus' crucifixion. Some churches stage ornate tableaux of the event, using a combination of human actors and life-sized clay figures. Photo *p135*.

Easter

Holy Name Cathedral, Colaba; St Michael's Church, Mahim; Mount Mary's Church, Bandra & across the city. **Date** 8 Apr, 2007; 23 Mar, 2008.
Easter is the most important religious festival of the Christian liturgical year, celebrated in March or April to mark the resurrection of Jesus. Easter eggs, made of marzipan and chocolate, are sold in confectionery stores across Mumbai.

Hanuman Jayanti

Across the city. **Date** Apr 2, 2007; Apr 20, 2008.
Hanuman Jayanti commemorates the birth of Hanuman, the monkey god and one of the most popular deities in the Hindu pantheon, admired for his agility, wit and unflinching devotion to Lord

Ram, whose story is related in the *Ramayana*. On this day, Hindu devotees venerate Hanuman with temple visits.

July-September

Ganesh Chaturthi
Lalbaug, Girgaum Chowpatty, Dadar & across the city. **Date** 27 Aug, 2006; 15 Sept, 2007; 3 Sept, 2008.
Ganesh Chaturthi marks the birthday of Lord Ganesha, the elephant-headed Hindu god of auspicious beginnings. During the 10-day festival, families install idols of the deity in their homes, while some neighbourhoods get together to erect tents (known as *pandals*) in which gigantic statues of Ganesha – some three storeys high – are enthroned. The idols are immersed in the sea or in lakes after either one-and-a-half days, three days, five days, seven days or ten days. But while they are in residence, the idols are treated to music concerts and films late into the night – or at least as late as noise regulations permit. It's Mumbai's most popular festival, but is a relatively new addition to the festive calendar. It was devised only in 1901, when a nationalist leader named Bal Gangadhar Tilak decided to create the festival to mobilise public opinion against British colonial rule. **Photo** *p133.*

Guru Purnima
Across the city. **Date** 29 July, 2007; 18 July, 2008.
On Guru Purnima, the day when the sage Vyasa, an avatar of Lord Vishnu, was born, gurus or teachers are venerated as gods. Students of all kinds traditionally present their teachers with flowers, sweets and coconuts, and their teachers bless them in return.

Janmashtami or Gokulashtami
Across the city. **Date** 16 Aug, 2006; 4 Sept, 2007; 24 Aug, 2008.
The birthday of Lord Krishna, the eighth incarnation of Lord Vishnu, is celebrated withprayers, plays and fasting. Clay pots of yoghurt are strung between buildings high above the street, and bands of young men form spectacular human pyramids in an effort to reach and break the vessels. Onlookers try to hamper their efforts by pouring buckets of water on them from out of their windows. Success brings the cheers of the crowd – and cash rewards too. **Photo** *p134.*

Pateti
Across the city. **Date** mid Aug.
Pateti is celebrated by Parsis on the eve of their New Year. Parsis visit fire temples or *agiaries*. After the *jashan* (prayers), sandalwood is offered to the holy fire. Parsi homes are decorated for the festival: white powder is used to fashion intricate designs of birds, flowers and fish (an art called *rangoli*) at the entrance to homes. Families exchange gifts and sweets and tuck into special dishes like *patra ni machchi* (fish wrapped in banana leaves), *sali boti* (meat with potato chips) and a sweet, milky drink called *falooda*.

Raksha Bandhan
Across the city. **Date** 4 Aug, 2006; 28 Aug, 2007; 16 Aug, 2008.
Raksha Bandhan commemorates the bond between brothers and sisters. Across India, sisters tie decorative bands – called *rakhis* – on their brothers' wrists to remind them that sisters need protection; in return, brothers give their sisters fancy presents. It isn't only siblings who celebrate the festival: girls can blunt the affections of ardent suitors by making them their symbolic '*rakhi*' brothers'.

October-December

Bhaubeej
Across the city. **Date** 23 Oct, 2006; 11 Nov, 2007; 30 Oct, 2008.
Bhaubeej (also called Bhaiduj), the day after Diwali, is when sisters pray for the well-being of their brothers (and receive gifts in return).

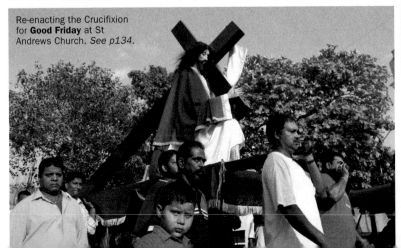

Re-enacting the Crucifixion for **Good Friday** at St Andrews Church. *See p134.*

Preparing an idol of the goddess Durga for **Durga Puja (Navratri)**.

Celebrate Bandra Festival

Across Bandra. **Date** Next due in Nov 2007.
In recent years, the once-sleepy northern suburb of Bandra has become the city's hottest neighbourhood, the ground zero of an explosion of nightclubs and chic restaurants. Every two years, the 'Celebrate Bandra' festival enlivens Bandra with events ranging from theatre and music to sports.

Christmas

Holy Name Cathedral, Colaba; St Michael's Church, Mahim; Mount Mary's Church, Bandra & across the city. **Date** 24-25 Dec.
Christmas in Mumbai is much like Christmas in the West – a midnight mass on Christmas eve, followed by an exchange of presents and a Christmas Day spent with the family. With temperatures reaching up to 25°C, white Christmases are unlikely; some make up for that by showering flecks of cotton over their carefully tended fir trees, while street urchins and vendors roam Colaba Causeway working up a sweat in red Santa hats.

Diwali

Across the city. **Date** 21 Oct, 2006; 9 Nov, 2007; 28 Oct, 2008.
Diwali (the 'festival of lights') celebrates Lord Rama's return to the kingdom of Ayodhya after he killed the demon Ravana, events that are described in the *Ramayana* epic. It's an Indian Christmas, marked by fireworks, sweets and merry-making. Diwali is also the day on which Indian businessmen open new accounts books for the year, and perform *puja* ceremonies at their places of work to invoke the blessings of Lakshmi, the goddess of wealth. The night before Diwali is spent gambling at cards, inviting luck to favour you for the rest of the year.

Dussehra

Across the city. **Date** 2 Oct, 2006; 21 Oct, 2007; 9 Oct, 2008.
Dussehra, the day on which Lord Rama killed the demon Ravana, symbolises the victory of good over evil. The slaying of the demon is recreated in colourful pageants called *Ram lilas*, which conclude with the burning of large effigies of Ravana.

Guru Nanak Jayanti

Four Bungalows, Andheri & across the city. **Date** early or mid Nov.
Celebrating the birth anniversary of Guru Nanak Dev, the founder of the Sikh faith, Guru Nanak Jayanti begins with early morning processions of devotees from *gurdwaras* (Sikh temples) performing *shabads* (hymns). The celebrations also include the three-day *akhand path*, during which the Sikh holy book, the *Guru Granth Sahib*, is read from beginning to end without a break.

Id-ul-Fitr

Mohammed Ali Road & across the city. **Date** 24 Oct, 2006; 13 Oct, 2007; 2 Oct, 2008.
Id-ul-Fitr, often referred to simply as Id, is an Islamic holiday that marks the end of Ramazan (or Ramadan), the month of fasting. Muslim men attend special prayers, after which there's a swirl of visiting friends and eating festive meals.

Navratri

Colaba, Andheri & across the city. **Date** Sep 23-Oct 1, 2006; Oct 12-20, 2007; Sep 30-Oct 8, 2008.
A popular festival with the city's Gujarati community, the 'nine nights' of Navratri are a countdown to Dussehra, the 'tenth day', on which Lord Rama killed the demon Ravana, as told in the *Ramayana*. Dance events, some attended by up to 10,000 people, are held on each night; couples holding batons in their hands dance the *dandiya raas* and the *garba*. They're a rare occasion on which teenagers are allowed to mix, unsupervised by their parents, with the opposite sex. (City legend has it that some plastic surgeons offer to perform hymenoplasties after the festival, to 'revirginise' women before their weddings.) For Mumbai's Bengali community, the period is celebrated as Durga Puja, with music and plays performed at *pandals* (tents) around the city.

Prithvi Theatre Festival

Prithvi Theatre, Juhu Tara Road, Juhu (2614-9546/www.prithvitheatre.org). **Date** Nov.
Since 1983, the Prithvi Theatre Festival – held in a cosy auditorium in Juhu, as well as in the National Centre for the Performing Arts complex downtown – has become the high point of the Mumbai theatre season. It showcases the talents of groups from around India, and often features international acts as well, with an emphasis on encouraging originality in local drama groups. Recently, the festival has started to make use of non-traditional spaces such as the picturesque Horniman Circle Garden.

Children

Finding entertainment for kids is no child's play.

At first glance, Mumbai looks like the world's worst city for kids. It's noisy, crowded, has few parks, terrible air pollution, and the pavements – where they exist – are too potholed to walk on. You'll rarely see parents with pushchairs in Mumbai; kids are carried, perched on the petrol tanks of motorbikes or – in wealthier families – strapped into the back seats of cars. There are very few clean public toilets and almost no facilities where babies can be changed, even in major stores, forcing hassled mums and dads to look for a vacant park bench (and good luck finding that park) to change a dirty nappy. Mumbai's maddening traffic congestion can be another downer for restless kids. Allow yourself plenty of time to get around, and make sure you're carrying plenty of drinks and snacks.

But take a second look and you'll see that Mumbai is not quite the worst city in the world for kids. It's probably only the fourth- or fifth-worst – and with a little imagination and persistence you can find activities to keep children amused, like a ride through the lion and tiger enclosures at Sanjay Gandhi National Park or a trip to Mani Bhavan, and the spectacle of festivals like Diwali and Ganesh Chaturthi make unforgettable experiences for young world travellers. And, not least, the weather is almost always glorious.

FESTIVALS AND EVENTS

January is crowded with activities for kids in the city-wide Mumbai Festival (*see p134*), closely followed by the Kala Ghoda Arts Festival (*see p132*). **February** sees a large flower, fruit and vegetable show hosted at the Victoria Jubilee Technical Institute grounds in Matunga by Friends of the Trees (2287-0860). World Book Day on **23 April**, Shakespeare's birthday, is marked by literary events for kids at the British Council Library at Nariman Point (2282-3530) and libraries and bookstores across the city. **June** brings in Environment Week, with events showcasing the region's flora and fauna organised by the Bombay Natural History Society (2282-1811) and the Worldwide Fund for Nature-India (2207-8105).

On the first Sunday after **8 September** the quiet lanes of Bandra come alive with a week-long fair around the Basilica of Mount Mary, Bandra, celebrating the birthday of the Virgin Mother. Also around September is Ganesh Chaturthi (*see p135*), when devotees throng Chowpatty Beach to immerse large, multi-coloured idols of the elephant-headed Ganesha in the Arabian Sea. In **October** or **November** Diwali, the Hindu festival of lights (*see p136*), turns the city into a giant fireworks display.

The great outdoors

Chowpatty Beach
Marine Drive, Girgaum. Charni Road station.
Spin on the creaking, hand-cranked merry-go-round (when was the last time you saw one of those?) and miniature Ferris wheels. Located at the northern end of Marine Drive, the beach is flanked by the Balodyan children's garden with play equipment.

Hanging Gardens
BG Kher Road, Malabar Hill (2363-3561). Grant Road station. **Open** 4am-9pm daily. **Admission** Free.
Hanging Gardens has broad lawns, entertaining animal-shaped hedges and breathtaking city views.

Juhu Beach
Juhu Tara Road, Juhu. Vile Parle station.
About 18 kilometres north of downtown, Juhu Beach beckons children with pony rides, air-rifle shooting, dancing monkeys and acrobats. Swimming isn't advisable in these waters, though.

Maharashtra Nature Park
Sion-Bandra Link Road, Sion (W) (2407-7641). Sion station. **Open** 10am-5pm daily. **Admission** Rs 5.
A charming nature trail along Mahim Creek, following leafy paths and chasing dragonflies and frogs. This park is lush with fragrant medicinal plants, under a thick canopy of trees.

Mumbai Port Trust Garden
Women Graduates Union Road, Colaba. Churchgate/CST stations. **Open** 5.30am-10am, 4.30-8.30pm daily. **Admission** Rs 2.
A beautiful 11-acre botanical park, with more than 450 flowering shrubs, spacious lawns, and woods with rose gardens and seashore flora. Kids get to play Tarzan on the hanging roots of banyan trees.

Sanjay Gandhi National Park
Western Express Highway, Borivali (E) (8860-0389). Borivali station. **Open** 8am-1.30pm, 2.30-7pm Tue-Sun. **Admission** Rs 4.
Mumbai has a beautiful forest on its northern fringe that makes an activity-filled day trip for kids. Highlights include bus rides through a lion and tiger enclosure, plus deer and snake gardens. Jungle trails lead past hundreds of species of spot birds, butterflies and reptiles. Also inside the park are the ancient Buddhist Kanheri caves (*see p80*).

Veermata Jijamata Udyan (Byculla Zoo)
Dr Ambedkar Road, Byculla (E) (2374-2162). Byculla station. **Open** 9.30am-5.30pm Thur-Tue. **Admission** Rs 2 children, Rs 5 adults.
Mumbai's lacklustre zoo, dating back to 1861, can be more depressing than educational, with animals confined in small, poorly maintained enclosures. But the surrounding gardens and paths are attractive and make a good spot for picnics. There's also a children's play area with slides and swings, and old statues from the era of the British Raj.

Indoor fun

Mani Bhavan
19 Laburnum Road, Gamdevi (2380-5864). Grant Road station. **Open** 9.30am-6pm daily. **Admission** Free.
Mahatma Gandhi lived here from 1917 to 1934, planning and co-ordinating the peaceful civil disobedience movement that led to an empire's downfall. The museum here is a perfect introduction to Gandhi for kids, with cute clay doll figures depicting scenes from the great man's life.

Monetary Museum
Pherozeshah Mehta Road, Fort (2266-0502). Churchgate/CST stations. **Open** 10.30am-5pm Mon-Fri, 10.30am-1pm Sat. **Admission** Rs 10.
Show them the money at the first-class Monetary Museum, with superb displays of ancient coins and crisp text explaining 'The Story of Money in India'.

Nehru Planetarium
Annie Besant Road, Worli (2492-0510). Mahalaxmi/ Byculla stations. **Open** 11am-5.30pm Tue-Sun. **Admission** Rs 35 adults, Rs 20 children under 12.
This recently renovated planetarium conducts high-standard sky shows in English starting at 3pm. There's also a 'Discovery of India' exposition on India's intellectual and cultural achievements.

Nehru Science Centre
Dr E Moses Road, Worli (2493-2667). Mahalaxmi/ Byculla stations. **Open** 10.30am-6.30pm daily. **Admission** Rs 20.
It's not a world-class science museum – and could do with a lick of fresh paint – but it does have interactive exhibits for kids explaining everything from how pulleys work to how the eyes see. Call direct or check *Time Out Mumbai* for the centre's regular kid-oriented workshops on astronomy, electronics, aero-modelling and rocketry.

Prince of Wales Museum
Mahatma Gandhi Road, Kala Ghoda, Fort (2284-4484). Churchgate/CST stations. **Open** 10.30am-6pm Tue-Sun. **Admission** Rs 300, children under 12 free.
Officially known as Chhatrapati Shivaji Vastu Sangrahalaya, the natural history section of this beautiful museum is a hit with kids and filled with whales, rhino, deer and birds from across the region. The armoury and the collection of Indian miniature paintings are also interesting – shame about the lack of explanation, though.

Taraporevala Aquarium
Marine Drive (2284-8985). Charni Road station. **Open** 10am-7pm Tue-Sat; 10am-8pm Sun & public holidays. **Admission** Rs 15 adults, Rs 10 children under 17.
Mumbai's only proper aquarium is poorly maintained, with display tanks packed to the gills with angel fish, freshwater sharks and turtles fighting for space. But kids love it anyway.

Film

Mumbai's other temples.

The innocence of cinema survives almost untouched in Mumbai. First-day-first-show fever still grips the city at noon every Friday, when crowds throng the city's 100-plus cinema halls to catch the first-ever public screenings of the latest movies. Over the years, the film industry has started to issue ever-more-sophisticated pre-release hype, but first-day-first-show audiences show up for the same reason they always did – a screening of a new movie is always an event.

Until the late 1990s Mumbaikars' hours in the flickering light were always spent in single-screen halls – spacious cinemas with an average capacity of 800 seats, with just one film show three or four times a day. Until multiplexes arrived, almost every neighbourhood had a cinema hall – usually located close to the train station – that screened either new movies, recent releases or re-issued prints of older movies. English movies were the preserve of a clutch of halls in the south of the city, including the still-extant Regal and Sterling cinemas. The intimate association between single-screen cinema halls and a single film meant that a box-office hit could ensure a cinema's success. For instance, Ramesh Sippy's action epic *Sholay*, released in 1975, ran for over five years at Minerva in central Mumbai. (When the movie was briefly re-released in 2004, it was at Minerva that *Sholay*'s posters first made their re-appearance.) Sooraj Barjatya's melodrama *Hum Aapke Hain Kaun…!* (*Who Am I To You...!*) helped yank the splendid Liberty Cinema out of the red by clocking just over 2,300 shows in 847 days (*see p140* **Silver screen, golden era**).

The relationship between movie and cinema hall is more fragmented in the day of the multiplex. Their pricing, improved sound and seating, and location – many are located inside shopping malls – make most multiplexes unaffordable to the city's underprivileged. The experience of going to the cinema – once India's great unifier – has now fractured, with the middle and upper classes visiting multiplexes while the city's poorest keep the single-screen cinema alive.

Apart from the weekly dose of new releases, Mumbai gets added shots of cinema from a handful of film clubs and cultural centres that bring international cinema of all hues to the

Not quite the walk of fame – **Cinema Road**, behind Metro Cinema.

city. Mumbai is also host to two international film festivals – the **Mumbai Academy of Moving Images Festival** (www.iff mumbai.org), between January and March; and the Asian cinema-focused **Third Eye Festival** (2413-1918, www.affmumbai.com) in October.

BUYING TICKETS

Multiplexes allow advance bookings by credit card via phone or website, or of course you can buy direct from the box office. You should book ahead for first-night shows to be sure of getting a seat. Single-screen cinema halls do not take advance bookings and you will need to buy direct from the box office in cash. **Note**: Hindi films generally do not have English subtitles.

> ▶ For more on Mumbai's cinema,
> *see pp34-37* **Bollywood**.

South Mumbai

Eros

Khambatta Building, Churchgate (2282-2335).
Churchgate/CST stations. **Tickets** Rs 40-Rs 100.
No credit cards.
Built during Mumbai's fascination with art deco,
Eros almost lives up to the romance of its name –
its one hiccup being the soggy *samosas*. With two
wings topped by a domed baby-blue ceiling, access
to its 1,000-seater hall is afforded by two grand
marble staircases. **Photo** *p141.*

Liberty

Chitralaya Exhibitors India, Liberty Building, 41/42
Marine Lines (2203-1196). Churchgate station.
Tickets Rs 45-Rs 100. **No credit cards.**
One of the most spectacularly designed and well-
maintained cinema halls in the city, Liberty's
interiors alone are worth the ticket price. Liberty
opened its doors in 1947, when India became free
from British rule, and it has screened some of Hindi
cinema's milestone movies over the decades.

Silver screen, golden era

The **Liberty Theatre** was constructed at a
time when they really knew how to make a
cinema hall; it was completed in 1947 – the
year of Indian Independence – hence the
name. Carved wooden gates lead to a foyer
arrayed with teak and white cedar panelling
and mirrors frosted with floral patterns. In
the auditorium, a silk-curtained screen, with
ornate mock fountains on either side, rises
to an impossibly high ceiling. Even before
the movie starts, Liberty always delivers
a spectacle.

Liberty is the Kohinoor diamond in
Mumbai's art deco crown, celebrated by
heritage conservationists, and taking pride
of place in David Vinnels' and Brent Skelly's
definitive book *Bollywood Showplaces:*
Cinema Theatres in India. And it all could
have been lost. In the early 1990s, the
theatre was well on the way to sharing the
fate of other *paan*-stained, peeled-paint pits
that were once the city's smartest single-
screen cinemas. But it was rescued in 1994
by a single movie, the surprise mega-hit *Hum*
Aapke Hain Kaun...! (Who Am I To You...!).

The film ran for 125 continuous weeks, with
a full house for 44 of them. The takings paid
for a restoration of Liberty's fading charms.

Liberty is the last survivor of a chain of 40
theatres once owned by the Hoosein family.
The business had become unmanageable by
the end of World War II and the chain was
consolidated into Liberty. It became one of
the city's most popular Hindi film theatres
and hosted several star-studded premières in
its heyday. 'Thousands would crowd outside
the theatre to gawk at the stars, and the cops
would often have to charge them with sticks
to keep them away,' recalls Nazir Hoosein,
Liberty's second-generation owner.

At just Rs 60 for an upper-stall seat, Liberty
still manages to draw a crowd – mainly from
families and college students, plus tourists
and heritage hounds – but profits are down
for the same reason the rest of India's single-
screen cinemas are suffering: a 45 per cent
entertainment tax on every ticket, something
from which multiplexes are exempt. 'I have no
problems with multiplexes,' says Hoosein,
'But if my government takes away 45 per cent
of my turnover with each movie,
how the hell do I survive?'

One day, Liberty may face the
same fate as its single-screen
art deco neighbour, Metro,
which was bought by the Adlabs
multiplex chain for reinvention
as the 'Metro Adlabs' multiplex.
Metro's stylish exterior will
remain intact, protected by
heritage rules, but its golden-
era interiors will be mercilessly
minced into multiple screens.
All the more reason to take
a taste of Liberty, while you
still can.

Regal
*Opposite SP Mukherji Chowk, Kala Ghoda, Colaba
(2202-1017). Churchgate/CST stations.* **Tickets**
Rs 60-Rs 150. **No credit cards**.
India's first cinema hall equipped with air-conditioning and an underground car park, Regal is
the pride of Colaba. It opened in 1933 and is
considered one of the city's finest examples of art
deco architecture. Although much of its thunder has
been stolen by multiplex parvenus, Regal remains
the queen of South Mumbai's single screens.

Sterling
Marzban Road, Fort (2207-5187). CST station.
Taxi *near CST station.* **Ticket** Rs 40-Rs 125.
No credit cards.
Location, rather than decor, is Sterling's biggest
advantage. Throw a piece of popcorn and you'll hit
both CST and the delights of Colaba. This 900-seater
screens mainly Hollywood movies. **Photo** *p142.*

Suburbs

Chandan
*Near Hare Rama Hare Krishna Temple, Juhu
(2620-0437). Andheri station.* **Tickets** Rs 40-Rs 70.
No credit cards.
Ye olde Chandan has held out against the snazzier
multiplexes in the neighbourhood. The cinema
screens Hindi and English films, has a strongly
middle-class crowd, and the excellent samosas are
worth the price of admission alone.

Chitra
*Dr BR Ambedkar Road, opposite Fire Brigade,
Dadar (E) (2418-2264). Dadar station.*
Tickets Rs 40-Rs 75. **No credit cards**.
Chitra suffered the same woes that beset other
single screens in the late 1980s and early '90s –
falling footfalls due to the video boom and
competition from multiplexes. It fought back by jazz-ing up its façade and pitching for new movie releas-es rather than 1980s re-runs.

G-7
SV Road, Bandra (W) (2642-6963). Bandra station.
Tickets Rs 35-Rs 100. **No credit cards**.
Triplets Gaiety, Galaxy and Gemini morphed into a
quasi-multiplex in the early 1990s by converting its
40-seater preview theatres into fully-fledged
auditoria. G-7 later added siblings Gem, Grace,
Gossip and Glamour.

Maratha Mandir
*Opposite Mumbai Central rail terminus (2307-0119).
Mumbai Central station.* **Tickets** Rs 40-Rs 60.
No credit cards.
If location is king, Maratha Mandir should be
wearing the crown with an unbeatable situation
bang opposite the busy Mumbai Central terminus.
However, Maratha Mandir has allowed lurid
B-grade flicks into its mirrored interior. But it still
screens some new Hindi movies.

Art deco veteran **Eros**. *See p140.*

Multiplexes

South Mumbai

Inox
*CR2 Mall, near Express Towers, Nariman Point
(5658-8888/www.inoxmovies.com). Churchgate/
CST stations.* **Tickets** Rs 89-Rs 200. **Credit** AmEx,
MC, V.
Art deco for fat wallets. Designed to resemble the
architectural style of its single-screen neighbours,
Inox screens Hindi and English movies through the
day, starting with morning shows at reduced rates.
As far as seating and sound go, it's one of the best
multiplexes around, though the snacks are only
so-so. **Photo** *p142.*

Suburbs

Cinemax
*Off Sion Circle, Sion (2404-1130/www.cinemax.
co.in). Sion station.* **Tickets** Rs 40-Rs 160.
Credit MC, V.
One of the biggest multiplexes in the city, Cinemax
aims to get middle-class bums onto seats. The chain
has been busy making sure that 'a cinema near
you' is a Cinemax one, with multiplexes in Sion,
Kandivali, Goregaon, Andheri, Versova, Thane and
Mira Road.

Inox. *See p141.*

Sterling cinem
See p14

Other locations: Sona Shopping Centre, Kandivali (W) (2864-7164); SV Road, near Goregaon Police Station, Goregaon (W) (2876-0505); Versova Infiniti Mall, New Link Road, Andheri (W) (2631-3355); Ghodbunder Road, Thane (W) (2589-9297); Beverly Park, Western Express Highway, Mira Road (E) (2811-0888).

Fame Adlabs

Crystal Plaza Building, New Link Road, Andheri (W). (5640-3600/www.famecinemas.com). Andheri station. Tickets Rs 70-Rs 250. Credit MC, V.
The exhibition wing of Shringar Films, which distributes and produces Hindi movies, Fame's purple-hued look and luxurious seats are clearly aimed at class over mass.
Other locations: Fame Malad, Inorbit Mall, Goregaon-Malad Link Road, Goregoan (W) (5649-0490); Fame Kandivali, Raghuleela Mall, SV Road, Kandivali (W). (2863-0500).

Fun Republic

Shah Industrial Estate, Veera Desai Road, Andheri (W) (5675-5675/www.funcinemas.com). Andheri station. Tickets Rs 70-Rs 180.
Credit AmEx, DC, MC, V.
Fame's rival in Andheri shares a strip with the offices of mega-producers Yashraj Films and music company major T Series. The multiplex often takes a break from Hindi and English movies to hold special screenings of international films.

IMAX Adlabs

Bhakti Park, Wadala (E) (2403-647/ www.adlabsmultiplex.com). Wadala station.
Tickets Rs 100-Rs 150; Dome Rs 125-Rs 225.
Credit MC, V.
Isolated in a hard-to-reach enclave in Wadala (E), India's first multiplex with an IMAX screen is a giant hi-tech globe surrounded by salt pans. It has a food court, gaming zone, and a Crossword bookstore. The IMAX screen is located in an auditorium that resembles a portal to another galaxy.

Meghraj

Sector 2, Plot No 22, Vashi (2782-7070/ www.meghrajmultiplex.com). Vashi station.
Taxi near Vashi bus depot. Tickets Rs 70-Rs 100.
No credit cards.
This multiplex in Navi Mumbai (also known as New Bombay) caters to the populace that lives in the township that came up in the 1980s. It screens Hindi, English and Marathi movies.

Other film venues

Alliance Française

Alliance Française Auditorium, Theosophy Hall, New Marine Lines, Churchgate (2203-6187/ www.afindia.org). Churchgate/CST stations.
Taxi next to Nirmala Niketan. Ticket free.
The French Consulate's cultural wing screens movies throughout the year. It also has a well-stocked movie library.

British Council

British Council Auditorium, Mittal Court, C wing, Nariman Point (2279-0126/www.british council.org.in). Churchgate/CST stations. Taxi opposite Vidhan Bhavan. Tickets free.
The British government's cultural wing in Mumbai has a vast library of DVDs available for rent, with the emphasis on British television and film. It also holds regular film screenings.

Ghetto

30 Bhulabhai Desai Road, Breach Candy (2353-8418). Mahalaxmi station. Tickets free.
Watch movies French-style – order a drink and light up a cigarette – at one of the city's oldest and grungiest pubs. Every Monday at 7.30pm, Ghetto casts a little movie magic with screenings of international classics. Seats are limited, so arrive early to ensure a good view.

Max Mueller Bhavan

Kala Ghoda, Colaba (2202-2085). Churchgate/ CST stations. Tickets free.
Max Mueller Bhavan waves Germany's cultural flag in Mumbai with German-language screenings of films that are as edgy and experimental as a government-supported centre can get. It also stocks a library of German-language films.

Vikalp

Bhupesh Gupta Bhavan, Leningrad Chowk, near Ravindra Natya Mandir, Sayani Marg, Prabhadevi (2437-4930). Dadar station.
Tickets free.
The only film screening space dedicated to Indian and international documentaries. Vikalp means 'alternative', and the organisation grew out of a protest movement by local documentary filmmakers against government censorship of the state-sponsored Mumbai International Festival of Films in 2004.

Arts & Entertainment

Art

Everyone's an art collector in Mumbai.

At one time, every other shop in Mumbai seemed to be a video parlour, hiring out everything from Bollywood blockbusters to pirated blue movies. When cable television killed that business off, they became cybercafés. When the prices of personal computers came down, they became clothing boutiques. Now, they're art galleries.

Along with the older, more respectable galleries, they cater to a huge new market of yuppies who have bought all the gadgetry they can fit into their handkerchief-sized flats in the new northern developments, and are now looking for some culture to hang on their walls. Non-resident Indians from the US and the UK are also lapping it up. The result is that Mumbai's art market is now booming as never before. When octogenarian artist Jehangir Sabavala had his first show in the 1950s, he had to hire out a Taj Mahal hotel ballroom, cover the walls with burlap and hang his show. Today, there's a line at his door, from art galleries to international auction houses to freelance curators. He's one of the handful of household names, along with Maqbool Fida Husain, Tyeb Mehta, Akbar Padamsee and Syed Haider Raza. (The dead artists' society includes Krishna Howalji Ara, Francis Newton Souza, Narayan Shridhar Bendre, Amrita Sher-Gill and Nasreen Mohammedi.)

Each week brings news of a new price barrier crossed. When veteran Hindi film actress Leela Naidu bought her first Raza in the 1960s, she paid a few thousand rupees. Today, a Raza of that vintage would fetch around Rs three million. For many of today's breed of nouveau riche art buyers, aesthetics are secondary to economics. Mumbai financial papers carry stories about the rise in Bendre's 'graph', the drop in the per-square-inch price of a Husain, and whether one should hold Anjolie Ela Menon or buy more. Each week brings a new breed of collector sniffing around, looking for an investment bargain that will also give its owner the aura of high culture. Now art show openings are social events filled with air kissing and shrieks of delight at seeing the same faces from the night before. No more will we have cheese sandwiches and orangeade; sponsored champagne and canapés are *de rigueur*.

Where can you see all this art in a public gallery? Unfortunately, nowhere. Mumbai was home to some of the biggest names in the business, including Mehta, Husain, Padamsee and Ara. Some of them were part of the very influential Progressive Artists Group (PAG; *see p144* **The Bombay Boys**). But the Indian government had no inclination to collect modern art when it was still affordable. Only the **National Gallery of Modern Art** has a small collection – but even it does not have a permanent display.

With the new boom, these works are now well out of the government's reach and out of sight, but it's possible to see some of the best contemporary work at established private galleries. With prices rising faster than the Sensex stock exchange, no one can be sure if or when the art boom will bust – but for now the euphoria of Mumbai's art scene mirrors that of a city riding on a seemingly unstoppable high.

Check *Time Out Mumbai* for details of the latest art shows.

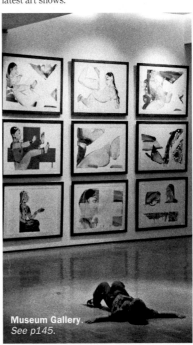

Museum Gallery.
See p145.

Colaba

Artquest

1 Daulat Building, Colaba (2215 0220/www.art questindia.com). Churchgate/CST stations. **Taxi** next to Colaba Post Office. **Open** 11am-7pm Mon-Sat. **Credit** MC, V.

A one-of-a-kind space in Mumbai with an emphasis on art made from found, restored and recycled objects.

Art Musings

1 Admiralty Building, Colaba Cross Lane, next to Sassoon Dock, Colaba (2216-3339/ www.artmusings.net). Churchgate/CST stations. **Taxi** opposite Dunne's School. **Open** 11am-7pm Mon-Sat. **No credit cards**.

A market-friendly gallery at the decorative end of the spectrum, this tiny space exhibited sell-out shows by established names like Akbar Padamsee, Anjolie Ela Menon and young, popular artists like Jitish Kallat, Baiju Parthan and Shibu Natesan.

Galerie Mirchandani + Steinruecke

2 Sunny House, 16/18 Mereweather Road, Colaba (2202-3030/www.galeriems.com). Churchgate/CST stations. **Taxi** behind Taj Mahal Hotel. **Open** 10am-6.30pm Mon-Fri; 10am-4pm Sat. **No credit cards**.

Mother-and-daughter team Usha Mirchandani and Ranjana Steinruecke closed their Berlin gallery and came back to Mumbai to open a space for mounting solos of major artists and high quality group shows.

Guild Art Gallery

2A Prince Chambers, first floor, Colaba (2218- 0057/www.guildindia.com). Churchgate/CST stations. **Open** 10am-6.30pm Mon-Sat. **Taxi** opposite Colaba Post Office. **Credit** AmEx.

Gallery owner Shalini Sawhney displays works by contemporary Indian artists from the Progressive Artists Group to works by the Bombay Boys, and also sells limited edition prints.

Kala Ghoda

Art Land

Esplanade Mansion, third floor, MG Road, Kala Ghoda (6635-0776/www.artlandindia.com). Churchgate/CST stations. **Taxi** next to Army & Navy Building. **Open** 10am-7pm Mon-Sat. **No credit cards**.

The Bombay Boys

When the Bombay Boys exhibition premiered in Delhi in December 2004, it not only showcased the work of 17 of Mumbai's hottest male painters but gave a name to a new breed of Indian artist. Curated by popular Mumbai artist Bose Krishnamachari, who also exhibited his work in the show, the Bombay Boys bowled over Indian buyers and lent the artists – Sudarshan Shetty, Riyas Komu, Justin Ponmany, Baiju Parthan, Anant Joshi, Chintan Upadhyaya, TV Santosh, Sunil Padwal, Sanjeev Sonpimpere and Jyothi Basu – the status of a brotherhood. 'They are all around the same age, most of them are from Kerala, they live around the same area in Mumbai and there is an obvious synchronicity in their work, which is contemporary and chic,' says Mumbai gallery owner Shireen Gandhy. There's an industrial and urban feel to their paintings, which explore themes of loneliness, sterility and artificiality in urban jungles and fantastical landscapes featuring robotic and 'genetically modified' human figures. The Bombay Boys diverge wildly from the erstwhile masters of Indian art, modernist painters like MF Husain and Tyeb Mehta of the Progressive Artists Group, who were primarily concerned with negotiating convergences and contrasts between traditional Indian art forms and Western styles such as Expressionism and Impressionism. The Bombay Boys have dropped that local preoccupation in favour of a 'global' type of art they consider accessible to viewers anywhere in the world. In that sense, the Bombay Boys represent the growing self-confidence of the Indian art market, in which artists want their work to speak for itself, rather than trading on the strength of being labelled 'art from India'. In the process, they've found a happy marriage with the art-hungry nouveau riche of the new Indian economy; speaking the same language as the urban elite but far removed from India's rural heartland.

Chintan Upadhyay's untitled robot-man.

Owner Sunil Chauhan opened this 800-sq-ft space as a platform for emerging Indian artists. Now renovated and extended, Chauhan hosts large shows and has widened the gallery's brief to include exhibitions by established artists like Prafulla Dhanukar, Padmanabh Bendre, Nayanaa Kanodia and Asit Kumar Patnaik.

Artists' Centre
Ador House, First Floor, 6 K Dubash Marg, next to Rhythm House, off MG Road, Kala Ghoda. (2284-5939). Churchgate/CST stations. **Open** 11am-7pm Mon-Sat. **No credit cards.**
Housed on the first floor of a heritage building, this was the first gallery to open in Mumbai's art district in 1950. It used to be the meeting point for renowned artists like KH Ara, FN Souza, MF Husain, SH Raza, S Bakre – the core of the Progressive Artists Group that took Indian art in a new direction (*see p144* **The Bombay Boys**).

Bodhi Art Gallery
28 K Dubash Marg, Kala Ghoda (6664-2554/ www.bodhiart.in). Churchgate/CST stations. **Taxi** near Rhythm House. **Open** 11am-7pm Mon-Sat. **No credit cards.**
One of the newest gallery spaces on the scene, which opened in April 2006. This three-storey gallery is a stunning space for art, with a repertoire running the gamut from cutting-edge to classic.

Gallery Beyond
130/132 Great Western Building, First Floor, Shahid Bhagat Singh Road, Fort (2283-7345/ www.gallerybeyond.com). CST station. **Open** 10.30am-6.30pm Mon-Sat. **Credit** AmEx, DC, MC, V.
Owner Vibhuraj Kapoor is committed to showcasing debut solo shows by young, emerging hot properties like Prajakta Palav, Minal Damani, Anu Agarwal and Preetam Bhatty.

Gallery Chemould
Jehangir Art Gallery, Kala Ghoda, Fort (2284-4356/ www.gallerychemould.com). Churchgate/CST stations. **Taxi** near Elphinstone College. **Open** 10.30am-6.30pm Mon-Sat. **Credit** MC, V.
Opened in 1963 by Kekoo and Khorshed Gandhy, Gallery Chemould has become central to the city's art scene and an informal meeting place for the art fraternity. Kekoo started with a frame shop ('Chemould' is a contraction of 'chemical mouldings') but became interested in the paintings he framed and began organising shows of emerging artists. His daughter Shireen is now director of the gallery and has a preference for artists working in unusual media.

Jehangir Art Gallery
MG Road, Kala Ghoda, Fort (2204-8212). Churchgate/CST stations. **Open** 11am-7pm Mon-Sat. **Credit** MC, V.
In the same building as Chemould, this is the largest art gallery in Mumbai, with four exhibition halls, an art shop and a café. Opened in 1951, it's now the city's most popular contemporary art space, with

Beyond Borders at the **NGMA**.

hundreds of visitors each day. But the Jehangir rarely offers the best of Mumbai's contemporary art. It's run by a trust that rents out the space on a first-come-first-served basis, often without careful attention to quality.

Museum Gallery
K Dubash Marg, Kala Ghoda, Fort (2284-4484). Churchgate/CST stations. **Taxi** behind Jehangir Art Gallery. **Open** 11am-7pm Mon-Sat. **No credit cards.**
Sharing a wall with the landmark Jehangir Art Gallery, this 1,000-sq-ft gallery is also a space-for-hire, but with more discrimination than its neighbour, and has hosted some of the city's best solo shows. **Photo** *p143*.

National Gallery of Modern Art (NGMA)
Cowasji Jehangir Hall, MG Road, Fort (2288-1969/ www.ngmaindia.gov.in). Churchgate/CST stations. **Taxi** opposite Regal Cinema.
Open 11am-6pm Tue-Sun. **No credit cards.**
The city's premier art gallery was renovated and reopened in 1996 and since then has hosted some pivotal exhibitions and group shows. One of the city's most interesting art spaces, it regularly mounts retrospectives of major Indian artists as well as shows from abroad.

Nariman Point

Jehangir Nicholson Gallery of Modern Art
National Centre for the Performing Arts, Nariman Point (2283-3737). Churchgate/CST stations. **Open** 10am-6pm Mon-Sat. **No credit cards.**
Housed within the National Centre for the Performing Arts building, the gallery is named

after legendary collector Jehangir Nicholson, who donated a significant part of his collection to the NCPA. The gallery is regularly rented out by curators and gallery owners for various exhibitions.

Fort

Fourth Floor
Kitab Mahal, fourth floor, DN Road, Fort (2207-9119/www.kitabmahal.org). Churchgate/ CST stations. **Open** 10.30am-7pm Mon-Sat. **No credit cards.**
Situated opposite Chhatrapati Shivaji Terminus, Fourth Floor is an 8,000-square foot event space with an avant-garde emphasis on the top floor of a heritage building, Kitab Mahal.

Pundole Art Gallery
369 DN Road, Flora Fountain (2204-8473). Churchgate/CST stations. **Taxi** next to American Dry Fruit. **Open** 10.30am-6.30pm Mon-Sat. **Credit** AmEx, DC, MC, V.
This gallery became the main building block of the Progressive Artists Group after its establishment in 1963. Run by Dadiba and Khorshed Pundole, this gallery specialises in the works of the PAG and you'll also find unique prints by these artists here.

Malabar Hill

Bombay Art Gallery
Ruia House, 19 Mount Pleasant Road, Malabar Hill (2367-5254/www.bombayartgallery.com). Grant Road station. **Open** 10.30am-6.30pm Mon-Sat. **No credit cards.**
Step inside the intricately carved iron gates of Ruia House, past the mansion and the luscious green lawns to an intimate gallery exhibiting works by a wide range of artists from new solo shows to video installations by Anita Dube to immense abstracts by veterans Mehli Gobai and Zareen Mistry.

Breach Candy

Cymroza Art Gallery
72 Bhulabhai Desai Road, Breach Candy (2367-1983/www.cymroza.com). Grant Road station. **Taxi** next to American Consulate. **Open** 10am-7pm Mon-Sat. **Credit** V.
The gallery exhibits works by emerging and young artists from across India.

Prabhadevi

Birla Academy of Art & Culture
Century Bhavan, Dr Annie Besant Road, Worli (2432-0316). Dadar station. **Open** 10.30am-8pm Mon-Sat; 4-8pm Sun. **No credit cards.**
This gallery reopened in 2005 with a fresh new look and an agenda to display works by debutant artists from across India. The quality level varies, but it's always interesting fare.

Worli

Gallery Art & Soul
1 Madhuli, Dr Annie Besant Road, Shivsagar Estate, Worli (2496-5798). Mahalaxmi station. **Open** 11am-7pm Mon-Sat; by appointment Sun. **No credit cards.**
Tarana Khubchandani's gallery, on the ground floor of a Worli seafront high-rise, is a platform for young artists, as well as a venue for talks by artists, art historians and critics.

Priyasri Art Gallery
4 Madhuli, Dr Annie Besant Road, Shivsagar Estate, Worli (93235-82303). Mahalaxmi station. **Open** 11am-7pm Mon-Sat. **No credit cards.**
Priyasri specialises in paintings, sculptures, installations and ceramics by artists from Baroda and Bengal, and is noted for spotting new art talent before the rest of the pack.

Tao Art Gallery
Sarjan Plaza, Dr Annie Besant Road, Worli (2491-8585/www.taoartgallery.com). Mahalaxmi station. **Open** 10.30am-6.30pm Mon-Sat. **No credit cards.**
Established by collector and artist Kalpana Shah, this gallery is known for large group shows spread over its three exhibition rooms. They've displayed work by contemporary tribal artists and young artists from Jammu and Kashmir, and regularly show the work of S H Raza, Akhilesh and A Anwar.

Lower Parel

Sakshi Gallery
39A/1 Sri Ram Mills Compound, GK Marg, Lower Parel (2491-0728/www.sakshigallery.com). Lower Parel station. **Open** 11am-7pm Mon-Sat. **Credit** AmEx, DC, MC, V.
Deep in the heart of Mumbai's mill lands, this warehouse-gallery features large installations, sculptures, video art and paintings by artists from all over India.

Khar

Dusk
Hotel Pali Hills, 14 Union Park, Khar (W) (2605-3536). Khar station. **Open** 6-11pm Tue-Sun. **No credit cards.**
A little isolated on the top floor of a hotel in a restaurant district, this new gallery usually shows work by masters such as Sunil Das, Jogen Chowdhury, Manish Chevda and Prajakta Palav.

Pradarshak
100 Kalpana Building, Plot No 338, 12th Road, Khar (W) (2646-2681). Khar station. **Open** 11am-7pm Mon-Sat. **No credit cards.**
The first gallery to open in Mumbai's suburbs, in 1995. Pradarshak mainly showcases realist works by lesser-known artists.

Gay & Lesbian

Not entirely in the closet.

Gay travellers in Mumbai are often confused. They've read warnings that homosexuality is illegal in India and that same-sex couples need to be discreet. But men keep looking at them in the street – and not just because they're foreign. That bold, direct look in the eyes seems to suggest something, but what?

It could be an invitation to sex; some Indian gay men see foreigners as a safe option, less likely to betray them to the local police. Some Indian gay guys have Cinderella fantasies of a foreign lover who'll take them far away from the problems of being gay in India. That gaze could also hold an acquisitive gleam. Male hookers hang around stations and the bylanes of Colaba, as do blackmailers looking for easy targets to set up for a scam (*see p148*). Or maybe that look doesn't mean anything. Perhaps he just wants to chat over coffee. Perhaps he wants to sell you a carpet.

Scratch the surface and you'll find Mumbai's gay scene is not as closeted as it might seem. Gay and lesbian support groups operate openly in the city through the internet and hold regular parties. Check out **www.gaybombay.org** to see if there's a party, trek or other event happening in the city during your stay.

Bookshops sell gay and lesbian books, and cinemas now show gay- and lesbian-themed films. In 2005, *My Brother Nikhil* won applause for its moving study of an Indian family dealing with a gay son who is HIV-positive. Bollywood remains wary of openly gay themes, but many gay people work in the industry and, slowly, more gay characters are showing up on screen. There's no gay pride parade as yet, but the city's gay and lesbian community have held open protests against Section 377 of the Indian Penal Code, which threatens prison terms of up to ten years for 'carnal intercourse against the order of nature'. And all this happens with the knowledge of the police, who are rarely interested. Despite the law, many gays and lesbians manage to live their lives openly, on their own terms.

Hijras (usually translated as 'eunuchs', although 'transgenders' is probably better these days) are the most visible face of Mumbai's queer community. You'll see them on the street: they are men dressed – with great style – as women, walking confidently through crowds and announcing themselves with a characteristic flat-handed clap as they solicit money. The community's deep roots in Indian

Hey, check out that *chikna*

Mumbai's gay slang.

Bhai a very butch lesbian or perhaps female-to-male transgendered person (literally, a 'brother'); **chakka** a derogatory term for *Hijra* (*see below*); **chammiya** an ultra-femme Indian lesbian; **chikna** a fair, good-looking young guy; **DPT** Dyke Passing Through, a tourist, leaving lube, hair gel and broken hearts in her wake; **double-decker** someone who's versatile – both top and bottom; **ghodhi** a policeman (literally, 'female horse'); **gud** a fag, very derogatory; **khavda** a blackmailer or troublemaker in general; **kothi** an effeminate man, usually a non-English speaker, usually a bottom; **panthi** a macho man, usually a non-English speaker, usually a top;

passport princess a rich Indian gay guy who's very out when abroad, but deep in the closet back home; he would go to Sydney for Mardi Gras and New York for Pride, but wouldn't be seen dead at a gay party in Mumbai; **satla** drag, to wear a sari, wig and bangles with lots of attitude; **snow queen**, an Indian guy who's exclusively into white guys.

A **hijra** is a transgendered man from a community with deep traditional roots. *Hijras* are the most visible face of the gay community, with an accepted, if marginalised, place in society. They are obviously men but are dressed – with a lot of care – in women's clothes.

traditions gives *hijras* the accepted place in Indian society that gays and lesbians still lack. This allows visibility and even access – *hijras* have stood successfully for elected office, claiming that their inability to have children would help counter the nepotism rampant in Indian politics. Yet acceptance is still marginal. *Hijras* are tolerated, even feared – watch how people who ignore beggars will shell out to them – but rarely respected. Regular employment is shut off to them, which is why they must beg or dance for a living, and many inevitably end up as prostitutes. Most *hijras* live in communal *gharanas* or houses, headed by a *hijra* guru who demands absolute obedience. It provides more security than many marginalised groups in India enjoy, but it's still firmly constrained.

Despite the city's relative openness, Mumbai's gay social scene is limited. There are no gay nightclubs or bars except for **Voodoo's** (*see p158*), which holds a special place in the hearts of the city's gay community for its gay nights, every Saturday after 10pm. The lack of venues is not just because of intolerance. Mumbai rents are sky-high, so any kind of niche venue is rare. The city's dyke community prefers to limit outsiders' access, for good reason. Indian women have a lot less access to public spaces than men, with highly protective families and Cinderella timings. Many lesbians are married and remain deep in the closet. But online groups do exist that are happy to introduce new members (*see p233*).

For the moment, a tacit understanding between the city and its gay and lesbian

community persists: you can do your own thing as long as you're discreet. This may sound repressive, but it's still much more than most Indian cities allow.

DOS AND DON'TS
Hotels in Mumbai usually don't bat an eyelid at two men or two women sharing a room. If you're a couple and don't want separate beds, insist on a double bed and they'll usually comply. Gay couples can run into problems getting into bars and clubs thanks to a near-universal 'no stags' door policy. You might want to try convincing the bouncers you're gay (we leave it to you to think of how) or you could persuade women friends to come as camouflage. **Indigo** (*see p111*) in Colaba, and **Olive** and **Zenzi** (*see p115*) in Bandra are gay-friendly bars.

There's been a disturbing rise in cases of blackmailers targeting gay men in Mumbai. Some of this is just opportunistic, but there's evidence that it's getting organised. Some use the internet to lure victims, so be careful with making online hook-ups. Take the usual precautions: don't carry too much money; if you're going somewhere with a new person make sure a friend knows; if you're bringing them back to your room make sure all valuables are locked up. A favourite scam with gay tourists is for the blackmailer to go back to your room and then pretend to be an undercover police officer threatening to arrest you for 'illegal sex', unless you pay him off. Don't buy this. Shout as loudly as you can, get the hotel manager, demand his identity card and say you'll go to the police – he'll have fled long before that.

Mind, Body & Soul

Open your third eye and take a peek.

Chakras feeling blocked? *Pranic* energy at a bit of a low ebb? India has a wealth of natural beauty, health and spiritual treatments for every conceivable need – and lots more you've never thought of. Most of them are available in Mumbai. The spectrum of practitioners is wide: a large, informal network of self-trained practitioners regularly visit patrons in their homes to teach yoga, correct breathing or *reiki*; even that small salon on the corner offers invigorating scalp massages and henna conditioning treatments; and plush new spas offer everything from lymphatic drainage and seaweed wraps to botox and weight reduction treatments.

The essentials are yoga, ayurveda and massage. Mumbai lacks the new fangled versions of yoga now popular in the West ('hot yoga' has yet to find any takers in Mumbai), but purists will enjoy authentic versions of the original practised at centres across the city. Be warned: most yoga centres are utilitarian and spartan, so leave the Louis Vuitton yoga tote at home and experience the science in its most unadorned form. Ayurveda is another ancient Indian science in which tradition is revered: rituals like the *shiro dhara* (a full-body massage in which a steady stream of warm medicinal oil is poured on the

forehead to awaken the 'third eye') are over 2,000 years old and continue to be popular today across the social spectrum. Meanwhile, beauty treatments incorporate a range of organic spices, herbs, fruit, flowers and vegetables. Even the wealthiest brides indulge in the pre-wedding custom of smearing turmeric paste over their bodies, and South Mumbai housewives dab La Mer cream on their cheeks only after first cleansing with all-natural rosewater.

A novelty not to be missed is the old Indian *tel maalish*, a vigorous scalp massage with coconut, olive or herbal oil that improves blood circulation, cures headaches and is often credited with giving Indian women their thick, healthy locks. But as the city becomes more global, so do its offerings: you can now choose from Swedish, Thai or Balinese massages, as well as shiatsu, reflexology and inventions like the 'octopus rub' and 'fire massage'. At the world-class **Jiva Grande Spa**, patrons undergo a full lymphatic drainage massage before being mummified in a herbal wrap while purifying Vedic verses are chanted. Spirituality is such an integral part of the Indian psyche that you won't have to look far to find other offerings of interest. Newspapers are flooded with classifieds advertising everything

Learning with the master – **Iyengar Yogashraya**. *See p152*.

from astrological readings to numerological consultations or *reiki*, hypnosis and tantric experts. Exercise some caution with these, but for the most part just go with the flow and don't worry: it's bad for your *chakras*.

Alternative therapies

Chakra therapy
Quan, JW Marriott Mumbai, Juhu Tara Road, Juhu. (6693-3000). Vile Parle station. **Open** 10am-10pm daily. **Credit** AmEx, DC, MC, V.
Chakra (Sanskrit for 'wheel') therapy involves balancing the body's seven *chakras* or energy centres. Located along the torso and on the head, these *chakras* can become blocked by stress and poor nutrition. At Quan they'll give you a bit of spiritual roto-rooting in treatment rooms with relaxing 30- to 75-minute sessions using massage, spiced oils, steam baths, and hot and cold stones. Treatments range from Rs 1,500 to Rs 4,500.

Laughter clubs
Dr Madan Kataria Laughter Club, A001, Denzil Building, 3rd Cross Road, Lokhandwala Complex, Andheri (W) (2631-6426/www.laughteryoga.org). Andheri station.
Take a stroll through Colaba Woods early in the morning and you're likely to spot groups of elderly folks laughing like drains at nothing in particular. But laughter clubs are nothing to laugh about. Oh all right, go ahead, it's good for you. According to Dr Madan Kataria, laughter enriches the blood by increasing oxygen flow, and improves lung capacity. Kataria has set up over 100 laughter clubs across the city, not to mention adding World Laughter Day to our calendars. Call or check online for a laughter club meeting near you. Most are free.

Palmistry
Savio D'Silva, 112 Shopper's Point, first floor, opposite Andheri station (W) (98202-62263).
Buried in the lines of our palms are the secrets of our personal and professional lives. Vedic sages began studying these lines as a means to understand the self and its relationships with others. Savio D'Silva is part of what is now a thriving Indian astro-palmistry industry.

Pranic healing
Pranic Healing Foundation of Maharashtra, Flat No 2, Sunny Side Building, Professor UU Bhat Road, Matunga (2416-0008/3137). **Open** 10am-6pm Mon-Sat. **No credit cards.**
The Chinese call it your *chi*. The Japanese named it *ki*. In Hebrew, it is known as *ruah*. In India it's *prana* – the universal life-force. Pranic healing uses the hands to transfer fresh, vital energy to diseased areas where the energy has 'gone bad'. Loyalists claim it readily alleviates minor aches and sprains, and can even treat serious conditions like heart problems and mental disorders.

Funny ha ha – a **laughter club** in action.

Vastu shastra
Maru Vastu Consultant, C6 MR Society, Juhu Tara Road, Santa Cruz (W) (2660-8135). Santa Cruz station. **Taxi** opposite Raheja College.
A sort of Indian Feng Shui, *vastu shastra* is the science of keeping your surroundings in order, bringing harmony to man-made spaces by aligning the forces of wind, water and fire. Based on the teachings of the ancient Vedas, it's used all over Mumbai in temples, homes, hotels, factories and corporate offices. *Vastu shastra* practitioners are consulted on everything from home-buying to career advice to improving sex lives.

Spas

Aquamarine Day Spa
202 Patel House, Bomanji Petit Road, Kemp's Corner (2381-1118). Grant Road station. **Open** 10am-7pm daily. **Credit** MC, V.
Mumbai's newest spa, Aquamarine was started by European beauty brand Thalgo and offers a range of treatments such as lymphatic drainage massages, facials, body wraps, hot stone therapy and others.

Butterfly Pond
58 Wodehouse Road, Royal Terrace, Colaba (2218-2516). Churchgate/CST stations. **Open** 10am-7pm Tue-Sun. **No credit cards.**
A wide range of facials and body treatments using all-natural aromatherapy products. We recommend a fresh fruit facial.

Centre for Colon Therapy
92 Lady Ratan Tata Medical & Research Centre, M Karve Road, Cooperage (3957-1781/ www.the coloncentre.com). Churchgate/CST stations. **Open** 10am-6pm daily. **Credit** AmEx, DC, MC, V.
Mumbai's only clinic dedicated solely to colonic irrigation, or hydrotherapy. Small, friendly and private, the centre employs the latest US-imported technology, which 'offers the most advanced methods in lower bowel evacuation'. Rs 2,500 per session, Rs 6,000 for three.

Franck Provost Spa & Salon
Aryston Centre, third floor, Juhu Tara Road (5502-1440). Vile Parle station. **Taxi** opposite

Sea, sand and saline drips

Why shell out $1,000 on a root canal in the US when you can just outsource the procedure to Mumbai for $100? And what's more, the money you save pays for a fabulous holiday in India.

Along with the Gateway of India, cheap laser eye corrections and hip replacements have now become compelling reasons to take a trip to Mumbai. In the West, long waiting lists for routine procedures and rising drug costs have helped to push India as a healthcare destination, where everything from heart surgery and knee transplants to dental care and cosmetic surgery can be had, at excellent facilities and performed by first-rate doctors.

Medical tourism is a growing industry that could be worth around $1 billion a year to the

Indian economy. Organisations like the Medical Tourism Council of Maharashtra (www.mahamedtour.com) are already wooing tourists with fixed packages that include travel, accommodation and medical expenses. On its website, the Apollo Group of Hospitals (www.apollohospitals.com) has a section devoted to international patients – explaining everything from blood screening standards to a virtual patient visit. In Mumbai, the private Lilavati, Jaslok and Hinduja hospitals (*see p233*) have state-of-the-art healthcare facilities that have been serving foreigners for years. Medical tourism could save you a fortune, but it's worth remembering that it's a new industry and poorly regulated.

JW Marriott Mumbai. **Open** 10am-7.30pm daily. **Credit** AmEx, MC, V.
French brand Franck Provost offers a range of hair, beauty and spa treatments over three floors. Luxury is the keyword and it offers packages for every conceivable occasion, including an indulgent couples' 'chocolate session' for Valentine's Day.

Kerala Ayurvedic Health Spa
Neelkanth, Marine Drive (2288-3210/98204-35344). Marine Lines station. **Taxi** outside Platform 1, Marine Lines Station. **Open** 8am-8pm daily. **Credit** AmEx, MC, V.
For an authentic and affordable taste of South India's natural ayurvedic treatments, visit this chain, the best-known for good reason. Sample the famous *shiro dhara* – a full body massage carried out simultaneously by two practitioners and a vessel full of medicinal oil that's slowly poured on to the forehead in a steady stream. It's an experience you'll want to sample at least once. Be warned: you don't get to keep your undies on.
Other locations: Garden View, J Mehta Marg, Nepean Sea Road (6608-7009). Grant Road station; Sun 'n' Sand Hotel, 39 Juhu Beach, Juhu (5502-4043). Santa Cruz station.

Lakme
Arsiwala Building, Wodehouse Road, Colaba (2218-1747/6631-5277). Churchgate/CST stations. **Open** 10am-7pm daily. **Credit** MC, V.
Lakme salons offer a range of beauty services, including waxing, threading and hot-oil scalp massages.
Other locations: Shop No 1, Kailash, Waterfield Road, Bandra (2643-7220). Bandra station.

Nail Bar
14 Union Park, Bandra (W) (5583-8464/8454). Bandra station. **Open** 10.30am-8pm daily. **Credit** AmEx, DC, MC, V.

This speciality nail salon offers you milkshakes and fresh lemonade as you get your hands and feet seen to. There are regular manis and pedis, as well as treatments such as a paraffin bath for hands and feet.
Other locations: 25 Off Arthur Bunder Road, Colaba (2287-6513/6514). Churchgate/CST stations.

Parcos
White Hall, Kemp's Corner (2364-3685). Grant Road station. **Open** *Store* 10.30am-7.30pm. *Studio* 10am-6pm. **Credit** AmEx, DC, MC, V.
This Clarins-run spa is small but neat, and offers signature face and body treatments.

Touch of Joy
Sethna House, Ground Floor, JA Allana Marg, Colaba (2204-5566). **Taxi** opposite Electric House. **Open** 10.30am-7.30pm daily. **Credit** MC, V.
This Colaba institution offers the gamut of beauty treatments for men and women, including possibly the best scalp massage in the city.

Massage

Moksh – The Wellness Place
Bhulabhai Desai Road, Breach Candy (2367-6990). Grant Road station. **Taxi** opposite US Consulate. **Open** 6am-10pm daily. **Credit** MC, V.
Moksh's therapists recommend the fire massage (don't worry – it's just hot oils) or a Swedish massage (Rs 800-Rs 950/hour), but if you're strapped for cash, go for the ones that lavish loving attention strictly on your feet (Rs 300 for half an hour). The real pampering happens in the individual bubble baths, complete with rose petals and essential oils. Treatments cost between Rs 300 and Rs 800. **Photo** *p152.*

Mustafa Mukth
Call 98201-44232 for details & appointments.

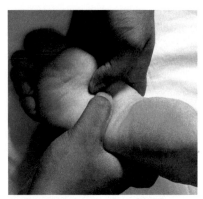

Get a loving foot massage at **Moksh**.
See p151.

A teacher of yoga and naturopathy, Mustafa Mukth makes house calls to the Mumbai elite (everyone from film stars to industrialists) to knead their knots in a variety of styles, including Swedish, Korean, shiatsu, Thai and Balinese. Massages start from Rs 500 an hour, plus travel expenses.

Specialist yoga

Ishwardas Chunnilal Yogic Health Centre – Kaivalyadhama
43 Netaji Subash Road, Marine Drive (2281-8417). Charni Road station. **Open** 7-10am, 4-7pm Mon-Sat. **No credit cards.**
The Kaivalyadhama at Marine Drive is part of a 60-year-old organisation set up by Swami Kuvalayananda to promote yoga for health and healing. Every year around 4,000 members flock to this roomy centre to study yogic practices. Rs 300 for a check-up.

Iyengar Yogashraya
Elmac House, Senapati Bapat Marg, Lower Parel (W) (2494-8416). Lower Parel station. **Open** 7am-4pm Mon; 7am-8pm Tue-Sat. **No credit cards.**
Come rain or shine, die-hard followers of BKS Iyengar yoga still show up at his institute in Pune to study under the guidance of the man himself. But in 2002, Mumbai got its own Iyengar Institute in Lower Parel. The warm and welcoming you-can-do-it-too attitude will put even the most insecure first-timer at ease. Not that the *asanas* are even remotely comfortable, but props designed by the master – wooden gadgets, belts and ropes – help tremendously. Prices range from Rs 276 to Rs 882. **Photo** *p149.*

Satyananda (Bihar) Yoga Centre
Individual classes only. Call 2364-0993 for details.
Practise yoga in the comfort of your hotel room under the guidance of private instructors from the Satyananda Centre. Founded by Swami Satyananda

Saraswati, the school integrates techniques from various traditional branches of yoga, including Raja, Bhakti, Karma, Hatha, Kundalini and Kriya. Around Rs 300-Rs 500 per class.

The Yoga Institute
Prabhat Colony, Shree Yogendra Marg, Santa Cruz (E) (2611-0506). Santa Cruz station. **Open** 6.30am-7.30pm daily. **No credit cards.**
If you want a serious crash course in the fundamentals of yoga, try the Yoga Institute's seven-day health camp (Rs 1,800 plus Rs 500 for accommodation), which includes an introduction to the philosophy of yoga and its practical applications. They also cover healthy diets and lifestyles, recreation and meaningful relationships. The centre combines traditional yogic values and techniques with Western science and educational methodology to spread the word about well-being. Put down the self-help book and register.

Ayurvedic healing

Ayush Therapy Centre
450B, 14th Road, Khar (W) (2649-0556). Bandra/ Khar stations. **Open** 9am-7pm daily. **Credit** MC, V.
Most Ayurvedic centres don't boast air-conditioning or a nice colour palette. And even in Bandra, few places can claim a fountain in the front yard. But this is Ayush, a top-flight centre with individually tailored meditation and yoga classes. Treatments range from Rs 300 to Rs 1,000.

Ayushakti
CTS 563 (1 & 2), Bandran Nagar, Cross Road 2, off SV Road, Malad (W) (2806-5757). Malad station. **Open** 10.30am-8pm Mon-Sat. **Credit** AmEx, DC, MC, V.
Dr Pankaj Naram is famous for diagnosing patients just by taking their pulses and then prescribing a customised combination of herbs, strange diets (sometimes nothing but pure ghee, or clarified butter) and much-needed detoxication. Legend has it Naram learned the art of pulse reading from a 115-year-old Tibetan monk. Today, the centre is spread over 15,000 feet in a leafy part of Malad and has a residential complex for long-term treatments (although you'll need to book at least two years in advance). Treatment sessions start at Rs 250.

Kerala Ayurvedic Health Spa
10A Louis Mansion, VS Road, Prabhadevi (2430-2336/98204-35344). Dadar station. **Open** 8am-8pm daily. **Credit** MC, V.
KAHS runs branches across the city and each spa offers a large variety of traditional Ayurvedic treatments including the popular *shiro dhara* (Rs 975) and the *ayushman bhava* (Rs 1,650) rejuvenation therapy. The clean but no-frills set-up feels cosy and authentic, thanks in large part to the Kerala sari-clad practitioners who studiously ignore the fact that you're naked. Treatments cost Rs 675 to Rs 1,650.

Music

On a *raga* trip.

Bollywood provides Mumbai's soundtrack – something that's evident every time you turn on a radio, climb into a rickshaw or go to a nightclub. New Hindi film music and reissues of old classics account for 60 per cent of recording industry sales. But strangely enough, Bollywood playback singers – the men and women who lend their voices to lip-synching actors – rarely perform live. That's because the Bollywood movie song is a cinematic spectacle – watching playback singers croon *Kuch Kuch Hota Hai* instead of Shah Rukh Khan and Kajol would just spoil the fantasy. The demand for live Hindi film song concerts is limited to nostalgia trips in which imitators of Mohammed Rafi, Kishore Kumar and other famous playback singers from the 1940s, '50s and '60s perform songs from the period.

So strong is Bollywood's hold over the city's music tastes that even though the arrival of MTV led to an Indian pop music boom in the mid-1990s, the genre has since been taken over by remixes of old Hindi film hits. Reality TV talent hunts like Sony TV's *Indian Idol* (a franchise of the UK's *Pop Idol*) have given Indian pop a recent boost, but established pop singers have to double up as playback singers to bring home the bread.

However, it's Hindustani (North Indian) and Carnatic (South Indian) classical music that dominates Mumbai's live music scene, despite accounting for just ten per cent of record sales. That's because of the improvisational nature of the music, in which a single *raga* (a fixed set of notes, somewhat akin to a scale) can last anywhere from ten minutes to two hours and sound utterly different each time it's performed, making each concert a unique event. Most classical concerts are organised by *sabhas*, or music circles, whose members pay an annual subscription fee to attend concerts arranged by the circle, which is usually associated with a particular venue. Non-members can also attend by paying a nominal guest fee (*see p154* **Buying tickets**). There are also larger concerts during the winter, the traditional classical music season, when famous names like Ravi Shankar and Zakir Hussain make their annual visit to the city for a series of appearances.

There's also a small Western classical music scene, which plays at just one venue – the **National Centre for Performing Arts**

Zakir Hussain.

'Jazzy' Joe Pereira.

(2282-4567, 6654-8135, www.ncpamumbai.com) at Nariman Point. But one of the city's most interesting live music experiences is only available once a year – the vibrant traditional folk music of Maharashtra. During the first, third, seventh, tenth and 11th days of the annual **Ganesh Chaturthi** festival (*see p135*) around September, the city streets are taken over with lines of devotees dancing to the sound of Nashik *bajas* – amateur bands who beat out frenetic rhythms on *dhols* (two-sided drums), *tashas* (copper drums), *jhanjs* (hand cymbals) and *lezims* (metal sticks with jangling metal plates).

Mumbai had a vibrant jazz music scene in the 1950s and '60s, when the erstwhile Churchgate Street (now Veer Nariman Road) was lined with venues, each with its own jazz band. Today, your last chance to catch some old-time Bombay jazz is at **Not Just Jazz by the Bay** (*see p114*), where the octogenarian Jazzy Joe and the Jazz Junkies play regularly. Mumbai also has one of India's biggest college rock scenes. Classic rock and extreme metal are the dominant sounds and, although most bands stick to covers, there are a handful of young acts putting out original (albeit derivative) music. Two of the biggest Mumbai bands are Zero and Pin Drop Violence, who play occasionally at college festivals (log on to **www.gigpad.com** for details), which are open to non-students for between Rs 50 and Rs 150 per ticket. There are also occasional larger festivals like **Independence Rock** (*see p156*). You can find Indian rock CDs at **BX Furtado** (*see p130*).

BUYING TICKETS

Check *Time Out Mumbai* and city newspaper supplements like *Bombay Times* to find out what concerts are on during your stay, or call one of the music circles (*see below*) direct for information on upcoming classical performances. Guests are welcome to attend music circle concerts for a fee of Rs 50 to Rs 100 payable at the venue on the night. Hindi film music nostalgia concerts usually take place around the birth or death anniversary of famous singers, composers and lyricists. Again, check *Time Out* or the newspapers. Tickets cost between Rs 50 and Rs 300. Except for larger concerts or performances at the NCPA, concert organisers generally do not accept credit cards or take advance bookings.

Music circles

Most of today's household names in Indian classical music made their debut at concerts organised by *sabhas*, or music circles, which emerged in the late 19th century to popularise

classical music. Indian classical music still lacks funding and music circles remain vital in supporting the form. Most of the venues listed below are small with simple facilities, and often lack air-conditioning.

Bharatiya Fine Arts Society

MS Subbulakshmi Auditorium, Plot H, Bhau Daji Road Extension, Sion (W) (2407-8888). Sion station.
The biggest classical names from Chennai, the hub of Carnatic music, perform here.

Dadar Matunga Cultural Centre

122A JK Sawant Road, near Ruparel College, Mahim (2430-4150). Dadar station.
One of the city's oldest music circles, it puts on at least one concert a month.

Fine Arts Society, Chembur

Sivaswamy Auditorium, Fine Arts Society, Fine Arts Chowk, near Chembur Flyover, RC Marg, Chembur (2522-2988). Chembur station.
One of the city's main venues for Carnatic classical music performances.

Indian Music Group

St Xavier's College Hall, St Xavier's College, 5 Mahapalika Marg (2263-4548). Churchgate/ CST stations.
Founded in 1974 by former students of St Xavier's College, the Indian Music Group organises four prestigious Hindustani concerts every year.

Kala Bharati

Karnataka Sangha, Dr Vishveshawarayya Samarak Mandir, CHM Marg, Matunga (W) (2437-7022). Matunga Road station.
Hosts a classical music or dance performance every Sunday morning in an air-conditioned auditorium.

Sri Shanmukhananda Fine Arts & Sangeet Sabha

Shanmukhananda Hall, Plot No 292, behind Gandhi Market, Comrade Harbans Lal Marg, Sion (E) (2407-8888). Sion station.
Carnatic music dominates this Sabha's calendar and the monthly list of performers includes both established and new artists. The Shanmukhananda Hall, with seating for over 3,000, has been rented out for performances by acts as varied as *ghazal* singer Jagjit Singh and British dinosaur rockers Jethro Tull.

Swar Sadhana Samiti

Mumbai Marathi Sahitya Sangh Mandir, Dr Bhalerao Marg, near St Mary's High School, Gaiwadi, Girgaum (2385-6303). Charni Road station.
Stages a monthly concert to showcase the work of upcoming Hindustani classical musicians.

Udayan

National Gallery of Modern Art, Sir CJ Hall, near Regal Cinema, Mahatma Gandhi Road, Fort (2288-1969). CST station.

Get your own guru

Want to be able to scat like Ella? Then Hindustani classical singing lessons might be just what you need. Over the past nine years, jazz singers from the US and Europe have been visiting Mumbai to learn how to sing *alaaps* and *nom-tom*, studying improvisation techniques employed in Indian classical music. For a few hours every week, they play the role of devoted *shishyas* (students) to their *guru* (teacher), Dhanashree Pandit-Rai of the Jazz India Vocal Institute. Although they visit for lessons, they don't actually move into the home of the mother of two, as they would have done in the good old days.

The *guru-shishya parampara* (literally 'teacher-student tradition') was a 3,000-year-old education system in which students lived with their teachers in an ashram and were taught the Vedas, ancient texts that dealt with everything from mathematics to medicine. Although the *guru-shishya* tradition has been replaced with the scholastic system, one-to-one oral teaching remains the main way of passing on skills in Indian classical music.

The name of your guru is still considered a keen indicator of how good you are. All the stalwarts of 20th-century Indian classical music, including sitar maestro Ravi Shankar and sarod virtuoso Ali Akbar Khan, are products of the *guru-shishya parampara*. If you'd like to learn the sitar, and are ready for the commitment, you could try and get your own *guru*. There are several *gurus* teaching both vocal and instrumental music in Mumbai. Fees range from Rs 200 to Rs 1,000 per lesson. Check music shops like Rhythm House and Bhargava's Musik *(see p129)* for directories of music teachers. There are also several city institutions teaching classical music; enrolments usually take place in June *(see p236)*.

Udayan organises classical music, dance and theatre performances every Saturday at the National Gallery of Modern Art at Nariman Point.

Music festivals

The most important events in Mumbai's musical calendar. Call ahead for the exact dates as performances often correspond to festivals and events in the Hindu calendar that vary from year to year.

Jan-Feb

Alla Rakha Khan Barsi Concert
Shanmukhananda Hall, Plot No 292, behind Gandhi Market, Comrade Harbans Lal Marg, Sion (E) (2407-8888). Sion station.
India's first family of percussion music pays tribute to the legendary tabla player.

Banganga Festival
Banganga Tank, Walkeshwar (2202-4482/ www.maharashtratourism.gov.in).
A legendary Hindustani classical musician performs at the bank of the picturesque Banganga tank.

JanFest
St Xavier's College Hall, St Xavier's College, 5 Mahapalika Marg (2263-4548). Churchgate/CST stations.
College kids outnumber the oldies at this concert organised by students of St Xavier's College and the Indian Music Group.

Jazz Utsav
Various venues.
The foremost exponents of Indian jazz perform alongside musicians visiting from around the world. Organised by Capital Jazz (email ashokgulati@vsnl.com).

Kala Ghoda Festival
Kala Ghoda, Fort (2387-5454/www.kalaghoda association.com).
The Kala Ghoda art district plays host to some of the country's most eclectic rock and jazz musicians.

Smriti Sandhya
St Andrew's Auditorium, St Andrew's College, St Dominic Road, Bandra (W) (2640-3041/ www.bimalroymemorial.org). Bandra station.
A concert of film music held in memory of one of India's greatest directors, Bimal Roy. Organised by the Bimal Roy Memorial Committee. **Photo** *p156.*

Arts & Entertainment

March/April

Alladiya Khan Festival

Balvikas Sangh Hall, Balvikas Sangh Marg,
near Gandhi Maidan, Chembur (2527-2388).
Chembur station.
This four-day concert pays tribute to the founder of
the Agra gharana of Hindustani classical music.

May/June

Aarohi

YB Chavan Centre, near Mantralaya, General
Jagannath Bhosle Marg (2285-2081). Churchgate
station.
Performances by the future stars of Hindustani
classical music. Organised by Pancham Nishad
(2412-4750).

Megh Malhar

Nehru Centre Auditorium, Dr Annie Besant Road,
Worli (2496-4676/nehrucentremumbai.com).
Mahalaxmi station.
Maestros perform romantic monsoon *ragas*.

Rabigeetika

Mysore Association Hall, 393 Bhau Daji Road, near
Maheshwari Udayan, Matunga (E) (2402-4647).
Matunga station.
A concert of Rabindra Sangeet, the music written
and composed by Bengali writer Rabindranath
Tagore. Organised by Rabigeetika (2262-4709).

July/August

Independence Rock

Various venues. www.gigpad.com.
Two adrenalin-charged days of headbanging,
courtesy of the country's best-loved rock and
metal acts.

Janmashtami Flute Concert

Brindavan Gurukul, Haridwar Marg, Versova-Link
Road, Andheri (W) (2646-3535/
www.brindavangurukul.org). Andheri station.
Legendary flautist Hariprasad Chaurasia and
his students perform a 24-hour concert at his
music school during the festival of Janmashtami
(*see p135*).

Khazana

Various venues. www.pankajudhas.com.
An annual ghazal festival organised by singer
Pankaj Udhas.

September/October

Lata Mangeshkar Tribute Concert

Various venues.
India's first family of playback singers pays tribute
to their most famous member. Organised by
Hridayesh Arts (2614-8556).

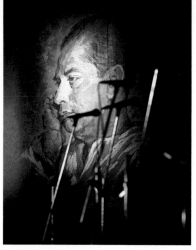

Smriti Sandhya pays tribute to the late
Bimal Roy. *See p155.*

Dhaval Nishad

National Centre for the Performing Arts,
Nariman Point (www.ncpamumbai.com).
Churchgate/CST stations.
An all-night concert celebrating Sharad Poornima,
the auspicious full-moon night during the month of
Sharad. Organised by Pancham Nishad (2412-4750).

November/December

A Festival of Festive Music

National Centre for the Performing Arts, Nariman
Point. Churchgate/CST stations.
Twelve choirs from around the country perform
Christmas music. Organised by the Stop Gaps
Cultural Academy (2421-2120).

Campus Rock Idols

MMRDA Grounds, Bandra Kurla Complex,
Bandra (E) (www.dnanetworks.com). Bandra station.
A battle of college bands. Organised by DNA
Networks.

Ruhaniyat

Horniman Circle Gardens, Horniman Circle,
Fort (2363-3561). Churchgate/CST stations.
A Sufi music festival. Organised by Banyan Tree
Events (2826-0674).

Sangat

National Centre for the Performing Arts,
Nariman Point (www.ncpamumbai.com).
Churchgate/CST stations.
A chamber music festival organised by the Mehli
Mehta Music Foundation (2382-3644).

Spiritual Morning

The Gateway of India, Colaba. Churchgate/
CST stations.
Morning *ragas* at the Gateway of India. Organised
by Pancham Nishad (2412-4750).

Nightlife

Dancing under a deadline.

In January 2006, Pete Gooding, the resident DJ at Ibiza institution Café Mambo, played a blistering set at Squeeze in Bandra that ran over the legal 1.30am deadline. It was a Thursday night and police stomped into the club as perplexed patrons looked on. The men in khaki recorded the faces of clubbers with a video camera, and refused to let anyone go until they'd got their names and numbers.

Club owners' palm-greasing of police, which had always allowed them to keep premises open beyond 1.30am, came to an abrupt halt in late 2005, sending Mumbai's burgeoning club scene into disarray. It's not that the Mumbai police had suddenly discovered their consciences; 2005 had been a public relations nightmare, with a high-profile case of a police officer raping a woman in a Marine Drive police booth being just the most striking example of decay in the force. In an attempt to regain some credibility, the police commissioner threatened to come down hard on corrupt officers. Enforcing the 1.30am deadline at Mumbai's clubs seemed like an easy way of showing that the force was doing its job.

The crackdown has made life extremely tough for a lot of city clubs. Punters rarely step out before 11pm, meaning there simply isn't time to make enough money before the 1.30am deadline kicks in. Many club owners still pay out bribes to sustain relationships with their local cops, but get little in return. Some canny promoters who run nightspots in Andheri have hooked cops as investors, ensuring that deadlines will never be a problem. But for the most part, the 1.30am cut-off is now strictly enforced.

And it had all been going so well; 20 new nightspots opened across the city in 2005 but they are now floundering, some killed off altogether. The beneficiaries of the new regime are the clubs run within luxury hotels, which have special licences to operate until 3am. Until the middle of 2005, the Taj Mahal Hotel club, **Insomnia** (*see p158*), had been thought to be on its last legs. Now, go there on the weekend and you're likely to get your ribs cracked in the crush.

The real tragedy of the 1.30am law has been its effect on creativity. With restricted business hours, club and bar owners are wary of experimenting with new music, and prefer catering to the lowest common denominator in a bid to maximise short-term profits. The result:

Enigma. *See p161.*

commercial Bollywood music sets that are indistinguishable from venue to venue, popular with the majority of clubbers, but sorely lacking in variety. Until a solution is found (one possibility is special late-night licences, under discussion when we went to press), Mumbai's nightlife is likely to remain stuck in a groove.

DOS & DON'TS

Mumbai nightclubs have notoriously complicated cover charges, depending on which night of the week you go, whether you are a male-female couple, a single woman or a 'stag' (a single male). Most cover charges range between Rs 600 and Rs 1,500 and include the cost of a few drinks. Clubs occasionally enforce no-stag policies on Friday and Saturday nights, but they're often more lax when it comes to (white) foreign men, thanks to the continuing popularity of the idea that foreigners add a touch of glamour – but don't count on this. Clubs are notorious for turning away black men; bouncers commonly assume that if you're black and in Mumbai you must be a) Nigerian and b) involved in the drug trade. If you suspect

Red Light.

that you're the victim of a racist entry policy, there's not much you can do except demand to see the manager and tell him you're going to call the local press – stories like that make club owners very uncomfortable.

The admission prices given in the listings are for male-female couples and stags, with the lower price applying on weekdays, and the higher price on Fridays and Saturdays. Single women can expect to pay about half that, or sometimes nothing at all.

Colaba

Insomnia

The Taj Mahal Hotel, Apollo Bunder (6665-3366). Churchgate/CST stations. **Open** 9pm-2am Tue-Sun. **Admission** Rs 600-Rs 1,500.
South Mumbai's tightest bodies and prettiest faces convene at the Taj's after-hours nightclub on weekends to meet, network and score work. The music is strictly commercial, though the DJs do push the boundaries if badgered enough. The club has several dimly lit chambers and ante-rooms, which fill up with punters looking to escape the hordes on the dancefloor. If you're hoping to party on a Saturday night, we suggest arriving early – or run the risk of being knocked unconscious by out-of-control drunk women doing the funky chicken. Trust us, we've seen it happen.

Polly Esther's

First Floor, Gordon House, Battery Street, Apollo Bunder, Colaba (2287-1122). Churchgate/CST stations. **Open** 9pm-3am Tue-Sun. **Admission** Rs 600-Rs 1,000.
A fun, roomy club that's part of the Gordon House Hotel, decked out with flower-power decor, posters of Rocky and a young Bollywood-starlet-of-yesteryear, Zeenat Aman, toking on a chillum. Most nights at Polly's are dedicated to retro at its purest – Prince, the Pet Shop Boys and the Bee Gees all do heavy-duty rotation – but there's also plenty of present-day fare for the satchel-and-apple crowd on Wednesdays. Spirits may be raised, but don't give in to your date's pleas to buy one of the Afro wigs worn by the waiters: they cost an oversized Rs 3,000.

Voodoo

Arthur Bunder Road, off Colaba Causeway, Colaba (2284-1959). Churchgate/CST stations. **Taxi** Near Radio Club. **Open** 8pm-1.30am daily. **Admission** Rs 200.
Voodoo is the most risqué little bar in South Mumbai. It's got girls a-plenty and they certainly do dance, but they also sit, talk and drink with the male clientele – a motley lot of minor-league businessmen, both local and visiting. In other words, you can look and you can touch. The lights are dim, the air is heavy and the atmosphere is sweaty, going on edgy. Unaccompanied males may feel intimidated by the attentions of predatory females and no one should go to the toilets on their own. Saturday night is gay night with plenty of equally predatory males on the prowl. For entertainment value, nothing beats it.

Fort

Red Light

Next to Khyber restaurant, 145 Mahatma Gandhi Road, Kala Ghoda, Fort (6634-6249). CST station. **Open** 7pm-midnight daily. **Admission** Rs 600-Rs 800.
A destination for the prettiest students in South Mumbai, paying for their drinks with plentiful allowances from daddy. The music at weekends is a mishmash of Hindi commercial grind (and you really have to like crowds), but the DJs serve up some old-school Snoop, Dre and Pac on Wednesdays, and there's plenty of Brit-Bolly-bhangra beats on offer for the city's bling bling crew. However, be warned: a clear head is necessary for a visit to the loos, where the mirrored corridor causes such disorientation that desperate and dazed patrons have been known to relieve themselves on the floor.

Lower Parel

Aziano

Phoenix Mills, Garden Court, Block 16, opposite Quorum, Senapati Bapat Marg, Lower Parel (2495-2879). Lower Parel station. **Open** 9pm-1.30am Wed-Sun. **Admission** Rs 1,000-Rs 1,500.
The latest addition to Phoenix Mills' continuing transformation from cotton mill to a midtown shopping-and-partying destination. They've retained the original sloping mill roof, now painted silver and black, for some post-industrial cred, but Aziano's best features are the open-air courtyard where live percussionists provide the soundtrack to romantic evenings, and the dinosaur eggshell sofas straight out of a 1970s sci-fi movie. The inside is long, narrow and crowded, with a non-stop commercial Hindi music soundtrack.

RA

Phoenix Mills Compound, 462 Senapati Bapat Marg, Lower Parel (6661-4343/4369). Lower Parel station. **Open** 9pm-1.30am Wed-Sun. **Admission** Rs 1,500.

Rock Bottom. *See p162.*

RA was supposed to be an exclusive members' club for regulars of nearby Lush (*see p114*) who could afford to fork out over Rs 100,000 for membership. It was so exclusive that members found themselves awkwardly clutching their cocktails in an empty lounge. So management roped-off an exclusive members' section and opened the rest to the public. It worked: RA has become a new playground for Mumbai's beautiful ones. The DJ spins contemporary chartbusters, Hindi as well as English – just the way the patrons like it. The Rs 1,500 cover charge is programmed onto an 'RA card' and redeemable at the bar for outrageously tasty cocktails at around Rs 400 a pop. But don't arrive before midnight – when RA's energy levels jump to max.

Bandra & Khar

Arabian Sea Lounge & Bar

ITC Welcom Group, Sea Rock Hotel, Land's End, Bandstand, Bandra (W) (2642-5454). Bandra station. **Taxi** opposite Taj Land's End Hotel. **Open** 8.30pm-3am Tue-Sun. **Admission** Rs 500 per couple.

The floral upholstery is straight out of the 1980s and so is the set list of the resident band, the Wayfarers, who perform on Saturday and Sunday nights. Luckily, the soft-rock quartet does more-than-decent versions of Crowded House and Guns 'n' Roses hits. When they pack up, a little after midnight, the action shifts to a long dancefloor next door that gets packed with punters getting down to hip hop sounds soon after the 1.30am deadline kicks in at other city clubs unfortunate enough not to be located in five-star hotels.

H2O: The Liquid Lounge

Sheetal Bukhara, off Linking Road, Khar (W) (2649-5151). Khar station. **Taxi** opposite Khar Telephone Exchange. **Open** 6.30pm-1.30am daily. **Admission** Rs 1,000.

Four split levels, three open-air terraces each with its own bar, walls in seven hues of blue and circular

One night in Colaba
The ultimate South Mumbai pub and club crawl.

These days the historic Colaba district is considered to have slipped into second place to Bandra when it comes to the city's nightlife. But for sheer variety, it takes some beating. Start off the night at **Gokul** *(see p111)*, a smoky back-room haunt that looks like it should be home to winos, piss artists and two-bit drunks but is actually a popular dive with a respectable crowd that includes suits, student types and, yes, even a few women. Saunter around the street corner to **Leopold Café** *(see p113)*, with its high ceilings, slow-spinning fans and turn-of-the-last-century charm. It's a hub for backpackers looking to exchange tips, sip on chilled suds and chow down on hearty fare. Or duck in to **Café Mondegar** *(see p111)*, a lively cheesecake-slice of a bar with an ancient jukebox playing unending '70s rock. Move on quickly to **Busaba** *(see p111)*, fondly known as Busa, with sultry red walls and chinoiserie love seats, for its trippy trance beats and great cocktails.

If you've dressed up nicely, pop next door to **Indigo** *(see p111)*, the celebrity hub of South Mumbai, where assembled lovelies and their banker boyfriends come to see and be seen. You'll find more of the city's pretty faces and lithe bodies at **Taxi** *(see p113)*, reminiscent of a luxurious Gothic castle. For a taste of Mumbai's only gay club, check out **Voodoo**

(see p158) on Saturday nights, with plenty of over-friendly girls thrown in.

Most Mumbai nightspots close at 1.30am so move on for some after-hours dancefloor action at **Insomnia** *(see p158)*, a plush nightclub with multiple sections where some of Mumbai's best DJs spin local and international hits. Retro freaks should visit Mumbai's tribute to the glitterball era, **Polly Esther's** *(see p158)*, where the waiters don fluorescent Afro wigs and the dancefloor lights up à la *Saturday Night Fever*. Still not had enough? Those looking for that one last beer or three should head straight to **Starlit Café** *(see p113)*, an open-air rooftop bar that's open 24 hours, with a grand view of the harbour and the Gateway of India.

Busaba.

Seven –
Anyone got a fire
extinguisher?

water-filled windows with colourful plants dancing in the currents. H2O is like an underwater lair from a Bond film (minus the bikini babes, unfortunately). The music is upbeat lounge in the early evening, followed by a smattering of house, ending up with Bollywood beats – standard Mumbai fare to keep the suburban punters bouncing.

Purple Haze
302 Landmark, Pali Naka, off Turner Road, Bandra (W) (5502-2200). Bandra station. **Open** 7pm-1.30am daily. **Admission** Rs 600-Rs 1,000.
Purple Haze, occupying two floors of the usually desolate Landmark Mall, is where the Bandra boys and girls go when they want to disco, instead of the usual retro ride on offer at almost every other Bandra joint. A mix of hip hop, bhangra and Bollywood packs in the dancefloor on Saturday nights. It looks like a 1970s vision of a nightclub of the future, complete with silver upholstery, pink floor lights and a staircase that connects the two levels via a tunnel of tubelights. On the lower deck, lounge around on the silver armchairs and sofas or swing in a love chair suspended from the 25-foot-high ceiling by purple ropes. Cocktails here are disappointing though; whatever you do, don't try the house special – the sickeningly sweet 'Purple Baby'.

Seven
Shopper's Stop Building, Sixth Floor, Linking Road, Bandra (W) (3951-1139). Bandra station. **Open** 8.30pm-1.30am Tue-Sun. **Admission** Rs 400-Rs 1,000.
Seven sits on the top of a Bandra shopping mall, with vast windows offering outstanding views of ugly building after ugly building – but, hey, this is Mumbai, so forget what's outside the window and dance. Seven is always packed, usually with the thirty- to fortysomething crowd and has an undeniable energy, with the not-quite-kids freaking out to green lasers, dry ice and commercial Hindi hits. A warning to barflies: for extra entertainment, the bar staff pour vodka on the stainless steel counters and set fire to them. What's that? Fire safety? Don't be a party-pooper. **Photo** *above*.

Squeeze
5th Road, SV Road, opposite Regency banquet hall, Khar (W)(2648-9311). Khar station. **Open** 9pm-1.30am Tue-Sun. **Admission** Rs 1,000-Rs 1,500.
You get plenty of build-up when you enter Squeeze. A set of giant red doors slide open off the street, onto a pathway lined with bamboo stems. Clipboard fiends lurk around a podium at the end of the walkway, which turns a corner and continues down another manicured stretch to an imposing door. Enter a cavernous (by Bandra standards) split-level nightclub of smooth black granite, leather couches and a soundtrack of hip hop-Bolly-bhangra mashups. They weren't kidding when they named this club – it's currently one of Bandra's most happening venues and attracts such a crowd that rush-hour suburban trains look roomy by comparison. If it all gets a bit too much you can try and escape into two soothing chill-out ante-chambers, with three-storey high ceilings and walls dripping with money plants. **Photo** *p162*.

Juhu

Enigma
JW Marriott Hotel, Juhu Tara Road, Juhu (6693-3000). Vile Parle station. **Open** 9.30pm-3am Tue-Sat. **Admission** Rs 500-Rs 1,500.
Enigma, the JW Marriott's super-club, has defied the competition by managing to keep pulling in the crowds almost continuously since 2003. Known as Bollywood's favourite nightclub, it tends to get filled up with paunchy movie producers, but you won't hear the girls complaining when they also get the chance to shake booty alongside regulars like movie stars Abhishek Bachchan and Fardeen Khan. The decor radiates an appropriate aura of cool: a dramatic chandelier is suspended above a large circular bar in the centre of a space decked out with dark-hued drapes, plush sofas, flickering candles and ottomans. The playlist is heavy on the Hindi, but Enigma is also one of the few city nightclubs to feature international acts. Thursdays are devoted to

Squeeze. *See p161.*

house, progressive, trance and drum 'n' bass, Fridays to R&B, bhangra and hip hop. Add regular sessions with local remix babes and tabletop twirling by girl bartenders from the Coyote Ugly bar in Dubai and it's easy to see why the boys love it. Photo *p157*.

J49

Hotel Juhu Residency, 148 B Juhu Tara Road, Juhu (2618-4546). Vile Parle station. **Open** 9pm-1.30am daily. **Admission** Rs 400.

In August 2002, three carbine-wielding gangsters unloaded 26 rounds into a wall outside J49, Juhu's oldest existing nightclub. It was a 'friendly' warning to the owners, who were caught up in a messy underworld feud. But the club refused to die. Hipper upstairs like Vie and Enigma have sprung up all over the neighbourhood but J49 has miraculously been able to bounce back and thrive. What's more, it's home to the city's most raging Sunday night scene: 'Bollywood Night' packs in the after-midnight crowd and the party doesn't end until early morning joggers are seen hitting the beach nearby.

Rock Bottom

Hotel Ramee Guestline, AB Nair Road, Juhu (6693-5555). Vile Parle station. **Open** 7pm-1.30am Thur-Sat. **Admission** Rs 500-Rs 1,800.

When Rock Bottom opened for business in late 2003, the hype was huge, with no less than living Bollywood legend Amitabh Bachchan seen regularly striding through this sleek Juhu nightclub. It remains the best-looking club in the city, with a cavernous dancefloor, vast screens over the DJ booth and a stellar sound system. Mini TV screens

above the men's urinals ensure that guys never have to miss a second of the revelry. Expect standard commercial fare as far as music is concerned – so what if it's the same songs every night? Photo *p159*.

Andheri

Avalon

Hotel Bawa International, Nehru Road Extension, Vile Parle (E) (2611-3636). Vile Parle station. **Open** 8pm-3am Tue-Sun. **Admission** Rs 400-Rs 2,000.

The hip hop-bhangra party rages late almost every night of the week at this decade-old club, making it a perennial suburban favourite, especially with middle-aged businessmen and their young girlfriends. In this city, where it's hard to find an inch of anonymity at mainstream nightspots, Avalon offers welcome relief. Patrons are unlikely to bump into anyone they know out here, which explains why so many of them unabashedly cut loose. The girls who look like hookers usually aren't and the ones who look like they're straight out of Bollywood-number remix videos actually are. Weekends draw in a more mainstream set, but everyone knows the rule on entering Avalon: leave your inhibitions at the door.

Club Escape

3A Crystal Plaza, near Fame Adlabs, New Link Road, Andheri (W) (5502-1692). Andheri station. **Open** 7pm-1.30am Tue-Sun. **Admission** Rs 500-Rs 1,000.

The designer of Club Escape clearly did everything he could to cover the entire place in black leather – and very nearly succeeded. The sofas, the walls, even the pillars are covered in the stuff. Add eight black-suited waiters sternly manning strategic points around the club, motionless but alert like FBI agents, and Club Escape starts to feel a bit like an aspiring S&M dungeon. The cocktails are excellent, so is the sound system and, boy, does the air-conditioning work. The DJs say they'll play anything guests demand, which means a little bit of everything for everyone.

Fashion Café

Dalia Estate, near Fun Republic, off Link Road, Andheri (W) (2673-3333). Andheri station. **Open** 7pm-2am daily. **Admission** Rs 500-Rs 1,000.

Fashion Café is one of the latest arrivals to a previously sleepy Andheri's swelling nightlife options. According to their publicity blurb, Fashion sets out to serve the needs of the aspiring local models – 'to give new talent an arena in which to express themselves and get themselves seen by the right people to further their careers.' As if. It's a little short on models, and the best-looking thing in Fashion Café is the place itself: a cavernous aircraft hangar bathed in pink light, with a spacious dance area and an elevated dining section resting on a translucent platform lit by red floor spots.

Sport & Fitness

Cricket knocks every other sport for six.

Mumbaikars like hockey and they're partial to football. But they love cricket. Cricket towers over other sports in the city and cricketers are adored like movie stars. Love it or hate it, there's no way to ignore it. When India went up against Australia in the 2003 World Cup final, Mumbai collectively took the day off to watch. Victories in important tournaments are celebrated like Diwali; defeats impose an uncharacteristic bout of depression.

No wonder, when cricket bats and balls are thrust into Mumbaikars' hands as soon as they're old enough to grip them, and when the city has produced so many Test cricketers for the national side, including the great Sachin Tendulkar. The fondest childhood memories for many Mumbaikars are of days spent at the **Wankhede Stadium**, watching the great Bombay cricket team crush opponent after opponent to win the inter-state Ranji Trophy 36 times since the trophy's inception in 1935.

Public parks and sports grounds are few, but do-it-yourself 'gully cricket' prevails in alleys and on patches of waste ground across the city. In South Mumbai, the **Oval** and **Azad Maidans** are packed with dozens of informal cricket matches, especially at weekends, and visitors are welcome to join in. When the monsoon begins in June, football takes over and the maidans turn into muddy battlegrounds. Bombay has a lively football league run by the Western India Football Association, in which sides with names like Maharashtra State Police battle Rashtriya Chemicals & Fertilisers at the **Cooperage** ground in South Bombay and at other venues. Hockey, once a thriving city sport that produced player after player for India's national side, now comes a distant third, with its heartland in the schools and colleges of suburban Bandra and Malad.

As they have done for over a century, private sports clubs and gymkhanas like the Bombay Gymkhana remain important, although privileged, centres for amateur and recreational sports like squash, tennis, badminton, cricket, rugby and swimming. Club memberships are expensive and waiting lists long, and these aren't accessible to visitors. But modern gyms have mushroomed in recent years, some offering short-term or day memberships.

Major events in the city's sporting calendar include the **Ranji Trophy** from October to January; the Royal Western India Turf Club **Derby** in February at Mahalaxmi Racecourse; and the **Mumbai Marathon** (www.thegreatest race.com), started in 2004 and sponsored by Standard Chartered Bank, now an annual January event that attracts thousands of runners for prize money of up to $30,000.

Spectator sports

Check *Time Out Mumbai* for details of sporting events, or call sports associations directly.

Cricket

Teeming maidans like **Oval Maidan** (Maharshi Karve Road, Churchgate) have become part of cricketing folklore for being training grounds for future superstars. Mumbai's biggest stadium is the 45,000-capacity **Wankhede Stadium** (next to Marine Lines Station, Marine Lines), home to Mumbai's Ranji Trophy team and the Mumbai Cricket Association. Call the Association on 2281-7820/2281-7876 for match details. Ticket prices vary from nothing for club-level matches to Rs 5,000 for international games.

Football

Mumbai has two major football venues, the largest of which is the **Cooperage** (Cooperage Road, Churchgate), a no-frills 12,000-capacity

Mumbai Marathon.

Go-karting at **Hakone** – no potholes.

stadium. There's also **St Xavier's Ground** (near Parel Flyover), Parel). Both the grounds are plain and functional, with simple facilities. Call the **Western India Football Association** on 2202-4020 for match details.

Hockey

Mahindra Stadium

Next to Marine Lines station, Marine Lines (W). Marine Lines station.
The Bombay Hockey Association's Mahindra Stadium is the only hockey stadium in Mumbai with an Astroturf surface. It hosts Mumbai Hockey League games and all the city's major tournaments, most famously the Bombay Gold Cup in April-May and the women's Tommy Emar Gold Cup in April. Call the **Mumbai Hockey Association** on 2281-1271 for match details. Entry is free.

Horse racing

Mahalaxmi Racecourse

KK Marg, Mahalaxmi (2307-1401). Mahalaxmi station. **Entry** Rs 25.
Mumbai has one of India's top horse racing venues at the Mahalaxmi Racecourse, also the headquarters of the Royal Western India Turf Club, equipped with the smart Gallops restaurant (*see p105*). The year's biggest races are the Indian Derby, the Poonawalla Breeders' Multimillion and the Indian 2000 Guineas, held every February. On these days, the racecourse becomes an Ascot-style photo-op for Bollywood stars and Page 3 celebs.

Active sports

Golf

Bombay Presidency Golf Club

Bombay Presidency Golf Club, Dr C Gidwani Road, Chembur (2520-5874). Ghatkopar/ Chembur stations. **Open** 6am-7pm Tue-Sun. **Green fees** Rs 500 Tue-Fri; Rs 1,000 Sat, Sun. **Credit** AmEx, DC, MC, V.

Mumbai's premier golf club has an 18-hole, 6,189-yard course, a swimming pool, gymnasium, billiards room and a cards room. Comfortable rooms are also available for visitors at Rs 2,400 a night. It also hosts major amateur and pro tournaments.

Go-karting

Hakone Entertainment

Haiko Mall, Level One, Hiranandani Gardens, Powai (2579-7373/www.hakonefun.com). **Open** 3-10pm daily. **Fees** Rs 230 for 10 laps. **No credit cards.**
Hakone has three high-quality tracks – a short junior track, a pro-track and a championship track – for different skill-levels. Kids over 12 years are welcome. The karts have four-stroke, nine bhp petrol engines with a remote-control link to a marshal who can steer or stop carts should the need arise.

Horse riding

Amateur Riders' Club

Mahalaxmi Racecourse, Gate No.8, Keshavrao Khadye Marg, Mahalaxmi (6600-5204). Mahalaxmi station. **Open** 9.30am-5.30pm. **Classes** Rs 500 for 30 mins. **No credit cards.**
Play at being a jockey and take a half-hour horse ride at the racecourse, or take a riding course pitched at your level. Choose from two modules: a beginner's course or an advanced course. But don't expect to spend all your time charging around on Seabiscuit; the courses are in-depth and you're also expected to take theory classes to familiarise yourself with horseback riding equipment as well as with the anatomy and psychology of the animal.

Tennis

Practennis

Hansraj Morarji Public School Grounds, Bhavan's College Campus, Andheri (W) (2624-3509/8553). Andheri station. **Open** 10.30am-3pm daily for non-members. **Fees** Rs 150 per hour. **No credit cards.**
Mumbai's premier tennis academy offers intensive tennis coaching classes. Practennis's director and instructor, Rama Rao, is a former coach of both the National Institute of Sports and the Maharashtra State Lawn Tennis Association.

Swimming

Bodyrhythm

Advent, 12A Gen J Bhosale Marg, Churchgate (2284-8011). Churchgate station. **Taxi** next to YB Chavan Auditorium. **Open** 7am-12.30pm, 3.30-9pm daily. **Fees** Rs 300 one visit; Rs 15,000 annual membership. **No credit cards.**
Look for the staircase at the right side of the Advent building for Bodyrhythm's 22-metre pool. Nothing fancy, but those who just want to hit the water will have no complaints.

Mahatma Gandhi Pool Camp

Mahatma Gandhi Public Pool, Veer Savarkar Marg, Shivaji Park (2445-2062). Dadar station. **Fees** Rs 40 one visit; Rs 1,990 annual membership. **No credit cards.**
Cheap, cheerful, and at 50m by 25m, the L-shaped MG pool is one of the city's biggest.

Watersports

H2O Water Sports Complex

Chowpatty (2367-7584/2367-7546). Charni Road station. **Open** 10am-sunset daily. **No credit cards.**
The H2O Water Sports Complex on Chowpatty beach offers waterskiing (Rs 1,600 for 15 mins), speed boating (Rs 170), kayaking (Rs 150-Rs 200 for 30 mins), plus jet skiing, parasailing and even beach volleyball. They also conduct week-long classes in wind surfing, waterskiing and rowing.

South Mumbai

Befit Zone

Amarchand Mansion, Madam Cama Road, near Regal Theatre, Colaba (2288-0055). Churchgate/CST stations. **Open** 6am-10.30pm daily. **Membership** Rs 1,300 one week; Rs 350 one visit. **No credit cards.**
Befit Zone is one of the city's biggest gyms, with cardio-vascular training, weights and steam rooms.

Euphoria

DSK Towers, opposite Taj President, Cuffe Parade (2262-4609). Churchgate/CST stations. **Open** 6am-11pm. **Membership** Rs 3,829 one month; Rs 2,755 two weeks. **Credit** AmEx, DC, MC, V.
Euphoria specialises in resistance, or strength training. But it also provides cardio-vascular

Kabaddi, kabaddi, kabaddi...

Mumbaikars' obsession with cricket has batted aside popular interest in most other sports, including traditional Indian ones like *mallakhamb, kabaddi* and *kho kho.* Fortunately there are a few pockets left where indigenous games are played – and the largest centre is ironically the spiritual home of Mumbai cricket: **Shivaji Park**, a giant public park in the heart of middle-class Dadar. Every weekday, about 800 children come here to learn traditional games, led by instructors from Shree Samartha Vyayam Mandir, an organisation dedicated to preserving India's erstwhile sporting culture.

Kabaddi is a kind of tag game played by two teams who score by touching or capturing players of the opposing team. The attacking side sends a raider who enters the opponents' half of the court chanting '*kabaddi-kabaddi*' repeatedly to prove he is not breathing in. His aim is to touch an opposing player (who is then out of the game) and return to his team's side of the court, all in one breath. Meanwhile, the defending team attempts to capture the raider and hold him until he's forced to take a breath, in which case he's also out of the game.

Another popular traditional sport is **kho kho**, also a tag game in which one side squats on their haunches while their opponents run around them. One gets up to chase and capture the opposing team and passes the job of chasing by touching his teammates' backs while saying '*kho*'.

On your marks, get set, *kho!*

But the most dramatic local sport is **mallakhamb**, a traditional form of Indian gymnastics involving intricate twists, turns, grips, coils and catches around a pole. 'In modern gyms you have different machines for each part of the body; *mallakhamb* allows you to work out every part with just one wooden pole,' says Uday Deshpande, head of the Shree Samartha Vyayam Mandir. Using both yoga moves and dynamic acrobatics, this 200-year-old Maharashtrian sport is a combination of body control, speed, strength, agility and grace. Climbing the greasy pole was never more fun.

Shree Samartha Vyayam Mandir

Shivaji Park Maidan, Dadar (W) (2445-7870). Dadar station. **Fees** Rs 30 per month, free trials available.

Arts & Entertainment

training, and has chiropractors and a full-time nutritionist on hand.

Fariyas Health Club
25, off Arthur Bunder Road, Colaba (2204-2911/www.fariyas.com). **Open** 7am-8pm daily. **Membership** Rs 15,120 six months; Rs 300 one visit. **Credit** AmEx, MC, V.
Compact to the point of being claustrophobic, this hotel gym does have some good equipment, as well as a steam bath, sauna and a pool.

Fitwell Fitness Centre
Colaba Police Compound, behind Buckley Court, Colaba (2288-2728). Churchgate/CST stations. **Open** 6-9.30am, 5-9pm daily; 10am-5pm women only. **Membership** Rs 1,500 one month; Rs 150 one visit. **No credit cards.**
This smart Colaba gym is open for both sexes in the morning and evenings (women-only 10am-5pm).

Gold's Gym
Garden View Chambers, opposite St Elizabeth Nursing Home, J Mehta Marg, Nepean Sea Road. (2367-9392/www.goldsgym.com). Grant Road station. **Open** 6am-10.30pm daily. **Membership** Rs 4,959 one month; Rs 3,306 two weeks; Rs 386 one visit. **Credit** AmEx, DC, MC, V.
Yes, *that* Gold's Gym. The Mumbai branch of the California-based chain offers international trainers, equipment, chiropractic massages, rehabilitation therapy and a tanning salon. It also sells sports clothing, hydration, meal-replacement drinks and a good range of energy food and supplements. **Other locations:** Landmark Residency, Pali Naka, Bandra (W) (6699-2291). Bandra station.

Inch by Inch
95 Parijat Building, Marine Drive (2282-8885). Churchgate station. **Open** 6am-10.30pm daily. Rs 561 per day or Rs 4,490 for one month. **Credit** AmEx, MC, V.
Gaze at the Arabian Sea as you work the treadmill at this airy, modern gym.

Suburbs

Talwalkar's
95K Khatau Mansion, Oomer Park, Bhulabhai Desai Road, Breach Candy. (2364-0966). Grant Road station. **Open** 6am-10pm daily. **Membership** Rs 3,637 one month; Rs 2,000 one week. **Credit** AmEx, DC, MC, V.
Mumbai's original fitness centre started from humble beginnings in 1932 before bench-pressing itself into a multi-branch chain of gyms with modern facilities.

10th Health Spa
19 Chateau Merdka, Pali Road, Bandra (W) (2644-2626). Bandra station. **Open** 6am-10.30pm daily. **Membership** Rs 2,650 one month; Rs 200 one visit. **Credit** AmEx, DC, MC, V.
A state-of-the-art steam room is the main feature at this spa, which also has a gym and a cardio-studio.

Martial arts

Judo

Cawas Billimoria
BJPC School, Charni Road (98211-35870). Charni Road station. **Open** 7pm-9pm Tue-Thur; 9-11am Sat, Sun. **Fees** Rs 300 one month. **No credit cards.**
Instructor and six-degree black belt Cawas Billimoria won a silver medal in judo at the 1992 Commonwealth Games and a bronze at the 1989 Asian Games.

Karate

Rajesh Thakkar
Fellowship School, Nana Chowk, Grant Road (98201-57738). Grant Road station. **Taxi** near August Kranti Maidan. **Open** 6.45-8.15am, 7-8.30pm Mon, Wed, Fri. **Fees** Rs 300 one month; free trial available. **No credit cards.**
Indian legend has it that karate originated in the *kalaripayattu* martial arts tradition of Kerala, based on animal moves, and was then taken to Japan by Malayalee Buddhist monks. Rajesh Thakkar, an instructor for the last 25 years, brought karate back to Mumbai with an emphasis on military-style discipline, but has softened up in recent years: 'These days we allow short breaks for water and visits to the bathroom. Not like the old days; the new generation just can't take the pain.'

Tae kwon do

Vijay Kumar
Call Vijay Kumar (98192-08504), Maker Towers, Cuffe Parade. Churchgate/CST stations. **Open** flexible hours Mon-Sat. **Classes** Rs 600 one month; free trial available. **No credit cards.**
Instructor Mahendra Mohan learned Tae kwon do from Jimmy Jagtiani, the man who introduced the art to India in 1972.

Tai chi

Rakesh Menon
98194-59694. **Fees** Rs 400-Rs 600 per month; free trial available. **No credit cards.**
Rakesh Menon teaches tai chi, the meditative Chinese exercise, at four locations across the city, with a regimen aimed at the older generation. 'As people age, it becomes harder to attempt flying kicks or do repeated push-ups,' reasons Menon. **Venues**: National Centre for the Performing Arts, Nariman Point. Churchgate station; St Andrew's School, Bandra (W). Bandra station; Holy Family High School, off MIDC Road, opposite Technopolis, Chakala, Andheri (E). Andheri station.

Theatre & Dance

Mumbai's spectacle takes to the stage.

Theatre

English-language theatre in Mumbai has come a long way since the 1980s, when it was mostly the preserve of somewhat self-indulgent wealthy South Mumbai actors who produced classic British and American plays and musicals, sometimes with Indian twists. Now a growing citywide movement, it has split into two halves – a growing cadre of writers producing original Indian drama in English, and those who look to fatuous Gujarati bedroom farces for inspiration. Either way, English drama still plays only a minor role in Mumbai's theatre scene, which is dominated by productions in Hindi, Gujarati and Marathi. Hindi and Gujarati theatre consists largely of commercial drama – mostly coarse bedroom comedies and Indian-adapted versions of Neil Simon plays. But Mumbai's most popular, exciting and innovative theatre is without doubt Marathi, which has a strong modern history of experimental drama (*see p168* **Marathi vérité**). One of India's most caustic and cutting-edge playwrights is the Mumbai-based Marathi playwright Vijay Tendulkar, whose plays are regularly performed in Mumbai theatres.

In recent years, an increasing taste for innovation has led theatre groups to move out of the usual venues for one-off performances and short runs in unconventional spaces like bars, libraries and out on the street – no mean feat in a desperately crowded city. In 2004 the Company Theatre, an experimental drama group, began putting on plays in private homes. Last year the Prithvi Theatre in Juhu, one of Mumbai's most popular, had performers take to the streets at its annual festival; in March 2006, the 19th-century David Sassoon Library at Kala Ghoda hosted a production of Shakespeare's *Much Ado About Nothing*. Frequent theatre festivals also offer a chance to catch independent drama from all over the country and the occasional visiting foreign company.

BUYING TICKETS

Check *Time Out Mumbai* and city newspapers for details of productions showing during your stay. It's also worth taking a look at *www.mumbaitheatreguide.com* – although their

The Mahatma's back – in *Sammy* at the **Sophia Bhabha Hall**. See p169.

listings are not exhaustive. There are no one-stop ticketing agencies and tickets usually must be bought direct from the box office in person. Except for the National Centre for the Performing Arts in Nariman Point, Mumbai's theatres do not accept credit cards. Theatre box offices are usually closed on Sundays unless there is a performance scheduled on that day. Calling the theatre in advance to enquire whether tickets are still available is always a good idea. Ticket prices vary considerably depending on the production, but expect them to cost between Rs 30 and Rs 400 each. International productions charge up to Rs 1,000.

Venues

South Mumbai

Mumbai Marathi Sahitya Sangh

Dr Bhalerao Marg, Gaiwadi, near Charni Road station, Charni Road (2385-6303). Charni Road station. **Box office** 5pm-9pm Mon-Sat. **No credit cards**.

Mumbai Marathi Sahitya Sangh is a theatre devoted to experimental Marathi work. The hall suffers from poor acoustics, compensated for by ridiculously low ticket prices – a mere Rs 30 – and high standards of performance.

National Centre for the Performing Arts

NCPA Marg, Nariman Point (2284-0633/ www.ncpamumbai.com). Churchgate/CST stations. **Box office** 9am-7pm Mon-Sat. **Credit** MC, V.

Mumbai's one claim to a world-class performance space. A complex of theatres, galleries and outdoor spaces, the NCPA includes the Jamshed Bhabha, Experimental, Tata, Little and Godrej Dance Academy theatres. The jewel in its crown is the Jamshed Bhabha theatre, resembling a Victorian town house, but the smaller Experimental Theatre remains the most popular venue for plays. Despite the name, the Experimental is indiscriminate in its line-up – romantic comedies and avant-garde drama all find a home here.

Nehru Centre Auditorium

Nehru Centre Auditorium, Dr Annie Besant Road, Worli (2496-4676/www.nehrucentremumbai.com). Mahalaxmi station. **Box office** 10am-6pm Mon-Sat. **No credit cards.**

A part of the Nehru Centre complex, the auditorium hosts plays and music concerts. The highlight of its theatre calendar is a month-long festival of plays in August.

Ravindra Natya Mandir

PL Deshpande Maharashtra Kala Academy, Sayani Road, Prabhadevi (2431-2956). Elphinstone Road station. **Taxi** near Siddhivinayak Temple. **Box office** 11am-10pm Mon-Sat. **No credit cards.**

Ravindra Natya Mandir and its smaller sister on the same complex, the PL Deshpande Hall, host performances from all the city's language theatres.

Marathi vérité

In Marathi playwright Sachin Kundalkar's riff on power in relationships, *Fridge Madhe Thevalele Prem*, a quarrelsome couple decide to preserve the meagre remnants of their love in the fridge. They consume a daily ration and top it up once a week. But when the husband demands a second helping, the system breaks down with disastrous consequences. Offbeat, funny and shamelessly absurd, *Fridge Madhe Thevalele Prem* finds few equivalents in the plays of Mumbai's other language theatres, but is nothing out of the ordinary in the effervescent Marathi theatre scene, which consistently outperforms other city theatre scenes in both originality and productivity.

That's partly thanks to the Maharashtrian community's long and distinguished heritage in the performing arts, with traditional forms like *sangeetnatak*, a kind of musical, and *tamasha*, which typically features raunchy dancing to risqué songs. Theatre-going remains a popular community recreation, with middle-class Maharashtrian families going to see plays in the way other communities go to the movies, swarming theatres from Thane to Dadar every weekend. That's fostered an audience accustomed to theatrical conventions and open to seeing them broken, giving rise to an energetic sub-culture of experimental Marathi theatre. It's a sub-culture that's produced Vijay Tendulkar, regarded as both the most controversial and greatest living Marathi playwright. Tendulkar is best known for *Sakharam Binder*, *Ghashiram Kotwal* and *Gidhade*, plays which altered the course of Marathi theatre in the 1970s with a furious critique of the Indian caste system and shocking depictions of violence and blasphemy on stage – something Maharashtrian theatre audiences had never seen before. Tendulkar was joined by other innovators like Satish Alekar, famous for his darkly witty *Mahanirvan* and the fantastical *Begum Barve*, and Mahesh Elkunchwar, whose gritty modern plays include the *Wada Trilogy*, *Party* and *Vasanakand*. Following in their footsteps, a new breed of young Marathi writers continue to push the boundaries with politically driven plots and experimental dramatic forms. But after Tendulkar, it's become harder to shock Maharashtrian audiences.

Vijay Tendulkar's *Sakharam Binder*.

The **Prithvi Theatre Festival** takes to the streets.

It also stages regular Bengali dance dramas and college theatre festivals.

Sophia Bhabha Hall

Sophia College campus, off Bhulabhai Desai Road (2353-8550). Grant Road station.
Box office 10am-6pm Mon-Sat. **No credit cards.**
This large, plush auditorium is a part of the palatial Sophia College campus, which was home to the Maharaja of Indore and subsequently the Maharaja of Bhavnagar between 1923 and 1940. The theatre offers a line-up of both serious and light English drama.

Tejpal Hall

Tejpal Road, August Kranti Maidan, Gowalia Tank. (2380-2679). Grant Road station. **Box office** 9am-noon, 4-7pm Wed-Sun. **No credit cards.**
Monopolised by Gujarati plays, Tejpal Hall is a spacious theatre tucked away in a quiet corner of Gowalia Tank. Dance dramas and plays in Bengali are performed at Tejpal during the Durga Puja festival *(see p136)*.

Suburbs

New Mahim Municipal School

Miya Mohammed Chotani Marg, Teesari Galli, Mahim (W) (2444-5871). Mahim station. **Box office** 7pm onwards Mon-Sat. **No credit cards.**
Awishkar, one of Mumbai's most active Marathi experimental theatre groups, operates out of this state-run school, and regularly performs plays by Vijay Tendulkar, the *enfant terrible* of Marathi theatre *(see p168 **Marathi vérité**)*.

Prithvi Theatre

Janki Kutir, Juhu Church Road, Juhu (2614-9546/ www.prithvitheatre.org). Vile Parle station.
Taxi near Hotel Tulip Star. **Box office** 10am-1pm, 2-7pm daily. **No credit cards.**
Built in 1978 to promote Hindi theatre, the Prithvi managed to snatch audiences away from the older, classier National Centre for the Performing Arts, despite being far away uptown in Juhu. An intimate 200-seater, Prithvi is partial to Hindi drama but hosts English and Marathi plays as well. It has a casual, cosy atmosphere with a leafy outside café that attracts the occasional Juhu celeb for its famous Irish coffees. In November, Prithvi hosts its annual theatre festival *(see p136)*, which includes performances at the picturesque Horniman Circle Garden in South Mumbai.

Rangsharda

Hotel Rangsharda, Bandra Reclamation, near Lilavati Hospital, Bandra (W) (2643-0544).
Box office 10am-6pm Mon-Sat. **No credit cards.**
Located in the basement of Hotel Rangsharda, the theatre hosts commercial plays in Hindi, Gujarati and English.

St Andrew's Auditorium

St Dominic Road, Bandra (W) (2645-9667). Bandra station. **Box office** 10am-6pm daily. **No credit cards.**
Musicals and English comedies take centre stage at this cavernous theatre, which boasts an excellent sound system.

Shivaji Mandir

Shivaji Natya Mandir, NC Kelkar Road, Dadar (W) (2438-9387). Dadar station. **Box office** 8.30am-11am, 5pm-8pm daily. **No credit cards.**
A pit-stop for those with a taste for ribald humour and slapstick, the mainstays of commercial Marathi theatre. Shivaji Mandir is also a venue for travelling *lavani* troupes. A Maharashtrian folk performance form, *lavani* features peppy dancing to risqué songs.

Dance

There are seven classical dance forms in India, but only four – *bharatanatyam, mohiniattam, kathak* and *Odissi* – are taught in Mumbai's established dance schools and regularly performed in the city. Traditionally, dances were performed in temples as an expression of devotion, later becoming courtly entertainment under Mughal rule in the 16th and 17th centuries. Most of the dances were performed by men; it was only in the 18th century that dancing became a socially acceptable pursuit for women, who today dominate the form.

Bharatanatyam was first performed in temples in the state of Tamil Nadu by *devdasis*, girls who devoted their lives to Lord Shiva. Its origins can be traced to the *Natya Shastra*, a 2,000-year-old discourse on dance and drama written by the sage Bharata. *Bharatanatyam* is characterised by powerful movements and an erect torso and is performed to Carnatic music played at an upbeat tempo. **Mohiniattam** (literally, 'enchanting dance') comes from Kerala. Unlike *bharatanatyam*, its postures are soft and delicate. *Mohiniattam* dancers sway gracefully in a traditional off-white sari with a coloured border, with movements that express love, pathos and *bhakti* (devotion).

Sculptures of women dancers and musicians discovered in caves in Udayagiri in Orissa suggest that **Odissi** dancing was being performed as far back as the 2nd century BC, but it gained acceptance as a classical dance form only in the 1950s, through the

efforts of celebrated male performers such as Pankajcharan Das and Kelucharan Mahapatra. Odissi is a subtle dance of lyrical, curving movements of the wrists and torso.
Kathak comes from North India and is a storytelling dance form (*katha* means 'story'). *Kathak* originated with the *kathakars*, dancers and musicians who travelled from village to village performing tales from the *Mahabharata* and the *Ramayana*. There are three *gharanas* or schools of *kathak*, Lucknow, Jaipur and Benares – each with a different style – but the form is characterised by vigorous, fast-paced footwork.

BUYING TICKETS
To find out what's on during your stay, check newspaper listings or look in *Time Out Mumbai*. Ticketed events are rare; most dance performances are arranged by cultural organisations for free or for a 'guest charge', typically Rs 50-Rs100, and guest passes can be bought on the night of a show or up to three days in advance of a performance from the box office. Tickets are also sold at the **Rhythm House** music store at Kala Ghoda (*see p129*). Credit card bookings are not available except at the Godrej Dance Academy at the National Centre for the Performing Arts.

Venues
Performances of all four classical dance forms are held at the following venues:

Godrej Dance Academy Theatre
National Centre for the Performing Arts, NCPA Marg, Nariman Point (2283-3838/ www.ncpamumbai.com). Churchgate/CST stations. **Box office** 9am-7pm daily. **Credit** MC, V.

Karnataka Sangha
Dr Vishveshawarayya Samarak Mandir, CHM Marg, near City Light Cinema, Matunga (2437-7022). Matunga Road station. **Box office** 10am-8pm daily. **No credit cards.**

Mysore Association Hall
Near Maheshwari Udayan, 393 Bhau Daji Road, Matunga (E) (2402-4647). Matunga/King's Circle stations. **Box office** 10am-6pm daily. **No credit cards.**

Nehru Centre Auditorium
Dr Annie Besant Road, near Shiv Sagar Estate, Worli (2496-4680/www.nehrucentremumbai.com). Mahalaxmi station. **Box office** 10am-6pm daily. **No credit cards.**

Sivaswamy Auditorium
The Fine Arts Society, Fine Arts Chowk, RC Marg, Chembur (2522-2988). Chembur station. **Taxi** near Chembur Flyover. **Box office** 10am-6pm daily. **No credit cards.**

Bharatanatyam.

Goa

Getting Started

Get *sussegad* in India's sunshine state.

Arriving in Goa from Mumbai is like entering a different country altogether, even though it's only 300 miles away. It's India's smallest state at just over 1,150 square miles, with a population of under 1.5 million. The air is clean, the skies wide, and life ambles along at a pace bordering on somnambulant. The maddening noise of the city dissolves into the insistent whisper of sea on sand, tower blocks give way to coconut palms, and traffic fumes fade under the perfume of cashew blossoms and ripening mango. No wonder it's India's most popular resort destination – not just for travellers from Europe, Israel and Russia, but for India's growing middle class, for whom Goa is famously summed up in the Konkani word *sussegad*, meaning 'laid-back' or 'relaxed'.

The best Of Goa

For a journey back in time
Old Goa was once one of the world's great cities – bigger than London or Paris – and home to adventurers and slave-traders. Now only spectacular Portuguese-built churches remain (*see p211*).

For India's only Latin quarter
Wander the narrow lanes of **Fontainhas**, a sun-kissed maze of brightly coloured colonial homes (*see p206*).

For a glimpse of the grandees
Take a privileged peek into the sumptuous world of the Indo-Portuguese aristocracy at the **Menezes-Braganza Mansion** in Chandor (*see p218* **Ain't life grandee?**).

For the neo-hippie experience
It's now 50 times bigger than originally intended. There's nothing else like the **Anjuna flea market**, a magic shopping mall, beer garden, live music venue and food court rolled into one (*see p192*).

For sunsets to remember
Take an evening cruise on the Mandovi river, with dolphins angling out of the water at the bow (*see p210*).

Goa's landscape is varied, ranging from the Western Ghats mountain range on its interior border through lush river valleys to the beaches of its 78-mile long coast. It has a tropical climate, with average temperatures of 25 to 30 degrees centigrade from November to April, and up to 40 degrees with high humidity in October and May. The Goan monsoon lasts from early June to late September, with the heaviest rains in July. Other than tourism, Goa's main industry is iron ore mining, which earns the state around $1 billion a year, much of it from China. Between highland mining areas lie protected reserves and forests, which lack tourism infrastructure but have great biodiversity, with animals such as tigers, elephants, crocodiles, boar and the bull-like gaur.

GOA TODAY

Goa's tourism development in the last 30 years has been anything but *sussegad*. The northern coastal strip from Aguada to Arambol has a vibrant, noisy, multinational resort culture, with restaurants lining winding access roads and hundreds of beach shacks crowding dunes. Tourists first started arriving in Goa in the 1970s, when a few hundred backpackers and hippies trickled in along an overland route from Europe. They found idyllic empty beaches fringed with thick coconut groves, and a local populace familiar with Westerners and happy to leave them alone. The so-called 'Goa Freaks' lived hedonistic lives on the cheap, giving the state its reputation as a party paradise.

In the mid 1980s, German charter operators began to operate regular flights to Dabolim from Europe, despite resistance from local activist groups, who warned of environmental and social damage from mass tourism. The first charter tourists to Goa stayed in five-star hotels, but hundreds of local entrepreneurs hastily threw up the small hotels and guesthouses that now form the main part of Goa's tourism infrastructure. Over two million foreign and domestic tourists now visit Goa every year – a number set to rise. In recent years, there's been a clear shift from budget accommodation to the boutique hotel, with some stunning and innovative properties like **Nilaya** (*see p190*) offering visitors exclusive surroundings with price-tags to match. Many foreigners have permanently settled in Goa in the last five years, taking advantage of the burgeoning economy and a high standard of living at affordable prices.

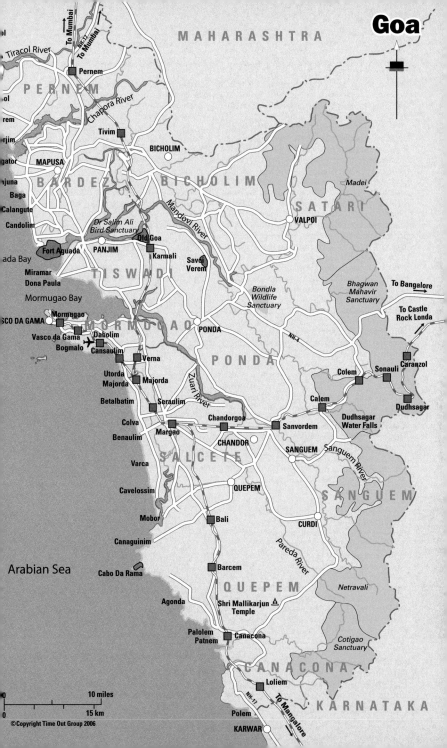

A giant new international airport planned at Mopa in North Goa will decisively shift the balance towards ever-greater mass tourism, with Indian developers racing to meet the projected demand. But many Goans bemoan what is happening to their formerly peaceful homeland. Mainstream Goan society is resolutely opposed to trance tourists, who are seen as self-indulgent drug users and an immoral influence on Goan youth. Responding to popular opinion, the Goa state government banned raves in the 2005/6 tourist season, though some underground parties took place in remote spots in the north and near Palolem. It's hard to predict what will happen next to the rave sub-culture that spawned Goa trance (*see p186* **Hippy and you know it**). It seems unlikely to recover its past glories, but parties are certain to continue as long as ravers keep coming, law or no law.

There is also widespread anger about illegal construction and the abuse of strict coastal land laws. Legislation forbids new permanent construction within 500 yards of the high-tide line and restricts it for another 500 yards. These laws have been blatantly flouted along Goa's entire coastline. The government claims to have over 300 cases ready for 'appropriate action', a claim that most Goans ruefully laugh at. The number of illegal developments is closer to 30,000, and includes many five-star hotels. With the state's real estate lobby hand-in-glove with local politicians, a serious effort to deal with illegal developments seems remote.

CULTURE AND COMMUNITIES

Except for the 250 years of the Portuguese Inquisition in Goa (*see pp176-178*), Hindus have always been the majority population of Goa, though you wouldn't guess it from all the whitewashed churches. Hindus make up around 65 per cent of the population, with largely the same caste divisions as the rest of India. In recent years, Goa has experienced a surge in right-wing Hinduism, part of a nationwide phenomenon, but the state remains relatively free of communal feuding. The situation turned tense in early 2006, when Goa experienced its first communal riot in Sanvordem, when a mob vandalised Muslim businesses and vehicles. Public reaction was near-unanimous in condemnation; Goa's various communities tend to respect each other's holy sites.

Christians in Goa have tenaciously hung on to their caste affiliations, though these have been adapted into three broad categories – Brahmin, Chardo (or Kshatriya) and Sudra (*see p30* **Caste in stone**). Despite the strictures of the Portuguese, strict Christian conservatism never took root in Goa. The majority of Goan Catholics continue to hold

on to indigenous influences that have helped create a mystical, goddess-centred Christianity.

Islam has a long history in Goa, but today Muslims have a small presence in the state, which has only recently grown through migration from surrounding states and Kashmir.

Konkani is the native language of Goa and remains widespread, despite efforts by the Portuguese to eradicate it. By law, all state-funded primary schools must be Konkani-language, but it is steadily losing out to the intense demand for English and Hindi (the latter of which comes to Goa via Bollywood movies). Portuguese remains surprisingly ubiquitous, though Goans will generally clam up rather than speak it around outsiders.

Getting there

More information on getting there and around is given in individual Goa chapters.

From Mumbai

By air

Over 20 direct flights make the short hop from Mumbai to Goa daily, mainly in the morning and early evening. India's emerging private mega-airline, Jet Airways (www.jetairways.com), offers impressive service and meals, but better deals are often available with start-up carriers like Kingfisher Airlines (1600-1800-101, www.flyking fisher.com), GoAir (1800-222-111, www.goair.in), SpiceJet (1800-180-3333, www.spicejet.com) and the very low-cost Air Deccan (3900-8888, www.airdeccan.net). State-owned Indian Airlines (1600-180-1407, www.indian-airlines.nic.in) flies to Goa from the international airport twice a week, which bypasses the slightly hectic transfer between Mumbai's domestic and international airports. One-way Mumbai-Goa flights cost Rs 2,000 to Rs 5,500. Book ahead in peak season.

By train

The Konkan Railway train, on its way to Kerala, chugs into Goa four times each day from Mumbai. The 11-hour trip offers magnificent views of the Ghats and the lush riverine plains of the Konkan coastline, or you can take the sleeper. The major stops are Thivim for North Goa, Karmali for Panjim and Margao for South Goa. Book at www.konkan railway.com. In peak season berths can be hard to come by, but there's a 'foreigners' quota' for one-way tickets (*see p230*). Return tickets with air-conditioning cost Rs 1,600 to Rs 3,500.

By bus

Dozens of bus services make the 12-hour trip from Mumbai to Goa each day, from decrepit decades-old coaches to comfortable modern behemoths with air-con and reclining seats. Go for the latter. Paulo Travels (022-2645-2624 Mumbai, 0832-243-8531/8537 Panjim, www. paulotravels.com) is the biggest coach company. Return fares range from Rs 1,000 to Rs 1,200.

Getting around

By bus

Goa has a well-connected bus network, with stops in every major village. Buses aren't particularly clean or punctual, but they are cheap (Panjim to Candolim costs Rs 10, for example). Non-stop Kadamba shuttle buses run regularly between major towns, charging Rs 7-Rs 20.

By autorickshaw

Unlike Mumbai, autorickshaws are neither plentiful or hassle-free; you have to bargain hard for a fair price. But they're useful for short trips and can usually be rented by the hour or day. A half-day rental costs around Rs 250.

By motorcycle

Goa's motorcycle taxis are known as 'pilots'. There's no way to know who is a pilot – they often wait for fares at village bus stops, or you can wave at passing motorcyclists until one stops, then hold on tight. Around Rs 13 per mile.

By ferry

Goa's rickety flat-bottomed ferries offer the most scenic way to cross the state's many rivers and pedestrians ride for free (two-wheelers Rs 10, cars Rs 15). Ferries on the Mandovi cross from Betim Jetty to Panjim; Ribandar to Divar; Chorao, Old Goa to Divar; and from Pomburpa to Chorao. On the Zuari, cross from Agassaim to Cortalim and on the river Tiracol from Keri to Tiracol.

Taxis & car rentals

Taxis routinely charge high rates in peak season, around Rs 200-Rs 300 for short hops. If you're planning to make several trips, hire one for the day for around Rs 1,000. Most car rentals include the cost of a driver and a drive-your-own deal offers negligible savings. You must have an International Driving Permit and third-party insurance, available from the rental company. Check the car carefully before you rent. Taxis and rentals are both available from Joey's in Panjim (0832-222-8989, fully insured Hyundai Santro Rs 1,000/day) and Vailankanni in Candolim (0832-248-9047/9658, Hyundai Santro Rs 800/day). Beware, parking can be a headache in North Goa's crowded tourist hotspots.

Motorcycle rental

Hundreds of individuals informally rent out motorbikes and scooters; you'll see them near the

The best Beaches

For idyllic lazing

Once deserted, **Palolem** is now firmly on the beaten track but in the off-peak season you can still taste the kind of beach experience that first put Goa on the map.

For following the hippie trail

The legendary paradise beach of the '70s hippie scene, **Arambol** retains plenty of counter-cultural atmosphere.

For getting back to nature

Morjim and **Ashvem** are a world away in atmosphere from the tourist hub of North Goa. Protected Olive Ridley turtles come here every year to lay eggs, fending off major construction in the process.

For getting away from it all

Oddly overlooked, **Utorda**'s broad stretches of clean, white sand stay tranquil throughout the year. **Agonda**, just north of Palolem, is peaceful and quiet even in high season.

For watching locals at play

Calangute earns sneers from beach snobs for its lines of shacks, but it's an upbeat spot loved by Indian holiday-makers.

bus stop in every village. Paulo Travels also offers two-wheeler rentals available from their agent's garage near the Mahalaxmi Temple in Panjim (0832-243-8531/8537; scooter Rs 300/day, 100cc motorbike Rs 350/day, Enfield Bullet Rs 450/day). Two-wheelers are perfect for Goa's narrow roads and parking is rarely a problem. But there are numerous attendant risks, and far too many visitors wind up in hospital (or worse) after misjudging Goa's roads and haphazard traffic. Exercise caution at night as road lighting is intermittent. Check the vehicle very carefully before renting – you'll be asked to pay for any damage to the bike.

Bicycle rental

Much of Goa's coast is flat and perfect for bikes. Cycle rentals are available for around Rs 25-50 per day; look for signs near village bus stands, or ask at the nearest gas station. Be careful at night and on major roads, where drivers show little consideration for cyclists.

Tourist information

Directorate of Tourism *Rua de Ourem, Patto, Panjm (0832-222-6515).*

Goa

Goa History

Souls, slaves and spices.

Goa has always been a gateway to India for foreign traders and travellers, and a window on the outside world for Indians. Until the arrival of Muslim invaders in the 14th century, the territory was exchanged between various subcontinental empires and then slumbered for 1,000 years under the home-grown Kadamba dynasty that reigned from their capital on the Zuari River. At that time the port of Goa was the main entry point for droves of Arabian warhorses into the disputed Deccan region. This trade had gone on for centuries, with many Arab traders settling in Goa. But the peaceable relationship changed in 1312, when Muslim armies from the Delhi Sultanate swept into power, destroying temples built by the Kadambas in their millennium in power. Just 30 years later, the Delhi Sultanate was itself challenged by a breakaway group from the Deccan, the Bahamanis, who unleashed another orgy of destruction. Both were finally displaced by the Hindu Vijayanagaris, who oversaw an interlude of prosperity and relative calm.

Successive waves of conquerors were lured by Goa's superb port and lucrative trade. By the late 15th century Goa had fallen under the control of the Sultanate of Bijapur, a splinter of the Bahamani Empire ruled by the Turkish-born Sultan Yusuf Adil Shah. Under his relatively enlightened rule, Goa developed once again into a rich trading post and crossroads between East and West, crowded by ships from Arabia and the Far East. But all this was soon to change. In 1497, the Portuguese explorer Vasco da Gama made an historic turn round the horn of Africa and set off towards the Indian coast. The Portuguese had recently emerged independent from Moorish domination and were determined to wrest control of the near-priceless spice trade from the Arabs and win souls for Christendom. On his first trip, Da Gama landed to the south of Goa in Calicut. There he harvested no souls but gathered plenty of black pepper – a treasure that was to spur future European colonial adventures in the Indian Ocean.

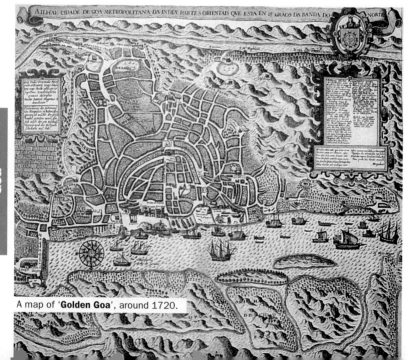

A map of '**Golden Goa**', around 1720.

Goa

Vasco da Gama never made it to Goa. But his successor, Afonso de Albuquerque, kept his eye on the territory on a trading voyage to Calicut, where he received word that Goan Hindus were unsatisfied with the rule of the Sultan of Bijapur. They were struggling under heavy taxes and would support a transfer of possession to these unknown foreigners should they manage to take control. Albuquerque duly seized the port on March 1, 1510. The Bijapuris briefly regained possession but were ejected by the Portuguese in a bloody rout nine months later.

The first land they took was Tiswadi, a promontory with two natural harbours between the Mandovi and Zuari rivers. In time, they added the territories of Bardez and Salcete, lands that became known as the 'Old Conquests'. By the middle of the 16th century, it had developed into a major outpost and a draw for foreign adventurers. A new elite of Portuguese (and other European) administrators and soldiers were married off to the widows and daughters of the erstwhile ruling class. Franciscan, Jesuit, Dominican and Augustinian priests arrived in Goa and were each granted territories in which to begin converting native Goans to Catholicism. A unique Luso-Indian cultural exchange began that would completely remake Goa with a hybrid of architecture, cuisine and customs.

Chillies first entered India via Goa, as did cashews, corn, potatoes, papayas and countless other imports now taken for granted, including Asia's first modern printing press, medical college and lighthouse.

THE ERA OF 'GOLDEN GOA'

By the end of the 16th century, the Portuguese-controlled city that mushroomed on the banks of the Mandovi was one of the richest places in the world, a crowded megalopolis bigger than London or Paris, and home to what are still the largest church and convent in Asia. It was known as *Goa Dourada*, or 'Golden Goa', of as much importance to the Portuguese court as Lisbon itself, and raked in such vast profits that it came under constant threat from envious newcomers to the Indian Ocean trade. The Dutch levelled crippling blockades against the city twice in the early decades of the 17th century, and then a series of plagues devastated the European population. Portuguese interest in the colony waned as the royal court became preoccupied with its new holdings in Brazil. The colony was occasionally threatened by the Marathas to the north, and was almost conquered by Shivaji's Maratha Confederacy before the Mughals distracted them away, but Goa remained in European hands.

Missing martyr

Almost as soon as the Indian government formally recognised the newly independent Republic of Georgia in 1991, bemused Indian officials received an urgent request from the former Soviet republic. It concerned the iconic Queen of Georgia, **Ketavan**, who was martyred in Shiraz, Iran, in 1624 after choosing death over conversion to Islam. The Georgians explained that her body was taken by Portuguese clerics, who most likely buried her in Old Goa, somewhere in the vicinity of the **St Augustine Tower** a few years after her death. 'Can we have her back?' the Georgians asked.

It's been a dozen years since a team of Indian state archaeologists first started looking for her, without success. They promise results soon, but Georgians had better not hold their breath.

St Augustine Tower –
Queen Ketavan's final
resting place?

From the 18th century, a native aristocracy steadily gained power and influence as willing proxies of a distracted ruling class in Lisbon. This cadre of converted upper-caste landlords and the offspring of Indo-Portuguese marriages embarked on a spate of estate building that left a permanent mark on Goa's landscape, a constellation of agrarian villages organised in a feudal manner, with a few landlords holding sway over large numbers of subject tenants. Unlike British India, there was never any emphasis on secular education, infrastructure improvement or the exploitation of natural resources. Goans began to leave their homeland to pursue opportunity elsewhere, initially to the Portuguese territories in Africa and Asia.

During the Napoleonic wars, when British troops were stationed in Goa to deter French attacks, the aspirations of ambitious Goans shifted to the British Empire. Thousands of Goans left to work in British cantons in India and in British East African colonies, where they became administrators, clerks, cooks, musicians and *ayahs* or nannies.

LIBERATION AND AFTER

At the end of World War II, the writing was on the wall for the European imperial project. India became independent in a cataclysm of sectarian violence in 1947, and the Portuguese immediately came under heavy pressure to hand Goa over to the new Indian government. But though there were only a few dozen Portuguese officials left in the territory, the fascist dictator Salazar declared that it would remain eternally Portuguese and embarked on an occasionally violent, occasionally lavish campaign to persuade Goans that their future lay with Portugal and not the Indian republic. The majority of Goans became increasingly impatient for change, and increasingly radicalised when Portuguese police responded to minor provocations with heavy-handed tactics, including firing on unarmed crowds and mercilessly beating peaceful protestors. In 1961, India's first prime minister, Jawaharlal Nehru, sent in the Indian army and took Goa virtually unopposed on December 19, at last ending the European colonial era on Indian soil. Almost immediately afterwards, Goan voters rejected a proposal to merge with the state of Maharashtra. On May 30, 1987, Goa finally became a fully fledged state of the Indian Union and Konkani became an official national language.

Bloody inquisitive

'If everywhere the Inquisition was an infamous court, the infamy, however base, however vile, however corrupt and determined by worldly interests, it was never more so than in Goa.' – Archbishop of Evora, Portugal

In 1542, Francis Xavier of Navarre, a Basque priest who co-founded the Jesuit order, arrived in Goa as an ambassador of the Pope. He was 35 and had most recently worked at the newly established Court of the Inquisition. Over the next few years he spent just six months in Goa, but it was enough time for him to form a deep distaste for the louche behaviour of its Portuguese residents and disgust at the newly converted Indian Catholics, whom he called 'half-baked, semi-pagan, Eurasian converts'. With characteristic impatience, he fired off numerous appeals to the Court of the Inquisition to export its cleansing offices to Goa. Eight years after his death, they did so.

The Portuguese Inquisition was imposed in Goa in 1560, and was formally renounced only in 1812, under pressure from the British. Officially, it was meant to seek out and eradicate religious heresy; in practice, it was a convenient tool for eradicating threats to Portuguese rule, suppressing dissent and ethnic cleansing. Confessions were extracted by the careful amputation of limbs and slicing-off of eyelids, done in a manner to keep the victim alive as long as possible. Bizarre and arbitrary laws were imposed on Hindus, including the banning of betel nuts, Indian musical instruments, the sarong-like *dhoti*, Sanskrit names and even the ritual feeding of the poor. Every few years, those deemed heretics were burned at the stake in an *auto da fe*, heralded by the tolling of a grand bell. The terror of the Inquisition in Goa – considered by many historians to be the bloodiest inquisition of all – prompted a mass exodus of Hindus and Christians alike from the region.

Ironically, St Francis Xavier today remains a deeply venerated saint in Goa. Xavier died on an island in the mouth of the Canton River in 1552, where his body was buried in a wooden coffin packed with lime to ensure its speedy decomposition. Ten weeks after, a Portuguese ship went to recover the body and – so the story goes – found it miraculously preserved and unmarked. The body was buried and disinterred yet again in Malacca, with similar tales of its incorruptibility. The body eventually made its way back to the seat of Portuguese power in Goa, where it is kept in the Basilica of Bom Jesus in Old Goa *(see p213)*. Every decade, the relic is displayed at an exposition which draws hundreds of thousands of pilgrims from across the world.

North Goa

Where hippydom survived.

This small sliver of the Konkan coast has been transformed in the four decades since the Goa Freaks first tumbled onto its sands. North Goa is now multicultural and multinational, with thousands of permanent expatriates from around the world, and over two million visitors a year. The beach stretches all the way from the **Aguada Plateau** at the southernmost tip to the **Tiracol Fort** on the Maharashtra border – a drive you can make in less than two hours. Charter tourism has invaded **Candolim**, the Indian middle class packing the sands of **Calangute**, while **Baga** is party central for the MTV generation. **Sinquerim** is known for the sprawling luxury villas of India's rich and famous. Further up the coast are the dream beaches of the '60s hippie trail, the first of which was **Anjuna**, where a few septuagenarian Goa Freaks linger on for its still-alternative vibe. There's also the more edgy **Chapora** and **Vagator**, where cafés are jammed with tokers openly puffing on smokestack-sized chillums under the watchful gaze of well-connected locals.

North of Vagator, the beaches begin to empty out – some are still deserted. **Morjim**, where protected Olive Ridley sea turtles come to lay eggs on the beach, now also hosts a thriving Russian sub-culture. **Ashvem**, with its rugged laterite rock outcrops and windswept sands, is home to Goa's best beach restaurant, **La Plage**. Beyond **Mandrem**'s unique marriage of swift-running fresh water and ocean surf, all roads lead to the legendary **Arambol**, where latter-day versions of the first flower children spend months living in the open under coconut trees. In peak season, your day on the beach here could easily be spent with 15,000 other travellers, with Hebrew as the lingua franca and waiters and peddlers the only visible Indians. Apart from the beaches, North Goa is also home to some of the most ambitious restaurants in India, including eateries offering Burmese, Turkish and French food – and the inevitable steak and kidney pie and mushy peas.

North Goa's attractions aren't just confined to the coast, extending to the hill-hugging cashew plantations that blanket much of **Pernem** district (Goa's feni-producing heartland), the noisy riot of colours that is **Mapusa** market in the heart of Bardez district, and the hidden, ancient Hindu temples of **Ponda**.

The fishing is divine at **Arambol Beach**. *See p200.*

Sinquerim & Fort Aguada

Goa tourism began here, at the tip of what was once a pristine four-mile stretch of broad golden sand lined with rolling dunes and backed by acres of coconut plantations. Long before strict coastal development laws, the hotel arm of the Indian Tata business house built a sprawling five-star hotel complex amid the crumbling ruins of an early 17th-century Portuguese fortress. The **Fort Aguada Beach Resort** opened the floodgates to mass tourism in 1972. By the late '90s the beach was lined elbow-to-elbow with beach shacks, concrete hotels, shopping centres, pubs, restaurants and massage parlours. The plateau atop the Sinquerim headland, near the modern, squat **Aguada Lighthouse**, offers one of the best ocean views in Goa, with the mouths of the Mandovi and Zuari rivers on one side, and the beach on the other. Next door sits its ancestor – the first lighthouse in Asia, built by the Portuguese in 1864.

Under the lighthouse is the grim low-rise complex of Goa's main prison, the **Fort Aguada Jail**, once packed with anti-colonial activists in the days of the Portuguese, now home to local crooks and two dozen or so foreigners busted under India's severe anti-drug laws. Back down along the tourism strip, the **Church of St Lawrence** (open for Sunday mass at 8am), built in 1630, commands another spectacular view of the Mandovi River, receding to the east.

Goa

Down the hill, past a curve overlooking the quiet **Nerul River**, tourist development takes over both sides of the road. The Fort Aguada hotel complex covers almost 90 acres sprawling on to the beachfront right up to the sister **Taj Holiday Village**. The Taj is now building a massive stone bulwark to protect the property from the rapid, destructive beach erosion that followed the grounding of the *River Princess* – a huge iron-ore cargo ship, during a storm in 2001. The rusting hulk is still stuck just off the beach; its powerful mining-company owner is fighting through the courts to ensure he never has to pay the huge cost of removing it. Off the road, just beyond the gardens of the Taj complex, is the palatial entranceway to **Kingfisher Villa**, the private pleasure palace of flamboyant brewery and airline tycoon Vijay Mallya (he makes Kingfisher beer). At New Year, and every few months, these gates are jammed with eager locals and frantic paparazzi clamouring to catch a glimpse of Mallya's Bollywood celeb-heavy guest list.

Where to eat & drink

Sinquerim and Fort Aguada are the most exclusive, expensive parts of the North Goan tourism strip, so expect high prices for good quality throughout. The **Banyan Tree** (Taj Holiday Village, 0832-564-5858, main courses Rs 250, open 12.30-2.30pm, 7.30-10.30pm daily), one of Goa's best Thai restaurants, sits beside a magnificent specimen of its namesake in the grounds of the Taj Holiday Village. North of Fort Aguada, there's **Santa Lucia** (Fort Aguada Road, 0832-561-5213, main courses Rs 150, open 6.30-10.30pm daily), a tiny, relaxed terrace restaurant serving zesty Italian and Swiss food.

Nightlife

Near the Taj Village is **Sweet Chilli Garden Restaurant and Lounge** (on the Lighthouse Road, 0832-247-9446, main courses Rs 120, open 11am-midnight daily), a popular open-air

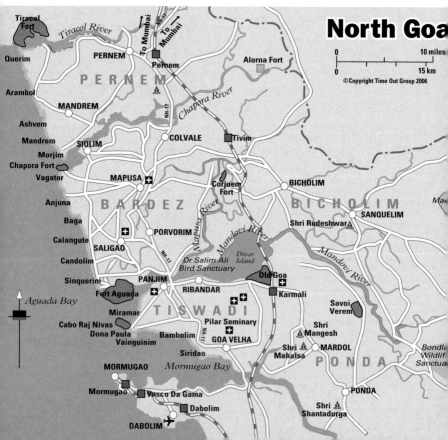

restaurant on several levels, with live music every night, like the lively jazz jams on Friday evenings.

Entertainment

Although Sinquerim beach has been cut to a third of its former breadth by the erosion caused by the marooned ore-carrier *River Princess*, it's still a good centre for watersports. Morgan D'Souza of **Thunder Waves** (on the beach near Fort Aguada, 982217-6986, open 9am-sunset daily) offers dolphin trips (Rs 400 per head for a half-hour excursion), speedboat-driven parasailing from the beach (Rs 1,000-Rs 1,500 for 3-10mins), and jetskiing (Rs 900 for 15 minutes). The Taj Aguada has one of the best spas in India: **Jiva** (0832-564-5858, open 8am-8pm daily), which offers popular Balinese massages for Rs 3,000 per hour, and a signature Jivaniya package (including spice scrub, wrap and deep-tissue massage) for Rs 3,650.

Where to stay

The **Fort Aguada Beach Resort** (Fort Aguada, 0832-564-5858, www.tajhotels.com, Rs 7,000-Rs 9,000 double), the luxury tourism pioneer, is showing its age but is still the playground for India's A-list, especially during New Year celebrations. But it's questionable whether the experience lives up to the hype. The **Taj Holiday Village** (0832-564-5858, www.tajhotels.com, Rs 8,000-Rs 9,000 double) offers attractive individual villas with private balconies. Near the Taj is the **Marbella Guesthouse** (Fort Aguada Beach Road, near Jojo's Corner restaurant, 0832-247-9551, Rs 1,100-Rs 2,500 double) with six eccentrically decorated but well-appointed rooms in a pretty house under a mango tree.

Getting there

Tivim is the nearest train stop to the north beaches; the half-hour taxi ride from Tivim to Sinquerim costs Rs 350. From Dabolim, it's Rs 650 and takes an hour. From Panjim, take the Mandovi Bridge towards Mapusa and turn left off the NH-17 at O Coqueiro junction. Turn left at St Alex Church and Sinquerim is 3 miles down the road. Taxis cost Rs 250 from Panjim.

Nerul (Coco Beach)

Before the beach road hits Candolim, a sharp right turn onto a narrow, scenic road leads to Nerul and Coco Beach on the Mandovi River, with views of the Panjim waterfront. Nerul feels slightly schizophrenic, alternating between the

A typical North Goan roadside shrine.

ultra-luxurious villas of Indian and foreign millionaires, and small village homes of local fishermen and farmers. The beach is popular with Goan families, wealthy Indians and older Europeans. The water off Coco Beach is a little murkier than that of Candolim or Calangute but it is clean and safe to swim 100 yards out.

Where to eat & drink

The **Bai Tereza Beach Camp** (behind Nerul Church, 98906-94138, www.beachcampgoa.com, sandwiches Rs 250, open 8.30am-9.30pm daily) is a smart outdoor restaurant with a Danish chef who concocts tasty sandwiches, grilled meats and pancakes. Under the Nerul bridge (which Matt Damon crashed a car off in the action flick *The Bourne Supremacy*) is **Amigo's** (0832-240-1123, main courses Rs 100, open 11am-10.30pm daily), a local-run restaurant in a beautiful spot on the mangrove-fringed riverbank, with strong ties with local fisherfolk – hence the super-fresh mussels, shrimp and estuarine crabs. Just beyond the bridge is **Rita's Bar** (no phone, main courses Rs 70, open 7-11pm Mon-Sat), a nondescript concrete box owned by a retired fishmonger, but worth the visit for the excellent seafood.

Candolim

Once a deserted expanse of banyan trees and soaring palm trees, Candolim is now ground zero in terms of Goa's mass tourism. It's a maze of lanes and byways lined with hundreds of guesthouses, shops and restaurants and choked with traffic in peak season. Candolim is the epicentre of the British invasion, both by budget travellers and expatriates, and fish-and-chip shops and pubs festooned with Premier League memorabilia abound. Candolim is as close as Goa gets to mass-tourism hotspots like Cancun and the Costa del Sol, but it's still reasonably relaxed and has some excellent restaurants hidden among the neon-lit also-rans. Unlike the beaches to the north, Candolim is a one-stop vacation destination – everything you need is within walking distance.

In the interior of the village, about a mile from the main road, the impressive **Our Lady of Hope Church** (open at 5.45pm for Sunday mass) sits on an elevated location with a good view of the carefully tended *bund* (earthen dam) system that keeps the acres of surrounding farmland protected from flooding from the Nerul marshes. The sluices for these bunds are called *kandoli* in Konkani – hence the name Candolim. The village played a prominent role in Goan history, and was the site of a major campaign of revolt against Portuguese rule in 1787, led by disaffected Catholic priests, including the clergyman father of the adventurer/hypnotist Abbe Faria (*see p208* **The Monk of Monte Cristo**). The revolt was put down, but locals proudly refer to the episode as the second anti-colonial uprising in history after the American Revolution of 1776. In the north of the village stands the **Casa dos Monteiros**, a beautifully preserved 17th-century private home. It can be approached from the road, but like the similarly impressive **Casa dos Costa-Frias** near Bosio Hospital, no visitors are allowed.

Where to eat & drink

Candolim has some of Goa's best restaurants, but the stand-out eatery here is **Bomra's** (Souza Vaddo, 98221-49633, 98221-34857, main courses Rs 200, open 7-10pm Mon-Sat, closed Apr-Sept), which serves innovative versions of Burmese and Kachin dishes, prepared by a London-trained Burmese chef. Opened in the 2006 season, Bomra's has received lots of attention and makes a

Feni for your thoughts

The French have their wine, the Greeks have their ouzo, but Goans have *feni* – and they don't really need anything else, thanks very much. Every April and May, the heavy scent of fermenting cashew drifts across the countryside, and traditional stills fire up to make the year's batch of this deeply loved drink – a drink as synonymous with Goa as beaches and fish-curry-rice. *Feni* (pronounced *fey-nee*) is a clear, powerful spirit that comes in two varieties: cashew and coconut. Coconut feni (also known as palm feni) is made all year round, mostly in South Goa, but is considered by purists to be an inferior version of the 'original' cashew *feni*, which can only be made after the cashew fruit harvest in March. The fruits are crushed and the juice left to ferment – it is then heated in large copper or earthen pots over firewood and the distillate collected through a coiled pipe. The first distillate is weak and makes a drink called *urrak*; it takes two or three distillations to make proper, strong *feni*, which is around 40 per cent alcohol.

Connoisseurs insist that good *feni* can be as smooth and nuanced as the finest single malt whiskies. It is by far the state's most popular drink, available at hole-in-the-wall taverns everywhere, which serve no-name homemade varieties poured from jerry cans or unlabelled plastic bottles. Hospadaria Venite in Panjim (*see p207*) sells an excellent home-produced *feni* by the bottle for about Rs 150, but there are lots of big-name brands like Big Boss (Rs 150 for 750 ml) available from wine shops everywhere. Drink it neat, with a squeeze of lime, a pinch of salt, or mixed with lemonade. It's also fabulous in fruit cocktails. A trip to Goa is not complete without at least one lazy peg of *feni*. Watch out – it has a kick like a gaur.

courses Rs 200, open 11am-2pm, 7-10pm daily, closed Apr-Aug), where a highly motivated staff working under German-Thai management turns out top-class Thai food in a garden setting.

Down on the beach, the pick of Candolim's endless line of shacks is **Calamari** (0832-309-0506, main courses Rs 150, open 9.30pm-8.30pm daily, closed May-Sept), where the motto is 'Bathe and Binge'. It has very friendly staff, great Goan-style seafood, and offers patrons an outdoor shower and free towels. A fabulous breakfast and lunch choice is **Café Chocolatti** (Fort Aguada Road, 0832-247-9340, main courses Rs 200), which specialises in superb salads, sandwiches and baked goods (with delicious cookies and chocolates for sale in the tiny attached shop). Highly recommended.

Nightlife

These days, nightlife in Candolim is relatively sleepy. Just next door to Bomra's restaurant is the relaxed **Havana** (Fort Aguada Road, Candolim, 0832-395-2973, open 7pm-midnight daily), a long bar with a full-sized snooker table and an open-air lawn – a nice spot for a pre-dinner drink. Opposite St Anthony's Chapel is the **Bar** (no phone, open 12pm-3am daily), a cosy bar with low cane seating, a couple of pool tables and a club-like feel, run by the effusive Anuj. Try his masala *feni*.

Furniture at **Sotohaus**.

credible claim to being one of the world's best Burmese restaurants. Another unusual eating option is **Cuckoo Zen Garden** (near Bob's Inn, Ximer 98221-26031, www.cuckoozen.com, main courses Rs 150, open 2-11pm Mon-Sat, closed Apr-Sept), Goa's only authentic Chinese restaurant, run by an eccentric commune of Taiwanese (with names like Soup and Elephant) who live in the shadow of Cuckoo, a Taiwanese acupuncturist and self-styled Zen master. Down the road, near the Tarcar ice factory, is **Lloyd's** (94224-38230, open 7pm-6am, main courses Rs 120), a basic space with dismal bathrooms that becomes extremely popular late at night for alcohol-soaked home-cooked dinners including legendary Goan-style spare ribs.

The beach road opposite the Tarcar ice factory leads to the Italian-run **La Fenice** (no phone, main courses Rs 150, open 11am-10pm daily). At the top of a long flight of stairs are some spacious, atmospheric terraces where you can dine on tasty and authentic Italian food – some of the best on offer in the state. Close to the Candolim Beach taxi stand is **Oriental** (Hotel Surf Side, next to Candolim Beach Taxi Stand, 0832-309-2809, main

Shopping

One of Goa's most popular shopping centres is the **Acron Arcade** (283 Fort Aguada Road, 0832-564-3671, open 10am-10pm daily). Downstairs, half the building is devoted to home decor from **Yamini**, an Indian chain of stores selling beautiful handmade fabrics and furnishings. It has a variety of men's and women's clothes with an emphasis on handloom, and reasonably priced designer labels from Pondicherry and Bangalore. Acron is also home to a well-stocked delicatessen offering everything from whole Scottish smoked salmon to pre-packaged pasta sauces. Down the road from the Tarcar ice factory, after La Fenice, is the **Literati Bookshop and Café** (98226-82566, 0832-227-7740), Goa's best bookstore and hangout for bibliophiles, in a charming old converted house. Not far away, the Swiss-owned store **Sotohaus** (1266F Anna Vaddo, Candolim, 0832-248-9983, www.sotodecor.com) offers beautifully worked iron-and-paper lamps, tables and other furniture, many made using found natural objects like banana, elephant-ear, papaya leaves, driftwood and even shed snakeskins, all under thick layers of lacquer.

Goa

Hippy and you know it

In 1969, Gilbert Levey left the Haight-Ashbury district of San Francisco and took the overland trail through Afghanistan and Pakistan, first to Bombay and then Goa. He'd been a roadie for Sons of Champlain, a pioneering acid rock band, but in Goa he adopted the saffron robes and matted hair of a Hindu *sadhu*, or wise man, and became Goa Gil – a pioneer of the early hippy scene at Anjuna Beach. Throughout the 1970s, Gil organised legendary parties at Anjuna – moonlight jams and ecstatic parties of non-stop music and drugs that lasted from Christmas Eve to New Year's day for a tribe

of fellow overland travellers who called themselves Goa Freaks. Gil describes these epic parties as efforts to 'tell the story of humanity'.

In the '90s, Gil started to use snippets from industrial music, ethno-techno, acid house and psychedelic rock to create Goa trance, dance music with a heavy spiritual accent. Today, Goa trance (sometimes known to fans simply as 604, a numerical approximation of the word Goa) has morphed into a global multi-million dollar industry and is played at clubs as far away as New York and Israel. Gil remains

Anjuna beach bums, 1975.

Where to stay

This is charter tourism country, so most hotels in Candolim are built to specifications dictated by travel companies – virtually everything is identical, clean and well-run but there are few non-full board options available. The pick of this bunch is the lovingly decorated **Aldeia Santa Rita** (near Kingfisher Villa, 0832-247-9868, Rs 4,000-Rs 7,500 double), close to the beach. Nearby is **Whispering Palms** (off Candolim main road 0832-247-9140, www.whisperingpalms.com, Rs 6,000-Rs 8,000 double), which has an excellent swimming pool and well-appointed rooms. More basic than either, though equally packed with British charter tourists, is the

Summerville Beach Resort (off Candolim main road, 0832-247-9075, www.summer villebeachresort.com, Rs 1,200-Rs 1,800 double), which has 20 well-maintained rooms, a pleasant rooftop restaurant and a small swimming pool.

Resources

Internet
Sify I-way, Bake N Byte, Laxmi Apartments, near Candolim Market (no phone). **Open** 9am-10pm daily.

Getting there

Taxis from Tivim take around 30 minutes and cost Rs 350. From Dabolim Airport, it's Rs 600

Goa

at the centre of the scene, DJing full-moon parties around the world that he calls attempts 'to redefine ancient tribal ritual for the 21st century' and 'uplift the consciousness of the participants', although a cynic might say that the drug ecstasy has as much to do with that as the music. For Gil, Goa trance is a logical continuation of what hippies were doing back in the '60s and '70s. 'The Psychedelic Revolution never really stopped,' he said. 'It just had to go halfway round the world to the end of a dirt road on a deserted beach, and there it was

allowed to evolve and mutate, without government or media pressures.'

But government pressure has finally caught up with the revolution in Goa. Because of their association with drugs, raves are viewed with suspicion by Goan authorities and were banned entirely in the 2005/06 tourist season. Still, underground raves do happen surreptitiously, sometimes starting at 4am on remote beaches or in forests. Ask staff at local bars and the 'pilots' who operate motorcycle taxis to find out when and where the next party is happening.

Goa Gil in 1972.

Full moon party at Anjuna, 1978.

and takes an hour; from Panjim, it's around Rs 200 for a 20-minute trip. When driving from Panjim, cross the Mandovi Bridge and go about two miles straight up the NH-17 highway towards Mapusa. Turn left at the O Coqueiro junction, and pass through Sangolda until you reach the Church of St Alex in Calangute. From there, turn left onto Candolim Road.

Calangute & Baga

Long before tourists washed up on Goan shores, **Calangute** was a seafront idyll for genteel Goan families from all over North Goa and Panjim. Through the hot summer months of April and May, they retired here to simple rented accommodation and borrowed villas to

take early morning 'sea baths' and evening walks along a rudimentary boardwalk. All that is long gone: Calangute's broad sands are as golden as ever but have been swamped with Goa's most congested tourist scene, with thousands of Indian visitors rubbing elbows with Scandinavians and Brits and a beach lined with paragliders, jetskis, speedboats and tightly packed sunbeds. The interior is just as crowded, with buses constantly disgorging Indian day-trippers from neighbouring states, and the usual collection of Kashmiri rug merchants, fast food outlets, and cheap souvenir shops.

It's hard to tell where Calangute ends and **Baga** begins. Baga is now one of the most famous party hotspots in India, with a range of

Goa

bars that pack in 20-something members of India's call-centre generation from Mumbai, Bangalore and Delhi, with money to burn and a taste for Bollywood music. Slightly quieter is Baga Creek, across a concrete bridge, where a long line of some of Goa's best eating options operate out of converted old houses just yards from the river bank.

A couple of reminders of the past do remain, notably the private home **Casa dos Proenças**, just north of the main Calangute market. It was built with several unusual features, including a gorgeous seashell-screened enclosed verandah and an ingenuous natural cooling system. Away from the beach, on the road towards Saligao, stands the spectacular rococo **Church of St Alex**, an 18th-century construction with a bulging dome and Indianised bell towers. Regular returnees to Calangute like to begin their vacation with a shave and a haircut in the barber shop (the sign reads 'Barberia') in the mirrored octagon in the centre of the Calangute market crossroads – a 200-year-old colonial customs post.

Where to eat & drink

Baga Creek has numerous exciting and ambitious restaurants, of which **J&A's Little Italy** (Baga Creek, 98231-39488, main courses Rs 350, open 6pm-midnight daily, closed Apr-

Waves, Calangute. *See p189.*

Sept), is easily the best, serving delicious Italian food with an emphasis on superb ingredients and flawless presentation. Close by is the hillside **La Terrasse** (Baga Creek, 0832-395-0832, www.laterrasse.in, main courses Rs 250, open 6.30-10.30pm daily, closed Apr-Sept) high up a couple of flights of steps with great views of the creek and authentic southern French food. On the same stretch is the brilliant daytime hangout **Lila Café** (0832-227-9843, main courses Rs 120, open 9am-6pm Mon, Wed-Sun, closed May-Sept), whose German owners keep a devoted crowd of regulars happy with fresh German bread, mushroom pâté, water-buffalo ham and other euro-treats.

Near the Baga Creek bridge, is the impeccable **Sublime** (98224-84051, main courses Rs 250, open 6.30pm daily, closed May-Sept). Its chef trained at the elite Culinary Institute of America, and turns out impeccable modern dishes with imported ingredients – try the fabulous medallions of beef. Heading towards the beach, there's old-timer **Britto's** (last corner on Baga Road, 0832-227-7331, main courses Rs 150, open 8.30am-10.30pm daily), a friendly Baga institution serving decent Goan dishes. Fifty yards inland from Britto's and much better is **Vasquito's** (near Kamasutra Lounge, Baga, 0832-395-2915, main courses Rs 150, open 7-11pm daily), whose chef serves up American deep-south barbecue staples like ribs and steak. A little further down the beach road towards Calangute is **Casa Portuguesa** (Beach Road, 0832-227-7024, www.casa-portuguesa-goa.com, main courses Rs 250, open 7-11pm Tue-Sun, closed May-Oct), a pleasant restaurant in a converted ancestral home specialising in authentic Portuguese food; it occasionally courts trouble by serving illegal wildlife dishes like wild boar and frog's legs.

Further along the beach road from Baga to Calangute, the next landmark is the unaccountably unsung **Le Restaurant Français** (Milky Way restaurant, Baga Road, 98221-21712, main courses Rs 200, open 7.30-10.30pm Mon, Wed-Sun, closed May-Oct), an experimental French restaurant. The huge screens painted with Parisian scenes are a bit incongruous but the food is stunning. Across the road is the lane that leads to **Tito's** (Tito's Lane, Baga, 0832-227-5028, 0832-227-6154, main courses Rs 250, open 7pm-midnight daily, closed May-Sept), the party hotspot that also serves decent pastas and steaks. Much better fare is available directly opposite at **Fiesta** (Tito's Lane, Baga, 0832-227-9894, 0832-228-1440, www.fiestagoa.com, main courses Rs 300, open 7-11pm Mon, Wed-Sun,

Brits on the beach in **Baga**.

closed Apr-Oct), a beautifully decorated open-air restaurant with a Caribbean feel and a German chef who makes superb wood-fired oven pizzas and outstanding desserts. Further down Tito's Lane towards the beach is the French-owned **Apple Pie** (0832-263-8898, main courses Rs 200, open 6-10pm Mon-Sat, closed May-Oct), which has won a loyal following for its homemade cheesecake and competent bistro fare. Nearby is the pick of Baga's beach shacks, **Zanzibar** (no phone, main courses Rs 175, open 9am-11pm daily, closed May-Sept), serving good Indian food with an emphasis on fresh fish and shrimp.

Just before the Calangute roundabout is the old Goan favourite **Infantaria** (0832-227-7421, main courses Rs 125, open 8.30am-10pm daily) which has been dishing up old-fashioned potato chops and croquettes to generations of day-trippers. All the way back in Gaurawaddo, in the part of Calangute that merges into Candolim, **Waves** (0832-227-6017, main courses Rs 200, open 7-10pm daily, closed May-Sept) is an unusual restaurant in the pleasant Kerkar Art Complex, serving Hindu Goan, or 'Gomantak' specialities. Next door is **Roma** (98905-55237, main courses Rs 200, open 11am-11pm daily, closed May-Oct), a Roman-owned restaurant serving authentic Roman food.

Nightlife

Calangute and Baga are home to some of Goa's most hectic nightlife; both beaches are crammed with chilled-out shacks serving drinks until late, and the streets behind are lined with hole-in-the-wall bars. Baga's (and maybe Goa's) most famous club is **Tito's** (Tito's Lane, Baga, 0832-227-9895, www.titosgoa.com, open 10pm-4am, admission Rs 500-Rs 600), a Baga institution that attracts hundreds of Kingfisher-fuelled boys and girls from Mumbai for Bollywood beats and dancing on three levels, with extra entertainment provided by professional dancers and the occasional magician. Just down the lane towards the beach is **Mambo's** (Tito's Lane, Baga, 0832-227-9895, open 7pm-3.30am, cover charge Rs 200-Rs 300), a wooden beach pub run by the Tito's management but with a more relaxed vibe. They usually play a mix of hip-hop and house, with some country music thrown in. A little further up the main road from Tito's Lane is **Congo** (Saunta Vaddo, Baga, 0832-561-6858, open 7pm-midnight, closed Apr-Sept), a stylish lounge bar and restaurant aimed at the Mumbai elite, with a fabulous sundeck for highly relaxing sunset drinks. **Kamasutra** (Saunta Vaddo, Baga, 98901-41879, open noon-midnight daily) is a laid-back bar serving food and cocktails to a progressive lounge soundtrack, popular with

Goa

Turn on, check in, drop out

Wildernest.

For years, visitors to Goa had to choose between beach huts and informal guesthouses with plenty of character but often little comfort, or sprawling five-stars where the reverse was true. But in recent years, Goa's hotel market has been energised by the rise of boutique hotels – small and stylish properties offering an exclusive experience much more suited to Goa's naturally laid-back vibe. Since 2000, the new boutique breed has become extremely popular, routinely charging more than the five-stars during the peak season around Christmas and New Year's Eve.

The grandfather of the trend is the **Nilaya Hermitage** (Arpora, 0832-227-6794, www.nilayahermitage.com, Rs 12,000-Rs 25,000 double), an ethereal fortress of laterite domes on an Arpora hilltop, with an eagle's-eye view of the jungle landscape below. The atmosphere is otherworldly – Arabian Nights meets New Age – with twelve exceptional rooms themed according to the 'cosmic elements', with names like 'sun', 'earth' and 'fire'. Under its largest dome

is a 'music room' decked out with white cotton mattresses and a superb sound system – a veritable temple of chill-out. Nilaya has attracted numerous famous guests, including Giorgio Armani, Kate Moss (who was snapped topless there by a *News of the World* paparazzo) and Richard Gere.

Pousada Tauma (Porba Vaddo, 0832-227-9061, www.pousadatauma.com, Rs 12,000-Rs 26,500 double) is a secluded dell of lush greenery and beautiful cottages around an attractive pool. It also has one of Goa's most enchanting restaurants with tables arranged along a laterite colonnade.

Getting away from it all is guaranteed at **Elsewhere** (Mandrem, 98200-37387, www.aseascape.com, Rs 6,100-Rs 24,000 per day, closed June-mid October), the ancestral home of Mumbai fashion photographer Denzil Sequeira and a stunning beach house-for-hire. It's set on an isolated strip of beach in Mandrem, with a verandah overlooking the surf, shuttered windows and servants on hand. The house overlooks a creek behind, and Sequeira has set up a few tents – the word doesn't really do them justice – each with hot and cold running water, a private jetty and a four-poster bed (Rs 2,300-Rs 5,700 per night).

Most unusual, and perhaps most stunning of all is Loulou Van Damme's creation, **Panchavatti** (Corjuem Island, 98225-80632, www.islaingoa.com, Rs 6,000-Rs 8,000 double, closed May-September), a magnificent hacienda on a headland above the coiled Mapusa River, blending design elements from Morocco, Latin America and the Caribbean. It's a retreat, Loulou says, 'for serenity, for you to redo your soul the right way'. Far inland, around 90 minutes' drive from Panjim, is **Wildernest** (Swapnagandha, Chorla Ghat, off highway to Belgaum, 0831-520-7954, www.wildernest-goa.com, Rs 2,500-Rs 5,500 double), a unique hotel complex of small wood-and-glass cottages located 800 yards above sea level in the mountains of the Western Ghats. Run by nature lovers, Wildernest offers secluded and highly comfortable cottages hidden away in the woods, with floor-to-ceiling glass windows that make you feel like you're camping out. Splash around the infinity pool, gazing out over the breathtaking Vazra Waterfall and the entire Mandovi River valley – then don your boots for a hike in the woods.

Panchavatti.

both Indians and Euro-kids. Open even during the depths of the monsoon, the bar at **Cavala** (Saunta Vaddo, Baga, 0832-227-6090, open 9am-midnight daily), an old Baga hotel, offers a warm welcome to a friendly (and older) crowd of locals, expats and regular returnees, with live music and retro nights most Fridays and Saturdays.

Where to stay

Pousada Tauma (Porba Vaddo, Calangute, 0832-227-9061, www.pousada-tauma.com, Rs 12,000-Rs 20,000 double), is a lush complex of villas set around an inviting pool with an enchanting restaurant beneath a laterite colonnade and a top-notch Ayurvedic spa. **Villa Goesa** (Cobra Vaddo, 0832-227-7535, www.villagoesa.com, Rs 1,700-Rs 2,700 double) is particularly close to the beach and set up in nicely maintained gardens. The nearby **Chalston Beach Resort** (Cobra Vaddo, 0832-227-6080, Rs 1,000-1,500 double) is a clean, reasonably priced option popular with Scandinavians. Its beach shack is one of the best on this stretch. On the road in the thick of Baga's action is **Cavala** (Baga main road, 0832-227-7587, www.cavala.com, Rs 600-Rs 1,700 double), not far from the beach and with attractive, great-value rooms.

Resources

Internet

Sify I-way, Shop No.1, Sunshine Complex, Baga Road (no phone). **Open** 9am-9pm daily.

Post office

Calangute Post Office, near St Alex Church (0832-227-6030). **Open** 9am-5pm Mon-Fri.

Getting there

Taxis from Tivim cost Rs 300 for the half-hour trip. From Dabolim Airport, it's Rs 650 and takes around 75 minutes. From Candolim, turn right at St Anthony's Chapel for Calangute; for Baga, take another right at the main traffic circle just before Calangute beach.

Anjuna

Anjuna is where the first tie-dyed '60s refugees came in search of freedom, sunshine and cheap drugs. Some never left: you can still find Eight-fingered Eddie (now in his 80s) playing ball on the beach he 'discovered' 40 years ago, and the spirit of the Goa Freaks lives on in the hundreds of raised chillums that hail each sunset on the beachfront. But Anjuna is also

Pousada Tauma.

Goa

Feed your inner hippy at **Zoories**, Anjuna. *See p193*.

home to writers and artists who simply like the vibe, and even has a straitlaced private school, the British-operated **Little Yellow School House** – by far the most expensive school in Goa, catering to expat children.

Long before the Goa Freaks skipped on to its beaches, Anjuna was a cosmopolitan trade outpost controlled by the Arabs (hence the name, derived from *hanjuman*, meaning 'trading post') in the tenth century. But most Muslim (and Hindu) traces were wiped out by the Portuguese zeal to Christianise the region as fast and as bloodily as possible. The sprawling **Church of St Michael the Archangel** (open for mass 7am Sun) dates back to that violent era.

Anjuna's famous **Flea Market** (South Anjuna, 8am-sunset every Wednesday) is a relic from the early hippie days in the '60s and '70s when hashish was legal and sold just like today's vendors hawk cheap T-shirts and wooden knick-knacks. The market's original avatar was small-scale, sometimes relied on barter rather than cash, and was mostly used by foreigners looking to raise the money to stay on or get home. Now tens of thousands converge on the flea market every Wednesday from October to April in a convoy of scooters, motorbikes and trucks that throws up huge clouds of dust. The market sprawls over a plateau by the beach with hundreds of stalls selling everything from tie-dye bikinis to chillums to sitars to cushion covers.

In the late '90s and early 2000s Anjuna became famous all over again for its moonlight parties and raves – legendary open-air happenings that sent trance beats pulsing out to the stars and drew thousands of wildly dressed revellers. That scene is on hold while the Goa government wrings its hands over a coherent policy towards rave tourists. But it seems unlikely that the rave scene will ever return to Anjuna in quite the same way again.

Where to eat & drink

All roads lead to **Curlies** (South Anjuna Beach, no phone, main courses Rs 100, open 10am-midnight daily), a low-slung beach shack in South Anjuna, where a tightly knit staff of Anjuna villagers watches over a veritable United Nations of tokers. Sunset on the steps feels like an ancient ritual, with dozens of packed chillums making the rounds while children and dogs caper in the surf a few yards away. Up the beach is **Café Looda** (0832-562-9323, main courses Rs 200, open 8.30am-11.30pm daily, closed May-Oct), perched on the rocks overlooking the beach, at its best after the flea market slows down on Wednesdays. Elvis, Looda's in-house guitarist, leads rollicking freestyle jams with anyone who shows up – from Aussie didgeridoo players to Swedish opera singers. Quite near both, behind a small chapel, is the Anjuna landmark **Xavier's** (Praia de San Miguel,

Chapora Fort. *See p195.*

0832-227-3402, main courses Rs 150, open 9am-11pm daily), once a small, basic shack and now a multi-cuisine establishment with three kitchens whipping up Indian, Chinese and continental dishes. Nearer to Anjuna village is **Bean Me Up** (Soranto Vaddo, 0832-227-3977, www.travelingoa.com/beanmeup, main courses Rs 120, open 9.30am-10.30pm daily), a world-class American-run vegetarian restaurant with super homemade tofu and salads. On the main Anjuna village road, the **Blue Tao Organic Restaurant and Café** (before Starco turn-off, 0832-309-0829, main courses Rs 100, open 9.30am-10.30pm daily) has an equally fervent following among Anjuna expatriates. It's a welcoming family restaurant selling homemade cakes and ice creams, great herbal teas and fresh juices, and tasty, healthy breakfasts.

At the far north end of Anjuna beach, near the Paradiso nightclub, is **Zoories** (no phone, main courses Rs 150, open 11am-11pm daily), with a stunning setting high on a cliff overlooking a rocky cove and a menu ranging featuring houmous, fajitas and enchiladas. A few minutes drive away from the beach is **Yoga Magic** (Grand Chinvar Vaddo, next to Bobby Bar, 0832-562-3796, 9370565717, www.yogamagic.net, main courses Rs 400, open 11.30am-1.30pm, 7-9pm daily, closed Apr-Sept), a popular eco-friendly getaway offering super 'Indian fusion' vegetarian meals to non-resident guests. Dinner bookings required.

Nightlife

Both **Curlies** and **Café Looda** (*see p192*) turn into lively beachside nightspots after sunset, with Curlies going heavy on the trance and ambient sounds for its stoner patrons. The **Shore Bar** (Anjuna Beach, no phone, open 8am-11pm daily), a few minutes' walk up the beach north of Café Looda, is pretty basic but very relaxed, with regular trance nights from 6pm to 11pm. Goa's most stylish club is **Club Cubana** (82 Xim Waddo, Arpora Hill, 98235-39000, www.cubana.net, open 9.30pm-5am, closed May-Oct, cover charge Rs 600-Rs 1,500), perched on an Arpora hilltop, a short drive from Anjuna. Cubana is a sprawling maze of levels and staircases, with terraces offering starry night views across Goa for its mixed crowd of Mumbai rich kids and European tourists. Trance is firmly rejected here in favour of hip hop, house and R&B. Towels are provided for patrons who fancy jumping into the swimming pool, and the drinks are unlimited once you pay the cover charge (it can hit Rs 1,500 each for stags around Christmas and New Year). Less fancy but even bigger is **Paradiso** (Anjuna, 93261-00013, open 10pm-5am, cover charge Rs 300-Rs 600), a huge club built on a series of psychedelically-painted laterite terraces overlooking the sea. Paradiso attracts some of India's best DJs and even the likes of Goa Gil (*see p186* **Hippy and you know it**). When

Goa

it's packed the energy level is hard to beat, pumped up by non-stop trance beats and the rhythm of the waves.

Underground Kingdom (Grand Peddem, Anjuna, no phone, open 10pm-6am, entry Rs 200) has got around the rave ban by burying itself in a large World War II-style concrete bunker in the middle of a forest, where DJs drop trance beats that echo insanely off the walls. Patrons can give their eardrums a break outside at relaxed open-air bars and canopies with soft cushions. The famous **Ingo's Saturday Night Bazaar** – a popular weekly night market at Arpora with food and live music seemed certain to end after the 2005/06 season. It faced stiff opposition from locals and it remains to be seen if the bazaar will return.

Where to stay

Anjuna is catching up the other beachfront villages fast in terms of the range and quality of its hotels and guesthouses. The most atmospheric of all is **Granpa's Inn** (Gaun Vaddo, 0832-227-3270, Rs 850-1750 double), the converted ancestral home of the Faria family. It has a great atmosphere, lovely gardens and terrace, and a pool. A similar, though more downmarket version is **Palacete Rodrigues** (Mazal Vaddo, 0832-227-3358, Rs 750-Rs 1,100 double), a converted 200-year-old house with the feel of a family home. Back in the present century, **Laguna Anjuna** (Soranto Vaddo, 0832-227-4305, www.lagunaanjuna.com, Rs 2,100-Rs 7,500 double) is Anjuna's best hotel, a stylish set of cottages around an attractive pool, although it is starting to look a little worse for wear. In the far north of Anjuna is **Lotus Inn** (Zor Vaddo, 0832-227-4015, www.lotusinn.com, Rs 1,000-Rs 4,500 double), a family-friendly modern hotel with a pool and a popular restaurant serving a mix of German and Indian food. Something different is offered by **Yoga Magic** (Grand Chinvar Vaddo, near Bobby Bar, 0832-562-3796, 93705-65717, www.yoga magic.net), an environmentally friendly, tented yoga camp (tents Rs 1,000 per person) which also offers a luxurious room (Rs 5,000 per night) in the main house.

Hidden temples

Shantadurga Temple.

For over a century after their arrival in Goa, the Portuguese conquistadors set out to destroy every single Hindu temple they could find, with one particularly zealous officer, Diogo Rodrigues, tearing down over 280 temples across 58 villages in 1567. By the turn of the 17th century, none were left standing.

But many of the precious idols housed within them were spirited away by loyal devotees, who stole across the rivers towards Ponda, a redoubt that didn't come under Portuguese rule until the 18th century, by which time their religious fervour had waned. There, nestled in thickly forested valleys, new temples came up to house the idols. As a result, today Ponda is home to some of Goa's most important Hindu sites.

The most famous of all is the **Shri Mangesh Temple** (Priol, north-west of Ponda on NH-4, open 7am-6.30pm daily), a popular stop for domestic and foreign tourists alike. The resident *shivalingam* (a clay symbol representing Lord Shiva) was brought across the Zuari River from Curtorim and is housed in a temple of Mughal-type domes, baroque flourishes adapted from Goa's churches, and an impressive octagonal tower that can be seen for miles. A few miles away is the **Shri Mahalsa**

Resources

Internet

Sify I-way, next to Tembi Café, Mazal Vaddo (no phone). **Open** 9am-9pm daily.

Post office

Anjuna Post Office, near Football Grounds (0832-227-3221). **Open** 9am-5pm Mon-Fri.

Getting there

The journey by taxi from Tivim takes 25 minutes and costs Rs 350. From Dabolim Airport, taxis take 75 minutes and cost Rs 750. From Panjim, take the NH-17 toward Mapusa and turn left near the Green Park Hotel. Follow the narrow road; Anjuna is signposted.

Vagator and Chapora

As Anjuna steadily turns more mainstream and family-friendly, the hard core of trance music pilgrims, drop-outs and committed stoners has shifted further north to the beaches and headland in the shadow of the rugged

Chapora Fort. The Portuguese rebuilt this bastion at the turn of the 18th century on the ruins of a much older fort built by Adil Shah (the name Chapora comes from *Shah-pura*, or 'Place of the Shah'). In the early 18th century, the son of the great Mughal Emperor Aurangzeb holed up here while scheming to topple his father in a pact with the enemy Marathas. The fortress is crumbling to bits and overrun with vegetation, but the views are magnificent, with the Arabian Sea on one side and the gorgeous harbour at the mouth of the Chapora River on the other. All this makes Chapora Fort one of the best sunset spots in Goa, often attracting hundreds of Indian tourists from neighbouring states.

In recent years, the winding palm-lined lanes of Chapora and the beaches of 'little' and 'big' Vagator have become home to a hard-edged sub-culture of Russians, Israelis, Italians and other Europeans. Many visitors stay for months, renting tiny no-frills rooms in the same local houses each year, watched over by a Goan mafia well-connected with the local police. The atmosphere can be a little off-

Temple (Mardol, north-west from Ponda off NH-4, open 7am-6pm daily). At the far end of a marble courtyard, there's a beautiful water tank fed by a freshwater spring, lined with coconut palms and traditional *ghats* used for ritual bathing (and for doing the locals' laundry).

South-west of Ponda, right on the edge of unbroken jungle, is Goa's largest and perhaps most important Hindu temple devoted to **Shri Shantadurga**, the Goddess of Peace (an avatar of Durga, Lord Shiva's consort), who remains one of Goa's most popular deities and is even venerated by Catholics. The temple was built by the Marathas in 1738, and is also influenced by Goan church architecture.

But if you can only visit one temple in Goa, it should be **Tambdi Surla** (seven miles north of Molem in Sanguem taluka, 30 minutes from Ponda along NH-4, take the left to Sancordem and follow signs, open 6am-4pm daily), a 12th-century survivor that escaped the Portuguese because of its remote, near-inaccessible location. Hewn from massive slabs of basalt that must have been carried across the mountains from the Deccan region beyond, it's a stunning and mysterious relic of the Kadamba era, the home-grown dynasty that ruled Goa until the 14th century.

Sri Mangesh Temple.

Goa

putting, with hundreds of foreigners jammed into pocket-sized tavernas and *chai* shops, openly smoking chillums under the watchful presence of those slightly menacing fix-it men and local minders. **Big Vagator**, a good swimming spot dramatically situated under the ramparts of the fort, is a lovely beach that gets crowded in high season (especially with Indian day-trippers). **Ozran** (aka **Little Vagator**), to the south, is where party folk congregate at beach shacks and the popular **Nine Bar**.

Where to eat & drink

There's a high turnover of restaurants in this area, but there are a few long-stayers like **Le Bluebird** (Ozran, 0832-227-3695, main courses Rs 250, open 9am-2pm, 7-11pm daily, closed May-Oct), a remarkable French restaurant with a very good (and pricey) wine list. There is also the trippy **Baba Yaga** (House 408, Main Road, Chapora, 0832-227-3339, main courses Rs 200, open 11am-midnight daily) in the middle of Chapora village. A short flight of stairs leads to a rooftop den painted with Russian folk murals where an all-Russian clientele enjoys a huge selection of vodkas along with *pelmenyi* (dumplings) and hearty Ukrainian-style borscht. There's also the local institution,

Britto's, Baga. *See p187.*

Primrose Café (Coutinho Vaddo, 0832-227-3210, open 9am-4am daily, main courses Rs 200) that fills up after 10pm. Another good option is the **Alcove** (no phone, main courses Rs 200, open 9am-9pm daily), a Goan restaurant on the cliff above Ozran.

Nightlife

Evenings kick off at **Nine Bar** (above Little Vagator Beach, no phone, open 6-10pm daily) a mini version of Paradiso, with a cliff-top sea view and a packed house of Indian and Euro-kids warming up to some intense trance (what else?). That finishes early, and since the clampdown on raves, open moonlight party venues like Disco Valley and Spaghetti Valley have fallen silent; instead, many opt for the **Primrose Café** (*see above*), a grungy indoor trance club with a heavy stoner contingent. The **Hill Top** (Vagator, 98221-51690, closed Apr-Oct) is an isolated hotel with a sprawling garden filled with fluorescent-painted palm trees – large enough for a few thousand revellers. They still manage the occasional rave; give them a ring to see if they're planning any. Charpora village is quiet late at night, but the friendly, Russian-dominated **Baba Yaga** (House 408, Main Road, Chapora, 0832-227-3339, open 11am-1am daily) chills out until late on comfy cushions to an ambient soundtrack.

Where to stay

Chapora and Vagator have a few professionally run guesthouses, including the bright **Bethany Inn** (538/6 Vagator Road, near Chinatown Restaurant, 0832-2273731, 0832-227-3163 www.bethanyinn.com, Rs 800-Rs 1,200 double), where each room has a private balcony and minibar. There are also two options run by the same management: **Julie Jolly** (near Ozran, 0832-227-3357, Rs 800-Rs 1,000 double), and the slightly more upscale **Jolly Jolly Roma** (Vagator Beach Road, 0832-227-3001, Rs 1,000-Rs 1,500 double). To the right of the road leading to Disco Valley is **Leoney's Resort** (0832-227-3634, www.leoneyresort.com, Rs 1,500-Rs 2,600 double), with Indo-Portuguese villas and cottages set around a pool. Leoney's doesn't take advance bookings for high season. Inland, ten minutes drive away, is the atmospheric **Siolim House** (Wadi, 0832-227-2138, www.siolimhouse.com, Rs 3,000-Rs 5,000 double), a converted 200-year old Indo-Portuguese mansion with a beautiful courtyard, huge rooms and a swimming pool. Check their website for 'silent auctions' that can get you a cheaper deal on a room.

Goa

Ashvem Beach. *See p198.*

Getting there

Taxis from Tivim charge Rs 350 for a 30-minute trip to Chapora. From Dabolim Airport, it's around Rs 750 and takes an hour. To get there from Anjuna, turn left at the crossroads just outside the village.

Morjim & Ashvem

Across the long Siolim Bridge into Pernem district, the landscape shifts into deep countryside. This part of Goa was annexed by the Portuguese much later than the lands to the south, after the chieftain Deshprabhu family accepted a royal title, Viscondes de Pernem, and allowed their holdings to be assimilated into the *Estado da India*. There is a distinct character to this part of the 'New Conquests', overwhelmingly Hindu rather than culturally mixed, and far less developed than Bardez district south of the river.

Until the bridge was built in 2002, mass tourism had never made it past the long queues for the ferries across the Chapora River. A few travellers made it to the strip of beach starting at **Morjim** and stretching north into **Ashvem**, but now that it's just a brisk 20-minute drive more development is on the way. The only thing holding back the hordes are the breeding

Siolim House. *See p196.*

habits of the migratory Olive Ridley Turtle. It's not a large nesting site (Orissa on India's east coast has far more) but this species is officially endangered and local officials have limited development in the area. In recent years, the influx of mainly Russian travellers has inhibited turtle hatchings to just two a year, but the government plans to turn the beach into a nature sanctuary, blocking plans to develop the village and the beachfront. Even now, this stretch of very broad sands feels empty, with casuarinas and palm groves standing untouched, and traditional fishing boats lining the northern and southern ends of the beach.

Nightlife

Morjim and Ashvem usually go to bed early, but a few folks keep going at the totally relaxed **Shivasati Café** (Ashvem, 982250-65093, open 6pm-2am daily), a small but beautiful space under a coolly-lit canopy on the sand.

Where to eat & drink

The Morjim/Ashvem culinary landscape is dominated by three very different eateries. The newest is **Glavfish** (Vithaldas Vaddo, 98812-87433, main courses Rs 300, closed 8am-midnight daily), an all-Russian hangout where patrons lounge on simple stone slabs and rough wooden benches. It specialises in seafood – three times as expensive as every other option on the beach. Just 100 metres away but radically different in atmosphere is the restaurant at **Montego Bay Beach Village** (Vithaldas Vaddo, 98221-50847, main courses Rs 150, open 8am-10pm daily), a Goan family favourite serving excellent food and staffed by friendly and helpful locals. The pick of the three is in a stand of mature coconut palms down the beach in Ashvem – **La Plage** (98221-21712, main courses Rs 250,

Mapusa market. *See p201.*

Goa

The great Goan land grab

'Goa is the next big overseas property destination... go for it sooner rather than later.' – www.50connect.com, Investment Guide for British Seniors.

India's economic boom has sent real estate prices rocketing in cities across the country, but even against that backdrop, Goa stands out for the sheer frenzy of its property market. Prices have more than doubled since 2003, with two-bedroom flats near Candolim now fetching around Rs 2 million. Demand for property still far outstrips supply. Indians from across the country – now wealthy enough to afford holiday homes – are snapping up virtually anything that doesn't move in India's premier resort destination. The market is also being fuelled by foreigners: over 25,000 Europeans, Israelis, Russians and North Americans have invested in Goan real estate since 2000, giving rise to growing foreign enclaves around Candolim, Baga, Anjuna and Morjim. They're still coming, and not just

retirees; the expatriate community now includes hundreds of young couples raising their children entirely under a Goan sun. Expat-oriented schools, shops and even doctors, lawyers and teachers are following in their wake.

If you catch the property bug, like countless others before you, get started by looking through the classifieds in the state's three English-language newspapers – *O Heraldo*, the *Navhind Times* and the *Gomantak Times*. You'll have to get to grips with some extremely complex rules governing foreign ownership of property in India, which some buyers have got around by setting up dummy companies in Mauritius or Panama that become the official owners of the property. Consult good lawyers at every step; land deals in Goa are notoriously unreliable and can collapse with investors losing all of their money. But if you do find that dream property, enjoy the seclusion while you can. You'll have lots of neighbours soon enough.

---

open 8.30am-10pm daily) with an outstanding menu that includes superb carpaccio, a zesty ceviche made with coconut milk, juicy tempura prawns.

Where to stay

This stretch of beach offers few options outside the informal huts and ultra-basic rented rooms. The warmest welcome is found at **Montego Bay Beach Village** (Vithaldas Vaddo, 98221-50847) which centres around a charming two-bedroom beach house (Rs 2,500-Rs 6,000), but also offers well-appointed tents with attached bathrooms (Rs 2,000-Rs 5,500) and air-conditioned rooms (Rs 2,500-Rs 6,000) with breakfast included. The friendly owner, Alwyn Fernandes, is a mine of information on Morjim. Well up the beach towards Ashvem is the beautifully designed **Papa Jolly's** (New Vaddo, 0832-224-4114, www.papajollys goa.com, Rs 2,500-Rs 10,000 double), an Austrian-run hotel with a superb location right on the beach.

Resources

Internet

Sify I-way, C-Shell Café, Mendonsa Vaddo (no phone). **Open** 9am-10pm daily.

Getting there

Taxis from Tivim Station charge Rs 500 for a 40-minute ride to Morjim and Ashvem. From Dabolim Airport, taxis cost Rs 850 and take around 90 minutes. From Panjim, take the NH-17 past Mapusa and turn left at Vrindavan Hospital for Siolim. Cross Siolim Bridge and follow the signs for Morjim. Taxis from Panjim charge around Rs 650 and take about an hour.

Mandrem

Mandrem still offers the secluded beach experience that first brought travellers to Goa, with friendly locals, communal games of football on the beach in the evenings and total quiet by late evening. Many of the miles of broad sand sweeping north towards Arambol are bounded by a narrow freshwater river running parallel to the ocean, and there's little development here, with a local economy that runs on fishing, toddy-tapping (*see p222* **Turn on the toddy tap**) and a calm, low-key tourist industry. In the centre of the village is the **Ravalnatha Temple**, which contains some centuries-old paintings and carvings, including an unusual depiction of Garuda, a divine eagle, here shown with a man's arms.

Goa

Where to eat & drink

There are few decent eateries in Mandrem but **Kimaya World Foods** (House 444, Junaswada, 0832-224-7604, open 8am-8pm daily), in the centre of Mandrem village, has all the ingredients for a perfect picnic on the beach. Run by the engaging Tanish Mahajan, Kimaya is a one-stop emporium for homemade products from an emerging local cottage industry in organic food. Grab bunches of peppery rocket, fresh multigrain bread, homemade tofu, pesto, brownies and peanut butter, and head for the beach.

Where to stay

One of Goa's most beautiful beachfront properties is the secluded **Elsewhere** (*see p190* **Turn on, check in, drop out**), the converted ancestral home of Mumbai photographer Denzil Sequeira, which also features luxury tents and three newly built guesthouses that mimic the original. Also enchanting is **Villa River Cat** (438/1 Junaswada, 0832-224-7928, www.villa rivercat.com, Rs 2,200-Rs 3,200 double), a highly individualistic riverside hotel run by fervent animal lover Rinoo Sehgal. It features 16 intensely decorated rooms, many with balconies and hammocks overlooking the shore, and a great rooftop terrace.

Getting there

Taxis from Tivim take around 45 minutes and charge Rs 500. From Dabolim Airport, taxis cost Rs 850 and take just under two hours. From Siolim Bridge, go straight on the 'new road' and look for signs for Mandrem after 5-6 miles. Taxis from Panjim charge about Rs 600 and take around an hour.

Arambol

Arambol was once the Holy Grail of the later hippy years, the dream beach for travellers seeking the precise location of the middle of nowhere. Arambol is the largest coastal village in Pernem district, with a wide beach clustered with shacks that hosts several thousand visitors a day in high season from November to March. It's become part of the well-beaten track that so many once came here to avoid, with endless lines of travellers hiking up the coastal path to the 'lakeside' beach – an arc of soft sand between the sea and an increasingly polluted freshwater lake behind. The lake is bounded by thick jungle where naked hippies still sleep under the stars like their '60s ancestors.

Where to eat & drink

A reliable standby is Dutch-owned **Double Dutch** (Beach Road, 0832-562-5973, open 8.30am-10pm daily, main courses Rs 250), which serves tasty quiches, pies, and generous salads and buffalo steaks. Unfortunately, the service can be a little frosty. Much more friendly is **Relax Inn** (Socoilo Vaddo, 98223-87618, main courses Rs 120, open 11pm-8am daily), a fun restaurant at the northern end of the beach run by five Goan brothers, serving excellent Italian dishes made from recipes handed down by an expatriate chef who has now returned to Italy. Great for seafood is **Fellini's** (Arambol Beach, no phone, main courses Rs 200, open 11am-11pm daily) a wildly popular Italian restaurant with outstanding homemade gnocchi and wood-fired pizzas. Decent Tibetan and other East Asian food is available at **Rice Bowl** (Socoilo Vaddo, 98507-27329, main courses Rs 150, open 8am-11pm daily), a Nepali-run restaurant which serves homemade noodles, dumplings and tempura.

Where to stay

Arambol's beach huts are basic compared to the sophisticated set-ups available at Palolem. The Naik family rents out over a hundred small huts with basic amenities (some have attached toilets, some do not) scattered across the cliffs on the northern end of the beach, with fabulous sea views. Call or ask at the Naik-run **Relax Inn** (Socoilo Vaddo, 98223-87618, huts Rs 500-Rs 750) for details. Modern, airy rooms are available at the Israeli-run **Lamuella Guesthouse** (Arambol Beach Road, 0832-561-4563, Rs 450-Rs 700 double), the smartest (and most expensive) guesthouse in Arambol.

Shopping

Down the beach in Khalcha Vaddo is **Arambol Hammocks** (House 564, no phone, www.arambol.com), a cottage industry set-up selling excellent handmade hammocks (from Rs 1,000) including extra-wide 'flying carpets'.

Resources

Internet
Famafa Hotel, Khalcha Vaddo (0832-229-2516). **Open** 9am-11pm daily.

Post office
Arambol Post Office, near Mount Carmel Church (0832-229-7665). **Open** 9am-5pm Mon-Fri.

North Goan beach shacks.

Getting there

Taxis from Tivim take an hour and charge Rs 600. From Dabolim Airport taxis cost Rs 850 and take just under two hours. On the 'new road' after Siolim Bridge, look for signs for the Arambol turn-off after ten miles.

Tiracol

From Arambol, the coastal road climbs to the top of a rugged laterite plateau, then descends through jungle back towards the shoreline and the pristine Tiracol river. Just before the tiny ferry point is **Querim**, a long sliver of shining sand untouched by development. You can spend hours here without seeing a soul, except at weekends when picnickers wander over from neighbouring Maharashtra. High on the headland **Tiracol Fort** stands sentinel over Goa's northern border. Now a heritage hotel, the fort courtyard contains a small, beautiful chapel which is still used by Tiracol villagers three times a week for mass. You can get there via the free ferry across the Tiracol (every 30mins 6.30am-9.30pm). Built by the Marathas in the 18th century and then snatched by the Portuguese, Tiracol Fort became the base for a disastrous anti-colonial insurrection in 1825 that ended in a bloody rout for the rebels. A plaque in the fort commemorates a later act of anti-colonial resistance in the Gandhian tradition of *satyagraha*, or 'truth force', by unarmed Goan freedom fighters in 1954. They took the fort and raised an Indian flag, but were later captured after Portuguese troops opened fire, killing two people.

Where to stay

In 2004, the **Fort Tiracol Heritage Hotel** (Tiracol, 0832-622-7631, Rs 4,500-Rs 6,000 double) was given a touch of glamour by new management – the owners of Nilaya, the stunning boutique hotel in Arpora (*see p190* **Turn on, check in, drop out**). It offers seven non-air-conditioned rooms decorated in ochre and black, including two suites, each with a turreted balcony and a cliff-top view of the Goan coast. It also has an impressive promenade lined with charpoys and tables for alfresco dining, and an excellent restaurant that welcomes day trippers. It's a little isolated, but a speedboat is on hand to take you to the busier beaches to the south.

Mapusa

A half-hour drive inland from the beaches is Mapusa, the commercial, administrative and transport hub of North Goa. Mapusa is a dusty smudge of urban India amid rich, sprawling agricultural lands, and hosts a raucous market spilling across several acres close to the city's main road. Much of Mapusa can be safely avoided, although the Friday market is lively and features an array of local produce trucked in from across the state. A little over seven miles east of the city is **Tivim**, the nearest stop on the Konkan Railway for North Goa's beaches. On

Where vindaloo comes from

*'Please Sir, Mr God of Death
Don't make it my turn today, not today,
There's fish curry for dinner.'
– Bakibab Borkar, Goan poet*

It tells you a lot about Goans that a common
way of asking 'How are you?' in Konkani is
'Nisteak kitem aslem?' which translates as:
'What fish did you have?' Food, particularly
seafood, is a Goan obsession – and far
removed in taste from familiar North Indian
staples like butter chicken and *biryani*. But
what Goans eat today would be almost
unrecognisable to a 16th-century Goan. The
cuisine was transformed by the arrival of
Portuguese colonists, who brought with them
a cornucopia of culinary treasures harvested
from previous adventures: chillies, tomatoes,
potatoes, pumpkins, fruits like guavas,
pineapples and *chikoos*, and cashews;
not to mention Iberian garlic sausages,
and *garrafãos* of vinegar, wines and olive oil.

As Portuguese influence took hold so did
their diet, edging out the traditional cuisine of
Saraswat dishes from the Konkan region. The
ubiquitous *vindaloo* (which tastes nothing like
the British version) is a corruption of *vinho e
alhos*, a garlicky Portuguese wine-vinegar
marinade. *Chouriço*, those chubby links of
spiced pork, are a Goan version of the Iberian
sausage. *Sorpatel* started off as *sarabulho*,
a Portuguese stew of pork meat and offal.

The Portuguese also introduced dishes and
influences from their journeys to South East
Asia, Africa and South America: like prawn
balchão from Myanmar and chicken *cafreal*
from Mozambique. Saraswat touches added
to the mix as a new Goan cuisine evolved –
turmeric, cumin, cinnamon and cloves found
their way into Portuguese *assados* or roasts,
coconut and semolina showed up in *bolos*
(cakes), and the local taste for strong spices

Sorpatel.

led to versions of Portuguese dishes with so
much chilli and vinegar that they would have
been intolerable to the colonisers' palates.

Today the staple dish remains fish-curry-
rice, the exact ingredients of which vary
widely from region to region, village to village,
and even house to house. For most of the
year, Goans tuck into prized estuarine shrimp
and tiger prawns, mussels, langoustines,
lobsters, pomfrets, kingfish and river perch –
and shark in the hot-and-sour *ambotik* curry.
In the monsoon, deep-sea fishing is banned
to allow stocks to replenish, and Goans take
to eating the *muddasho* (ladyfish), a slender
fish with a buttery taste. Other speciality
Goan curries include the mild *caldine*, a
children's favourite often made with eggs or
vegetables, and the complex, vinegary *xacuti*,
usually made with chicken, goat meat or beef.

The original Saraswat cuisine did survive
as 'Gomantak' cooking, as it's now known.
Goa's hidden cuisine generally consists of
thick-grained, nutty, reddish par-boiled rice
taken with fish or shellfish that has been
curried or fried. It's accompanied by mildly
spiced seasonal vegetables, all flavoured
with dark palm sugar (jaggery) and tamarind,
with lashings of coconut in every form. Mud
vessels and wood fires gave the food its
characteristic smoky aroma – now best
captured in a steaming bowl of *canjee* (rice
gruel) with a wicked piece of mango pickle.

Always leave room for dessert, an area
where Goan cuisine truly excels. Along with
bebinca, a layered cake made with dozens
of egg yolks, comes *bolo sans rival*, a cake
made with the left-over whites. Many sweet
dishes are heavy on the coconut, including
the *batika* cake and steamed coconut-jaggery
festival favourite *pattoyos*, which come
wrapped in a segment of banana leaf.

Bebinca.

the eastern edge of the city is the 'Milagres' ('Miracles') church, **Our Lady of Miracles** (open for mass at 7.30am daily), built on an ancient, sacred site where a Hindu temple once stood and now worshipped at by Goans of all religions.

Where to eat & drink

The **Golden Oven** (opposite Mapusa Market, 0832-226-4210, open 8am-8.30pm Mon-Sat) is a highly popular and attractive bakery-café serving freshly made baked goods – try the delicious beef patties (Rs 19) or the Goa sausage pizza (Rs 24).

Where to stay

The tourism strip's myriad options are a short drive away. But if you absolutely have to stay in Mapusa, the **GTDC Mapusa Residency** (opposite Kadamba bus stand, Mapusa, 0832-226-2794, Rs 550-Rs 750 double) offers barely adequate en suite rooms, and has a convenient tourist information kiosk in the lobby.

Shopping

Goa's most interesting bookshop lurks in an undistinguished building on the slope of Mapusa Hill. The **Other India Bookstore** (near Mapusa clinic, 0832-226-3306, www.otherindiabookstore.com, open 9am-5pm Mon-Fri, 9am-1pm Sat) has over 1,000 books on Goa and Goan history, organic farming, environmentalism, and what seems like every anti-globalisation text ever written.

Getting there

From Panjim, take the NH-17 straight to Mapusa. Taxis usually charge around Rs 200 and take 20 minutes. From Tivim by taxi, it takes around 20 minutes and costs Rs 300. From Dabolim, it's Rs 650 for the one-hour trip.

Resources

Hospital
Vrindavan Hospital, off NH-17 Highway (0832-225-0022). **Open** 24 hrs.

Internet
Sify I-way, Angod, near market, opposite the mosque. **Open** 9am-9pm Mon-Sat.

Police
Mapusa Police Station, near Municipal Gardens, Mapusa. Emergency Number 100.

Post office
Mapusa Post Office, next to Mapusa Police Station (0832-226-2881). **Open** 9.30am-1pm, 2-5.30pm Mon-Sat.

Tourist information
Goa Tourism Development Corporation Information Office, Mapusa Residency Hotel lobby, opposite Kadamba Bus Stand, Mapusa (0832-226-2390). **Open** 9.30am-5.30pm Mon-Fri.

Driving to cover makes fielders' lives difficult at **Morjim Beach**. *See p198.*

Goa

Sleep in.

Dive in.

Panjim & Old Goa

Golden Goa's ancient heart.

It's easily the most laid-back state capital in India, a raffish colonial set piece on the headland between the **Zuari** and **Mandovi** rivers that retains plenty of old-world charm even as it spills its borders in all directions. Don't expect a bigger version of Calangute or Colva, or even a smaller version of Mumbai – Panjim is more genteel than any of them. The city began to emerge around the late 18th century and by the 1820s had become the bustling administrative centre of the Portuguese *Estado da India* and home to the colony's most senior officials. Beautiful buildings from this period still crowd many of the old neighbourhoods and give the city its Latinate character. In recent years many of these architectural jewels have been restored and brightly repainted in characteristically Goan pastel shades.

The city is best explored on foot. Wander along the broad boulevard along the Mandovi riverfront, take a stroll under the overhanging street arcades of **18th June Road** and amble through the old quarter of **Fontainhas** – a Latinate labyrinth of sun-kissed ochre and magenta buildings, pocket-sized balconies and tiny plazas, and trees laden with ripening papayas and guavas.

The original colonial capital, now known simply as **Old Goa**, is an area of broad lanes and ancient churches. It's a few kilometres away, linked to modern Panjim by an old causeway that stretches through backwaters that have been converted to salt pans, and passes through the early colonial architecture of **Ribandar**.

Panjim

City centre

Panjim's commercial centre is dominated by the baroque **Church of the Immaculate Conception** (*see p207*), near the Municipal Garden. A huge church sitting atop criss-crossing whitewashed stairways, it has become an instantly recognisable symbol of the city, and looms over the road leading to the **Altinho Hill**, with the **Garcia da Orta Garden** on one side. Along the Dada Vaidya Road that hugs the Altinho Hill is the **Mahalaxmi Temple**, the first new Hindu temple that was allowed in Portuguese territory after the Inquisition was finally abandoned in the early 19th century after pressure from the British (*see p178* **Bloody inquisitive**). During the time of the holy terrors, the idol of the goddess Mahalaxmi now kept here was trucked around in the hinterlands in a bullock-cart by devotees anxious to save it from desecration. Just down the road is the attractive **Boca de Vaca Spring**, where fresh water flows year-round from a cow's-head spigot.

A shrine on the **Panjim waterfront**.

Goa

Panjim's old Latin quarter and heritage district is **Fontainhas**, where strict development laws now preserve hidden gems after senseless demolition in the '70s and '80s. A beautifully restored colonial mansion now houses the **Fundaçao Oriente** (Filipe Neri Road, 0832-223-0728), a European NGO founded on vast amounts of casino lucre from Macao, which works to maintain the city's colonial architectural legacy. Nearby is the small

Club Portugal

Colonial-era Panjim lingers on under the high ceilings and slow-spinning fans of the **Clube Vasco da Gama**, near the Municipal Garden. Established in 1909, Clube Vasco was a social club reserved for the Catholic landowners and government officers of the Portuguese-speaking elite until Liberation in 1961. After that, they faced resentment and suspicion from Indian nationalists, and many emigrated first to Portugal and Brazil, and later to the UK, Canada and Australia. Those who stayed behind self-consciously stepped into the shadows: they stopped speaking Portuguese in public, and bent over backwards to prove that they were as Indian as everyone else.

Over 40 years later, such families still reside in the houses they built in the city's sleepy Latinate neighbourhoods of Altinho, Campal, Fontainhas and Sao Tome. And Clube Vasco remains at the centre of social life. Members still congregate there every day, to while away idle afternoons enjoying the steady breeze through the French windows, prop up the bar with glasses of *feni*, the local cashew liquor, and to listen to live music or sing karaoke in the evenings. Tourists are made more than welcome. The afternoons are particularly atmospheric: the clock ticks slowly, the roast tongue sandwiches on distinctive Goan bread go down well with *feni*, and the next thing you know, it's sunset.

In a newly self-confident India, Portuguese-speaking Panjimites feel a lot less reticent about expressing their hybrid identity. It'll only take a little prodding to hear nostalgic stories of life in Goa before the Indian 'invasion', when goods were imported tax-free from Europe, Panjim's roadways and marketplaces were clean, and law enforcement had an efficient, fascist bite.

For Clube Vasco da Gama listing, *see p207*.

heritage inn complex run by the Sequeira-Sukhijia family, that neatly includes **Panjim Pousada**, a restored traditional Hindu home; **Panjim Inn**, a quirky old Goan two-storey house; and the more upmarket **Panjim People's High School**.

A short walk along the river leads to two iconic Panjim restaurants: **Horseshoe**, where Chef Vasco Silveira turns out superb Luso-Indian food, and the more modest **Avanti**, serving delicious home-style Goan food with an accent on pork and seafood.

Nearby is the landmark **San Sebastian Chapel** that houses the large wooden crucifix that once towered over the bloody deliberations at the old Palace of the Inquisition in Old Goa. The collection of altars and paintings here is one of the best in Goa, gathered by refugees who fled the plagues that decimated Old Goa throughout the 17th century. The **Afonso Guesthouse** near here has a rooftop terrace where you can sip coffee and get a bird's eye view of the neighbourhood. Literally in the middle of the crowded block, accessible only by narrow pathways, is the charming, family-style **Viva Panjim** restaurant.

Across the concrete walkway that crosses the **Ourem River**, a short walk brings you to the ugly concrete high-rise locality called Patto and the **Goa State Archaeological Museum** (*see p207*). A leisurely amble through Fontainhas towards the Mandovi riverfront brings you to the delightful **31st January Road**, which is lined on both sides with colonial-era buildings, many adorned with public shrines. In the evenings, these icons of Mary and ornate crosses are often visited by groups of hymn-singing supplicants, a village tradition that has survived the shift to the city. At the end of the street is the seashell-encrusted entrance to **Hospedaria Venite**, a popular backpacker hotel and restaurant, whose friendly owner, Luis, is always happy to talk about the neighbourhood and Goa's history.

A couple of minutes' walk towards the waterfront, on one side of the Secretariat, is a low, crumbling two-storey maroon building still owned by the Mhamai Kamat family, a Hindu clan that made its fortune trading opium, African slaves and socks (yes, socks) throughout the Portuguese colonies. Their 250-year-old ancestral home is now slowly falling apart and is subdivided like a rabbit warren, but you can still peer through open wooden doors to the colonnaded inner courtyard distinctive of palatial Hindu architecture. Right opposite is a statue of **Abbe Faria**, a charismatic 18th-century Goan abbot, political radical and hypnotist (*see p208* **The monk of Monte Cristo**).

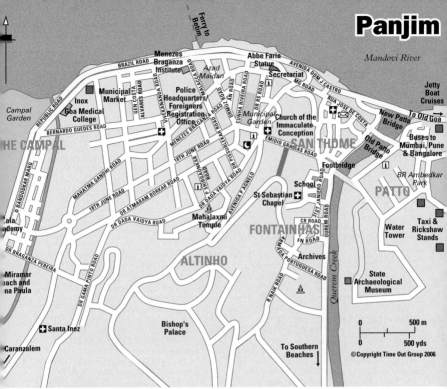

Panjim

Mandovi River

Church of the Immaculate Conception

Church Square, Emidio Gracia Road, near Municipal Garden.

A symbol of Portuguese ambition and power when it was built in 1541, with gilded and ornate interiors. The church was then expanded repeatedly, most recently in 1871 to accommodate a huge bell that once hung at the Tower of St Augustine in Old Goa. The church hosts one of the most popular Goan feasts in December, the Feast of Our Lady of the Immaculate Conception, when the nearby square is lit with thousands of candles.

Goa State Archaeological Museum

Near the State Bank of India building, Patto.
Open 9.30am-1.15pm, 2-5.30pm Mon-Fri.
Admission free.

A threadbare museum with a random collection of exhibits, but a few intriguing pieces as well, like the huge table used by the Grand Inquisitor in Old Goa, and an unusual antique lottery machine imported from Lisbon by the colonial administration for weekly state lottery draws.

Where to eat & drink

There's a smorgasbord of eateries in Panjim offering excellent Goan cooking, with an emphasis on super-fresh seafood. In Fontainhas there's **Hotel Avanti** (Rua de Ourem, 0832-242-7179, closed Sun, main course Rs 100-Rs 200), Panjim's most character-filled restaurant, staffed by old Goan aunties with an expert home-style touch. Nearby is the great value **Horseshoe** (Rua de Ourem, Fontainhas, 0832-243-1788, closed Sun, main course Rs 100-Rs 150) where Chef Vasco Silveira crafts Luso-Indian dishes with flavours from his years in Portugal and the Angolan army. **Viva Panjim** (off 31st January Road, Fontainhas, 0832-242-2405, main course Rs 100) is a backpacker favourite with excellent Goan fare and a sweet courtyard for alfresco dining. The charming, 50-year-old **Hospedaria Venite** (31st January Road, 0832-242-5537, closed Sun, main course Rs 200-Rs 300) has old oak shipwreck timbers for a floor, tables-for-two on balconies and great food. They also sell fabulous *feni* for Rs 150 a bottle. Near the town centre, the popular **Ritz Classic Family Restaurant** (18th June Road, 0832-564-4796, main course Rs 50-Rs 150) is always packed with Panjimites, there for its super-fresh seafood at great prices. **Ernesto's** at **Clube Vasco da Gama** (Souza Towers, opposite the Municipal Garden, 98230-15921, closed Sun, main course Rs 100-Rs 150) is better for atmosphere than food; a relaxed social club with views of the Municipal Garden (*see p206* **Club Portugal**). For great pastries and snacks, visit the nearby **Mr Baker** (Jesuit House, opposite Municipal Garden, 0832-222-4622, closed Sun), a landmark Panjim bakery since 1922. Try the *bebinca*, a rich Goan dessert.

Shopping

In Fontainhas, **Velha Goa** (4/191 Rua de Ourem, 0832-242-6628, www.costavin.com) is a sweet boutique selling *azulejos* – hand-painted tiles made in the Iberian tradition – and has a nearby studio where you can watch their artisans at work. Not far away, **Sosa's** (E245, Rua de Ourem, 0832-222-8063) offers clothes by top Indian designers, including funky retro designs by Goa's own Savio Jon, all at reasonable prices. Make the equivalent of a quick trip to Lisbon by popping into **A Nau** (Jesuit House, near Municipal Garden, 0832-222-4567), a cheerful store filled with Portuguese food and drink imports. Over at Azad Maidan, **UK Traders** (0832-242-7172) sells super Goa-grown cashew nuts for around Rs 300 per kilo.

The monk of Monte Cristo

On the Panjim waterfront near the Secretariat building stands a 60-year-old bronze statue of **Jose Custodio Faria** looming with his arms outstretched over a hypnotised woman. It's an unusual piece of public art celebrating an unusual man. Faria was an abbot, military adventurer and pioneering 18th-century hypnotist, and one of the first Indians to become famous in the West.

Faria was born in Candolim in 1746. At that time, the priesthood was the only career with any prospects for ambitious Goans, and the young Faria followed his father into the Church. Sensing that the young man's prodigious intellect and charisma would be stifled in the colonies, Faria's father took him to Europe, where he was enrolled in Rome's elite Propaganda Fide college. Within a few years, his studies in theology had made him famous. He was invited by the Pope to deliver a Pentecost sermon at the Sistine Chapel, and soon after to preside over mass at the Royal Portuguese Court at the Queluz Palace near Lisbon. Faria was struck with stage-fright at the sight of the queen and her dazzling courtiers, but a strange whispered phrase in Konkani from his father – '*Hi sogli bhaji, kathor re bhaji*' ('They're all vegetables, just cut the vegetables') – unfroze the young abbot. It was an early lesson in the power of suggestion that set Faria on the path to groundbreaking ideas about hypnotism.

Historical details are sketchy, but Faria and his father were later discovered plotting to expel the Portuguese from Goa and were forced to flee the Portuguese Court, turning up in 1787 in Revolutionary France. There Faria plunged headlong into the turmoil, commanding a battalion in a campaign against the anti-Royalist National Convention that was crushed by the young Napoleon Bonaparte, before being locked up in the Bastille. During his time in jail, Faria supposedly invented the modern version of the board game draughts, further developed his scientific study of hypnotism and became so notorious that Alexandre Dumas even included a fictional version of him as the 'mad abbe' in *The Count of Monte Cristo*.

Faria emerged from prison at the beginning of the 19th century to engage in an acrimonious public debate with Anton Mesmer about the nature of hypnosis. The Frenchman had popularised the theory that hypnosis was the result of an exceptional 'animal magnetism' exuded by the hypnotist. Faria challenged this, declaring that the hypnotist merely implanted suggestions in the mind of the subject, and that hypnosis was a kind of compact in which the subject's own imagination was paramount. Faria's idea was later proved essentially correct, and is now known as 'post-hypnotic suggestion'. But although Faria provided a crucial insight that underpins modern psychoanalysis, it is his rival Mesmer who remains celebrated in the West with the word 'mesmerise'. Guess 'faria-ise' doesn't roll off the tongue.

Where to stay

The **Directorate of Tourism** (Rua de Ourem, Patto, 0832-222-6515) has a list of private homes open to paying guests. The Fontainhas heritage district offers several attractive places to stay, including the family-run **Afonso Guesthouse** (San Sebastian Chapel Square, 0832-222-2359, Rs 600-Rs 700 doubles) with an attractive terrace. Nearby are the **Panjim Inn, Panjim People's** and **Panjim Pousada** (31st January Road, 0832-222-6523, www.panjiminn.com, Rs 2,000-Rs 5,500 doubles), three atmospheric heritage hotels with the same management, nestled together at a crossroads in the heart of the district. Near the centre of Panjim is **Manvin's Hotel** (Souza Towers, opposite Municipal Gardens, 0832-222-4412, Rs 1,000 doubles), an unremarkable hotel with basic rooms but pleasant river views. The modern **Nova Goa** (Borkar Road, 0832-222-6231, www.hotelnovagoa.com, Rs 2,500 doubles) is excellent value, given its location in the centre of town.

Getting there

From Dabolim airport, pre-paid taxis for a ride into Panjim can be hired for around Rs 500 from a counter just outside the arrivals hall. The nearest Konkan Railway stop to Panjim is **Karmali** (also called **Carambolim**) about 13km away. Taxis charge Rs 200-Rs 250 for a ride to Panjim, auto-rickshaws Rs 150-Rs 200.

The Waterfront

The Mandovi riverfront road that links the district of **Sao Tome** to the rest of Panjim, and then to **Campal** and **Miramar**, is named after Dayanand Bandodkar, Goa's charismatic first chief minister after local government was established in 1963. A pleasant river walkway runs along almost the entire length from the quayside where innumerable brightly lit tourist cruisers are berthed. Near here the waterfront is dominated by the **Idalcao Palace**, now known as the **Old Secretariat**, a pretty 400-year-old mansion. Further down D Bandodkar Marg is the **Mandovi Hotel**, once the city's premier hotel and still good-value accommodation. Nearby is the down-at-heel **Central Library** and **Menezes-Braganza Institute**, occupying one corner of a massive structure that also houses a dozen government offices and the Panjim police headquarters. Just outside is **Azad Maidan**, a cheerful open space teeming with schoolboys playing cricket throughout the day. It holds a pavilion of Corinthian columns salvaged from Old Goa that

A view from **Azad Maidan**, Panjim.

shades a **memorial to Tristao Braganza Cunha**, the most important Goan anti-colonial freedom fighter. Further up on DB Road is the vibrant **Municipal Market** (*see p210*), still holding on to its traditional patch in the face of efforts to shift vendors to a new building. Across the lane is the recently renovated **Goa Medical College**.

The pretty, aristocratic locality of **Campal** houses a set of the grandest houses in the city. They're all out of bounds for visitors, but an upper floor of one has been converted by Goan designer **Wendell Rodricks** (*see p210*) into an airy boutique selling elegant couture and all kinds of accessories from furniture to skin cream. Across the road stands a statue of **Francis Luis Gomes**, an eloquent orator who was the lone Goan representative in the Portuguese parliament, and argued passionately for pan-Indian nationalism 50 years before the freedom movement began.

The statue overlooks the entrance to the **Campal Children's Park**, a beautifully situated public garden that spreads right to the bank of the river under the shade of hundreds of casuarina trees. It's a great place to people-watch in the evenings, with Goan families from across the social spectrum happily wandering the curving pathways and hoisting ecstatic youngsters onto swings and slides. A similar riverfront garden is located a bit further down the road in the grounds of the **Kala Academy**

Goa

(D Bandodkar Marg, Campal, 0832-242-0451, 9am-9pm daily), where you can buy a cup of coffee for Rs 5, and relax on lawns and benches overlooking the river. The complex was designed by Charles Correa, the internationally-renowned Goan architect. It's a couple of miles on to **Miramar Beach**. The beach centres on **Miramar Circle** where middle-class Panjimites gather every evening for walks and streetside snacks. Unfortunately the water isn't clean enough for swimming, but the beach is pretty, with sweeping views of the mouth of the Mandovi River and the Aguada headland.

A few miles further down the riverfront highway is Dona Paula, home to the huge **National Institute of Oceanography** at Dona Paula Circle (0832-245-0450, public science seminars every Thursday) a world-class research institute and the leading authority on the biology of the Indian Ocean. Here there is also the tiny **British Cemetery**, left over from a brief occupation during the Napoleonic Wars. Further up, the road leads to the **Cabo Raj Nivas** – the mansion of the Goa state Governor. The complex includes a magnificently situated chapel on a jutting promontory between the Zuari and Mandovi rivers. Visitors can only enter for Sunday services (from 8am) and Midnight Mass on Christmas Eve, but the effort is worth it for the location, the beautiful chapel and a rousing choir that's considered to be the best in Goa.

Idalcao Palace/Old Secretariat
Panjim Waterfront
A mansion built as a summer palace in the early 16th century by the Bijapuri ruler Yusuf Adil Shah. It stood virtually isolated on the island for centuries until Panjim began to grow around it under the rule of the Portuguese, who used it as the seat of the viceroys of the Portuguese East Indies for over a century. The grand arch over the main entrance used to carry the viceroy's ornate crest; it now displays India's national symbol, the Ashoka *chakra*. Plans are underway to convert it into a museum.

Menezes-Braganza Institute
Malacca Road, opposite Azad Maidan. **Open** 9.30am-1pm, 2-5.45pm Mon-Fri. **Admission** free. Before 1961, the Institute was named after Vasco da Gama. The entranceway still holds a mesmerising floor-to-ceiling mural of hand-painted tiles commemorating the colonisation of the Indies, adorned with stanzas from the epic *Os Lusiades* written by the Portuguese national poet, Luis Vaz de Camoens.

Where to eat & drink

At Azad Maidan, **Delhi Darbar** (0832-222-2544, main course Rs 150-300) is the best of Panjim's tandoori restaurants, with excellent service. Also on the Maidan is **Farm Products**

(0832-222-5287), a cute three-seater snack shop run by octogenarian Goan freedom fighter Alvaro Pereira, who serves a clientele of old Panjim characters.

Nightlife

For Indian tourists in Panjim the evening river cruises departing from the Santa Monica pier are a must-do. Boats leave regularly every evening, starting from 5pm, and chug up to the mouth of the Mandovi with an enthusiastically corny song-and-dance routine to entertain passengers en route (Rs 100 per person). Night cruises depart from 8.30pm. Contact the **Goa Tourism Development Corporation** (0832-222-3396, www.goa-tourism.com) for further details. Panjim's only proper nightclub is **O-Zone** (Goa Marriott Resort, Miramar, 0832-246-3333, www.goamarriottresort.com, closed before 7pm, Rs 500 cover charge Sat), a bit on the small side but coolly lit and decked out in white. Open throughout the year, it's popular with Panjim's rich kids but usually comes into its own when there's nothing else to do – in the tourist off-season, from May to September.

Shopping

Municipal Market
D Bandodkar Marg, Panjim waterfront.
Open from dawn to dusk daily.
Lively and crowded, Goa's municipal market is packed with Goa-grown produce like Alphonso, Mankurade, Ilario and Monserrate mangoes and dozens of bananas from delicate fingerlings to enormous green plantains. Early mornings here are the best time to visit, with fisherwomen in full voice and baskets spilling over with white river prawns, estuarine fish and baby sharks.

Wendell Rodricks Design Space
Campal, near Francis Luis Gomes garden (0832-2238-177/0832-242-0604/wendellrodricks.com).
Open 10am-6.30pm Mon-Sat. **Credit** AmEx, MC, V.
Elegant couture by Goa's most celebrated designer and favourite of the Bollywood set.

Entertainment

A floating casino, the **MS Caravela** (0832-223-4077, Rs 1,300 per person, departs 9pm, no shorts/sandals) sails from the **Fisheries Building** opposite the Mandovi Hotel for a couple of hours of gambling on a short cruise up the river, with a buffet and drinks included in the price. For the die-hard gambler, there's the considerably less atmospheric **Chances** casino in Dona Paula (Vainguinim Valley Resort, Machado Cove, 0832-245-2201,

11am-4am). Alternatively, save your money and
check out the latest Bollywood offerings at the
INOX Cinema (behind Goa Medical College
building, Campal, 0832-242-0999), a modern
multiplex built for the first International Film
Festival of India in 2004.

Where to stay

The **Mandovi Hotel** (D Bandodkar Marg,
0832-242-6270, www.hotelmandovigoa.com,
Rs 3,000 doubles) on the riverfront road was
once Panjim's most exclusive hotel. These
days it's an art deco oldie in need of renovation,
but still provides good service and value.
It's been supplanted by the **Goa Marriott**
(Mandovi waterfront, Miramar, 0832-246-3333,
www.goamarriottresort.com, Rs 6,000 doubles),
easily the most luxurious hotel in Panjim and
a kind of clubhouse for Goa's moneyed elite,
with an unbeatable location on the waterfront.
Contending for the top spot is the excellent
Cidade de Goa (Vainguinim Beach, 0832-
245-4545, www.cidadedegoa.com, Rs 4,000
doubles), with its own private beach. A little
cheaper is **Prainha** (Dona Paula 0832-245-3881,
www.prainha.com, Rs 2,000-Rs 3,000 doubles), a
cantilevered hotel with a secluded private beach
and a lovely outdoor pool.

Old Goa

Old Goa was the original capital of the
Portuguese colony, a European-style
metropolis whose grand architecture reflected
its tremendous power, wealth and prestige.
Known as *Goa Dourada* or 'Golden Goa', it
made a fortune in spices and slaves. In the
western part of the city lay a huge barracks,
the first European-style hospital in Asia, a
foundry and a vast arsenal. In the east was
its sprawling marketplace and waterfront slave
market, which sent African slaves across Asia.
And dominating the centre were churches,
cathedrals, monasteries and convents built by
the Franciscans, Dominicans, Augustinians and
other religious orders. Plague outbreaks in the
17th century forced residents to flee. Today,
only soaring architecture remains.

On the crest of the city's tallest hill sits
the **Chapel of Our Lady of the Mount**
(*photo p212*), one of the earliest Portuguese
buildings in Goa, commissioned by Afonso de
Albuquerque after he took control of the city
in 1510. It's built on the site of a fierce battle
between Bijapuri troops and the Portuguese.
The chapel has been restored and hosts a

The **Chapel of Our Lady of the Mount**. *See p211*.

The **Museum of Christian Art** at the Convent of Santa Monica.

classical music festival (*see p214*) every March. Come here at sunrise (around 7.30am) to enjoy a magical view of slanting sunlight slowly illuminating the churches' forlorn façades in the distance below. Perched on the slope of Holy Hill is the fortress-like **Convent of Santa Monica**, the largest convent in Asia. Access is restricted, but if you ask nicely, you might be allowed into the private chapel at the rear, which is covered with stunning 17th-century frescoes. One wing open to the public houses the **Museum of Christian Art** (0832-228-5299), a beautiful if poorly curated collection of intricate chalices and other Catholic ritual objects, along with beautiful period Christian paintings.

Opposite the Convent of Santa Monica a stone tower, now known as the **St Augustine Tower**, is all that's left of a grand church complex of the Augustinian mission. There were once eight chapels, plus a convent and library, and the imposing tower housed a huge bell that now tolls at the Church of the Immaculate Conception in Panjim. Over the centuries the entire complex gradually collapsed, with the last sections crumbling in 1942. All except that solitary tower, which now watches over a team of state archaeologists searching for the tomb of Queen Ketavan of Georgia (*see p177* **Missing martyr**).

Nearby is the **Royal Chapel of St Anthony**, another mid-16th century church (dedicated to the patron saint of Portugal) that declined in decrepitude until it was restored in 1960. The simple painted idol of St Anthony kept here was treated as a full captain in the Portuguese army and each year was taken for a ceremonial ride through Old Goa to collect his officer's wages from the colony's treasurer.

Just behind is the **Chapel of Our Lady of the Rosary**, one of the first buildings built by the Portuguese in Goa, on the site of a pitched battle that Alfonso Albuquerque considered the turning point in his campaign for a foothold in the subcontinent. Down the hill along Rua Das Naus de Omruz is the World Heritage Site precinct of the **Basilica of Bom Jesus**, Goa's most famous church, and resting place of the body of St Francis Xavier. Each decade, his body is removed and put on public display at the impressive **Se Cathedral** (7am-6pm daily) across the central square from the Basilica of Bom Jesus (*see p178* **Bloody inquisitive**). This huge Dominican-built church remains the largest in Asia, despite one of its towers collapsing after being struck by lightning in the 18th century. Its typically Corinthian interior includes a barrel-vaulted ceiling and two long side aisles, and a masterpiece of a gilded altar.

Across the road towards the riverfront from the Se Cathedral sits another baroque architectural jewel, the **Convent & Church of St Cajetan**. Further on, at the riverfront, new arrivals to the colonies first set eyes on the fabled Goa Dourada through the granite-faced **Arch of the Viceroys**.

Arch of the Viceroys

Near the riverfront, Old Goa.
This dilapidated stone gateway is the Portuguese equivalent of the Gateway of India built by the British in Mumbai – but this one came first, by 200 years. It was built by Vasco da Gama's great-

grandson, Francisco da Gama, who became viceroy of Goa at the end of the 16th century and promptly erected this tribute to his ancestor. It was the main entranceway to the city and the symbolic spot where Portuguese supreme commanders of the Indies handed responsibility to their successors.

Basilica of Bom Jesus

Rua das Naus de Ormuz, opposite Se Cathedral, Old Goa. **Open** 7am-6pm daily.

Goa's most well-known church and the only one whose façade and layout show no local influences – it has a clearly Italianate look. The last of the Medicis, Cosimo II, the Grand Duke of Tuscany, financed the opulent altar that now holds the body of St Francis Xavier. It was sculpted by the Florentine artist Giovanni Batista Foggini. He took ten years to carve the three tiers of marble and jasper with intricate scenes from Xavier's life (*see p178* **Bloody inquisitive**). Inside, in a silver casket, lies the 'incorruptible' body, whose face can be seen through a glass window. The body has become an object of pilgrimage that draws hundreds of thousands to a solemn Exposition held once every decade, with the last one held in 2004.

Chapel of Our Lady of the Rosary

Near St Augustine Tower.

Built by Hindu and Muslim workmen inherited from the Bijapuri kingdom, the church developed a unique hybrid style of Eastern flourishes and decorative detail combined with a Western layout. The chapel's style was later widely copied across the new territory, a crucible for the fusion architecture now called Luso-Indian.

Convent & Church of St Cajetan

Rua Direita, near the Arch of the Viceroys, Old Goa.

Built by a team of Italian friars dispatched to India by Pope Urban III, this is the last domed church in Goa, shaped like a Greek cross and supposedly modelled on St Peter's in Rome. At its centre lies a mystery, a large slab of stone that covers a well purportedly belonging to a Hindu temple that once stood on this spot. The story of the temple is lost to history, as is the reason why the well was given such prominence in its Catholic replacement. The church altar is an exuberant work of art, with angels and cherubs rising to a spectacular gilded crown. In the crypt below, sealed caskets hold the remains of senior Portuguese officials who never made it home.

Where to eat & drink

An ambitious renovation has given new life to **Solar Souto Maior** (Old Goa, 0832-561-4524, 9am-6pm daily) a palatial mansion with an impressive garden once owned by wealthy Spanish grandees. Now it's a kind of rest stop on the way to Old Goa with a tea room and pleasant café serving snacks and home-made ice-cream. **Star Bar** (near Goa Institute of Management, Ribandar, no phone, main course Rs 100) has bad service, lousy decor and an undistinguished location, but its mussels and fresh fish are legendary – Goans will drive across the state for them.

If they Cannes, why can't Goa?

Panjim's historic riverfront road is a lot prettier than it used to be. In 2004, with a rapidity unusual for Goa, the crumbling old colonial buildings were renovated and painted in pretty pastel shades, new roads and pavements were installed, and a long line of elegant street lamps erected. Almost overnight, a shiny multiplex cinema appeared and the modernist Kala Academy arts complex on the banks of the Mandovi River was fully refurbished. The cause was the **International Film Festival of India**, or IFFI, now held in Goa every November.

The first festival was held in a frenzy of publicity, with accusations of shady dealing in the multi-million dollar infrastructure improvements and complaints that the money could have been better spent. After the mayhem (editorials in the Goan press called it 'IFFI in a Jiffy'), the festival settled down into a fun event that has improved

each year, with a bonanza of alternative cinema from India and around the world. To become a delegate, you need to prove that you have some connection to the film industry or the visual arts (see the IFFI website at www.iffi.nic.in) and pay a fee of around Rs 200. Even if you can't attend, it's well worth visiting Panjim during the festival for the free carnival along the riverfront, with dozens of live music acts and other street performances, and an open-air film screening on Miramar Beach.

Delhi bureaucrats and the Goa government would love to see IFFI become a world-class event, modelled on the festivals in Cannes, Venice and Berlin. They've still got a long way to go, but there's no denying the potential of a film festival held in the premier resort of the world's biggest movie-going nation. *International Film Festival of India, Panjim (www.iffi.nic.in). Every November.*

Old Goa is about six miles from Panjim on a scenic road alongside the Mandovi River. Taxis routinely charge an exorbitant Rs 300 one-way, auto-rickshaws Rs 200. Buses leave from the Kadamba bus stand (Patto, opposite Ambedkar Garden) every half-hour. A one-way fare to Old Goa is Rs 20.

Festivals

Carnival
Panjim waterfront. **Date** Feb.
Southern European-style bacchanalia with an evening parade of colourful floats along the waterfront. It's followed by a charming fancy-dress ball on the city streets behind.

Monte Music Festival
Chapel of Our Lady of the Mount, Old Goa. **Date** Mar.
One of Goa's best annual events, a festival of Indian and Western classical music. Concerts take full advantage of the stunning setting: both inside the church and in a small amphitheatre nearby. Call Fundaçao Oriente on 0832-243-6108 for details.

Shigmo
Panjim Waterfront. **Date** Mar.
Shigmo is a spring festival, celebrated as Holi in other parts of India. This is the time that Goa's Hindu hinterland takes centre stage on the capital's streets with vibrant, noisy, colourful displays and floats.

International Film Festival of India
Kala Academy/Inox cinema, Campal, Panjim (www.iffi.nic.in). **Date** Nov.
A pleasantly chaotic Indian version of Cannes. The festival encompasses two weeks of non-stop movie viewing on Panjim's waterfront, usually accompanied by some Bollywood and foreign movie-star glamour, and a crowded, democratic jamboree of entertainment and exhibitions along the riverfront road.

Fontainhas Festival of the Arts
Fontainhas, Panjim. **Date** Nov.
A week-long event in which the heritage houses of India's only Latin Quarter turn into temporary galleries showcasing Goa's best artists, with excellent free music concerts as well.

Feast of Our Lady of the Immaculate Conception
Panjim Church Square. **Date** 8 Dec.
The largest of Panjim's feast day celebrations. Street stalls crowd the roads in front of the church selling everything from peanuts to plastic buckets to candles as big as your arm. There are fireworks displays after dusk every evening.

Resources

Hospital
Vintage Hospital & Medical Research Centre Caculo Enclave, St Inez (0832-564-4401/ www.vintage3.com). **Open** 24hrs daily.

Internet
Reliance Infocomm Campal, near Kala Academy (0832-243-8176). Open 10am-8pm Mon-Sat.

Police
Police Headquarters *Opposite Azad Maidan, Panjim. Emergency number 100.*

Post office
Old Tobacco Exchange building, Sao Tome, Panjim. (0832-222-3704/3706). **Open** 9.30am-1pm, 2-5.30pm Mon-Sat.

Tourist information
Directorate of Tourism Rua de Ourem *Patto, Panjim (0832-222-6515).* **Open** 9.30am-1.15pm, 2-5.45pm.

Carnival time on Panjim waterfront.

South Goa

Last stand of the grandees.

Goa's lower half is arguably its better half. It has the state's finest old architecture and its most beautiful beaches. Fifteen miles of shining, uninterrupted white sand stretches from **Cansaulim** to **Mobor** under the spectacular ruins of the **Cabo de Rama Fort** looming over a rugged stretch of coastline. Further inland there are the astounding Mesolithic carvings at Usgalimol, the thick jungles of the **Cotigao Wildlife Sanctuary** and the lush rice-growing interior of **Quepem**.

Rich farmland and hundreds of millions of dollars in mining income have so far kept South Goa from replicating North Goa's party strip. It's sleepier, less crowded and relatively untouched by large-scale development. It's also the home turf of the fading Luso-Indian grandees – the aristocracy whose mansions still line the streets of **Margao** and where Portuguese is still widely spoken. These days, the south's idyllic character is under threat from development. Indian construction companies and real estate entrepreneurs have snapped up stretches of land all the way down to the Karnataka border, and though it will probably take years to become as hectic as the north, large-scale development looks inevitable as more travellers gravitate to the south's superior beaches.

But while it lasts, the south offers a glimpse of an older Goa, where farmers work the same fields and orchards that their families have tended for centuries. Spectacular rococo and baroque whitewashed churches gleam amid emerald paddy fields. Old colonial-era houses are still meticulously maintained, and locals retain the gracious culture and beautiful manners that still count in Goa.

Bogmalo

Right in the path of approaching jet-liners, the hidden cove-like beach of **Bogmalo** is becoming more popular with both foreign and Indian visitors who want no-frills sun-and-sand holidays without the crowds of the north strip. Goans also come here to party when other beaches get too crowded, and there's a long line of bars trailing up Bogmalo Beach. It's relaxed and uncluttered, with a few family-run hotels and the somewhat dilapidated five-star **Bogmalo Beach Resort**. The beach road ends at **Joet's Bar & Restaurant**, a local institution that started out as a beach shack run by a fisherman serving his day's catch. Now it's a friendly bar/restaurant run by his son, with a clean, good-value guesthouse at the back and the neat **Coconut Creek Hotel** a few hundred yards across the road. If you had just one day in Goa and couldn't stray far from the airport, Bogmalo would be your beach.

Where to eat & drink

Joet's Bar & Restaurant
Bogmalo Beach (0832-253-8036). **Open** 8am-midnight. **Main courses** Rs 300. **Credit** MC, V.
Clean and bright, with a non-stop rock 'n' roll soundtrack, this is one of Goa's best beachfront hangouts and a favourite with locals, who will drive across the state to while away an evening here.

Chapel of Our Lady of Mercy, Margao. *See p225.*

Goa

Zeebop by the Sea in Utorda. *See p217.*

Where to stay

Coconut Creek
Bimut Ward, near St Cosme and Damian Church, Bogmalo (0832-253-8090). **Rates** Rs 3,950 double. **Credit** AmEx, MC, V.

Getting a room here can be tough in peak season because it's heavily booked up by repeat customers. The loyalty is well-deserved: the staff at Coconut Creek go the extra mile with warm, friendly service (including keeping the bar open 'until the last guest leaves').

Entertainment

It's worth taking a 15-minute drive north from Bogmalo to Vasco's Baina Beach for **H2O** (Baina Beach, 0832-394-6052, closed after sunset), which offers a range of water activities including parasailing (Rs 900), kayaking (Rs 150 for 30mins), jet skiing (Rs 250 or 5mins), glass-bottomed boat rides (Rs 150 for a 30min tour) and speedboat rides (Rs 450 for a six-seater for 5-10mins). The highlight is a Jules Verne-style underwater walk 12 feet down, in a giant fish-bowl helmet (Rs 1,500 for 20mins).

Getting there

A taxi from Dabolim Airport to Bogmalo takes about ten minutes and costs around Rs 200. From Margao Station, it's a 40-minute taxi ride for around Rs 400.

Cansaulim to Betalbatim

South of Bogmalo, the beach turns to rock for a few kilometres before descending onto a 15-mile stretch of white-sand beach from **Cansaulim** to **Betalbatim** and beyond through **Utorda** and **Majorda**. Much like North Goa, the entire beach is lined with palm-thatched restaurant-bar beach shacks, backed by thick coconut palms yielding to acres of well-tended paddy fields. The **Park Hyatt** in Cansaulim is arguably the state's most luxurious hotel but unfortunately it is loomed over by the colossal Zuari Agrochemical plant, a hideous industrial complex. **Zeebop by the Sea**, a restaurant in Utorda, is a pretty shack with tables on the sand and perfect sunset views.

Another couple of kilometres down the surf's edge and you're in **Betalbatim**, another popular hangout for Goans. One big reason is **Martin's Corner**, a kitschy and hugely popular Goan restaurant five minutes' walk from the waterline. If you feel like a change of scene, take a five- to seven-minute ride inland to **Casa Walfrido Antao** (next to the turning for Nanu Resorts), a whimsical Indo-Portuguese home with windows made of oyster shells, unfortunately closed to visitors but worth admiring from the outside.

Where to eat & drink

Fusion
Majorda Beach Road, Majorda (0832-288-1694). **Open** *Oct-Apr* 7pm-11.30pm Mon-Sat. **Main courses** Rs 250. **Credit** MC, V.

A romantic outdoor setting and unusual food, prepared by a Brazilian chef who trained in France and has a knack for fabulous steaks and other grilled meats. The closest you can get to South American churrasco in India.

Martin's Corner
Betalbatim (0832-288-0061). **Open** 11am-3pm, 6.30pm-midnight daily. **Main courses** Rs 200. **Credit** MC, V.

A beloved South Goa institution, with a devoted Indian clientele that includes the great Indian cricketer Sachin Tendulkar (his favourite dish is the king crab, if you want to know). Dine under arches of red laterite and bamboo thatch under the smiling gaze of caricatures of Goan folk. Serving mostly Goan seafood, Martin's cooking is not outstanding but it is decent – and there's nothing else worthwhile around for miles.

Zeebop by the Sea

Opposite Kenilworth Beach Resort, Utorda Beach (0832-275-5333). **Open** *Oct-Apr* 10am-10pm daily. **Main courses** Rs 250. **Credit** MC, V.

One of the best beach shacks in Goa, on an empty, atmospheric stretch of white-sand beach. It's by far the most popular beach restaurant for Goan families, who pile in at weekends and stay late into the night for regular live music performances and lots of well-prepared Goan seafood.

Where to stay

Despite the shadow of a monstrous agrochemical plant nearby, the **Park Hyatt Goa Resort and Spa** in Cansaulim (Arossim Beach, Cansaulim, 0832-272-1234, www.goa.park.hyatt.com, Rs 9,000 double) has won a clutch of awards for its magnificent landscaped grounds, and offers every imaginable facility, including optional private gardens and the largest swimming pool in India. Further south in Utorda, the **Casa Ligorio** (near Kenilworth Beach Resort, Utorda, 0832-275-5405, www.casaligorio.com, Rs 2,000 double) isn't attractive to look at but offers great value, with nine well-appointed rooms, each with its own balcony, set in pleasant gardens. In Majorda there's the **Kenilworth Beach Resort** (Majorda Beach,

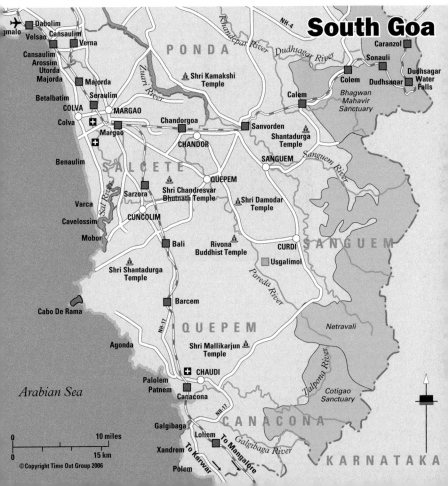

Ain't life grandee?

Just like the Spanish colonists in Latin America, the Portuguese administrators of Goa managed their holdings using the ancient Roman system of *latifundia* – landed estates parcelled out to trusted supporters of the regime. Important native collaborators, staunch mestizo allies, and loyal compatriots who wished to settle permanently were granted vast estates that functioned as fiefdoms, with all authority ceded directly by fiat. This hybrid aristocracy of grandees served as an instant class of intermediary rulers, and as the Portuguese court's interest switched to its colonies in Brazil, they steadily gained in power and influence.

In South Goa, particularly in the rich agricultural lands of Salcete, this ambitious cadre of landowners celebrated their flourishing fortunes by constructing grand, luxurious mansions. The front rooms were designed for spectacular entertainment on the European model, with ballrooms and raised stages for orchestras, and imposing dining rooms for lavish banquets and receptions that were imagined to be exactly like those in faraway Europe.

After Goa's liberation in 1961, land reform took back their vast agricultural holdings and dismantled the feudal system that supported them. Many of the *palacios* survive in various states of disrepair, with absentee owners now in Portugal or Brazil. Of the surviving grand mansions, the gorgeous **Figueiredo Mansion** (House No 376, Loutolim, donations accepted), a 15-minute drive from Margao, is the most beautiful home open to visitors. Owned by a pair of septuagenarian sisters, Georgina Figueiredo and Maria de Lourdes de Albuquerque, the house retains much of its former grandeur,

Maria serves it up at **Figueiredo Mansion**.

with magnificent collections of antique furniture and porcelain. One wing, the Heritage Inn (0832-277-7028, oldheritage inn @rediffmail.com, Rs 2,200-Rs 3,150 doubles), is open for paying guests, although it has not been very well restored and feels a little ramshackle. Or you can take a taste of the grandee way of life with a full Indo-Portuguese meal (minimum six people, Rs 600 per head) in the formal dining room, complete with liveried service and century-old family crockery.

Even more imposing is the spectacular **Menezes-Braganza House** in old Chandor (25 minutes drive from Margao, 0832-278-4201, admission Rs 100). Here gargantuan chandeliers dominate an opulent salon with marble walls and floors, filled with museum-quality antique furniture and Chinese porcelain. The east wing contains a famous private chapel, containing a sacred relic – a sliver of St Francis Xavier's fingernail, encrusted with gold and diamonds.

Still undergoing restoration but well worth a visit is the 200-year-old **Palacio do Deao** (30 minutes' drive from Margao, opposite Holy Cross Church, Quepem, 98231-75639, www.palaciododeao.com), on the banks of the Kushavati River in Quepem. Built by a clergyman from Braga, Portugal, it lay half in ruins until a young Goan couple, Celia and Ruben Vasco da Gama, agreed to take over its upkeep from Church authorities.

Celia and Ruben keep the house and its overgrown but pretty gardens open to visitors, who are also welcome to stay for a traditional Goan meal in an attractive covered courtyard behind the house (10am-6pm Mon-Sat, around Rs 250 per head).

0832-2754180, www.kenilworthhotels.com, Rs 6,700 double), a luxurious five-star just yards from the beach, with a huge swimming pool and a modern spa specialising in Ayurvedic massages and treatments. Outstanding facilities make the difference at the **Majorda Beach Resort** (Majorda Beach, 0832-275-4871, www.majordabeachresort.com, Rs 7,500 double), which has everything you would expect and more, including separate gymnasiums for men and women, indoor and outdoor pools, squash and tennis courts.

Entertainment

The Go Kart Race Track (Belloy-Nuvem, just off NH17, 98225-89313, open from 4pm Mon-Sat, closed Sun) is perhaps India's finest go-karting track – a quarter-mile of asphalt with fabulous views of the coastline and the Arabian Sea. Spin around at speeds of up to 60kmph in four-stroke, 6-horsepower karts. Ten laps cost Rs 120.

Getting there

Taxis from Dabolim Airport or Margao Station to Cansaulim, Utorda or Majorda both take around 20 minutes and cost Rs 300.

Colva

Like Calangute, its spiritual doppelganger in the north, poor old Colva gets a bad rap in Goa. Part of the reason is that, just like Calangute, it was once a favoured getaway for the landed elite during the summer months, and has now been taken over by tourists – mostly Indians from neighbouring states who paddle in the

surf in their saris, and middle-aged Europeans. But Colva has broad, beautiful sands and plenty of room for everyone. There are no deckchairs hogging the sand at high-tide mark, and few vendors hawking rugs and massages. It's still a working beach: dozens of fishing boats depart each day from here before dawn. There is a downside, though; the dunes have been levelled, and the area of the beach near Colva bus stand is strewn with garbage.

Where to eat & drink

Kentuckee
Shop No 28, Colva Beach (0832-278-8107).
Open 24 hours. **Main courses** Rs 200.
Credit MC, V.
The best of an undistinguished scrum of beach-front restaurants and shacks. One of the original Colva institutions, with a decades-old reputation for good seafood.

Where to stay

A great location sets the excellent-value **Longuinho's** (Colva beachfront, 0832-278-8068, www.longuinhos.net, Rs 1,400 to Rs 1,700 double) apart from the pack, on a prime spot of beach with lawns leading right up to the sand. The **Star Beach Resort** (near football ground, 0832-278-8166, www.starbeachresortgoa.com, Rs 800-Rs 1,400 doubles) is a newly-built hotel offering good value rooms, many with pleasant views over nearby rice fields, and the best pool in the area. **La Ben** (Colva Beach Road, 0832-278-8040, www.laben.net, Rs 450-Rs 850) offers spick-and-span rooms in a modern building, with a breezy rooftop restaurant.

Taj Exotica, Benaulim. *See p221.*

Nightlife

The **Boomerang** (4th Ward, Colva Beach, 0832-278-8071) has a circular bar right on the beach and attracts a crowd of locals and older Brits with regular live music and karaoke. **Gatsby's** (Colva Beach Road, 0832-278-9745, open 9pm-2am, entry Rs 250 incl 2 drinks) is Colva's only 'nightclub'; a tiny, dark disco with mirrored walls playing house and hip hop for euro-tourists.

Resources

Internet

Hello Mae, Colva Beach Road (0832-278-0108). **Open** 7.30am-11pm daily.

Getting around

Taxis from Dabolim Airport take around 45 minutes to Colva and charge Rs 450. From Margao, it's a 15-minute ride for around Rs 150.

Benaulim

According to the *Skanda Purana*, an ancient Hindu text, Goa was created by Lord Parashurama, an avatar of Lord Vishnu. He stood atop the mountains of the Western Ghats and shot an arrow far into the sea, and commanded the waters to retreat to where it landed. That legendary spot is 'Bannali', or 'where the arrow landed' – now named Benaulim. Just a decade ago, this beach was deserted, used mainly by fishermen whose decorated wooden boats still line the sand. But tourism is steadily taking over as Benaulim's main trade as travellers branch out from the behemoth **Taj Exotica** resort to a range of new hotels. New holiday homes and apartment complexes aimed at Indian and European retirees are mushrooming. Just beyond Benaulim village, the 'monte' (hill) is crested by the **Church of St John the Baptist** (open for Mass at 8am daily). Built at the turn of the 16th century, it's one of the prettiest examples of classic neo-Roman church architecture in Goa.

Where to eat & drink

As you'd imagine for a working fishing village, Benaulim's many shacks and restaurants all specialise in super-fresh seafood from the catch of the day. First among equals is **Johncy's Beach Shack** (Benaulim Beach, 0832-277-1390, main courses Rs 220, open 7am-1am daily) which features excellent tandoori specialities. **Fiplee's Bar and Restaurant** (off Benaulim Beach Road, near Maria Hall, 0832-277-0123, main courses Rs 200, open noon-3pm, 7pm-2am daily) is more of an entertainment magnet than a restaurant. Very popular with locals, it features an air-conditioned pub, a multi-cuisine menu, a cybercafe and 'leisure' zone complete with snooker tables and dart boards. **Joecon's Garden** (near Taj Exotica, 0832-277-0099, main courses Rs 250, open 11am-midnight daily) is another favourite.

Cuba Beach Café, Palolem. *See p225.*

Goa

Where to stay

Camilson's Beach Resort (Sernabatim Beach Road, Colva, 0832-2771582, Rs 1,000-Rs 2,500 doubles) has a great location just off the beach and offers clean double rooms with private terraces and a well-maintained garden. The super-cheap **Succorina Guesthouse** (1711 Vas Vaddo, Benaulim, 0832-277-0365, Rs 200 doubles) is about as low-budget as you can get, offering total peace and quiet, friendly service and small rooms with distant sea views. A few minutes' walk from the beachfront are the secluded, family-run **Palm Grove Cottages** (Tamdi Mati, 149 Vas Vaddo, Benaulim 0832-2770059, www.palmgrove goa.com, Rs 850-1,050 double) with spacious, airy rooms overlooking the greenery and a good restaurant. Set on over 50 acres of headland, with access to the prettiest part of the beach, is the sprawling **Taj Exotica** (Cal Vaddo, Benaulim 0832-277-1234, www.tajhotels.com, Rs 12,000-Rs 18,000 double) resort, offering private villas and luxurious facilities.

Nightlife

Benaulim is quiet in the evenings, but **Pedro's** (Benaulim Beach, near the Beach Road, 0932-277-0563) has live music every Tuesday and Saturday evening. Nearby, **Coco's Beach Shack** (Benaulim Beach, 20 yards north of Beach Road, 98224-88079) has live music every Friday and Monday evening. **Joecon's Garden** (near Taj Exotica, 0832-277-0099, closed midnight-11am daily) has live music every night.

Resources

Internet

New Horizon, 1595, Beach Road (0832-277-1218/ 1219). **Open** 9am-11pm daily.

Getting there

From Dabolim Airport, taxi rides to Benaulim take 50 minutes and cost Rs 500. From Margao it's a 20-minute trip for Rs 200.

Varca, Cavelossim & Mobor

The beachfront runs straight down to **Mobor**, trailing through giant five-star complexes around Varca and the charter-tourist destination of **Cavelossim**. The beaches are beautiful but the fishing villages here have never been prosperous, and there's little to do outside the five-star hotels. Beyond Mobor, the

Usgalimol

In 1993, a group of villagers led a team from the Archaeological Survey of India to a football field-sized shelf of laterite near a bend in the Kushavati River at Usgalimol. Scraping away some of the silt that regularly accumulates in the monsoon months, the villagers revealed ancient carvings of hulking bison and deer, some with the shafts of spears sticking from their sides. The astonished archaeologists went on to uncover over 100 carvings spread over 600 square yards, many of them depictions of hunts. They most likely date back to the Upper Paleolithic or Mesolithic eras between 20,000 and 30,000 years ago. Alongside the animals are elegant line etchings of human figures, including an energetic 'dancing woman', and several strange triskelions, concentric rings that archaeologists speculate may have been used as rudimentary clocks. Large reproductions of the carvings are on display at the Goa State Archaeological Museum in Panjim (*see p207*).

The site is hidden in the rural interior of South Goa, about an hour's drive from Margao (around Rs 1,000 to Rs 1,200 in a taxi). Take the NH-17 south from Margao to the Tilamol crossroads, from where you head towards Rivona. From Rivona, head south through the tiny village of **Colomb** (also the last stop for toilets, food and drink) until you see a round red and green Archaeological Survey of India sign that points to the site along a winding dirt track.

An Usgalimol triskelon.

beach tapers off at the junction with the Sal River estuary where another cluster of five-stars have sprouted along with charmless fast-food outlets, imitation pubs and air-conditioned malls.

Goa

Where to eat & drink

Outside the five-stars and beach shacks, **Fisherman's Wharf** (near Leela Hotel, Cavelossim, 93261-29810, main courses Rs 175, open 11am-midnight daily) is a smart restaurant with a pretty wooden interior and tables overlooking the calm River Sal. Better still, take the free ferry boat across the river to Betul and the charming **Hotel River Sal** (near Cutbona jetty, Betul, 0832-309-6313, main courses Rs 150, open 7am-midnight daily) which specialises in ultra-fresh seafood straight from the next-door trawler jetty. Instead of the ferry, simply wave from the beach next to the Leela hotel – they'll happily send a boat over for you.

Where to stay

Once part of the Marriott chain, the ostentatious **Ramada Caravela Goa Resort** (Varca beach road, Varca, 0832-274-5200, www.caravelabeachresort.com, Rs 8,250-Rs 15,000 doubles) looms over its surroundings with an in-house casino and a nine-hole golf course. A favourite with charter tourists is **Dona Sylvia** (opposite shopping mall, Mobor

village, 0832-287-1321, www.donasylvia.com, Rs 7,000-13,000 doubles), with spacious cottages in large, manicured gardens. The **Holiday Inn Resort** (next to the Leela Hotel, Mobor, 0832-287-1303, www.holiday inngoa.com, Rs 6,500-Rs 9,500 double) is an undistinguished five-star but located very close to the beach. Second only to the Park Hyatt for outrageous luxury is The **Leela** (Mobor beach, 0832-287-1234, www.ghm hotels.com, Rs 9,000-Rs 20,000 doubles), a massive hotel complex built despite strong opposition from local environmental activists. It has seven restaurants, a spa, tennis courts and a 12-hole golf course.

Entertainment

Dolphin rides & deep-sea fishing

Boat rides to view the dolphins that frolic in Goan waters (the silvery Indo-Pacific humpbacked dolphin is the most common) are available through most hotels. Expect to pay around Rs 400 per person for an hour and a half on the water in the early morning, leaving around 7am. **Betty's Place** (near Leela beach, Mobor, 0832 -287-1456, www.bettysgoa.com) offers dolphin boat rides departing at 8am

Turn on the toddy tap

It's not as common as it once was, but keep an eye on the tops of palm trees for toddy-tappers and if you spot one, ask him for a drink. Toddy is a fermented, mildly alcoholic drink made from the sap of the coconut palm. Using nothing but their hands and feet, and occasionally a strap of cloth for support, toddy-tappers cut small holes in the trunk between the branches and attach clay gourds to collect the sap. The fresh sap is sweet and colourless, and can be drunk straight away, often at breakfast, or left to ferment. Within eight hours, the sap turns into fresh toddy, a white, sweet-sour drink with a strong smell and taste and about the same alcohol level as a European beer – about five to six per cent. It has to be drunk that day, or it rapidly ferments into a palm vinegar that Goans use as a major ingredient in cooking. A lot of the palm sap collected in Goa is also distilled into a palm *feni* (see p183 **Feni for your thoughts**). There's no organised toddy manufacturing – toddy tappers are itinerant workers – but ask at your hotel to see if they can arrange to get some for you. It's very cheap, usually around Rs 40 for a litre bottle.

Don't try this at home – toddy tapping.

Sea views from **Cabo de Rama Fort**.

and 10am (Rs 300 per person for around two hours) and deep-sea fishing (Rs 500 per person for four hours).

Cycle tours
The British expat-run **Cycle Goa** (Shop 7, Mobor Beach Resort, Cavelossim, 0832-287-1369, 98223-80031, www.cyclegoa.com, open 9am-1pm, 2-6pm) conducts a variety of rides, including pretty half-day village tours (Rs 750) and day-long rides pitched at different fitness levels. The beautiful ride up to the Cabo de Rama Fort costs Rs 1,800. They also do a two-week cycling tour of Goa covering around 25 miles a day. They supply bikes, lunches and a back-up vehicle in case it all gets too much.

Getting there

Taxis from Dabolim Airport to Varca and Cavelossim take around 75 minutes and cost Rs 650. From Margao, it's a 30-minute ride (Rs 400), which takes you along the coast past Benaulim, then off a turn through Varca and Carmona.

Agonda

South of Mobor, a winding coastal road see-saws through valleys cut with rice terraces and coconut and areca nut palm groves. On the way, the road forks right to the forbidding **Cabo de Rama** fortress, which overlooks the sea from a dramatic headland. Leaving the cape, the road to Palolem cuts through cashew plantations and rice fields until it reaches another right turn leading to **Agonda**. This road is not officially marked, but look for signs advertising beach shacks. Agonda is one of Goa's best beaches, a small stretch of tranquillity that has escaped

major tourist development thanks to local opposition. It's perfect for lazy beach days, and from October to April there are a few temporary shacks here offering food and drinks.

Cabo de Rama Fort
Off the Palolem Road.
The Cabo de Rama had already been a prized fortress for centuries when the Portuguese seized it in 1763. According to Hindu mythology, Lord Rama, the hero of the epic Ramayana, rested at this fort after being exiled from Ayodya. A decrepit gateway leads to a copse of fruit trees alive with wide-eyed Hanuman langur monkeys. On one side are the remains of the battlements, still mounted with a rusting cannon, which afford spectacular views up and down the coastline. Walk past the monkeys and tangled vegetation, and you emerge on a small plateau that offers more superb views.

Palolem

The old coastal road is the most enchanting way to arrive in Palolem; turn a corner near the summit of the hill for an unmatched view of the beach's graceful arc far below. Palolem is the stuff of picture-postcards – a beautiful bay lined with rippling golden sand dunes and fringed by stands of coconut palms, with thick jungle rising from the southern end into the foothills of the Western Ghats. Once well off the beaten track, today Palolem is the beach of choice for young backpackers and European families. Palolem heaves with visitors from October to April, peaking at around 10,000 visitors during Christmas and New Year. Around 50 shacks line the bay like beads on a necklace, many of them run by expat foreigners – it's now easy to find wood-fired pizzas, home-made houmous, and artery-clogging English breakfasts.

Agonda beach. *See p223*.

Bhakti Kutir, Palolem.

Where to eat & drink

The restaurant scene in Palolem shifts wildly from season to season and even month to month, as itinerant entrepreneurs and chefs pick up and leave whenever they feel like it. One reliable institution is **Smuggler's Inn** (Palolem Beach Road, 98229-86093, main courses Rs 250, open 9am-10pm daily), a Brit-run eatery with friendly local staff offering very decent euro-fare including roasts, mountains of mashed potatoes and old-fashioned bangers. Another is **Magic View** (Colomb Cove, no phone, main courses Rs 150, open 10am-10pm daily) on a slope with a great view of the ocean, featuring excellent Italian home cooking including very tasty pizzas. A leisurely 15-minute amble down the rocky coastline from Palolem, **Home** (Patnem Beach, 0832-264-3916, main courses Rs 140, open 8.30am-5.30pm) is a spotless, professionally run guesthouse and café offering Lavazza coffees, super-fresh salads and brilliant homemade desserts. **Dropadi Beach Restaurant & Bar** (98226-85138, Palolem Beach road, main courses Rs 200, open 8am-10pm daily Apr-Aug) is a popular eatery for everything from lasagna to tandoori chicken.

Where to stay

Easily the best place to stay in Palolem is **Bhakti Kutir** (south end of Palolem Beach, take the fork right near the mosque and look for a sign, 0832-264-3469, www.bhaktikutir.com, Rs 1,200-Rs 2,200 double). Run by an idealistic Goan-German couple, the hotel has a strict environmentally friendly philosophy, with non-AC cabanas entirely fashioned from local materials like rice straw, bamboo and mud. Most rooms have Indian-style squat toilets. Cleanse yourself with wheatgrass juice and mud baths at the Ayurvedic healing centre. Of the beach huts, **Ciaran's Camp** (Palolem Beach, 0832-264-3477, www.ciarans.com, Rs 1,500-2,500 double) is the most attractive, with a smart lawn and well-designed cottages with walk-in showers. The sea-facing cottages command higher prices, at Rs 2,000 to Rs 2,500 a night. A pleasant 12-minute stroll from the beach is **Oceanic** (Temba Vaddo, Palolem, 0832-264-3059, www.hotel-oceanic.com, Rs 1,500-Rs 2,000 double), run by a British expat couple to a good standard, with spacious and clean rooms equipped with mosquito nets. It's perfect for kids, with a good restaurant and the only swimming pool in Palolem. Slightly off the beaten track, a couple of minutes' walk from the beach across a bamboo footbridge is **Ordosounsar** (98224-88769, north end of

Palolem Beach, Rs 400-Rs 800 cottages), a collection of 12 huts that feel nicely isolated from the rest of Palolem.

Nightlife

Rave parties do happen in and around Palolem – its remoteness makes it easier to evade late-night music bans. When and where gets circulated by word of mouth at the innumerable shacks along Palolem Beach. Otherwise, Palolem's nightlife is dedicated to shameless chilling out. Daytime beach parties sometimes happen outside **Café Del Mar** (Palolem Beach, 98232-76520), one of the most popular of Palolem's beach shacks and a sprawling, deeply relaxed wood-and-bamboo den serving hookah pipes, cocktails and snacks to an ambient soundtrack. Further down the beach is the **Cuba Beach Café** (Palolem Beach, 98221-83775), another popular lounge-vibe shack on a wooden platform on the sand, with sofas and chairs and a house guitar for late-night strumming.

Resources

Internet

Bliss Travels *Near main gate, Palolem Beach. (0832-264-3912).* **Open** 9am-11pm daily. **Rates** Rs 50 per hr.

True Value *Beach Road (0832-264-4896).* **Open** 9am-11pm daily. **Rates** Rs 50 per hr.

Getting there

The nearest major train stop for Palolem is Margao. From Margao station you can then take a taxi to Palolem for about Rs 800. The trip takes approximately an hour. From Dabolim Airport taxis charge Rs 1,000 for the 105-minute journey. From Panjim, taxis charge around Rs 1,200 and take 90 minutes.

Margao

Margao is a small city with a big opinion of itself. In the early 20th century, it was a town of opulent mansions that styled itself as a centre for scholars and the arts, and its grandee families prided themselves on their sophistication and refinement. After the 1961 liberation of Goa by Indian troops, many left for Portugal and Brazil and their huge estates were redistributed to tenant farmers. Residents still like to talk of Margao as Goa's second city after Panjim, but today much of Margao's character has been written over by modern concrete sprawl and its narrow streets are choked with traffic.

Leopards, tigers and sloth bears, oh my!

In April 2006, an adult 50-kilo male leopard wandered into the heart of residential Miramar in Panjim, causing panic until he was brought down by a tranquilliser dart. But what's most surprising is that it doesn't happen more often. Nature preserves and sanctuaries cover a fifth of Goa's land – unspoiled jungle filled with a wide variety of wildlife. Tigers often stray into Goa's forests from Karnataka and Maharashtra and border villages are frequently plagued by stray elephants that gorge on sugarcane and other crops. Leopards are even more common; every year around half a dozen have to be rescued from wells or trapped by rangers after eating dogs near human settlements.

Although the state's sanctuaries are open to visitors, most lack basic tourist facilities like trained guides, visitor centres or even bathrooms. Of all Goa's reserves, the **Cotigao Wildlife Sanctuary** is perhaps the most accessible and rewarding, and is only 20 minutes from Palolem by road (along the NH-17 to Karwar, entry fees Rs 5 per person, plus Rs 100 car, Rs 50 motorbike, Rs 50 camera charge). Stretching across 33 square miles of mixed deciduous forest, Cotigao is home to large numbers of gaur (the world's largest kind of cattle), langur and macaque monkeys, wild boar, porcupines, leopards, jackals and even a few sloth bears.

Right on the edge of Cotigao Sanctuary is one of Goa's best hotel options for wildlife enthusiasts – a converted spice plantation named **Pepper Valley** (0832-263-3370, 98504-51714, www.peppervalley.com, Rs 500 cottage). Perfect for trips into the sanctuary, Pepper Valley is a simple but charming row of huts and cottages on the Talpona riverbank, under a cool stand of areca nut palms, all run by enthusiastic Irish expat Sinead McManus.

A walk around the **Largo de Igreja**, the old church square surrounding the impressive **Church of the Holy Spirit** (closed after 11.30am daily) in the centre of town yields a glimmer of Margao's former glory, lined with ornate colonial-era buildings. The baroque church has seen better days, but the façade is still impressive. Down from the church square the road skirts some old grandee *palacios*, not open to visitors but worth a look from outside, particularly the so-called **House of Seven Gables**, a mansion that has lost four of its famous pitched roofs to generations of neglect since the days of the grandees. There's not much else to see in Margao other than the pretty **Chapel of Our Lady of Mercy** on the Monte Hill.

Where to eat & drink

The Margao branch of **Café Tato** (behind Collectorate, 0832-273-6014, main courses Rs 30, open 7am-10pm Mon-Sat) serves fabulous vegetarian thalis and *puri bhaji*. **Banjara** (De Souza Chambers, behind Grace Church, 0832-271-4837, main courses Rs 200, open 11am-3pm, 6pm-11pm daily) is the best North Indian restaurant in the south, serving particularly good tandoori breads. **Gaylin** (behind Collectorate, BB Road, main courses Rs 190, open 10am-3pm, 6.30-11.30pm daily) is a popular restaurant offering decent Indian-Chinese food.

Where to stay

Nanutel

Rua Padre Miranda, opposite Clube Harmonia, Margao (0832-270-0900/www.nanuindia.com).
Rates Rs 1,100 single, Rs 1,200 double.
Credit MC, V.
Only if you absolutely have to stay in Margao. A standard, uninspiring hotel but conveniently close to Margao Station and the Apollo Victor Hospital.

Entertainment

Crocodile spotting

Crocodile Station (61 Thana, Cortalim, 98221-27936, 0832-255-0334, Rs 750 per person) runs lazy rides up the ancient Cumbarajua Canal to view the two dozen or so resident crocodiles lazing around on the mud flats and canal banks. They promise your money back if you don't see a croc – and haven't had to pay a penny back yet.

Getting there

Margao Station on the Konkan Railway line running from Mumbai to Kerala is the main

Palolem Beach. *See p223.*

station for South Goa. Buses run regularly to the station from Panjim (Rs 30, 1hr) and Calangute (Rs 50, 90mins). Or you can take a taxi from Panjim to Margao (around Rs 800, 50 minutes) or from Calangute (around Rs 1,000, 1hr). Taxis from Dabolim Airport charge around Rs 450 for a 40-minute trip.

Resources

Hospital

Apollo Victor Hospital, near Carmelite Monastery, Aquem, Margao (0832-272-8888). **Open** 24hrs daily.

Internet

JR Cyberworld, Sheesh Mahal, Shop 12, near Saraswat Bank, Combao (0832-271-3061).
Open 8.30am-9pm daily.
Phoenix, Apna Bazaar, behind Collector's Office (0832-271-2430). **Open** 8.45am-9pm Mon-Sat.
Cyberocks, Shop 5, Reliance Residency, Colmarod, Navelim (0832-270-2407). **Open** 9am-9pm daily.

Police

Police Station, near Municipal Gardens, Margao. Emergency number 100.

Post office

Margao General Post Office, Municipal Gardens, Margao (0832-271-5791). **Open** 9.30am-1pm, 2-5.30pm Mon-Sat.

Tourist information

Goa Tourism Development Corporation Information Office, Margao Residency lobby, behind Municipality building, opposite Municipal Gardens (0832-271-5528). **Open** 9.30am-5.30pm Mon-Fri.

Directory

Features

Getting Around

Arriving & leaving

By air

Chhatrapati Shivaji International Airport

2615-6000/www.airportsindia.org.in/aai/mumbai.
Mumbai's international airport is located off the Western Express Highway about nine miles north of Mumbai Central and 19 miles from Colaba. For transit to the domestic airport, there is a free **fly-bus** that runs every 15 minutes between the international airport and the domestic airport. The Brihanmumbai Electric Supply & Transport (BEST) runs buses from the airport to Nariman Point and Backbay Depot in Colaba every hour 24 hours daily from Terminal 2C (arrivals). All stop at the Taj Mahal Palace and Towers in Colaba, the Hilton Towers and the Oberoi at Nariman Point, and the Taj President at Cuffe Parade both to and from the airport. A single fare is Rs 16.

Chhatrapati Shivaji Domestic Airport

2617-6738/www.airportsindia.org.in/aai/domestic_airport/operational/juhu.htm.
The domestic airport at Santa Cruz is about three miles south of the international terminus. The state-run Indian Airlines flies out of Terminal 1A while private carriers use Terminal 1B. The domestic airport is well connected to destinations across India.

Taxis from the airports

Most five-star hotels offer pick-ups from the airport. If your hotel doesn't, you can hire a **pre-paid taxi** from a counter just before the exit from the Arrivals lounge. The standard charge for a ride into Colaba is Rs 330. Regular taxis and blue air-conditioned taxis called 'cool cabs' are also available from the taxi stand outside. Ignore the shouts from touts and take a place in the queue. A trip from the airport to Colaba in a metered taxi costs around Rs 250-Rs 300 (Rs 400 in a cool cab). Drivers routinely overcharge and demand inflated 'luggage charges'. Ask for the tariff card to check the fare (*see p229* **Taxis**).

Airlines

Terminals are shown in brackets.

International

Air France (II-C)
2495-4348/2682-8072/www.airfrance.com/in
Air India (II-C)
2279-6666/www.airindia.com
British Airways (II-A)
98925-77470/www.britishairways.com/india
Cathay Pacific (II-A)
5657-2222/www.cathaypacific.com/in
Delta Air Lines (II-A)
2826-7000/www.delta.com
El Al Israel Airlines (II-C)
2215-4701/www.elal.co.il
Malaysia Airlines (II-C)
5650-5757/in.malaysiaairlines.com
Qantas (II-A)
2200-7440/www.qantas.com.au
Singapore Airlines (II-C)
2202-8316/www.singaporeair.com
South African Airways (II-C)
2282-3450/www.flysaa.com
Sri Lankan Airlines (II-C)
2282-3288/www.srilankan.aero
Swiss International Airlines (II-A)
2287-2210/www.swiss.com
Virgin Atlantic (II-A)
2280-1289/www.virgin-atlantic.com

Domestic

Air Deccan (I-B)
2661-1601/www.deccanair.com
Go Air (I-B)
1800-222-111/www.goair.in
Indian Airlines (I-A)
2202-3031/2202-3131/indian-airlines.nic.in
Jet Airways (I-B)
3989-3333/www.jetairways.com
Kingfisher Airlines (I-A)
5646-9999/www.flykingfisher.com
Spicejet
3989-3333/www.spicejet.com

By road

If you are getting to Mumbai by road, there are three entry points. The Western Express Highway runs in from the north-west through Borivali to the airports and the western suburbs. If you're coming in on the highway from Pune, you'll hit the eastern suburb of Chembur and then on to the city's central suburbs. The Eastern Express Highway enters from the north through Thane. A toll of Rs 20 is levied on this road if you're in a car.

By train

Mumbai is well connected to most parts of India through an extensive railway network divided by region. The Western Railway (2200-5388, www.wr.indianrail.gov.in) and Central Railway (2262-1450) have their headquarters in Mumbai.

Maps

General maps of the city and road maps are available at the Maharashtra Tourism Development Corporation kiosk in Nariman Point (Madam Cama Road, opposite LIC Building, 2202-7762). Other city maps are sold at bookstores and at stalls at major railway stations. The most detailed city map is published by Eicher, priced Rs 250. For our maps, *see pp248-255.*

Public transport

Mumbai's tourist and business district is located at its southern tip in Colaba, Fort and Nariman Point. Taxis and buses are a good way to get around this part of the city, although much of Colaba and Fort can be covered on foot. For travel north into the suburbs, especially if you're heading past Dadar, the local train service is far quicker than trying to beat the traffic in a cab. A train from Churchgate to Bandra takes less than 25 minutes; the same journey from Churchgate by car in rush hour will take at least one-and-a-half hours.

Buses

Mumbai's public bus system is run by the Brihanmumbai Electric Supply & Transport, whose red double- and single-decker buses are marked with big 'BEST' signs on the side. They're efficient across city districts. BEST runs 3,380 buses on 335 routes, carrying 4.5 million passengers every day. A short trip costs Rs 4. The tourism department also runs open-top 'Nilambari' buses on a heritage tour (*see p58*).

Local trains

Mumbai's suburban train network has three lines – **Western**, **Central** and **Harbour**. The Western line starts from Churchgate and ends at Dahanu Road outside Greater Mumbai. The Central and Harbour lines start at Chhatrapati Shivaji Terminus. The Central line has two branches, which extend to Khopoli on the mainland in the south-east and Kasara to the north-east. The Harbour line also has two branches running to Andheri in the north and Panvel in the north-east. Mumbai's trains are reliable, efficient and frequent – you'll rarely wait more than ten minutes for a train. The service carries six million commuters a day and the general compartments are densely packed in rush hours (9-11am, 5-8pm) and can be a highly uncomfortable, sweaty experience. First-class compartments have padded seats and are less crowded because fewer people can afford the fares. There are separate compartments for women, marked 'Ladies 24 hours' which are usually less crowded and highly recommended for women travellers. For a map of the suburban railway network, *see p256*.

Tickets

Travel in the general compartment is cheap, at just Rs 6 from Churchgate to Bandra, for example, jumping to Rs 50 for first-class travel. Tickets are sold only at railway station counters. Return tickets are valid for return travel up to the following day. You can save a lot of time waiting in queues by buying a booklet of travel coupons instead of tickets for individual journeys. Just punch coupons to the value of your ticket in a red machine near the ticket counter before you travel. Fares for different destinations are displayed on a chart at each station. If you're staying for a while, you could buy a monthly or three-month standard or first-class pass, which allows unlimited travel between the stations you choose for great savings. A single route pass allows travel only on either the Central, Western or Harbour line, or you can buy a 'two-route' or a 'three-route' pass which allows for universal travel.

Auto-rickshaws

Auto-rickshaws (often locally called 'ricks' or 'autos') are three-wheeled taxis that operate in the suburbs beyond north of Bandra in the west and Sion in central Mumbai. Drivers are not allowed to ply in South Mumbai. Many rickshaws are mobile art installations, with colourful upholstery, movie-star images adorning the cabins and blaring Hindi film music. The minimum fare is Rs 9 for 0.9 mile. Each additional tenth of a mile adds one rupee to the fare. To figure out your total fare at your destination, multiply the number on the meter by ten, and subtract one. So if the meter shows 1, the fare is Rs 9; if it reads 1.9, the fare is Rs 18. Between midnight and 5am, there's a 25 per cent 'night

charge'. Ask the driver for the tariff card to verify the fare.

Taxis

Mumbai's distinctive black-and-yellow Padmini taxis are elderly, but built like tanks. In the 1990s their petrol engines were converted to compressed natural gas, as an environmental measure. They charge Rs 13 for the first mile and Rs 1.50 for every additional 0.6 miles. As with rickshaws, there's a 25 per cent 'night charge' for travel between midnight and 5am. Although many cabbies are honest, some will hike their prices dramatically for foreign tourists. Ask for the tariff card ('*card dikhao*') to check.

Long-distance

Coaches

An array of new luxury coach companies have made long-distance bus travel comfortable, though all Indian buses still lack toilet facilities. Be warned that 'video coaches' will blare Bollywood films almost non-stop until you get to your destination.

Amey Travels *Shop No 4, Arun Building Compound, Agarwal Estate, Madhavi Society, Mughal Lane, Matunga (W) (2430-3228/0122). Dadar station.* **No credit cards.**
Gohil Travels *64/66 Gohil Sadan, SJ Marg, Lower Parel (W) (2496-1211/1113/gohiltravels.com). Lower Parel station.* **Credit MC, V, AmEx.**
Maitri Tours & Travels *Tejpal Building, Plot No 37, second floor, Pan Galli, near Cumballa Hill Hospital, Kemp's Corner (2871-2852/93222-13316). Grant Road station.* **No credit cards.**
Neeta Travels *19 Saraswati Niwas, Rokadia Lane, SV Road, Borivali (W) (2890-2666/2888-3335). Borivali station.* **No credit cards.**
Sachin Travels *Nirmal Sagar, first floor, near Sena Bhavan, next to Aswad Hotel, LJ Road, Shivaji Park, Dadar (2432-3235). Dadar station.* **No credit cards.**
Sagar Hills Tours & Travels *192/1 Pathare Mansion, LJ Road, Mahim (2444-3899/2017). Dadar station.* **No credit cards.**

Saraswat Travels *Room No 9,*
Second Floor, Parvati Niwas,
Mahant Road, Vile Parle (E)
(2618-0220). Vile Parle station.
No credit cards.

Swami Tours & Travels
Saraswati Niwas, Rokadia Lane,
opposite Gokul Hotel, Borivali (W)
(2890-4646/4747). Borivali station.
No credit cards.

Swarmeet Travels *41 Ganga*
Niwas, Ranade Road, Dadar (W)
(2432-7366). Dadar station.
No credit cards.

Travel Today *104 Sapna, SK Bole*
Road, Agar Bazaar, Dadar (W)
(2430-3686/2437-0801). Dadar
station. **No credit cards.**

Vartman Travels
Shop No 3, Sagar Shopping Complex,
near Ram Mandir, MG Road,
Vile Parle (E) (2615-3191/5876).
Vile Parle station. **No credit cards.**

Trains

Long-distance trains are a
slow but relatively comfortable
way to travel long distances.
Seats or berths on popular
routes like Mumbai-Goa are
often booked weeks in advance
in peak season (November-
March). For foreign travellers
there is a **foreigners' quota**
of seats reserved for tourists
that can be bought up to 60
days before the day of travel
from the **Chhatrapati
Shivaji Terminus** first-floor
booking hall (window 52). It's
open from 8am to 11.50pm,
1.10pm to 2pm, and 2.30pm
to 9pm (Mon-Sat). A passport
is required as proof of foreign
nationality. US dollars, British
pounds, euros and travellers'
cheques are accepted, but if
you pay in rupees you may
be asked to show your foreign
exchange receipt. Tickets can
also be reserved and bought
online from **www.indian
rail.gov.in**, which offers e-
ticketing on select routes. If
you're doing a lot of travelling,
you can also buy an **Indrail
pass**, which offers unlimited
rail travel across India for up
to 90 days. These are available
from the Tourist Information
Counter at Chhatrapati Shivaji
Terminus. As well as first-
class berths, which are often
as expensive as air tickets,

there are second-and third-
class berths available, further
divided into air-conditioned
and non-air-conditioned
categories.

The difference between AC
and non-AC is much more than
simply whether the carriage is
air-conditioned. Second-class
AC carriages have padded
bunks, complimentary bedding
and cleaner toilets than
second-class non-AC carriages.
They're also more expensive,
sometimes ten times the price
of non-AC tickets.

Driving

Indians drive on the left,
usually. Mumbai motorists
often prefer to adopt a more
flexible interpretation of
such pesky rules. Driving
in Mumbai can be a nerve-
racking experience; traffic
is heavy and many roads are
badly maintained. With few
decent pavements, pedestrians
are forced to walk on the road,
and often wander in front
of traffic without looking,
apparently in the expectation
that any approaching motorist
will be equipped with good
brakes. Motorists make ample
use of the horn to warn other
drivers of their approach,
jostling aggressively for
position with routine disregard
for lanes and other vehicles
to the sides or behind. Do not
expect other motorists to check
what's behind them before
pulling out. To drive you will
need both a valid driving
licence and international
driving permit both issued
in your home country. Don't
forget to carry them with
you whenever you drive.
Drunk driving is an offence:
drivers found with over 0.03%
alcohol in their blood can be
prosecuted. It is also an offence
to drive without a seatbelt or
while using a mobile phone.
Helmets are now mandatory
for motorcycles and scooters.
Traffic is intense during rush

hours, usually 9.30am to noon
and 5.30pm to 9.30pm.

Car hire

Mumbai doesn't have any
agencies that rent out self-
drive cars; only chauffeur-
driven vehicles are available.
A typical rental fee is about
Rs 1,000 for eight hours or 50
miles, inclusive of driver, fuel
and insurance, with surcharges
for every additional hour/mile.
You should check carefully for
terms and conditions, and any
regional limits on where you
can take the vehicle.

Car Care
42 Kedia Apartments, 29F Dongersi
Road, Malabar Hill (98210-12685/
2367-7724). Grant Road station.
Open 24hrs daily. **Credit** AmEx.

Orix Car Rental
IL&FS Financial Center, Bandra-
Kurla Complex, Bandra (E)
(98192-54244/2653-3141).
Bandra station. **Open** 24hrs daily.
Credit AmEx, DC, MC, V.

Royal Cars
7/27 Grant Building, Arthur
Bunder Road, Colaba (2283-
2928/1844). Churchgate/CST
stations. **Open** 24hrs daily.
No credit cards.

Satnam Travels
Shop No 10, Plot No 769, Tharu
House, 3rd and 4th Road junction,
Khar (W) (98210-32606/5575-
8505). Khar station. **Open** 24hrs
daily. **No credit cards.**

Walking

Getting around parts of
Mumbai on foot can be
difficult – many roads do
not have pavements and
where they exist they
are frequently broken or
obstructed by vendors' stalls.
Watch out for hazards like
open manholes. But walking
is a good way to enjoy heritage
parts of the city such as Colaba
and Fort, where pavements
are in better condition. *Fort
Walks* by Sharada Dwivedi
details picturesque walks
through the Fort district
(*see p240* **Books**).

Resources A-Z

Addresses

Addresses usually begin with the flat number of the building or the housing compound, followed by the name of the house or building, followed by the street number and finally the street name and district, with an E or W in brackets indicating whether the address is on the eastern or western side of the local railway line. For example, *31 Pluto Building, 36 Turner Road, Bandra (W)*. Addresses also often contain a reference to a local landmark such as 'opposite Mahalaxmi Racecourse', and a Mumbai postal code, locally called a 'pin number', which is a six-digit number beginning with 4.

Age restrictions

The legal age for drinking varies according to the drink: you have to be 21 to knock back a beer, and 24 to drink spirits and wine. In practice, proof of age is rarely asked for. The age of sexual consent is 18; the driving age is 18. It's illegal for shopkeepers to sell cigarettes to anyone under 18.

Attitudes & etiquette

Mumbaikars are usually very warm and hospitable towards foreign visitors, and often have a great interest in their opinions of the city. Shaking hands is a common greeting, but Indians also touch their palms together in front of the chest and say the Hindi greeting '*Namaste*', or '*Namaskaar*' in Marathi. This can be a more appropriate way to greet the elderly and women from traditional families.

Mainstream society does not look fondly on the idea of a man greeting a woman who is not his wife with a kiss, even on the cheeks, although many upper-class Mumbaikars will have no problem with it – stick to shaking hands and '*Namastes*' if in doubt. Be aware that some Indian men labour under the idea that Western women are more open to casual sex than their Indian counterparts. This is unlikely to cause serious problems; rapes and sexual assaults against foreign tourists are rare in Mumbai. Still, women travellers should be careful of getting into potentially risky situations.

Mumbai is a fairly liberal city and you will see women dressed in a variety of styles. Dress for the occasion: if you're going to a nightclub or a posh restaurant then a tight skirt or a skimpy top is fine; but if you're going for a bus ride or a walk on Chowpatty Beach then dress more conservatively if you don't want to be the focus of stares. When visiting religious sites, both men and women should cover their arms and legs, and remove their shoes before entering. Don't forget to cover your head before entering a Sikh *gurdwara* or a mosque.

Punctuality is not considered a great virtue in India and you can often expect to be kept waiting, even in business contexts. That's partly because Indians are very flexible with their schedules, which can be an advantage if you need to see someone senior at short notice. If you're being kept waiting, whether it's for a bus or an official, there is usually little to be gained from showing your anger about the delay – it will only cause resentment and embarrassment. Anticipate from the outset that tasks are likely to take longer than you would expect.

Although Mumbaikars are in general a friendly lot, this is a big, crowded city and they don't have time to waste on niceties. You may be surprised at the cursory, sometimes rude way that Mumbaikars deal with servants, waiting staff and other people in service jobs – 'pleases' and 'thank yous' are often not bothered with. On trains, buses and in traffic, Mumbaikars are cut-throat in jostling for an inch of space. Queuing does happen at railway stations and banks, but is not universal – just as on the road, the biggest and fastest get to the front first.

Couriers & shippers

Prices vary considerably, but the price of sending a 5kg package from India to the UK is around Rs 5,000 to Rs 5,600 inclusive, subject to customs.

Blue Dart Express *Sunder Mahal, ground floor, next to Ambassador Hotel, Veer Nariman Road, Churchgate (2282-8064/www.bluedart.com). Churchgate station.* **Open** 10am-8.30pm. **Credit** MC, V.

DHL Worldwide Express *Nazir Building, ground floor, Calicut Street, Ballard Estate (2262-3548/www.dhl.co.in). CST station.* **Open** 8am-10pm daily. **Credit** AmEx, DC, MC, V.

FedEx *108/110 Khadija Hasanji Sultanji Building, ground floor, Mint Road, near Reserve Bank of India (2269-2812/www.fedex.com/in). Churchgate/CST stations.* **Open** 10am-9pm daily. **No credit cards**.

Customs

Personal items can be brought in duty-free as long as they'll be consumed or taken out of the country upon return. Up to 200 cigarettes or 50 cigars or 250 grams of tobacco and up to one litre each of spirits and wine are permitted. For more information on customs see www.mumbaicustoms.gov.in.

Disabled

Bad pavements, heavy crowds and intense traffic all make

Malaria

Malaria is a potentially fatal disease that is spread by the bites of infected mosquitoes. Malaria-carrying mosquitoes breed in Mumbai and Goa around areas with stagnant water, particularly at construction sites. Around 14,000 people a year are infected with malaria in Mumbai, with the riskiest season being the monsoon, from June to September. The typical incubation period is one week to one month, but travellers can fall sick up to one year after being infected, often long after returning home from India.

Symptoms include fever, body aches, chills, sweating, exhaustion, headaches, nausea and vomiting. Typically, malaria attacks last between six to ten hours and repeat after a period of abatement. The onset of malaria can be difficult to spot because the initial symptoms are flu-like and the disease must be diagnosed by a blood test. Consult a doctor immediately if you develop malaria-like symptoms. Severe cases can lead to seizures, comas, fluid in the lungs, hallucinations, kidney failure, respiratory problems and death.

Your chances of becoming infected on a short holiday to Mumbai or Goa are low, but both the UK foreign office and the US state department advise travellers to India to protect themselves against infection with anti-malarial drugs. Recommended drugs for India include chloroquine (sold under brand names like Nivaquine and Avloclor), taken once a week. There are some chloroquine-resistant strains of malaria

present in India, so you should supplement that with a daily dose of proguanil. Start taking your medicine one week before travel and for four weeks after you return. The more expensive Malarone, a new-generation anti-malarial drug, combines atovaquone and proguanil, and is taken daily with food or milk; start taking it two days before travel and for a week after you return. Bring enough medicine to last the duration of your trip; drugs like proguanil and Malarone will not be easily available.

Some anti-malarial drugs are associated with mild side effects, including stomach pains, mouth ulcers, nausea, itchiness, vomiting, sleep disturbances and headaches. Try switching to a different type if you suffer heavy side effects. Some drugs are not recommended for pregnant women, those with existing medical problems like epilepsy or those taking other drugs – consult your doctor.

You can also protect yourself by using an insect repellent containing diethyltoluamide and by wearing diethyltoluamide-soaked wristbands and ankle bands. Use insecticide sprays in your room, sleep under a mosquito net (buy a light-weight one before you travel), keep windows closed at night and cover your arms and legs. Pyrethroid coils to burn are readily available in India, as are repellents that can be plugged into electrical sockets. Mosquitoes can bite through thin clothing, but you can spray a permethrine insecticide on your clothes, which offers protection for up to two weeks.

Mumbai a challenge for travellers with disabilities. There is no legislation making it mandatory for shops, restaurants, hotels or office buildings to offer wheelchair access, and most do not offer it. Nor do any of the city's public transport systems.

Drugs

Cannabis and other recreational drugs are illegal in India, and penalties for possession are severe, with prison terms of up to ten years. But that hasn't hampered a widespread drug culture across Mumbai's social classes. Hashish, locally known as *charas*, finds its way from Himachal Pradesh and Kashmir onto Mumbai's streets. In Colaba, tourists are likely to be approached by dealers peddling hash and heroin, and occasionally cocaine.

Electricity

The Indian domestic electricity supply is 230-250V, 50 Hz. UK appliances work with just a basic adaptor, but US 110V appliances will need a transformer as well. Both round three-pin and flat two-pin plug sockets are in use.

Embassies & consulates

Australia *36 Maker Chambers VI, 220 Nariman Point (5669-2000). CST/Churchgate stations.* **Open** 9am-5pm Mon-Fri.

Canada *Fort House, sixth floor, 221 DN Road, Fort (5549-4444). Churchgate/CST stations.* **Open** 9am-5.30pm Mon-Thur; 9am-3pm Fri.

Israel *Earnest House, 16th floor, NCPA Marg, Nariman Point (2282-2822). Churchgate/CST stations.* **Open** 9am-5pm Mon-Thur; 9am-3pm Fri.

Italy *First floor, Kanchanjunga, 72 Peddar Road (2380-4071/sedi. esteri.it/mumbai). Grant Road station.* **Open** 10am-1pm Mon-Fri.

South Africa *Gandhi Mansion, 20 Altamount Road, Cumballa Hill (2351-3725/ 3726).*

Grant Road station. **Open** 8.30am-5pm Mon-Fri.

United Kingdom *Maker Chambers IV, second floor, 222 Jamnalal Bajaj Road, Nariman Point (5650-2222). Churchgate/CST stations.* **Open** 8am-4pm Mon-Thur; 8am-1pm Fri.

USA *Lincoln House, 78 Bhulabhai Desai Road, Breach Candy (2363-3611/ mumbai.usconsulate.gov). Grant Road station.* **Open** 8.30am-5pm Mon-Fri.

Emergencies

To report an emergency, dial 100. For more information, consult www.mumbaipolice.com.

Ambulance Service *102*
(Rs 200 per hour)
Children distress line *1098*
Fire Brigade *101*
Mumbai Police *100*

Gay & lesbian

Under section 377 of the Indian Penal Code, homosexuality is still a crime in India. But the city has a vibrant and active gay and lesbian community, and activists continue to campaign strongly for a change in the law. Some of these organisations meet regularly. *See also p147* **Gay & Lesbian**.

Aanchal *www.aanchal.org* Aanchal provides counselling and support for Indian women questioning their sexuality. Contact Geeta Kumana at aanchaltrust@gmail.com.

Gaybombay *www.gaybombay.org* Gaybombay aims to create safe spaces for the gay community in Mumbai through its website and mailing list (gaybombay@yahoo groups.com), and regular meetings on the first, third and fifth Sundays of each month, with parties, film screenings, treks and more.

Humjinsi Helpline *2343-5700 (3pm-6pm Tue & Thur)/www. humjinsi.org.* Humjinsi provides counselling, meeting spaces and awareness-raising for lesbians and bisexual women.

Humsafar Centre *Girish Kumar (administrator), Post Box No 6913, Santa Cruz (W) (2667-3800/ www.humsafar.org). Santa Cruz station.* **Open** noon-8.30pm Mon-Sat. India's oldest organisation supporting sexual minorities. Its focus is communication and support on HIV/AIDS for gay men.

Symphony In Pink *www.symphonyinpink.com* Symphony In Pink is an online discussion group for women only, to highlight issues relevant to lesbian and bisexual women in Mumbai. It also holds trips and meetings.

Health

Accident & emergency

In case of accidents, call 102.

Bombay Hospital *Bombay Hospital Road, Marine Lines (2206-7676/www.bombayhospital.com). Marine Lines station.* **Taxi** behind Metro Cinema.

Cumballa Hill Hospital & Heart Institute *93/95 August Kranti Marg, Cumballa Hill (2380-3336). Grant Road station.*

Jaslok Hospital *Peddar Road, near Mahalaxmi Temple (2352-3333). Mahalaxmi station.*

JJ Hospital *Ibrahim Rehamatullah Road, Byculla (2373-5555). Byculla station.*

Lilavati Hospital & Research Centre *A791 Bandra Reclamation, Bandra (W) (2642-1111/ 2655-2222). Bandra station.*

PD Hinduja National Hospital & Medical Research Centre *Veer Savarkar Marg, Mahim (2445-2222/2444-9199). Mahim station.*

Pharmacies

Open 24-hour

Bombay Hospital Pharmacy *Bombay Hospital, New Marine Lines (2206-7676 ext 356/252). Marine Lines station.*

Dava Bazaar *32 Kakad Arcade, near Bombay Hospital, New Marine Lines (6665-9079/6655-9557). Marine Lines station.*

Hospital Chemist *Prarthna Samaj, Harkishondas Hospital, near Opera House, Charni Road. (2386-9219/ 2389-5553). Charni Road station.*

Other pharmacies

Bombay Chemists *Kakad Arcade, near Bombay Hospital, New Marine Lines (2200-1173). Marine Lines station.* **Open** 8.30am-11.30pm daily.

Colaba Chemist *27 Arthur Bunder Road, Glamour Building, Colaba (2284-8029/2283-2848). Churchgate/CST stations.* **Open** 8am-11pm daily.

Real Chemists *Kakad Arcade, near Bombay Hospital, New Marine*

Lines (2200-4211). Marine Lines station. **Open** 8am-10pm daily.

Red Cross Chemist *41/43 Kakad Arcade, near Bombay Hospital, New Marine Lines (5631-5766/ 2203-2410). Marine Lines station.* **Open** 8am-11pm daily.

Royal Chemist *41/42, Liberty Cinema Building, New Marine Lines (2200-4051/4052). Marine Lines station.* **Open** 8.30am-8.30pm Mon-Sat.

RN Kapadia & Company *199B Gopal Bhavan, near Parsi Dairy, Shamaldas Gandhi Marg (2201-9659/2205-4824). Marine Lines station.* **Open** 9am-8.30pm Mon-Sat.

Insurance

India has no reciprocal healthcare agreements with other countries and you should take out a medical insurance policy before you travel.

Vaccinations

You should consult your doctor at least three months before you travel to India. Vaccinations recommended for India are hepatitis A, typhoid and diphtheria. Even if you had polio immunisation as a child, you may still need a booster vaccine before travelling. Ensure you're up to date with tetanus shots and, for extended trips, consult a doctor about vaccinations against tuberculosis, hepatitis B, rabies and Japanese B encephalitis.

Water

Water is not safe to drink straight from the tap and you should always drink bottled water or water that has been filtered or thoroughly boiled. Good bottled water brands include Himalayan and Bisleri. Always ensure that the bottle seal has not been tampered with – it's not unheard of for vendors to fill mineral water bottles with tap water and then resell them. Avoid salads unless they have been washed with boiled or filtered water and decline ice that hasn't been made with boiled or filtered water.

Directory

Internet

There are cybercafes across the city, with many clustered around the Fort area in South Mumbai. Fees vary, but are usually in the range of Rs 20 to Rs 30 for one hour of surfing at good connection speeds. Many hotels are hooked up, but usually at higher rates than those offered by cafes. Local service provider MTNL (mumbai.mtnl.net.in/instant) offers instant dial-up services from any landline using the user's phone number as the username and 'MTNL' as the password. Internet surfing charges (32p per minute at 128 kpbs) are added straight to the user's telephone bill.

Asiatic Business Centre
124 Mint Road, Cama House, near Reserve Bank of India, Fort (2261-4492). Churchgate/CST stations. **Open** 9am-10pm daily.

PC Zone
2 Himmat Mansion, 236 Lady Jamshedji Road, Shivaji Park, Dadar (W) (2446-0667/9786). Dadar station. **Open** 9am-10pm daily.

Reliance Webworld
Opposite Akbarally's, Dadabhai Naoroji Road, Fort (3094-0950). Churchgate/CST stations. **Open** 10am-8pm daily.

Wembley Cybercafe
Building No 261, Bilquies Mansion, near Citibank, DN Road, Fort (2262-5728/2261-1299). Churchgate/CST stations. **Open** 9am-11pm daily.

Language

Mumbai is the capital of the state of Maharashtra, the dominant language of which is Marathi. Although Marathi is commonly spoken in Mumbai, the lingua franca across the city's mix of communities is a form of Hindi known as Bambaiyya Hindi, which comprises elements of Gujarati, Marathi, Hindi and English, and is a bastardised version of the pure Hindi

spoken in north India. English is commonly spoken, sometimes mixed with Hindi and other languages in an argot known as 'Hinglish'. Most public signs and notices across the city, and travel announcements at train stations and airports, are given in both English and Hindi. Although Mumbaikars always appreciate efforts by foreign visitors to speak in Hindi and other Indian languages, English is common enough to allow you to get by without them. For help with communication in Indian languages, *see p232* **Translators & interpreters**

Legal help

For legal assistance, contact your consulate or embassy (*see p232*) in the first instance.

Media

Newspapers

Mumbai has a rambunctious daily press in seven languages, and is home to India's oldest newspaper, the Gujarati-language *Mumbai Samachar*, founded in 1822. But foreign visitors reading the English-language press are often struck by how flippantly the front pages of the city's broadsheets juxtapose political reportage with celebrity gossip; articles about the state of Britney Spears's marriage and Kate Moss's love life are common features in even the so-called quality press. The dumbing-down started about a decade ago, when the venerable *Times of India*, founded in 1838, decided to practise what it called 'aspirational journalism', focussing on beauty contests and society parties (*see p25* **The other page 3**), allowing stories about poverty and infrastructure onto its pages

only grudgingly. With a circulation of 700,000-plus, the *Times* is by far Mumbai's largest and most influential English-language newspaper.

Until recently, the feisty *Indian Express*, which prides itself on its investigative stories, especially about official corruption, was the *Times*'s only real competition. the *Asian Age*, notable for its wide international coverage (reproduced mainly from the *New York Times*), is weak on local affairs. But the last year has seen the birth of two new newspapers. While the multi-coloured *Daily News and Analysis* has seemed content to ape the *Times*'s infotainment model, the local edition of the Delhi-based *Hindustan Times* has begun to win fans for putting serious issues back on the agenda. For many Mumbaikars, the long train journey home after work affords the opportunity to browse through one of the two afternoon tabloids (a broadsheet would be impossible to read in a cramped compartment): the *Afternoon Despatch and Courier* is mainly read by an older audience who have fond memories of its late founder-editor Behram Contractor, a man who fancied himself as an Indian Art Buchwald and went by the pen name Busybee. *Mid-Day*, meanwhile, is a zesty mixture of shocking crimes, political scandal and showbiz tattle.

Radio

It's expensive to start up a radio station and more so to keep it running, and private radio stations in India aren't allowed to broadcast news. As a result, Mumbai's young breed of FM stations have been unable to appeal to niche audiences. Most stations seek the widest audience by playing the same songs as their competitors. *Radio City 91FM, Red 93.5FM, Go 92.5FM, Radio Mirchi 98.3FM* and *All India Radio Rainbow 107.1FM* are the most popular stations, playing Hindi film numbers and Indi-pop songs.

Television

TV sets started appearing in India only in 1959, and it wasn't until the 9th Asian Games in Delhi in 1982 that colour TV was introduced. But it was only in 1992 that private channels were allowed. Until then, Indian viewers had to make do with the state-run *Doordarshan* channel, which had a strong focus on education and socio-economic development. New channels *MTV*, *Star Plus*, *BBC* and the Hong Kong-based *Star TV*, gave Indians new options. *Zee TV*, the first privately owned Indian channel, brought a bevy of regional channels.

A few years later, *CNN*, *Discovery Channel* and *National Geographic Channel* came in. Star also expanded its bouquet introducing *Star World*, *Star Sports*, *ESPN* and *Star Gold*. Regional channels flourished along with a multitude of Hindi channels and a few English channels. By the late '90s, *HBO* and *Cartoon Network* made their appearance, as did *Nickelodeon*. *MTV*'s popular international music channel VH1 came only in 2005, but it has enamoured audiences previously unexposed to international rock, hip hop and pop acts.

A boom in news broadcasting in 2003 has left the market crammed with nearly 20 news channels. Of these *NDTV* (with *NDTV India* in Hindi and *NDTV 24x7* in English) employs the most recognisable and experienced faces in Indian broadcast journalism. *CNN-IBN* formed as a breakaway from *NDTV* in 2005 and *Times Now*, a

collaboration between the *Times* Group (which owns the *Times of India*) and *Reuters*, have novice reporters and tacky graphics. Other channels such as *Headlines Today* (*India Today* Group) and *Channel 7* rely heavily on sensational pieces of gossip, crime and trivia-based news. Regional news channels all follow the trail of *Aaj Tak* (*India Today* Group). India's first 24-hour Hindi news channel, *Aaj Tak*, focuses on rural stories.

Money

India's currency is the rupee (short form Rs, although one rupee is written Re 1), which comprises 100 paise (p). Coins come in 50p, Re 1, Rs 2 and Rs 5 denominations. Paper money comes in denominations of Rs 5, 10, 20, 50, 100, 500 and 1,000. At the time of writing the tourist exchange rate was approximately Rs 78 for £1, Rs 45 for $1 and Rs 54 for €1. Avoid money-changers offering black market rates – it's illegal and they are frequently scamsters looking to short-change their victims.

ATMs

Most banks have 24-hour ATMs, often marked by an 'ATM' sign. They can also be found in shopping malls and some train stations. They dispense rupees only. Some are only for customers of certain banks, so look for the symbol of your card company. Links with international networks like Visa and Cirrus are common. You may be charged a small fee. Many ATMs are guarded by watchmen, but exercise basic caution and discretion if withdrawing large sums.

Banks

The banks below have branches throughout the city.

BNP Paribas India

French Bank Building, 62 Homji Street, Fort. (2266-0822/ bnpparibas.co.in). Churchgate/CST stations. Open 9am-6pm Mon-Fri; 9am-2pm Sat.

Citibank

Bombay Mutual Building, DN Road, Fort. (2269-5757/ www.citibank.co.in). Churchgate/CST stations. Open 10.30am-2pm.

HSBC

52/60 MG Road, Fort (2498-2424/www.hsbc.co.in). CST/Churchgate stations. Open 9.30am-5pm Mon-Sat.

ING Vysya

Mittal Towers, A Wing, ground floor, 210 Nariman Point (2288-2616). CST/Churchgate stations. Taxi near Vidhan Bhavan. Open 10.30am-4.30pm Mon-Fri; 10.30am-1.30pm Sat.

Standard Chartered

23-25 MG Road, opposite VSNL, Fort (2204-4444). CST/Churchgate stations. Open 9am-6pm Mon-Fri; 9am-4pm Sat.

Foreign exchange

Thomas Cook

Thomas Cook Building, 324 DN Road, Fort (2204-8556). Churchgate/CST stations. Also at Terminal IIA, Chhatrapati Shivaji International Airport, Andheri (E) (2682-9217). Andheri station. Open 9.30am-6pm Mon-Sat.

ABN Amro Bank

Sakhar Bhavan, near Oberoi Shopping Centre, Nariman Point (5656-3800/www.abnamro.com). Churchgate station. Open 10am-7pm Mon-Fri, 10am-3pm Sat.

Travelex

Nagina 2, Kartar Bhavan, Arthur Bunder Road, Colaba (5637-8575). Churchgate/CST stations. Open 10am-6pm Mon-Sat.

Credit cards

MasterCard (MC) and Visa (V) are accepted at many shops, restaurants and hotels. Some will also accept American Express (AmEx) cards, while a rare few accept Diners Club (DC) cards.

To report a lost or stolen credit card call these 24-hour helplines:

Directory

American Express *98926-00800*
Diners Club *2834-4653*
MasterCard *Call the card issuer in your home country.*
Visa *000-117-866-765-9644*

Natural hazards

Mumbai's famously moderate weather seems to have turned a little nasty in recent years. The days between April and June are increasingly scorching and the monsoon between June and October causes floods every year. Bring plenty of sunscreen, and dress in a T-shirt and loose pants to avoid sweat retention. Drink lots of water, but don't take it straight from the tap. Boil it first or buy bottled water. Mosquitoes are a perennial problem in Mumbai due to the humid weather. Arm yourself with a repellent and keep windows shut after sunset.

Opening hours

General stores open at 9am and close between 7pm and 8pm. Closed days vary and many businesses remain open on Sundays. Many liquor stores are shut on Thursdays. Banks generally open at 9.30am and stay open till 5pm on weekdays. Banks close at around 2pm on Saturdays and are closed on Sundays.

Postal services

Post is delivered once a day from Monday to Friday. The city's main post office, the main General Post Office near Chhatrapati Shivaji Terminus in Fort, is open from 10am to 8pm from Monday to Saturday but most branches close at 3pm. Stamps can be bought from post offices and some general stores. Most post offices also rent out post office boxes for a minimum of one year (Rs 185). See www.indiapost.gov.in for other postal services. *See also p232* **Couriers & shippers**.
General Post Office *St George Road, behind Chhatrapati Shivaji*

Terminus, Fort (2262-0956). CST/Churchgate stations. **Open** 10am-8pm Mon-Sat.
Colaba Post Office *SBS Marg, RC Church, Colaba (2215-3833). Churchgate/CST stations.* **Open** 10am-3pm Mon-Sat.

Safety & security

Mumbai is a remarkably safe city. Muggings, robberies and other serious crimes against tourists are rare, although pickpockets do operate in crowded areas. Still, it's always a good idea to take basic precautions, especially at night. Keep an eye on your luggage when travelling. In an emergency, dial 100.

For up-to-date information – including the latest news on safety and security, health issues, local laws and customs – contact your home country government's department of foreign affairs. For the UK, see www.fco.gov.uk/travel; for the US, see http://travel.state.gov. *See also p233* **Emergencies**.

Smoking

Mumbai is generally tolerant of smoking, and non-smoking areas in public places are rare, though smoking is not permitted on railway station platforms or trains. It is frowned upon to smoke in or near temples and other places of religious importance. Under Indian law, selling cigarettes to persons under the age of 18 years is illegal.

Study

India follows a 15-year education format – four years of primary school, six years of secondary school, followed by two years of higher secondary education. This normally precedes a three-year bachelor's degree university course. Indian masters degree courses usually take two years. Student visas are granted for the duration of the academic course

of study up to five years on the basis of letters of admission from the educational institution.

University of Mumbai

Founded in 1857, the University of Mumbai offers a massive number of masters and diploma courses, including one in Yogic Education, but it lags behind in teaching quality.
Fort Campus *Mayo Road, next to Mumbai High Court (2265-2819). Churchgate/CST stations.*
Vidyanagari Campus *Kalina, Santa Cruz (E) (2652-6388). Santa Cruz station.*

Studying music

There are several institutions in Mumbai teaching Hindustani and Carnatic classical music courses.
Bharatiya Vidya Bhavan's Sangeet Vidyapeeth *KM Munshi Marg, near Wilson College, Girgaum, Chowpatty (2369-8085). Charni Road station.*
Fine Arts School of Music & Dance *Fine Arts Society, Fine Arts Chowk, near Chembur Flyover, RC Marg, Chembur (2522-2988/www.faschembur.com). Chembur station.*
Jazz India Vocal Institute *nmjazz@vsnl.com.*
Professor Deodhar's School of Indian Music *Mody Chambers, Pt Paluskar Chowk (2382-1940/www.deodharmusicschool.com). Charni Road station.*
Sangeet Mahabharati *A6, 10th Road, Juhu Scheme, Vile Parle (W) (2620-7283). Vile Parle station.*
Shanmukhananda Music School *Sri Shanmukhananda Fine Arts and Sangeet Sabha, Plot No 292, Comrade Harbans Lal Marg, Sion (E) (2407-8888). Sion station.*
SNDT University *1 Nathibai Damodar Thackersey Road, New Marine Lines (2203-1879). Marine Lines station.*
University of Mumbai Department of Music *Vidyapeeth Vidyarthi Bhavan, B Road, Churchgate (2204-8665). Churchgate station.*

Telephones

Dialling & codes

The country code for India is 91 and the area code for Mumbai is 022. To dial India, dial the country code and drop the zero of the area code, followed by an eight-digit number, for example 91-22-2123-4567. You do not need to dial 022 from within the city except when dialling from a mobile phone. Most Mumbai landline numbers have eight digits. In 2002, MTNL, India's public sector telecom provider added an extra '2' to the start of all landline numbers, but many people, websites and other sources of information still quote the old seven-digit numbers. Just add the '2' and the number should work. Some fixed phone service providers like Tata Indicom and Reliance Infocomm have eight-digit phone numbers beginning with 5 and 3. Some numbers prefixed with 5 are being changed to 6 – try replacing it if the number you have doesn't work. To find phone numbers, try these 24-hour directory enquiry services:

Just Dial *2888-8888/2222-2222.*
Times Infoline *2600-5555.*

Calling long distance

Kiosks across the city marked 'STD' (Standard Trunk Dialling) offer facilities to make calls around India and internationally. Rates depend on where you are calling and at what time.

Public phones

There are numerous pay phones around the city and every second shop is likely to have one. Look for yellow 'PCO' (Public Call Office) signboards on street stalls and outside shops. Local calls cost Re 1 for 90 seconds.

Mobile phones

Contact your local mobile phone provider for details of roaming facilities in India. Mobile phones are now widespread in India. There are

several providers that offer SIM cards with pre-paid/top-up billing. To buy one, you'll need two passport-size photographs and a photocopy of your passport.

Airtel
Shop No 4, Yusuf Building, Veer Nariman Road, next to Akbarally's, Fort (98929-33400/98920-98920). Churchgate/CST stations. **Open** 10am-8pm daily.

BPL
Rajmahal, ground floor, near Ambassador Hotel, Veer Nariman Road, Churchgate (98210-99800). Churchgate station. **Open** 9am-8pm Mon-Sat.

Hutch
Shop No 3, Indian Merchant Chambers, 76 Veer Nariman Road, Churchgate (98200-98200). Churchgate station. **Open** 10am-7pm Mon-Sat.

Reliance Webworld
33/34 Veer Nariman Road, opposite Akbarally's, Fort (3094-0950). Churchgate/CST stations. **Open** 10am-8pm daily.

Time

Indian Standard Time is GMT +5 hours and 30 minutes. India does not use Daylight Saving Time.

Tipping

In restaurants, a five to ten per cent tip is appreciated, but not expected. Mumbaikars rarely tip in taxis and rickshaws.

Toilets

There are two styles of toilets in use in Mumbai – the Western-style toilet and the Indian 'squat' toilet. Squat toilets usually have ribbed areas to place your feet; stand on them and sit with your back to the hole. Although squat toilets take a bit of getting used to, it's worth the effort as the lack of a seat makes them more hygienic to use. Traditionally, toilet paper is not used; Indians usually clean themselves with a mug of

water using the left hand. Public toilets in Mumbai are rare and where they exist, are poorly maintained and frequently unhygienic. However, most major stores and malls keep their toilets clean. Walking into bars and restaurants just to use the toilet is frowned upon.

Tourist information

Maharashtra Tourism Development Corporation
Madam Cama Road, opposite LIC Building, Nariman Point (2202-6713/2202-7762/ www.maharashtratourism.gov.in). Churchgate/CST stations. **Open** 10am-5.30pm Mon-Sat.

Visas & immigration

All foreign visitors to India require a visa except for citizens of Nepal, Bhutan and the Maldives. There is no provision for granting visas upon arrival in India and you should apply to the Indian embassy or high commission in your home country. Visitors planning to stay over 180 days should register with the Foreigners' Regional Registration Office (*see p238*) within 14 days of arrival.

Depending upon the purpose of your stay in India, you should apply for one of the following visa categories: **Tourist** six months, multiple entry. Tourist visas cannot be extended or converted into other visa types; **Business** valid for one year or more, multiple entry. Applications should be accompanied by a letter from a sponsoring organisation indicating the nature of business, probable duration of stay, places and organisations to be visited; **Employment** valid for one to two years, multiple entry.

Applicants are required to submit a copy of a contract of employment; **Student** valid for the duration of the academic course of study or for a period of five years, whichever is less. Proof of admission from an Indian educational institute is required. Student visas cannot be converted; **Transit** issued to transit passengers for a maximum of 15 days, single/double entry; **Missionary** valid for a non-fixed duration at the discretion of the Government of India, single entry; **Journalist** issued to professional journalists and photographers, usually for three months, single entry; **Conference** issued to attendees of conferences/ seminars/ meetings held in India. Applicants are required to submit a letter of invitation from the conference organiser.

Temporary Landing Permits

Temporary Landing Permits can be granted to foreigners without visas coming to India in an emergency such as the death or hospitalisation of a relative. A cash payment of US$40 (Rs 1,935) is required. Permits can also be granted to foreigners in transit with confirmed onward journey tickets departing within 72 hours. This facility is not available to citizens of Sri Lanka, Bangladesh, Pakistan, Iran, Afghanistan, Somalia, Nigeria, Ethiopia and Algeria.

Foreigners' registration

Registration is compulsory for all foreigners intending to stay in India for more than 180 days. It should be done within 14 days of arrival.

Foreigners Regional Registration Office

Special Branch Building, third floor, Badruddin Tayabji Lane, behind St Xavier's College, Fort (2262-1169). Churchgate/CST stations.

Weights & measures

India uses the metric system. Indians also commonly use the terms **lakh** for 100,000 and **crore** for 10,000,000. For example, 'Rs 1 million' is usually written as 'Rs 10 lakh', and 'Rs 1 billion' is written as 'Rs 100 crore'.

What to take

Mumbai has a tropical climate, so pack light summer clothes, but also take a thin sweater or thick shirt for cool January and February evenings. Clothes and shoes are widely available at cheap prices but with a limited range in larger shoe sizes for men. The sun is bright and burning, so bring a hat, sunglasses and sunscreen. Open shoes or sandals are a good option, but closed shoes are a must if you're coming in the monsoon, between June and October, as is an umbrella (easy to purchase in Mumbai). Foreign tourists are notorious among Mumbaikars for looking unkempt and dirty; Indians always make an effort to look neat and you should pack at least one smart ensemble for going out or for visiting an Indian home.

Many medicines are available in Mumbai over the counter without a prescription, so only bring specialised personal medication. Essentials include luggage locks (bicycle locks are good for securing luggage on long train journeys), a money belt, insect repellent, photocopies of important documents like passports, spare batteries and an electrical adaptor. You might also consider bringing candles, a penknife (put it in your check-in luggage, not your hand luggage, or it will be confiscated at the airport), a phrasebook, toiletries, sanitary towels and tampons, and an anti-bacterial hand gel.

When to go

Climate

The 'winter', from December to February, is generally considered the most pleasant time to visit Mumbai, when average daytime temperatures dip to around 24°C (75°F) with low humidity. It can get very hot and humid in April and May, when temperatures peak at 35°C (95°F). In June, the monsoon begins, bringing torrential rains and intermittent flooding across the city right through until September and early October, with the heaviest rains in July and August. In October, the temperature and humidity rises again after the monsoon, cooling off by November.

Public holidays

New Year 1 Jan.
Makar Sankranti 14 Jan.
Muharram 20 Jan 2007; 10 Jan 2008.
Republic Day 26 Jan.
Maha Shivratri 16 Feb 2007; 6 Mar 2008.
Holi 3 Mar 2007; 22 Mar 2008.
Mahavir Jayanthi 8 Mar.
Rama Navami 27 Mar 2007; 14 April 2008.
Good Friday 6 Apr 2007; 21 Mar 2008.
Easter 8 Apr 2007; 23 Mar 2008.
Baisakhi 13 Apr.
Maharashtra Day 1 May.
Buddha Punima 2 May 2007; 19 May 2008.
Independence Day 15 Aug.
Janmashtami 15 Aug 2006; 4 Sept 2007; 24 Aug 2008.
Parsi New Year 20 Aug 2007; 19 Aug 2008.
Ganesh Chaturthi 27 Aug 2006; 15 Aug 2007; 3 Sept 2008.
Mahatma Gandhi Jayanti 2 Oct.
Dussera 2 Oct 2006; 21 Oct 2007; 9 Oct 2008.
Diwali 21 Oct 2006; 9 Nov 2007; 28 Oct 2008.

Directory

Bhaubeej 23 Oct 2006; 11 Nov 2007; 30 Oct 2008.
Id ul Fitr (Ramzan) 25 Oct 2006; 13 Oct 2007; 2 Oct 2008.
Guru Nanak Jayanti 5 Nov.
Christmas 25 Dec.

Women

Mumbai's women are not shrinking violets. Many are independent, assertive and are strongly represented in senior roles in industry and other walks of life. Women generally earn the same salaries as their male colleagues, but the glass ceiling persists at high levels of government and the corporate hierachy. The level of independence that Mumbai's women enjoy varies for different classes and ethnic groups. Despite the ever-present lurid Bollywood movie posters of skimpily-clad women, conservative dress for women is considered the norm – short skirts and tight tops are generally reserved for the upper classes, although jeans and T-shirts are the city's college student uniform. 'Eve-teasing' is how Mumbaikars refer to cat-calls, sexual harassment and worse by men, which occur with distressing frequency, although rapes and other sexual crimes are not as common in Mumbai as compared with Delhi, for example. Foreign women visitors are very often likely to be the objects of curiosity for some, and occasionally of lascivious attention, and it's best to avoid revealing shorts and skirts (*see p231* **Attitudes & etiquette**).

Working in Mumbai

Foreigners are not allowed to work in India without an appropriate visa (*see p237* **Visa & immigration**).

What's on the menu?

A beginner's glossary.

Ingredients

aloo potato; **badam** almond; **bhindi** okra or lady's finger; **bombil** small, soft-boned fish also called Bombay duck; **brinjal** aubergine or eggplant; **chana** chickpeas; **gobi** cauliflower; **ghosh** mutton or lamb; **imli** tamarind; **kala mirch** black pepper; **jhinga** prawns; **kesar** saffron; **kothmir** coriander or cilantro; **malai** cream; **methi** fenugreek; **mirch** chillies or peppers; **mosambi** a mild citrus fruit also known as 'sweet lime'; **murgh** chicken; **palak** spinach; **paneer** Indian cottage cheese; **pista** pistachio; **pomfret** a popular, delicately-flavoured fish; **pudina** mint; **rawas** Indian salmon; **sabzi/sabji** vegetable, or a vegetable dish; **sitaphal** a knobbly green fruit also known as 'custard apple'; **surmai** kingfish.

Dishes & styles

chivda a term for dry savoury snacks like Bombay mix; **dahi batata puri** crispy shells filled with yoghurt, potato, onion, chilli and sweet date chutney; **dal chaval** a staple meal of steamed spiced lentils and rice; **dal makhani** a classic, rich and creamy Punjabi dal; **dosa** a South Indian crisp pancake, commonly stuffed with spiced potato; **dhansak** a classic Parsi meal of strained vegetables and dal, usually served with mutton; **farsan** dry savoury snacks; **gassi** Mangalorean curry, made with coconut and fish, crab or prawns; **idli** a steamed savoury rice cake, eaten with a dal and coconut chutney; **kachumba** an

accompaniment mix of onion, tomato, fresh coriander and chilli; **kheema** spicy ground mutton or beef; **khichdi** a mixture of rice and dal; **kolhapuri** a very spicy masala; **makhanwala** cooked in butter; **navratan korma** literally, 'nine jewels' korma – a mild, creamy dish from the Mughal era made with nuts and raisins; **pani puri** crispy hollow shells filled with tiny chickpea dumplings, mung sprouts and spiced water; **paratha** flat bread commonly stuffed with onion, potato, fenugreek or ground meat; **pao bhaji** spicy puréed vegetables eaten with buttered bread; **pulao** mixed vegetables, meat or prawns sautéed with rice; **raan** a rich, tender leg of lamb slow-cooked overnight; **rasam** spicy South Indian soup made with tamarind; **tangdi** leg of chicken; **thali** a way of serving food common to many Indian cuisines, in five or six *katoris* (small bowls) on a circular metal plate. 'Unlimited *thali*' means it's all-you-can-eat; **vada pao** a fried, spicy mashed potato patty in a soft roll.

Desserts

falooda a rich, cold drink with nuts, vermicelli and soft sago balls, often flavoured with rose or saffron; **gulab jamun** balls of fried chickpea flour soaked in sugar syrup; **halwa** ground carrot, pumpkin or flour mixed with fruit and nuts; **jalebi** coiled strands of sugar syrup deep-fried in batter; **kulfi** frozen milk dessert, often with saffron and nuts; **mishti doi** a Bengali yoghurt dessert.

Directory

Further Reference

Books

Fiction

Chandra, Vikram *Love and Longing in Bombay* Five stories that offer a glimpse of Mumbai's passions and ghosts.
De Souza, Eunice *Dangerlok* A finely etched portrait of an ageing English Lit professor struggling with life in a distant Mumbai suburb.
Desai, Anita *Baumgartner's Bombay* A German Jew, who has long made a new life in a distant port city, runs into a wild hippie from his homeland.
Mistry, Cyrus *Radiance of Ashes* A young Parsi market researcher makes his way through the city's underbelly.
Mistry, Rohinton *Tales from Ferozeshah Baug, Such a Long Journey, A Fine Balance* and *Family Matters* explore the anxieties and joys of Mumbai's fast-diminishing Parsi community.
Nagarkar, Kiran *Ravan and Eddie* Mumbai's much-vaunted spirit of cosmopolitanism is stretched and tested in this brilliant novel, set in a tenement.
Roberts, Gregory *Shantaram* An Australian convict finds redemption in this simplistic New Agey narrative, purportedly based on real life.
Rushdie, Salman *Midnight's Children, The Moor's Last Sigh* and *The Ground Beneath Her Feet* Careen through Mumbai (with tangents shooting through time and space) as India's best-known writer pays tribute to the city of his birth.
Suri, Manil *Death of Vishnu* A fascinating snapshot of life in a city apartment complex, as a beggar lies dying on the stairway.
Tyrewala, Altaf *No God in Sight* A cinematically constructed journey through the heart of the Muslim community of central Mumbai.

Poetry

Chaudhuri, Amit *St Cyril Road and Other Poems* Reflections on Bandra's Roman Catholic community, and other meanderings.
Ezekiel, Nissim *Collected Poems 1952-1988* Ezekiel's poems in Indian English display a verbal litheness that could only have been inspired by multilingual Mumbai.
Kolatkar, Arun *Kala Ghoda Poems* One of India's most famous English-language poets looks out across the city's most famous square.

Subramaniam, Arundhathi *Where I Live* It's a 'city of L'Oreal sunsets…of septic magenta hairclips…of hope and bulimia', says the poet.

Non-fiction

Dalmia, Yashodhara *The Making of Modern Indian Art* A lavishly illustrated, incisive look at the painters of the Progressive Artists Group, who invented a new idiom in the early years of Independence.
D'Monte, Darryl *Ripping the Fabric: The Decline of Mumbai and its Mills* An analysis of how the shuttering of Mumbai's textile mills has undermined the city's social and economic health.
Dwivedi, Sharada and Mehrotra, Rahul *Fort Walks* An indispensable guide to the buildings of the the Fort district.
Dwyer, Rachel *Yash Chopra* Surveys the pastel-shaded success of this legendary Bollywood director, and is an insightful guide into the workings of the Indian film industry. *100 Bollywood Films* tells you which movies you simply can't afford to miss.
Garga, BD *So Many Cinemas* A superbly researched history of Indian cinema, supported by film stills from the earliest movies.
Guha, Ramachandra *A Corner of a Foreign Field: The Indian History of a British Sport* Set largely in Mumbai, the home of subcontinental cricket, this book is a social history of India, told through its favourite sport.
Gupt, Somnath *The Parsi Theatre: Its Origins and Development.* A study of a 19th-century theatre form that established the conventions still followed in Bollywood films.
Hansen, Thomas Blom *Wages of Violence: Naming and Identity in Postcolonial Bombay* How the nativist Shiv Sena party unleashed fundamentalist forces that polarised India's most cosmopolitan city.
Hoskote, Ranjit *The Complicit Observer* A showcase of the work of Sudhir Patwardhan, who paints Mumbaikars travelling on the train, on the street and sitting in Irani cafés and who delights in finding the extraordinary in the mundane.
Kabir, Nasreen Munni *Guru Dutt: A Life in Cinema* A biography of the brilliant director and actor who re-imagined formulaic Hindi cinema in the 1950s.
Kapoor, Shashi and Gehlot, Deepa *Prithviwallas* The story of how India's most famous film family built the auditorium that

now is the nerve centre of Mumbai's theatre scene.
Khote, Durga *I, Durga Khote* The journey of an upper-class woman, through the vaguely disreputable world of Indian cinema. Khote made her debut in 1931 and acted in more than 200 films through her career.
London, Christopher W *Bombay Gothic* A pictorial history of Mumbai's fascination with a style that had its origins thousands of miles away.
Manto, Sadat Hasan *Mumbai: Stars from Another Sky* A catty collection of pieces from the time that one of the greatest Urdu writers worked as a film journalist.
Mehta, Suketu *Maximum City* A painstakingly researched, magnificently written book about the numerous worlds that make up Mumbai. Arguably the best book about the city ever.
Michell, George *Elephanta* A guide to the famous sixth-century rock-carved caves on the island just off Mumbai.
Moraes, Dom *A Variety of Absences* The shimmering memoirs of the famous poet and journalist.
Neuwirth, Robert *Shadow Cities* An American writer takes up residence in shanty towns on four continents, Mumbai among them.
Patel, Sujata and Thorner, Alice *Bombay: Metaphor for Modern India* and *Bombay: Mosaic of Modern Culture* are collections of academic articles that examine the city's past – and make prescriptions for its future.
Pinto, Jerry and Fernandes, Naresh (editors) *Bombay Meri Jaan* An anthology of writing and poetry about India's most vibrant city.
Seabrook, Jeremy *Life and Labour in a Bombay Slum* The author finds optimism amid the squalour of Mumbai's shanty colonies.
Sharma, Kalpnana *Rediscovering Dharavi: Stories from Asia's Largest Slum* A study of life in the neighbourhood that has come to symbolise the urban policy that ensures that half of Mumbai's population has no hope of moving out of slums.
Virani, Pinky *Once There Was Bombay* Interlinked stories of lives in a city that the author insists is on the verge of death.
Zaidi, Hussain S *Black Friday: The True Story of the Bombay Bomb Blasts* A pacy reconstruction of the conspiracy that resulted in the explosions that killed 257 Mumbaikars on March 12, 1993.

History

Dwivedi, Shardha and Mehrotra, Rahul *Bombay: The Cities Within* An immensely readable tale of how seven malarial islands grew into a major metropolis, with lots of pictorial evidence.

Edwardes, SM *Gazetteer of Bombay City and Island* The ultimate administrators' handbook to the city, completed in 1909, has sections on the city's history, trade patterns, headgear, and even lists of distinctive hawkers' cries.

Farooqui, Amar *Opium City: The Making of Early Victorian Bombay* Opium, as much as cotton, boosted Mumbai's fortunes, says the author.

Marg Publications *Bombay to Mumbai: Changing Perspectives* An eclectic selection of articles, including pieces on early photography in Mumbai, 19th-century homes and the city's art deco architecture.

Menon, Meena and Adarkar, Neera *One Hundred Years, One Hundred Voices. The Millworkers of Girangaon: An Oral History.* A compelling history of how tumultuous changes in Mumbai's mill district shaped events across India.

Tindall, Gillian *City of Gold: The Biography of Bombay* A delightful stroll through the city's British history, told with a novelist's eye for detail.

Film

See also p34 **Bollywood**.

Aar Paar (1954) 1950s tragedy king Guru Dutt directs as well as stars as a working-class taxi driver who loses his job, starts working at a garage, has a run-in with gangsters and is the object of two women's affections.

Taxi Driver (1954) Chetan Anand's rambling tale of the relationship between a taxi driver Dev Anand and a runaway singer, Kalpana Kartik, was a grand excuse to shoot Mumbai's urban vistas.

Boot Polish (1954) Prakash Arora tells the story of Rattan Kumar and his sister, who survive on the streets of Mumbai by scrabbling for food and a few dimes at railway stations. Raj Kapoor bankrolled this landmark movie, the first mainstream production to show children making a living off the streets.

Shree 420 (1955) Raj Kapoor's guileless tramp trips into Mumbai singing. The poor welcome him with open arms but he loses his way and starts working for a businessman who wants to raze the slum where his comrades and lady love Nargis live.

Mr and Mrs '55 (1955) This is loaded with playfulness, amazingly inventive camerawork and a modern spirit. Made by Guru Dutt in the decade when the post-independence bubbly still hadn't gone flat, this is a satire on the feudal upper classes.

CID (1956) *CID*'s magic lies in its taut storytelling, business-like characters and snappy editing. Plus, this Bollywoodian film noir story has the unofficial Mumbai anthem: 'Yeh Hai Bombay Meri Jaan'.

Aakhri Khat (1966) Chetan Anand's precursor to 1994's *Baby's Day Out* follows the adorable little Bunty as he stumbles about the city looking for his mother. Brilliantly shot, mostly in Mahim, with a jazzy soundtrack.

Chhoti Si Baat (1975) Basu Chatterji paints Mumbai as a truly romantic city, full of possibilities and a love of life. Amol Palekar's Arun meets Prabha every day at the bus stop. He's madly in love but has no confidence until he takes courtship lessons from a retired colonel.

Deewar (1975) Directed by Yash Chopra and carried by Amitabh Bachchan, this has been interpreted by film theorists in different ways – some see it as an obtuse comment on the Emergency – but it also happens to be a city film and a comment on how money-driven Mumbai drives a wedge between two brothers.

Don (1978) Amitabh Bachchan is Don, the head of an international smuggling ring based in Mumbai. He gets killed in an encounter and is replaced by a Bhojpuri-speaking lookalike who is tasked by the police with infiltrating his gang.

Jaane Bhi Do Yaaron (1983) In this cult slapstick satire, directed by Kundan Shah, two bumbling photographers stumble onto a scam being hatched by corrupt builders and municipal officials, and embark on a series of madcap adventures to unearth the truth.

Ardh Satya (1983) Govind Nihalani's gritty cop story takes on a debate over violence, authority and control, with a hard-edged story unfolding through the eyes of a Mumbai police inspector, played by Om Puri.

Saaransh (1984) Possibly Mahesh Bhatt's best film, and one of the few Hindi films to subtly explore the Shiv Sena's reign of terror in the city.

Nayakan (1987) Mani Ratnam's Tamil classic, also dubbed into Hindi, combines a respectful hat tip to Francis Ford Coppola's *The Godfather* with a loosely based biopic of Vardharaj Mudaliar, the infamous smuggler who operated in Dharavi in the 1960s.

Salaam Bombay! (1988) Many Mumbaikars hate this movie, and dismiss it as urban exotica, but Mira Nair's debut is a moving portrait of the city's underbelly, seen through its street children, whores and pimps.

Tezaab (1998) N Chandra's movie is a great visual dictionary for the city: it has street lingo, gangster brawls, tough love and hip-shaking songs. Anil Kapoor plays Munna, an aspiring naval officer whose journey to gangsterhood is told in flashback.

Salim Langde Pe Mat Ro (1989) Saeed Mirza tackles issues faced by Mumbai's marginalised Muslims in this beautifully shot movie, set in the teeming alleys of central Mumbai.

Parinda (1989) A successful assimilation of the Hollywood film noir genre. *Parinda* remains Vidhu Vinod Chopra's most evocative film and one of the most well-crafted gangster films in recent times.

Sadak (1991) Eunuchs, taxi drivers, prostitutes, pimps, thugs. *Sadak* is the apogee of Mahesh Bhatt's series of films featuring street characters. Sanjay Dutt gives his all, and is brilliant, in a sort of neurotic tribute to Martin Scorsese's *Taxi Driver*.

Rangeela (1995) Light at heart and on the feet, *Rangeela* is Ram Gopal Varma's ode to the magic of the movies. Urmila Matondkar plays Mili, a film extra who dreams of being a star. She's spotted by the reigning superstar Raj Kamal (Jackie Shroff) who falls for her and breaks the heart of her childhood buddy Munna (Aamir Khan).

Bombay (1995) One of the few films to look squarely at the 1992-1993 Mumbai communal riots, Mani Rathnam's love story has been dissected and dissed for its portrayal of events and characters – for example, the violence in the film is always initiated by a Muslim.

Satya (1998) Through the character of Satya, a man with no background who emerges from the stone corridors of Chhatrapati Shivaji Terminus into the arms of the underworld, Ram Gopal Varma trawls through shoot-outs, betrayals and revenge. Bloody good fun, and a modern gangster classic.

Dil Chahta Hai (2001) *Dil Chahta Hai* mostly plays out in spacious homes replete with leather sofas, electronic gadgetry, colour-coordinated walls, chic furniture and the kind of luxury you'd find in Nepean Sea Road or Juhu. Then the plot moves to Goa and Sydney, but the heart is local; the portrait of the well-heeled universe is non-judgemental and accurate.

Munnabhai MBBS (2003) *Munnabhai MBBS*, a comedy about a street thug who teaches doctors a thing or two about treatment, isn't the first film to put Mumbai's street lingo into a film script. But it is the first to use the language almost as a living, breathing character.

Index

Note page numbers in **bold** indicate section(s) giving key information on a topic; *italics* indicate photographs.

Advertisers' Index

Please refer to relevant sections for
addresses and /or telephone numbers

Place of interest and/or entertainment ...	
College/Hospital/University	
Railway station/Bus depot	
Ruins	
Parks	
River	
Beach	
Main Road	
Pedestrian road	
Airport	✈
Church	✚
Temple	🛕
Synagogues	✡
Hospital	✚
Post office	✉
Mosque	☪
Tourist information	ℹ
Area name	FORT
Hotels	❶
Restaurants & Cafés	❶
Pubs & Bars	❶

Maps

Mumbai

GORAI BEACH GORAI NAGAR DOKALI
Borivali
SANJAY
Kanheri Caves
MNADA
Kandivali LOKMANYA NALPADA
NAGAR
KHAREGAO
AKURLI GANDHI
Tulsi Lake Wagle Industrial
Estate THANE Kalw
Malad NATIONAL PODWAL NAGAR Thane
PATHANWADI
RAM NAGAR
DINDOSHI PARK
DONGARPADA Goregaon Mulund MHADA
ERANGAL Film City COLONY Airo
BEACH Bhandup
MADH VIHAR Lake
BEACH VERSOVA LAXMI NAGAR Bhandup FRIENDS
BEACH OSHIWARA COLONY Rabale
Jogeshwari Mahakali Caves NOCIL
Powai Lake Kanjurmarg COLONY
AZAD NAGAR SEEPZ Ghansoli
Andheri
JUHU SAKI NAKA Vikhroli Kopa
BEACH Khaira
Vile
Parle Chhatrapati Shivaji
International Airport Ghatkopar HAVI
Arabian Sea Domestic Airport MUMBA
Santa Cruz Vidyavihar
AIRELI VAKOLA San
Khar Road Kurla Tilak Nagar SHIVAJI NAGAR
BANDRA Chembur Vashi
Bandra Govandi HERDLI
p249 Sion Chunabhatti DEONAR Mankhurd COLON
Mahim Mahim Sion Fort CIDC
Fort GTB Nagar WADAVALI UPPER COLO
Bandra Fort Matunga King's Circle ANTOP HILL TROMBAY
Road Matunga PANCHAVATI
Worli Fort Shivaji Park Dadar MAHUL COLONY
PRABHADEVI Wadala Road TROMBAY
Elphinstone Parel
Road
Sewri
Lower Parel Currey Road
Chinchpokli Cotton Green
Mahalaxmi Beay Road
Mumbai Central Byculla
Terminus Dockyard Road Butcher Island NHAVA
CUMBALLA p254-5 Grant Road Sandhurst Road Elephanta
Charni Road Masjid Bunder Island
Chowpatty Cross Island
Beach Chhatrapati Shivaji
Marine Lines p252-3 Terminus
Back Bay FORT Churchgate
NARIMAN Gateway of India
CUFFE PARADE
COLABA p250-1 Harbour URAN

0 ——— 3 miles
0 ——— 4 km
© Copyright Time Out Group 2006

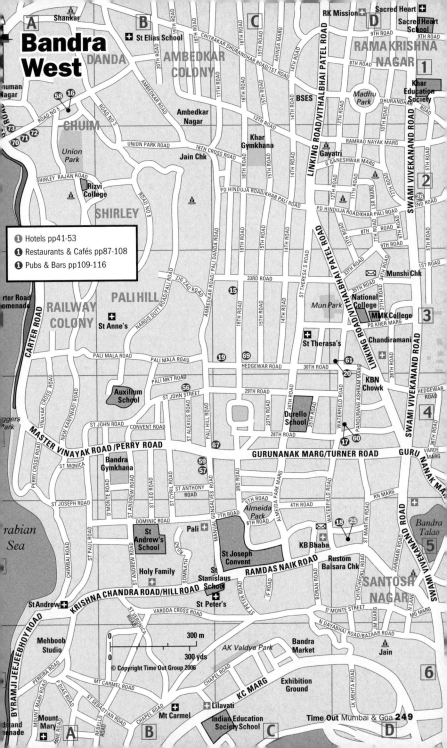

Bandra West

A

Shankar

B

St Elias School

AMBEDKAR COLONY

C

CHITRAKAR DHURANDHAR ROAD/1ST ROAD

AHINSA MARG

RK Mission

D

Sacred Heart

Sacred Heart School

RAMA KRISHNA NAGAR

1

DANDA

CHUIM

Ambedkar Nagar

Khar Gymkhana

Jain Chk

Madhu Park

Khar Education Society

BSES

Gayatri

RAMRAO NAYAK MARG

6 GANESHWAR MARG

2

Union Park

Shirley Rajan Road

Rizvi College

SHIRLEY

PD HINDUJA ROAD/KHAR PALI ROAD

PD HINDUJA ROAD/KHAR PALI ROAD

Munshi Chk

Hotels pp41-53
Restaurants & Cafés pp87-108
Pubs & Bars pp109-116

PALI HILL

St Anne's

RAILWAY COLONY

33RD ROAD

Mun Park

National College

MMK College

3

Carter Road Promenade

St Theresa's

PG KHER MARG

Chandiramani

Pali Mala Road

Pali Mala Road

HEDGEWAR ROAD

30TH ROAD

KBN Chowk

KBN Chowk

Auxilium School

Pali Mkt Road

ST JOHN STREET

29TH ROAD

Durello School

4

ST JOHN ROAD

CONVENT ROAD

28TH ROAD

MASTER VINAYAK ROAD/PERRY ROAD

GURUNANAK MARG/TURNER ROAD

GURU NANAK MA

Bandra Gymkhana

ST ANTHONY ROAD

Arabian Sea

ST JOSEPH ROAD

DOMINIC ROAD

Pali

4TH ROAD

Almeida Park

5TH ROAD
6TH ROAD

KB Bhaba

Bandra Talao

5

St Andrew's School

Holy Family

St Joseph Convent

RAMDAS NAIK ROAD

Rustom Balsara Chk

SANTOSH NAGAR

St Andrew

KRISHNA CHANDRA ROAD/HILL ROAD

St Stanislaus School

St Peter's

VARODA CROSS ROAD

Jain

Mehboob Studio

300 m

300 yds

© Copyright Time Out Group 2006

AK Valdya Park

Bandra Market

6

Mount Mary

MT CARMEL ROAD

Mt Carmel

Lilavati

Indian Education Society School

KC MARG

Exhibition Ground

A   **B**   **C**   **D**

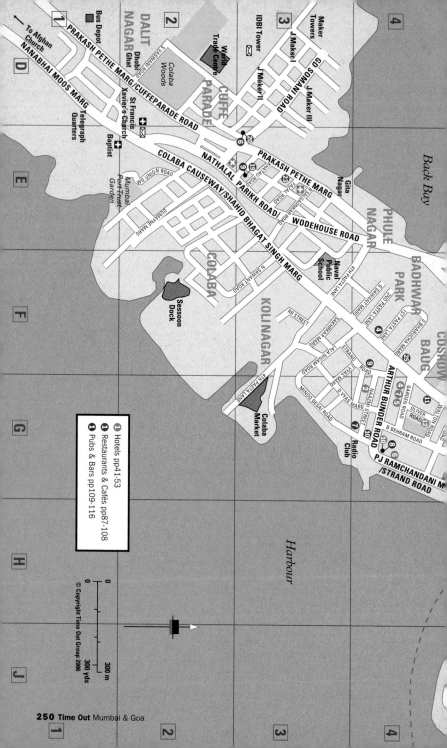

Bus Depot

PRAKASH PETHE MARG /CUFFEPARADE ROAD

NANABHAI MOOS MARG

DALIT NAGAR

Dhobi Ghat

St Francis Xavier's Church

Baptist

Telegraph Quarters

To Afghan Church

Maker Towers

IDBI Tower

J Maker I

J Maker II

World Trade Centre

Colaba Woods

S YASWANT ROAD

CUFFE PARADE

GO SOVANI ROAD

J Maker III

PRAKASH PETHE MARG

NATHALAL PARIKH ROAD

COLABA CAUSEWAY /SHAHID BHAGAT SINGH MARG

Gita Nagar

AZAD NAGAR ROAD

V B UNION ROAD

Mumbai Port Trust Garden

COLABA

DUMANE MARG

WODEHOUSE ROAD

Naval Public School

4TH PASI LANE

3RD PASTA LANE

2ND PASTA LANE

1ST PASTA LANE

6 SAWANT MARG

5 SAWANT MARG

N SAWANT ROAD

Sessoon Dock

KOLINAGAR

RR STREET

SARKHAWE MARG

LALA NIGAM ROAD

STRAND

D VYAS MARG

MINGO DESAI ROAD

PHULE NAGAR

Back Bay

BADHWAR PARK

COSSOW BAUG

S BHARUCHA MARG

ARTHUR BUNDER ROAD

NAZIM STREET

GARDEN ROAD

OLIVER ROAD

WALTON ROAD

B BEHRAM ROAD

PJ RAMCHANDANI M /STRAND ROAD

Colaba Market

Radio Club

Harbour

- **1** Hotels pp41-53
- **1** Restaurants & Cafés pp87-108
- **1** Pubs & Bars pp109-116

0   300 m
0   300 yds

© Copyright Time Out Group 2006

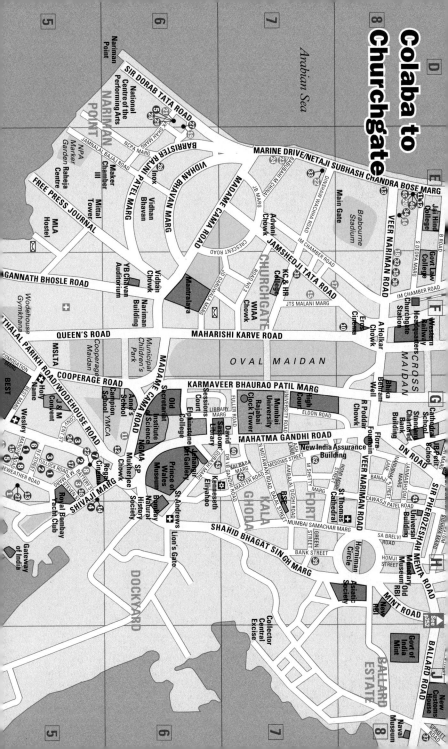

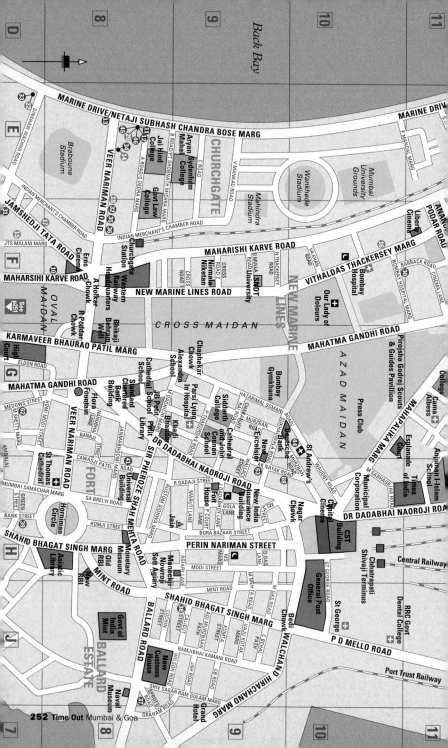

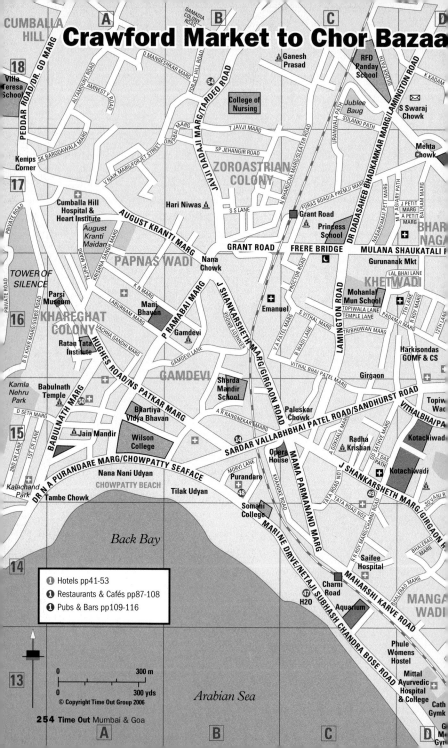

Crawford Market to Chor Bazaa

18
Villa Teresa School

GAMADIA COLONY ROAD

Ganesh Prasad

RFD Panday School

K KADAM

D MANGESHKAR MARG

FORJET HILL ROAD

College of Nursing

Jublee Baug

S Swaraj Chowk

17
Kemps Corner

Cumballa Hill Hospital & Heart Institute

Hari Niwas

ZOROASTRIAN COLONY

Mehta Chowk

S S LANE

FORAS ROAD/A PREMJI MARG

Grant Road

M P AGIARY PATH

Princess School

J PETIT MARG
A PETIT MARG

BHAR NAGA

AUGUST KRANTI MARG

GRANT ROAD

FRERE BRIDGE

MULANA SHAUKATALI R

Gurunanak Mkt

TOWER OF SILENCE

PAPNAS WADI

Nana Chowk

KHETWADI

LAL BHAI LANE

16
KHAREGHAT COLONY

Parsi Museum

Mani Bhavan

Emanuel

Mohanlal Mun School

TOPIWALA LANE
TEMPLE LANE

Ratan Tata Institute

Gamdevi

Girgaon

Harkisondas GOMF & CS

GAMDEVI LANE

Kamla Nehru Park

Babulnath Temple

GAMDEVI

Sharda Mandir School

Paluskar Chowk

15
D SETH MARG

Jain Mandir

Bhartiya Vidya Bhavan

Wilson College

Opera House

Radha Krishan

Kotachiwad

SARDAR VALLABHBHAI PATEL ROAD/SANDHURST ROAD

Kotachiwadi

Kalachand Park

Nana Nani Udyan

CHOWPATTY BEACH

Tilak Udyan

Purandare

Somani College

14
❶ Hotels pp41-53
❶ Restaurants & Cafés pp87-108
❶ Pubs & Bars pp109-116

Back Bay

MARINE DRIVE/NETAJI SUBHASH CHANDRA BOSE ROAD

Saifee Hospital

Charni Road

H2O

Aquarium

MANGA WADI

MAHARSHI KARVE ROAD

Phule Womens Hostel

Mittal Ayurvedic Hospital & College

13
0   300 m
0   300 yds
© Copyright Time Out Group 2006

Arabian Sea

Mumbai Rail Network

Central Railway Main
Central Railway Harbour
Western Railway
Thane-Vashi Shuttle

Virar-Dahanu Shuttle
Vasai-Diva/Kalyan Shuttle
Kalyan-Panvel Shuttle
Indian Railway IR

© Copyright Time Out Group 2006
Map not to scale